AF540265

Secularism Under Siege: Revisiting the Indian Secular State

Secularism Under Siege: Revisiting the Indian Secular State

Edited by

Zaheer Ali

Secularism Under Siege: Revisiting the Indian Secular State
Edited by Zaheer Ali

First Published 2016

ISBN 978-93-5002-416-4

Published by
AAKAR BOOKS
28 E Pocket IV, Mayur Vihar Phase I, Delhi 110 091
Phone : 011 2279 5505 Telefax : 011 2279 5641
aakarbooks@gmail.com; www.aakarbooks.com

Laser Typeset at
Arpit Printographers, Delhi 110 032

Printed at
Mudrak, 30 A, Patparganj, Delhi 110 091

Contents

Editor's Note

It is contentious to estimate whether secularism as an ideology is entirely a Western construct and its introduction in the Indian Constitution as an operative principle of governance entails cataclysm in political processes and societal interactions. The Indian Constitution that came into force more than six decades ago was endowed with the spirit of secularism despite the fact that during the first 26 years of its existence and functioning, the word secular was not used to denote as a descriptor of the nature of the state. Nevertheless, it was widely acknowledged that because of the presence of an interrelated set of certain components such as freedom of religion, citizenship rights to all irrespective of faith, race etc., absence of a state religion and separation of state and religion in core areas of governance and politics, the constitution makers had created a secular state in an excessively religious and essentially traditional society. This disconnect between a modern-secular state and a conservative society has always been a detrimental factor in the attainment of the ideal of a secular-democratic polity. Added to this is the burden of the past centuries that the independent nation of India has to carry on its young shoulders. There are political factions in India that invent their own historical narratives to advance their political agenda. This exercise coupled with political and economic contestations leads to social dissensions and communal hatred, the ugliest manifestation of which is communal violence that occasionally takes on the form of anti-minority pogroms.

It must be made clear that there has never been a consensus on the issue of efficacy or desirability of the idea of secularism among the political elite in India. Despite being accorded the status of one of the constituent values of the philosophy of the Constitution, secularism has never been made the genuine operative principle of governance largely because of the compulsions of competitive politics. Yet, until the 1980s, secularism was being acknowledged as one of the desirable ideals of Indian democracy which, it was expected, the nation would ultimately attain with the spread of modern, scientific education and maturity of democratic processes. In retrospect, it seems that it was a flawed expectation. The ideal of secularism has been under siege for more than two decades thanks to the political ascendancy of fascist and communal forces, which are determined to do away with the very idea of secularism and transform India into a theocracy favouring the religious aspirations of the majority.

An alarming offshoot of the rise of the anti-secular political narrative is the concerns and misgivings about the concept of secularism put across by some academicians and public intellectuals who are not remotely connected with communal and divisive political forces. The main thrust of their argument is that since the concept of secularism is imported from the West it is not compatible with Indian society and state. It is obvious that it is a disingenuous criticism to say the least. An objective analysis can reveal that almost all the constituent values of the Indian Constitution—the ideas of nation, democracy, socialism, rule of law, parliament, executive, judiciary, bureaucracy—are of Western origin. Then why single out secularism?

Secularism as an ideology is under siege currently not only in India but all across the world in the aftermath of 9/11 attacks. Most countries have declared officially or unofficially 'wars on terror which, in practical terms, means surveillance and religious profiling of minorities, in particular, the adherents of Islam. This global trend has provided a fillip to the anti-Muslim socio-political groups in India to demonize the largest religious minority of India and goad the state agencies to treat most of its members as potential terrorists. Consequently, innumerable cases of violation of human rights of the members of the minorities have been reported and there seems to be no let up in the trend. More importantly, the idioms in which the political discourses are presently conducted both at national and regional levels, especially by the votaries of the Hindu Right have distinct linkages with religion. For them whatever is Hindu is essentially national. They also argue that terms like religious or cultural minorities are in actuality misnomers in the Indian context for all inhabitants of the country are Hindus and minority religions including Islam and Christianity are strands (*panths*) of all-encompassing Hindu *dharma*. A member of a minority faith, say for instance a Muslim, therefore, should identify himself, in the opinion of the Hindu Right, as Hindu by faith and Muslim by sect.

The role of the Muslim socio-religious-political elite, nonetheless, is far from encouraging to promote the idea of secularism among the largest minority of the country. It is an undeniable fact of modern Indian history that a major section of the Muslim middle class and under its influence the Muslim masses always responded favourably to the political ideas deeply soaked in the religious stream. For instance, Jinnah was a nonentity for the Muslims when he was a staunch secular leader of the Indian National Congress; he became the darling of the Muslims when he reappeared as the leader of the Muslim League holding a weapon of religion in his hand and the slogan of 'two nations' on his tongue. Abul Kalam Azad, despite being an outstanding religious scholar could not win over the Muslim middle class or the masses because he was talking about the unity of all Indians, the composite culture and a secular political order. Possibly it could be because of the fear of the overwhelming majority of the Hindus whom many Muslims in undivided India perceived as their enemies or the loss of political power or because of the failure of the Muslim liberals, the large number of Muslims always had a propensity to seek protection in Islam whenever confronted with a socio-political crisis. This weakness of the Muslims had always been exploited to the hilt by the orthodox *ulema* to advance their obscurantist ideology invariably based on anti-secularism and hatred of the non-Muslims.

In the post-partition scenario, most mullahs and the self-seeking political leaders belonging to various political parties started 'affirming' faith in the idea of secularism as a political strategy. They do not have any other option. Accordingly, the irony is that essentially Muslim communal parties such as the Indian Union Muslim League, which is confined to Kerala and the Majlis-e-Ittehadul Muslimeen (MIM), which seems to be spreading its tentacles beyond Telangana, vociferously declare their 'commitment' to secularism. The emergence of MIM in recent times as the preferred political alternative of the Muslim masses seems to be an upshot of the ascendancy of the Hindutva forces. The victory of the BJP in the 16th Lok Sabha elections has made the religious minorities, in particular, the Muslims extremely desperate as most of them foresee a bleak and dreadful future for the community. The MIM is out to exploit the Muslim desperation to its advantage and it has also registered a modest success by winning two Assembly seats in Maharashtra. This phenomenon reinforces the argument that Hindu and Muslim communalists need each other for their political survival. There are reports that the MIM is being deliberately promoted and financed by the anti-secular Hindu outfits to decimate the secular challenge. The point to ponder is how the MIM, which was hitherto confined only to Hyderabad, has suddenly emerged as a political force to reckon with in the aftermath of BJP's victory? It only shows that there is a clandestine nexus between the MIM and the Hindu political parties. By exciting the gullible Muslim masses with fiery and emotionally charged speeches, the leaders of the MIM are only polarizing Indian society on communal lines.

In view of these developments of the last two and a half decades there is a widespread belief that secularism in India is under siege and there is an urgent need to revisit the secular credentials of the Indian state. All those who are committed to see India as a truly secular-democratic state and who hold the Constitution of the country in high esteem subscribe to the view that the challenges before the Indian secular state are mammoth and they must be dealt with utmost seriousness and candour. One way of doing it is to reaffirm our faith in the secular foundation of the Indian state. The crucial posers are: Can the Indian state take apart the siege under which the idea of secularism has been forced to be? Or, as some observers point out, is the state itself part of the problem?

In order to address the challenges before secularism and reexamine the secular attributes of the Indian state, the Centre for Promotion of Democracy and Secularism (CPDS), a non-profit organisation, organised a three-day national seminar sponsored by the ICSSR, New Delhi and in collaboration with the Rajiv Gandhi Centre for Contemporary Studies, University of Mumbai, in Mumbai between December 18 and 20, 2014. The event proved a huge success in which more than fifty delegates from all over India made presentations. The present volume comprises the selected papers that were greatly appreciated during the proceedings of the seminar.

I owe gratitude to a number of individuals who helped me organise the seminar and edit this volume. I thank Ms. Alka Srivastava, NIS in-charge, ICSSR, New Delhi, because without her objective consideration of the CPDS's proposal the seminar would not have met with such a colossal success. Similarly, I express my gratitude to Dr. Gautam Gawali, the then Director of the ICSSR (Western Region) and Professor, Department of Applied Psychology, University of Mumbai for his keen interest in making the seminar a memorable event. Thanks are also due to Dr. Chandrakant Puri, Director, Rajiv Gandhi Centre for Contemporary Studies, University of Mumbai, for collaborating with CPDS and offering the maximum possible assistance. Likewise, Dr. Surendra Jondhale, Professor and Head, Department of Civics and Politics, University of Mumbai must be thanked for helping me in myriad ways.

I also take this opportunity to thank Mr. Mahesh Bhatt, who despite being a celebrity and having an extremely busy schedule of engagements, inaugurated the seminar and delivered an erudite address. In the same manner, I express my gratitude to Professor Rajeev Bhargava of the Centre for the Study of Developing Societies, Delhi, who not only delivered an insightful keynote address in the opening event of the seminar but also contributed another scholarly article to this volume. The transcript of his keynote address is reproduced here as the *Foreword* to the book. I am indebted to Dr. Ram Puniyani, Chairman of the Centre for the Study of Society and Secularism, Mumbai for chairing the inaugural function of the seminar and contributing an article to this volume. Likewise, I am grateful to Mr. L.S. Herdenia, Convener, All India Secular Forum, who despite his advanced age took the trouble to travel from Bhopal to Mumbai to deliver the valedictory address. Mr. Harsh Mander, Director, Centre for Equity Studies, New Delhi, must also be thanked for his brilliant presidential address in the valedictory programme. Lastly, I profusely thank Mr. Firoz Ashraf, a veteran social activist and Ms. Jyoti Punwani, a senior journalist who dexterously conducted the Open Session of the seminar.

Among my colleagues and friends associated with CPDS, I would like to express my gratitude to Dr. Afaq Khan, Vice-President, Mr. Abdul Majeed, Secretary, Mr. Sibtain Naqvi, Treasurer and Dr. Munawwar Ali Razvi, the Member of the Executive Committee who helped me in many ways on innumerable occasions.

Zaheer Ali

Mumbai
December 1, 2015

Foreword

Rajeev Bhargava

The secular state is besieged in India. But it is a mistake to think that the siege began with the coming to power of the new government, though it cannot be denied that forces have been unleashed more recently that attack the secular ethos of our society in a manner that is more blatant, persistent, frontally direct and shamelessly open. However, wittingly or unwittingly, deliberately or unintentionally, various groups in our society have been chipping away at the secular edifice, so that gradually, overtime, its moral legitimacy has been eroded. To put it differently, although secularism has long been facing an external threat by those who vigorously oppose it and this challenge has been political, social, cultural and intellectual, secularism has also been facing an internal threat in the sense that, the myopia, neglect, complacency, propensity for ritual hyperbole, weakness of will or failure of nerve of its proponents has also undermined it. This internal threat has also been political, social, cultural and intellectual.

My focus today is on such internal, intellectual factors that have led to the moral delegitimation of secularism. More specifically, I speak of the conceptual flaws in the understanding and defence of secularism. It is important to point out that I do not believe that internal, intellectual reasons contributed more to the crisis of secularism. Far from that. Indeed, their role may be less significant than external, non-intellectual factors. But internal factors are more in our control; we can do something immediately about them. Besides, I don't think secularism can be rescued without some course correction which in turn is impossible without self-reflexivity and self-criticism. So, where have we gone wrong?

As part of this answer, I will here state five propositions. In keeping with the mood generated by Mahesh Bhatt's semi-autobiographical inaugural address and Zaheer Ali's evocative introductory remarks, I will draw you into my first point by asking you to join me in a thought experiment. So imagine you are in a situation where along with others in your society, you are facing the usual problems of life, problems that emanate from both natural and social causes. You are at the mercy of wild natural forces, confronting disease, death, separation, violence, and social oppression and therefore have a yearning to move beyond, transcend this situation, somehow, somewhere, sometime. A feeling of being trapped in our current condition and a metaphysical longing to overcome it, exists regardless of whether we believe in God or some other world. And all these people find themselves in their midst a brilliant and empathetic person full of wisdom and insight about the human condition. People get attracted to his teachings—his because the time of which I speak had only men with such capacity and standing—and over time become his dedicated followers. Let us call this step 1. Over time, they begin to recognize each other as followers of this teacher or his teachings and a vague, fuzzy sense of community emerges among them. Call it step 2. The next step, 3, involves the organization of this community and giving it an institutional structure. In other words, step 2 to 3 marks the birth of an institutionalized community. Now a distinction begins to develop between those who play an important formal role in this structure and all those who, though outside this formal structure, also sincerely follow these teachings. Some of these institutional, semi-professional and literate men are given or take upon themselves the task of elaborating and systematizing the 'original' teachings. This invariably means interpretation and the introduction of the views and biases of the interpreters who, taking their professional expertise seriously, change these teachings into an intellectual doctrine. (Step 4) Ordinary people no longer have direct access to the original teachings. They can only reach them mediated by the doctrines enunciated by literate, professionals.

Overlaid now on community relations are twisted, distorted relations of power, particularly between those who claim to know more and those with the belief that they know less. These powerful men not only organize their community tightly around a rigid intellectual doctrine but become gate keepers, defining rules of entry and exit into this institutionalized community, now more closed and bounded. Call it step 5. As different peoples living in the same or different regions take the same steps 1-5, many such communities develop, each defining itself in opposition to the other, viewing each other as rivals, asking everyone to choose between one or the other, asking for exclusive allegiance on the ground that their doctrine is the best, that they alone have access to Truth. All the others are false. (step 6).

In this imaginary reconstruction, I have, in effect, traced, in an outrageously brief and sketchy manner, the development of modern, confessional religions that are (a) mutually exclusive and (b) seek exclusive allegiance. It is my view that steps 4-6, particularly steps 5 and 6 were taken more decisively and firmly if not irrevocably only in the aftermath of the breakdown of Latin Christendom and during the wars of religion that erupted in Europe in the 16th/17th century. In contrast, the history of the development in South Asia of something akin to confessional religion or of a broader conception that subsumes or encompasses what the West calls religion did not, unsurprisingly, lead to the formation of confessional religion, at least until the 19th century. To be sure, a few strands here and there did threaten to turn in that direction. But contrary features in the social imaginary pulled them back, contained them or steered them on an altogether different track. Thus, the history of the subcontinent is littered with millions of individuals and groups having taken one, two or three steps and then seen the futility, irrelevance, self-defeating nature of the next steps. The idea of a bounded community seeking exclusive allegiance was at best marginal, not centre stage. Fuzzy communities, multiple allegiances, and fluid, hybrid and composite identities were possibly the norm. The sudden induction of fully grown confessional religions had a dramatic, somewhat disastrous impact on religious formations in India.

Since there is greater movement between and within non-confessional religions and because they contain, albeit implicitly, the idea of respect for all religions, it would be tragic and socially explosive if the idea of confessional religion overwhelms this other freer, more fluid conception. I believe this process of confessionalization is reversible, however, for two reasons. First, other religious formations are still very much around and have a fairly stable presence. Second, confessionalization is an emerging phenomenon, far from complete and therefore still unstable and relatively weak.

Reversing the confessionalization of faith, (and ritual and philosophy) should be one of the primary tasks of the secular project in India. Secular practice has partially recognized this but the issue has never found a forceful, general and normative formulation. This is my first proposition in this lecture.

From here on, I accept that at least a partial confessionalization of faiths has taken place in India and therefore the contemporary relevance of the more modern, confessional idea of religion and move to my second claim: Those who defend secularism have frequently lost sight of the whole point behind a secular state, what secularism is for. More specifically, they do not fully understand what it was that gave Indian secularism its point and what made it distinctive., even unique. To elaborate this issue, allow me to furnish some examples:

- A woman is burnt at the stake because she is believed to be a witch.
- A man is stoned to death for heresy.
- A woman is not allowed to enter a temple because she is more than 15 and less than 55 years old, a time span in which she is menstruating and hence 'polluted'.
- A man from the lowest caste, believed to be an untouchable is not allowed to take water from the well.

What is common to all these examples? In all these cases, (a) some person is discriminated against, excluded, marginalized, intimidated, oppressed or humiliated on grounds of religion or somewhere along the chain of reasoning behind it, a religious rationale is cited. (b) In each of these cases, both the victim and the perpetrator are from the same religious community. Call this intra-religious domination.

Intra-religious domination takes other forms too as when (a) Ahmedias are deemed to be non-Muslims and their places of worship prevented from being called 'mosques', (b) when Catholics are persecuted by Lutherans or (c) a Shaivite temple is desecrated by Vaishaivites, Take another set of examples.

- A tax is imposed on Hindus but not on Muslims.
- Churches are attacked by intolerant Hindus or militant Muslims.
- Catholic schools are subsidized by the state but Hindu, Muslim, Protestant and Jewish schools are not.
- A person called Hussain is unable to get a house on rent in metropolitan cities.

Here again we have (a) discrimination, exclusion, marginalization, oppression or humiliation on grounds of religion but (b) victims and perpetrators come from different religious communities. Call this inter-religious domination.

The point I wish to make through these examples is that secularism must be seen as a critical social perspective not against every religious formation, or against religiosity or religion per se but against all forms of institutionalized religious domination. Political secularism is a narrower perspective, according to which a state should be so designed as to reduce institutionalized religious domination in both its forms, inter- and intra-religious. Its main claim is that if institutionalized religious domination is to be reduced, then states should not be captured by or align themselves with a particular religious community or a section thereof. Some form of separation between state and institutionalized religion is necessary. Now, this idea that secularism is not anti-religious but against different forms of institutionalized religious domination was novel, a conception that was invented under very special circumstances that had emerged in India specific conditions in India before and at the time of its independence from colonial rule.

The story of what happened in the first half of the 20th century in India is familiar to all of us but it is still worth recalling. Sections of Hindu and Muslim elites had at that time been sucked into what can be called a majority-minority syndrome, a diseased network of neurotic relations, so completely poisoned and accompanied by a such a vertiginous assortment of negative emotions (envy, malice, jealousy, spite, and hatred) that, collective delirium and cold-blooded acts of revenge, sending groups on a downward path of deeper and still deeper estrangement are mindlessly, alternately, cyclically, generated. It is a feature of this syndrome that, groups make demands on one another that can rarely be fulfilled, conjure up imaginary grievances, insist precisely on that which hurts the other most, at one time obsessively desires the very same thing that the other wants, at another time the exact opposite, always with the sole purpose of negating the claims of the other. In this condition animosity between groups circulates freely, adding layer upon layer of grievances and antagonistic games are played with no end in mind except the defeat and humiliation of the other. Ambedkar provides several examples: 'Hindus and Muslims make preparations against each other', he tells us, 'without abatement reminding one of a race in armaments between two hostile nations. If the Hindus have the Banaras University, the Musalmans must have the Aligarh University. If the Hindus start the *Shuddhi* movement, the Muslims must launch the *Tablig* movement. If the Hindus start *sangathan*, the Muslims must have the *Tanjim*. If the Hindus have the RSS, the Muslims must reply by organizing the *Khaksars*.' A group of Muslims had psyched themselves into a state of paranoia that was only partly grounded in fears of inter-religious domination but which got exacerbated and became a very real prospect after the formation of Pakistan.

But a majority-minority syndrome had another consequence. In the 19th century, a number of freedom- and equality-centred reform movements had been initiated within Hindus and Muslims. But a majority-minority syndrome set off by inter-communal rivalry forestalled these reforms, intensifying anti-reformist tendencies. Once again, Ambedkar grasped this point well: "When people regard each other as a menace, all energies are spent on meeting this menace. The exigencies of a common front against one another generates a conspiracy of silence over social evils. Internal dissent and conflict is squashed in favour of the idea that everyone must close ranks or the community would weaken." In other words, prospects of intra-religious domination had also grown at the crucial moment of India's independence.

It was in such a context replete with continuing inter- and intra-religious domination that independent India had to decide the character of the newly instituted state and its relationship with religion. It had two options: either to have a majoritarian religion centred state that consolidates both forms of inter-religious domination, a patriarchal, upper caste dominated Hindu majoritarian state or a state that contains these tendencies and tries to reduce both these forms of domination. In 1950, when India was declared a republic, it chose to have a secular state *despite* the massacre and displacement of millions of people on ethno-religious grounds, not to offer 'a final solution' by expulsion or liquidation of all but the dominant religious group but with the explicit objective of dealing with tensions generated continuously by deep religious diversity. In doing so they developed a distinctive conception of secularism.

Why is this secularism distinctive? Because unlike say the French or Turkish model, it was not anti-religious. In the French state, for example, (a) religion is not officially recognized, (b) It becomes a target of active disrespect by a state that excludes religion, from its affairs but retains the power to intervene in religion, (c) is removed from the public domain, i.e. privatized, (d) qualification of citizenship, both membership in the state and all rights are made wholly independent of religious affiliation. As I shall explain below, Indian secularism is very different. Likewise, it is also unlike the American model in which (a) the non-recognition of religion is accompanied by a different understanding of what separation means. Here, religion and state are mutually excluded from each other—none has the right or the power to intervene in the affairs of one another. Thus (b) the state has no power to intervene in religious affairs. (c) There is no active disrespect but rather continues to favour unqualified passive respect for religion, and (d) qualification of citizenship, both membership in the state and all rights are made wholly independent of religious affiliation. Indian secularism is also different from Western European states where many states remain weakly but constitutively linked to one dominant religion. While individual rights are independent of religious affiliation, the state, in all kinds of ways, one dominant religion. All 'Western' states grew out of the need to respond to the challenge posed to individuals and non-religious groups by a politically meddlesome and socially oppressive church in a context of virtual religious homogeneity. In India on the other hand, (a) a distinction is drawn between the identity of the state which is made entirely independent of religion and an important but limited sphere where religion is officially recognized (Articles 25-30 in the Indian Constitution). (b) The state is required to be equally (well- or ill) disposed to all religions. No religion is supposed to be politically dominant or favoured by the state. The state is meant to challenge not support inter-religious domination. (c) Religion is understood to be a complex, morally ambiguous phenomenon—some aspects of which require negative state intervention—ban on untouchability, the order that all temples be opened to all sections of Hindus, the law that seeks to keep religious restrictions away from the exercise of basic individual rights of women—(state against intra-religious domination), some aspects require positive intervention—exemption to Sikhs from wearing standard headgear in the army or the police, and still other aspects that require that the state keep entirely away from religion, a space must exist where religious individuals and communities are entirely free to do as they believe are required by their religion. (d) There is no blanket disrespect towards religions nor an unqualified respect for them but rather an attitude of critical respect. (e) Unlike both the French and American models, the state is not strictly separated from religion. Instead, the state keeps a policy of principled distance from all religions and (f) The qualification for citizenship qua membership in the state is made wholly independent of religious affiliation and although most rights are independent of religion, some are dependent on membership in religious communities.

To restate my second proposition: Most Indian secularists have frequently defended not this complex, sophisticated, very Indian model but instead some very limited and partial version of it or worse, one or the other Western variants. They have alternatingly defended a secularism that is anti-religious—alienating the religious by failing to treat them as citizens worthy of equal respect, sometimes put their force behind an areligious secularism—failing to understand that no modern state can keep itself aloof from religion, especially in places like India where religion cannot easily be separated from the social and the cultural, and sometimes chosen to support a multi-religious secularism that has a high propensity to tolerate indefensible socio-religious practices and that cries foul every time the state intervenes in religion. This has got defenders of secularism into a mess. They have intervened in religion when they should not have, intervened when restraint was desperately needed and frequently continued to respect aspects of religion not worthy of respect and disrespect those facets that deserved respect. An acute understanding of the complex and variegated ways in which inter-and intra-religious domination persists in the interstices of Indian society has been elusive and therefore has been challenged, if at all, only half-heartedly.

One manifestation of this misunderstanding is the complete and exhaustive identification of secularism with a defence of minority rights, as if the only purpose of secularism is to equally respect all religions and to provide support to all of them—my third proposition. On this view, fighting inter-religious domination seems to be the only raison d'etre of secularism. But this forgets that an equally important purpose of Indian secularism and indeed the primary purpose of all Western secularisms has been to counter intra-religious domination. That one function of a secular state is to encourage freedom, equality and justice-centred reforms in every religion, to protect individuals from oppression by their own fellow co-religionists, indeed, to rescue ordinary Hindus, Muslims, Christians and Sikhs from their own religious extremists, to liberate religion from bigotry and fanaticism, simply slips off the radar of secularism. The marginalization of socio-religious reform in the agenda of Indian secularism and the resulting exclusive focus on minority rights lends credence to the mostly unjust charge of minorityism. If secularism is seen as concerned solely with the defence of minority rights, it can be viewed as a tool to protect the interests of Muslims and Christians, and having little to do with Hindus. It can then be twisted to appear as pro-Muslim and anti-Hindu. But secularism is needed as much to protect Hindus from their own extremists and homogenizers and from the exclusionary instincts of its traditional power wielders that have cared little in the past for Dalits and women.

Put differently, the reduction of secularism to a minority-protection device and the disconnection of minority-rights discourse from feminist and Dalit discourses has led to the weakening of the politics of all vulnerable sections of society. Instead of standing together and complementing one another, today, secular, feminist and Dalit discourses, in many contexts, confront one another as competitors, if not opponents. The strength of Indian secularism—its defence of minority rights—is easily made to appear as its weakness and the burden of its defence, rather than be shared by all citizens, falls on the minorities and 'pro-minority' secularists. This is both unfair and unnecessary.

I now come to my fourth proposition: The misunderstanding of Indian secularism, especially as an anti-religious doctrine has meant that secularists have not maintained a proper distinction between the communitarian and the communal. A communitarian position is one that an individual is at least partly defined by his or her religious/philosophical commitments and traditions (community) and therefore that there is nothing inappropriate in proclaiming that one is a Hindu/Muslim/Sikh/Christian/Marxist/Advaita and so on. Indeed, in some instances, a person may even take legitimate pride in one's community and community identity—as long as the person is also prepared to be openly ashamed when there is good reason to. A communitarian position is different from a communal one. A communal perspective is one in which one's community identity is defined in opposition to, not in dialogue with, other communities (Recall the modern conception of confessional religion that I alluded to earlier) such that the existence and interests is necessarily viewed as being at the expense of other communities and community identities. It is communal to believe or act in a way that presupposes that one can't be a Hindu without being anti-Muslim or vice-versa. Communalism is communitarianism gone sour. Perhaps, very much in line with the tone and substance of the paper, communal is also a term that can be legitimately used for communitarian excesses that thwart individual interests and autonomy.

The conflation of communitarian and communal in India has often meant that secular persons with a Hindu background or identity have not found a way of articulating the religious or socio-religious interests of Hindus without sounding communal and have often appeared to have defended the Muslim faith and interests in bad faith, as if in doing so, they were really being communal but this was permissible given the vulnerability of minorities in a representative democracy dominated by Hindus. The fact is that there is nothing wrong in articulating and defending some Hindu, Muslim and Christian interests when they do not come into conflict with one another. This can be done without guilt or shame. However, sadly, Indian secularism has rarely sorted out this issue and dispelled this confusion. Lack of clarity and honesty has bred indefensible swings from one communal position to another and a lot of avoidable hypocrisy. Proponents of secularism have managed to avoid this problem occasionally, sporadically, inconsistently, somewhat superficially and half-heartedly but had to and will have to do so with greater understanding of each other's religious tradition, consistently, all the time.

This brings me to my fifth and final point, one that I make with less certainty but feel compelled to put on the table, all the same. This relates to my remark about the general ignorance of religious and philosophical traditions, both one's own and of the other. There continues to exist deep fault lines in our education system. We have universities in India where there are no religious studies, and universities without departments of comparative religion. This means that students come out of the university system without a deeper, critical understanding of the great religious traditions of the world. As a result, both the critique and defence of our own religion and that of the other is at best shallow and frequently mischievous. This is so unlike the 'secular' West where the study of comparative religions is done seriously in institutions of higher learning. Some of the best studies of ancient Hindu traditions and medieval and modern Hinduism have emanated from university departments. I simply wish to flag this issue because

I believe it needs greater attention, discussion and debate, not secularist posturing.

Furthermore, and this is true as much of the West as it is of countries such as India, the study of religion is not seen as central to humanities and the social sciences. In parts of the West, religion could be studied separately because at some point in their history, it became identified with doctrine and belief and belief came to be viewed not as love, allegiance or trust, as when one still says that I truly believe in him or his word, but rather something to do with propositional claims or assertions; Quite like, I believe that it is raining, I would say, I believe that God exists. A belief, on this view, is an idea in the head which can be true or false. This view of religion was neither prevalent in pre-modern Europe nor captures the complex phenomenon that it is meant to in the South Asian context, where religion is inscribed in the institutional, cultural and linguistic matrix of the whole society. It follows that here in India what we today call religion must be made integral to the social sciences.

My final, brief remark: Defenders of secularism need to do three things simultaneously and consistently. Their (a) defence of minority rights must always be accompanied by (b) a robust critique of minority extremism and all forms of communalisms and both of these must always reflect (c) a deeper understanding and defence of the best of every religious tradition. Our critiques of minority extremism and majoritarianism must reflect that we know minority and majority religious traditions from the inside.

1

Secularism: The Idea, Indian Version and Challenges

Zaheer Ali

Introduction

I have to underline one point at the outset that the claim that secularism is exclusively a Western concept or the 'gift of Christianity' has gone uncontested for too long. Despite so many scholarly studies, there appears no consensus on the absolute definition of the idea. There are banks of principles that may be associated with secularism. It is true that the political facet of secularism, particularly the principle of separation of religion and state, is essentially Western. Nevertheless, secularism is not entirely about political processes. It has linkages with religion, culture, philosophy and ethics too. It is in these areas that the Eastern religions and intellectual traditions have contributed substantially to the concept of secularism.

Another aspect of this paper is to delineate the Indian version of secularism and to distinguish it from different modes of the idea that are collectively known as the Western concept of secularism. The Constitution of India does not exclusively deal with the definition of the concept of secularism even after the 42nd Constitution Amendment Act. During the freedom struggle though there was an unstated understanding among the prominent leaders of the Indian National Congress (INC) that an independent India would be a secular state, no prominent leader exclusively dealt with the concept of secularism either in his writings or speeches. What relevant material, therefore, we get from that period is the resolution of the INC passed in its Karachi session in 1931 and stray references about the idea in the speeches and writings of some leaders, notably Gandhi and Nehru. Consequently, in exposing the contours of Indian secularism, I have made use of the religious, intellectual, historical inputs of India as well as the ideas of the leaders of the freedom struggle that ultimately got expressed in the pertinent provisions of the Constitution.

It must also be made clear that there has never been complete conformity on the definition, efficacy or desirability of secularism among the scholars who chose to write on the concept and among the statesmen or popular leaders who made it official policy to run political affairs in their respective states. Therefore, posers like what is secularism or is there a universally accepted definition of it cannot be definitely answered because there is no solitary version of secularism. Another problem is that the term 'secularism' entered into the lexicon of social discourse only in the middle of the 19th century while quite a few values and ideas such as atheism, agnosticism, religious tolerance, justice, freethinking, humanism, freedom of religion, worldly laws, non-theocratic state, natural morality and even separation of state and religion that are directly or indirectly associated with secularism are very old. This confounds things further. Does secularism denote any one specific value of these or all of these? Or does a specific value of these constitute the core and the rest of them or a couple of them are the minor components of the concept?

If we look up the Oxford English Dictionary, we are informed that secularism is the doctrine that morality should be based solely on regard to the well-being of mankind in the present life to the exclusion of all considerations drawn on belief in God....This is an extremely narrow view of the concept underlying only secular morality and disregarding various other topics linked to secularism. Candidly speaking, secularism cannot be defined in absolute terms. For instance, the attitude that may also be called secular has always been the thrust of thoughts and way of actions of some individuals whom we call freethinkers. Such people had always been present in almost all societies.[1]

Although, the broad vision and all-inclusive outlook of the freethinkers over the ages may be symptomatic of a particular value or a couple of values that secularism promotes, it per se cannot be termed secularism. Then there are certain philosophical (even religious) and intellectual inputs that have hugely contributed in fashioning the idea of secularism that has close linkages with the institution of the state and the policies of its agency, the government. This is essentially a pronounced political dimension of the notion that we call the Western concept of secularism. As we know it has been a subject of intense debate for more than two centuries.

Secularism, in its Western mode is a contentious issue in many Eastern societies. It, as some of the scholars make us believe, explains why it has remained a distant ideal in the popular psyche of Indians. It is also true that even in the West the concept of secularism never had a sole, uncontested definition at any point of time. The perspectives about secularism kept changing and by the time the Indian elite got to know about it in the latter part of the 19th century, the concept had largely denoted two things, one, freeing the education system from the thraldom of religion and two, separation of religion from the state. As we shall see, in the course of discussion, that none of these modes of secularism has been adopted as an ideal in its entirety by the makers of the Constitution of India.

The Western mode of secularism is a product of European history, more accurately the logical culmination of the Renaissance and the Reformation, advancements in the fields of knowledge, science, technology and the consequent surfacing of liberal democracy. As regards the meaning of the term 'secularism' it is adequate to know that it is derived from the Latin word '*saeculum*' that essentially refers to 'time and space'. It implies indifference to transcendental or spiritual affairs and concentrates solely on this-worldly affairs. Traditionally, the word saeculum was used to mean the liberation of man's reason and language from the clutches of religion. Gradually, the term came to be known as a channel to build on an ethical system based on the principle of natural morality that should be necessarily independent of religious precepts. In this sense it epitomizes the right of an individual to question the bases of obligation, the existence of God, the immortality of soul, the Hereafter, etc. In its Western variety that is excessively political, secularism underlines separation of Church and State.

The Middle Ages witnessed violent conflicts between Church and State in Europe that ultimately led to the collapse of the Holy Roman Empire and the consequent separation of temporal affairs from those of spiritual. During the 15th and 16th centuries, at the height of the Renaissance, the grip of religion over the minds of the people weakened considerably and man appeared to embark on exploring a new world of new possibilities without the crutches of religion. The intelligentsia gradually began confronting and sometimes openly attacking the Roman Catholic Church, as for instance, Voltaire exhorted, "let us crush the infamous."[2] In the 18th century, in the post-Kantian Europe, ecclesiastical matters were rendered superfluous and the focus shifted to material reality and rational thinking. Consequently, by the end of the 18th century the spheres of Church and State were distinctly earmarked and the elite of respective spheres somehow kept sustaining an edgy rapport.

It was in the USA that the idea of secularism got a firm foundation for the first time as it was enshrined in the federal Constitution. In point of fact, the idea of building 'a wall of separation between the Church and the state' got widespread currency after the enactment of the American Constitution. The French Revolution had set in motion the process for the establishment of an egalitarian, democratic and secular republic. However, it took more than two centuries to change France from an intensely religious country to a truly secular state with the enactment of the Law of Separation of Church and State of 1905. Turkey is another country that has strengthened the concept of secularism by introducing it in a predominantly Muslim society after the First World War. Though Turkey was not made a secular state by a truly democratic process, its transformation from the seat of the Caliphate and the centre of Sunni orthodoxy into a secular state was astonishing.

The idea of secularism had always been under attack for varied reasons mostly by the priest classes all across the world.

Nonetheless, in recent years it has to face a two-pronged assault from the religious orthodoxy as well as from the post-modernist intellectuals who are not necessarily religious apologetics. The latter group of critics are quite vociferous in India in the changed political scenario in the country wherein the Hindu Right has emerged as a formidable force to reckon with. The major area of concern in the context of India is the growing influence of communal politics that has severely eroded secular values from society and even from some state institutions.

I

Most Western scholars claim that secularism is a product of Christendom. This is factually inaccurate. Etymologically the term might have been drawn from 'saeculum' a word associated with the Christian literature but the secular ideas predate Christianity. For instance, as a noteworthy strand of philosophical thought secularism was deeply ingrained in the thoughts of the thinkers of ancient Greece and Rome. The Greek philosopher Epicurus (342 BCE-circa 270 BCE) contemplated that the cardinal aim of philosophy was to facilitate for the people a happy and serene life that should ensure the presence of peace and absence of fear and pain. He believed that death denoted the end of body as well as soul and did not seem to have faith in the Hereafter. Epicures' worth in the context of secularism lies in his contribution to promote objectivity and scientific method. He forcefully taught that nothing should be believed unless it was passed through the tests of observation and logical deduction. In this respect he furnished a scientific foundation to speculative philosophy.

Similarly, Roman Emperor, Marcus Aurelius (121-180), a Stoic philosopher who had acquired the reputation of a philosopher-king in his lifetime itself, did not give credence to the prevailing religious norms and customs of his times while meting out justice. He was a thoroughly judicious ruler and in administrative matters he would always stick to logic and reasoning.

Ideas refuting the life after death or negating the existence of God that form the core of the Western concept of secularism did find expression in Indian philosophical traditions and religious doctrines. It is believed these thoughts were advanced as part of the protest movements against the extremely rigid and irksomely ritualistic social order that had emerged in India by the 5th century BCE because of the complete dominance of the priest class. In this context we must refer to an atheistic and materialistic school of philosophy, the Charvakas, which is usually classified as 'heterodox' or the *nastika* system of Indian philosophy. The school is believed to be named after its founder, Charvak who had authored a philosophical treatise, the *Barhaspatya-sutras*.

Charvakas, like Buddhism and Jainism, rejected the sanctity and authority of the Vedas. Religion and God, the Charvakas emphasized, were the creations of the human mind that were fervently propagated by the class of the priests that had emerged as a consequence of these superstitious ideas because it had vested interests in hoodwinking the susceptible masses. Charvakas had fearlessly blamed the Brahmins for spreading superstitious ideas as divine truth and making a living out of it. They did not make a distinction between body and soul and for them death denoted the end of everything for the deceased. Thus, they believed only in the material world and reflected solely about its affairs. The Charvakas advocated that every human being had a right to lead a happy, successful and fruitful life as there was no life after death. Significantly, the Charvakas attacked the caste system because for them, like religion and God, it was also a man-made, fake and exploitative institution. They argued that naturally all human beings were born equal and their social stratification was a conspiracy of the priest class.

India has a unique distinction of producing two religions that do not recognize the existence of an omnipotent, omnipresent and supernatural entity called God. A major world religion like Buddhism and another nationally significant religion, Jainism, refute the sanctity and authority of the Vedas and for that reason the mainstream schools of Hindu philosophy typify them as *nastika*, materialistic and atheistic schools of thought. The Buddhist teachings primarily focus on the issues of the worldly life and its suffering. Having attained nirvana, the Buddha was believed to have first taught the Four Noble

Truths viz. a) life leads to suffering; b) suffering is the result of craving; c) suffering ends when craving ends; d) one can achieve enlightenment or liberation by following the Noble Eightfold Path as shown by the Buddha.

An analysis of the path shown by the Buddha reveals that among those eight noble truths worshipping a supernatural god who would dole out rewards and punishments to men in the Hereafter does not figure at all. The Eightfold Path recommends that man must rely on his wisdom to comprehend the true nature of things; must be prepared for renunciation to be truly free; must always speak the truth; must not harm anyone by his actions; must earn a non-harmful livelihood; must strive to improve himself; must be conscious of the present reality of his existence; and train himself for meditation. In fact, it is a kind of universal moral code devoid of the superstitious ideas that are usually promoted by most religions.

The Buddha, as per the experts, had refused to respond to the metaphysical posers. In the context it is worthy of note to refer to a part of the dialogue between Buddha and the Brahmin Potthapada cited by B.R. Ambedkar:

"Then in the same terms, Potthapada asked (the Buddha) each of the following questions:

1. Is the world not eternal?
2. Is the world finite?
3. Is the world infinite?
4. Is the soul same as the body?
5. Is the soul one thing and body another?
6. Does one who has gained the truth live again after death?
7. Does he neither live again, nor not live again, after death?

And to each one the exalted one made the same reply: It was this.

That too, Potthapada, is a matter on which I have expressed no opinion."[3]

It is because of Buddha's silence on ecclesiastical and transcendental issues that Buddhism is usually classified as an agnostic faith. The Buddhist position is that insight in such matters comes from the experience, critical enquiry and reasoning of the seeker and not by having a blind faith in the paranormal phenomena. It is quite surprising that many

Buddhist canons are so rational and scientific that they surpass the ideas that are regularly trumpeted as the contribution of European Age of Enlightenment. The Buddha advises his followers not to accept anything merely because it is part of the tradition or finds expression in scriptures. Also one must not accept something as true because it fits in his pre-conceived notions. The Buddha recommends that one must accept and believe in things only when he finds them moral, blameless, exemplary and conducive to happiness on account of his personal experience and reasoning. This is, in fact, the essence of secularism that flourished in Europe in the second half of the 19th century.

Though Jainism too is believed to have come up as a protest movement against the Brahmanical orthodoxy, the Jain sources account otherwise. It is believed to be a very ancient religion, perhaps the oldest one that has survived till the present. The Jain scholars claim it predates Hinduism because Mahavir (6th century BCE) was the 24th *tirthankara* while the Parshva, the twenty-third one lived and preached in the 9th century BCE and the first one Rishaba or Adinath belonged to pre-history. It is probably the only atheistic religion of the world and in this respect it is the first important philosophical source that has contributed in shaping the idea of secularism. The individual and his deeds are of primary importance in Jainism for every living being achieves the divine consciousness only through self struggle. Any soul that succeeds in conquering its inner demons is bound to experience spiritual bliss that makes him a supreme being, *Jina* (conqueror). Jainism believes that every soul is potentially capable of reaching the stage of Supreme Being through the right actions, *karma*.

Rooted in this precept is the most significant principle of Jainism i.e. *Ahimsa* or non-violence. Since every soul is potentially qualified to be a supreme being, therefore, every living being must regard other living beings as herself/ himself/ itself; thus, using violence against the other living being will mean harming the self. A living being can perform the right actions, *karma*, by sticking to the three gems of Jainism viz. right faith, right knowledge and right conduct. Jainism clearly emphasizes that *there exists no supreme, supernatural or sacrosanct creator, preserver or destroyer of the Universe. The Universe is self-existent and self-regulated.* This is a remarkably scientific approach to comprehend the cosmos that has been the core of Jainism for centuries. We, therefore, cannot overlook the canons of Jainism while exploring the philosophical legacy of secularism.

It seems quite difficult for many, in the backdrop of the emergence of very powerful Hindu chauvinist forces represented by the RSS, the BJP, the VHP and a host of other organisations collectively known as the *Singh Parivar* since the last decade of the last century on the socio-political horizon of India, to imagine that Hinduism is as compatible to the idea of secularism as some other major religions of the world. The issue gets further complicated when one makes an attempt to comprehend a sole and authentic version of Hinduism and fails miserably.

The faith that is now popularly known as Hinduism, the anglicised growth of the Arabic word Hindu applied to the people of India first by the Arab traders and later by the Muslim conquerors, was believed to be called the *Sanatana Dharma*, which can roughly be translated as 'perpetual faith', is not a single religion in the customary sense of the term but it is a confederation of various faiths and modes of worship practiced by numerous communities of the Indian subcontinent and South Asia. According to an estimate of the Anthropological Survey of India there are about 2,800 communities in India which can be distinguished from each other on the bases of their beliefs and religious practices. The reasons are that Hinduism was not established by any prophet or the representative of God, it has no set of core beliefs and it does not have any specific mode of worship. This diversity of the faith is not its weakness but its strength because it gives its followers total freedom in matters of belief and mode of worship. Hinduism gives liberty to each of its followers to believe in the deity of his choice, *ishta-devata*, to be selected from a huge pantheon of innumerable gods and goddesses.

Another distinct feature of Hinduism is its opposition to proselytism, which is in direct contrast to other organised religions such as Buddhism, Christianity and Islam. The logical corollary of the principle is tolerance of, if not respect shown to, other religions. In the light of these characteristics, we may argue that the complete liberty enjoyed by the Hindus in matters of beliefs, choice of deity, mode of worship, absence of compulsion to adhere to a specific faith and tolerance of other faiths makes Hinduism a faith perfectly conducive to the idea of secularism because all these principles do constitute the major features of secularism that is currently prevalent the world over. Nevertheless, it is only the half truth.

The flip side of the story is that while Hindu philosophical traditions are very non-interventionist, the society that ultimately emerges in a predominantly Hindu geographical region such as India is extremely exploitative, regressive and inhuman. The reason is a rigid and hierarchical caste system that primarily defines a Hindu society. The debate whether the caste system has always been the integral part of Hinduism or it emerged later as a consequence of conflicts between the Dravidians of the Indus valley civilization and the Aryan invaders of Central Asia is irrelevant because caste system has been a domineering force in Hindu society for centuries. The free-thinking principles of Hinduism, or rather Hindu philosophy, mentioned above apply only to the *suvarna* castes that are part of the Hindu caste hierarchy. The *Chandals* and the tribal people (the untouchables, *Dalits* and the *Adivasis*) do not figure anywhere in the scheme of Hinduism. In fact, these people have always been forced to live a sub-human life.

Added to this, is the rise of political Hinduism that emerged as an organized force during the British period most probably with the covert patronage of the foreign masters to vertically divide Indian society on religious lines and thus ensure the security of the Raj. A chauvinist organization such as the RSS and a fascist political party like the Hindu Mahasabha had actually laid the foundation of militant Hinduism. It was V. D. Savarkar who coined the term *Hindutva*, which may be loosely defined as a *Hindu Rashtra* or the justification for such a state that is now the favoured agenda of all the organizations of the Hindu Right. In order to accomplish the agenda, the fascist Hindu forces intend either to annihilate the religious minorities, in particular the Muslims and Christians, or to reduce them to the level of third class citizens.

The concept of secularism has largely acquired political undertones (distinct from philosophical ones) since the second half of the 19th century and in that respect it essentially implies separation of religion and state. Now, if we refer to the New Testament we come across this guidance that Jesus gave to his disciples: "Render therefore to Caesar the things that are Caesar's, and to God the things that are God's."[4] It is, therefore, widely believed that Christianity has clearly separated the domains of religion and politics, which enables a religious man to be perfectly comfortable in a secular state by keeping his religious beliefs to himself and as citizen of a state should abide by its laws.

Though most Christians seem to concur with the counselling of Jesus and regard religion as a private affair, many others contest this position and argue that the Lord did not intend to put up a 'wall' of separation between the church and the state. The conservatives and now the neo-conservatives in the USA forcefully reject the secular foundation of the US Constitution on the ground that it was Thomas Jefferson who in a letter to the Danbury Baptist Association, Connecticut, had casually mentioned a 'wall' between church and the state as a decorative metaphor that was later misconstrued as the inalienable philosophy of the Constitution.

Recently, the State Board of Education, Texas, USA, passed a resolution that made it mandatory for students to learn that the words "separation of church and state" are not mentioned in the Constitution and that the US government should be referred to as a "constitutional republic rather than a democratic republic" in the social study textbooks. The resolution further insisted that the students be made aware of the Judeo-Christian background of the Founding Fathers of the nation.[5] Likewise, the Catholic Church vehemently opposes the idea of treating religion as a private affair because they argue, in accordance with theism, that God not only rules over the individuals but also over societies. Accordingly, the political concept of secularism has not been universally accepted by all in the West, which is predominantly Christian.

The correlation between Islam and secularism is really vexed. Like Christianity or any other major religion, there are two main discourses of Islam, one, orthodox and second, liberal. Now, there may be variants of orthodox and liberal discourses from extreme to endurable depending on time-space variability. In reality, no religion except Buddhism (agnostic) and Jainism (atheist) can entirely endorse the concept of secularism; at best a liberal religious interpretation might encourage peaceful coexistence of all religions by respecting the religious sentiments of all. This is exactly what we witness in most Western nations. It does not mean that Christianity, the predominant faith of Western societies, encompasses secularism as a core principle of the faith. If there is one advice to separate the domains of God and Caesar in the New Testament there are many others, for instance ("Far above all principality and power and might and dominion, and every name that is named, not only in this age but also in that which is to come. And He put all *things* under his feet, and gave him *to be* head over all *things* to the church."[6]), which negate the separation of state and church.

Western liberalism and religious tolerance are the logical consequences of religious reformation, renaissance, age of enlightenment, industrial revolution, secular and socialist movements and secularization of society that were the upshots of European history. Such revolutionary movements or ideas could not get penetrated in Eastern societies particularly those which came under the sway of Islam. Ironically it was the works of a Muslim, Ibn Rushd (known by Latinized corruption, Averroes, in the West) that set off the process of enlightenment in Europe. While the West embraced Ibn Rushd and consequently benefited tremendously, the Muslim world deviously ignored him and suffered a lot. We will return to Ibn Rushd a little later. So far as the issue of tolerance of other religions is concerned there are two verses of the Quran that exactly connote the idea:

"There is no compulsion in religion."[7] and

"Unto you your religion and unto me my religion."[8]

These verses invariably find expression in the liberal discourse of Islam of every hue. The issue of political secularism, nevertheless, is quite dicey. The orthodox version of Islam makes absolutely no distinction between the temporal and religious domains. For it every aspect of human life comes under the purview of Islam and, therefore, political activity must be conducted in accordance with the Quran, *ahadis* and *sharia*. The last two sources mentioned here are not universally accepted by all Muslims. They are latter compilations that have taken in many patriarchal, regressive, misogynic and irrational social practices and ideas that were prevalent in the Middle East during the first and second centuries of Islam.

Another problem with ahadis and sharia is that they do not have a single narrative. Though there are more than seventy sects of Islam the broader ones are two, the Sunni and the Shia. Both the sects have different sets of ahadis and sharia. A liberal discourse of Islam invariably suggests discounting ahadis and sharia for their contentious character and approves of tolerance of all religions in the light of Quranic injunctions cited above. It must, however, be admitted that liberal voices in the Muslim world are not as strident as they are in the West. Accordingly, barring a few Muslim nations, secularism does not figure as a cherished political principle of most Muslim-dominated countries.

Most scholars agree that one person who has actually instituted a secular school of thought in Europe and thus ushered in an era of enlightenment and liberalism in the thick of the Dark Ages was Muhammad Ibn Ahmad Ibn Rushd (1126-1198) whom the Western world refers to as Averroes and his philosophy as Averroism. A colossal genius who contributed immensely to philosophy, logic, politics, psychology, medicine, astronomy, physics, geography, mathematics, celestial mathematics, music, Islamic jurisprudence and Islamic theology was born in Cordoba, Andulas, present-day Spain. At a time when Christian Europe was immersed in the cesspool of superstitions and intellectual bankruptcy, Ibṇ Rushd could carry on research freely in areas such as philosophy, sciences, law, theology and so on mainly because he lived in the Muslim-controlled region of Spain. At the side of his original contributions, he also retrieved and introduced the intellectual sources of Hellenistic civilization, in particular, the writings of Aristotle and Plato, a legacy that was lost to the world under the albatross of the Holy Roman Empire. Averroism played a pivotal role in liberalizing Europe and ultimately heralding the European Renaissance.

Ibn Rushd consistently argued against the religious restriction over philosophy, science or any field of intellectual activity. This is exactly the line of reasoning that was replicated six centuries later by Holyoake as the founder of the movement of secularism and for that reason Ibn Rushd is rightly called the father of the modern concept of secularism. Ibn Rushd, notwithstanding the dominance of orthodoxy over Islamic theology, forcefully stipulated an analytical interpretation of the Quran. This was indeed a ground-breaking approach that should have been applied to all religious scriptures, not just the Quran. Having applied an analytical methodology in the study of the Quran, Ibn Rushd surmises that Islam is purely a rational religion and advises the Muslims to develop rational thinking and a scientific spirit which are in tune with the message of their religion. Had the Islamic world taken hold of his advice in the 12th century, it, rather than Europe, would have been the leader in philosophy, science and technology.

As a political philosopher, Ibn Rushd recommends that the philosophers should have a dominant role in decision-making and at the same time disapproves of the involvement of theologians (the so-called *Ulema*) in political affairs. He emphasizes that the very presence of theologians poses a serious threat to the institution of the state and urges the rulers to maintain a strict check over their activities. This clubbed with his rationalism and naturalism expounds a philosophical principle that implies separation of religion and state. It continues to be the core value of political dimension of secularism today.

Machiavelli (1469-1527), a realist political thinker of the Renaissance period, is credited to free the discipline of political science from the firm grip of ethics and religion and thus making it a true modern social science. Taking a cue from Ibn Rushd, he too criticizes the role of corrupt religious institutions and these associated with them and believes that their involvement in politics gives rise to corruption and breaks up the state into vicious groups. Since the thrust of Machiavelli's political thought is prudence and expediency, he does not rule out completely the intermixing of religion and politics. He advises the ruler to exploit people's religious susceptibilities to keep them subdued.

The point that gets underlined, however, is Machiavelli's insolence for the institution of religion. He treated it as a mere exploiting tool in the hands of the ruler. According to a scholarly estimation, "In his (Machiavelli's) cool, calculating cynicism, his frank and undisguised naturalism, his extreme individualism, his pragmatism, his devotion to classical antiquity, in his rejection of religion and of supernatural sanctions in favour of a 'here and now' philosophy and a hedonistic morality___in all these things he is characteristic of the Renaissance and, to a very considerable extent, of the modern mind."[9]

"It (religion) is the opium of the people." This is perhaps one of the most famous statements ever made about the institution of religion. The author of the comment, Karl Marx (1818-1883), the revolutionary philosopher and economist, had become an atheist early on in his youth. In 1848, he in collaboration with Friedrich Engels published a booklet, *The Communist Manifesto,* which was to change the course of history in the next century. Together with *The Manifesto* some other writings of Marx constitute the revolutionary doctrine known as Marxism, which offers a completely radical worldview wherein religion is rendered redundant.

The famous remark cited above may sound unpleasantly anti-religion. It is not if read as part of the passage, which appears in *Introduction to a Contribution to the Critique of Hegel's Philosophy of Right*. The preceding sentences to the remark are: "*Religious* distress is at the same time the *expression* of real distress and the *protest* against real distress. Religion is the sigh of the oppressed creature, the heart of a heartless world, just as it is the spirit of a spiritless situation. It is the opium of the people" (emphasis of the author). Marx, therefore, concedes that religion did play its role in human history as a solace to the poor and the wretched by promising them a better life in the Hereafter. The promise is illusory, however, dawns upon people who rely on rationality rather than blind faith.

Marx rejects religion because: a) it is irrational, b) it makes human beings servile and forces them to accept the status quo and, c) it is hypocritical for it might profess equality of human beings in the kingdom of god but in practice supports powerful oppressors and exploiters. In a socialist society, the ultimate stage of human development that Marxism envisages, religion will inevitably disappear along with the state and classes. It must, therefore, be underlined that Marx does not specifically write about secularism or recommend a premeditated and violent opposition to religion as Bradlaugh does; for Marx religion will peter out inexorably like other superstitions in a rationalistic-socialist society.

Though the nuances and the implications that are usually associated with the concept of secularism as discussed above, are quite old, the term is of recent origin. It was George Jacob Holyoake (1817-1906), a British activist and writer who first used it in 1851 to denote a movement that he had launched to provide a rational base to the worldly affairs and free them from the clutches of instinctive and irrational theology. The movement aimed at popularizing a code of duty concerning the worldly life with an emphasis on human intelligence. It appealed mostly to those who were sceptical of Christian theology.

It was, in fact, a protest movement against the rigid theological canons that accentuated only transcendental issues. Holyoake established the Central Secular Society through which he aimed at improving the worldly life by material means. He and his supporters like Charles Southwell, Thomas Cooper, Thomas Patterson and William Chilton laid great emphasis on science and reasoning. Secularism for Holyoake was a way of thinking that taught us about practical astuteness of natural ethics without depending upon the Church.[10] Holyoake's movement of secularism called attention to rationality and freedom of thought and expression. He was of the opinion that like scientific research, religious research should be carried out in a free atmosphere and for his finding a research scholar should not be persecuted either by the laws of state or the edicts of the Church.[11] The Central Secular Society was to be the vehicle to promote the doctrine of secularism that essentially implied:

(a) The real driving force of human activity must be science.
(b) Morality should not spring up from religion but from

the secular conduct of man.

(c) Reason must be the sole criterion for authorized actions and thought.

(d) A secular society must guarantee freedom of thought and expression.

(e) All human actions should be directed towards the improvement and progress of the worldly life.

Though Holyoake never explicitly declared himself an atheist, his critics insisted that by coining the term 'secularism' he actually intended to endow legitimacy to atheism. Holyoake could have been an agnostic for he ignored and advised others to ignore religion and its major related topic, god. For him to promote secularism it was not necessary to attack religion or deny the existence of god. His approach was that in order to put across the secular argument, the negation or condemnation of religious arguments was gratuitous. What Holyoake actually intended was to accentuate people's natural right to be free from the canons and restrictions imposed on their freedom by religion and its agents, the priests.

Holyoake's secular movement made attempts to create a society that would render the institution of religion superfluous. He elaborates his indifference towards religion and total commitment to his movement thus: "Secularism is not an argument against Christianity; it is one independent of it. It does not question the pretensions of Christianity; it advances others. Secularism does not say there is no light or guidance elsewhere, but maintains that there is light and guidance in secular truth, whose conditions and sanctions exist independently, and act forever. Secular knowledge is manifestly that kind of knowledge which is founded in this life, which relates to the conduct of this life, conduces to the welfare of this life, and is capable of being tested by the experience of this life."[12]

According to Holyoake, there are three essential principles of secularism: (a) the worldly life has to be made better by making progress in all fields of human activity making use of material means; (b) scientific research must be carried on and scientific temperament ought to be developed because Science is the key to all human progress and happiness; (c) it is always good to act good irrespective of the presence or absence of other good. Holyoake also dismantled the edifice of ethics founded on religion by theologians. He delinked ethics from religion and believed that secular ethics was essentially natural morality which formed the quintessence of humanity. On this issue he refused to needlessly get embroiled in the debate that whether it was crucial to completely demolish the institution of religion to create a true secular society and a set of secular ethical principles.

His attitude of indifference rather than hostility towards religion had annoyed some of his friends, in particular, Charles Bradlaugh (1833-1891), an atheist and a firm believer that a true secular society could only come into being if religion was completely destroyed. Bradlaugh was committed to the view that the logical outcome of secularism is complete denial of the institution of religion and God. He defined secularism as a movement that was fundamentally opposed to religion. He believed that it was inevitable for a secularist to be antagonistic towards religion.[13] Such a hostile attitude towards religion, in particular about its operation in socio-political matters, abounds in Communist literature. A classless socialist society ought to be a secular society in the sense that the institution of religion is absolutely taken apart in it. Among the prominent Indian thinkers, M.N. Roy was perhaps the sole exception whose concept of secularism was closer to this particular school.[14]

Bradlaugh actively promoted atheism during the 19th century and because of his complete dedication to the cause could succeed in winning over numerous supporters, some of them quite prominent such as William Ewart Gladstone, T.P. O'Connor and George Bernard Shaw. In 1866 he, in collaboration with Annie Besant, established the National Secular Society that served as a major force in channelizing secular and atheistic ideas in British society. It was Bradlaugh's unflinching faith in atheism as opposed to the institution of religion that distinguished Holyoake's concept of secularism from that of Bradlaugh's. To put it plainly, Bradlaugh's brand of secularism is essentially anti-religion which refuses to concede any space for religion in the lives of the people. Bradlaugh was elected to the House of Commons from Northampton as many as five times in succession but on four occasions he had to surrender his seat because of his refusal to take the oath in the name of god. The fifth time, i.e. in 1886 he was allowed to take the oath of affirmation and two years later it was because of his activism a new Oath Act was passed that recognized the right of affirmation for the members of Parliament.

Charles Bradlaugh's version of secularism found favour with Communist Parties (not necessarily Marxist), the vanguards of revolution, in many parts of the world. After the Bolshevik Revolution, therefore, the Communist Party of the Soviet Union banished religion and imposed an anti-religion secular mode in the country. About three decades later the policy was replicated by Chairman Mao in China. Though the situation was reversed in Russia after the collapse of the Soviet Union in 1990, China continues to stick to the brand of secularism that actively represses religious freedom.

Despite differences, the secular movements of both, Holyoake and Bradlaugh, forcefully advocated that the state and its operative agency, the government, desist from supporting any religion directly or indirectly and the state laws must not accommodate religious precepts but they be the creation of the wisdom of the legislators. In a nutshell, secularism insisted on complete separation of the state from religion. This particular aspect of secular movement firmly established the linkages of secularism with political actions. Though the secular movement did succeed in secularizing English society to a considerable extent, it failed to convert the state into a secular one. Technically, the United Kingdom is not a secular state as the Anglican Church continues to be its official religion.

A reference must also be made about Max Weber (1864-1920), the German sociologist and political economist whose brilliant works dealing with rationalization and exploration of natural phenomena helped European society to imbibe a scientific outlook and objective thinking—traits that determine a secular culture—to a great extent. He advocated a scientific and value-free approach in the analysis of natural phenomena, social actions and religious institutions. He did not negate nor did he reject religion. He also refrained from condemning or extolling the religious beliefs of the people. Nonetheless, his writings proved instrumental in secularizing Western society. He is credited for coining and making popular the phrase 'disenchantment of nature' by which he roughly means liberating nature from religion. The notion underlines dismissing unscientific ideas while exploring nature. Nature is not a divine entity but a physical phenomenon and man should freely exploit it for his needs and bringing about development. The 'disenchantment of nature' reduced nature to merely a thing of utility for man and this idea was one of the most significant views that helped secularize the Western world.

II

For many Western scholars and for quite a few South Asian writers too, the starting point of a discussion on secularism in the Indian context is the arrival of the European colonists, in particular, the British. By boasting about the Christian roots of secularism and misconstruing the policy of the Raj as neutral, the Western 'experts' condescendingly declare that though the concept of secularism is essentially Western, rather Christian, the Eastern and non-Christian countries such as India are making efforts to establish a secular state. As the discussion above makes it amply clear that most values that may be allied with secularism originated in the East and some of them predate Christ. As far as the policy of the Raj is concerned we will shortly see it was hardly neutral. And who decides what is Western? Do Jesus and Christianity, both of Middle Eastern origin, qualify? Making claims such as, "The secular state is, in origin, a Western and not an Asian conception..."[15] is considered to be scholarship and mostly goes uncontested.

The truth is what Amartya Sen says: "As the first millennium of the Muslim Hijri calendar came to an end in 1591-2, Akbar engaged in a far-reaching scrutiny of social and political values and legal and cultural practice. He paid particular attention to the challenge of inter-community relations and the abiding need for communal peace and fruitful collaboration in the already multicultural India of the 16th century. We have to recognize how unusual Akbar's policies were for the time. The Inquisitions were in full swing and Giordano Bruno was burnt at the stake for heresy in Rome in 1600 even as Akbar was making pronouncements on religious tolerance in India."[16]

The intellectual contribution of Indian religions such as Buddhism and Jainism to secularism has already been referred to above. It is, however, necessary to briefly review the policies of two emperors, one from the ancient and the other from the medieval periods of Indian history from the point of view of secularism. Incidentally, these are the only two rulers among a long list of Indian sovereigns, viz. Ashoka and Akbar whom the historians remember by the honorific, 'the Great'. Though they were truly great considering the overall efficacy of their rule, their religious policies deeply ingrained in tolerance and humanism set them apart from other rulers of India who neither had the vision nor the inclination to rise above their personal religious prejudices.

Ashoka the Great was the last emperor of the Mauryan dynasty whose rule spanned from 269 to 231 BCE. About 264 BCE he embarked on a policy of expansion and invaded Kalingas, a kingdom in eastern India in and around the present-day state of Odisha. The consequent bloodshed and destruction moved him so much that in his remorse he embraced Buddhism and took a vow to strictly follow a policy of non-violence. He also made attempts to proselytize Buddhism for which he sent emissaries to different parts of India and abroad.

He also spread the humanistic content of Buddhism by inscribing it on rocks and pillars. Apparently it was a religious activity for which he should be condemned rather than praised from a secular perspective. Nevertheless, the edicts engraved on rocks and pillars do not preach any specific religion; they are essentially moralistic and humanistic and speak of tolerance and respect of all religions. Some of the inscriptions are: "All religions should reside everywhere for all of them desire self-control and purity of heart." [Rock Edict Nb7 (S. Dhammika)][17]. Another one conveys: "Contact (between religions) is good. One should listen to and respect the doctrines professed by others." [Rock Edict Nb 12 (S. Dhammika)][18].

Thus, despite being a passionate Buddhist, Ashoka followed a policy of religious tolerance. Romila Thapar, is of the view that Ashoka's definition of social ethics is based on a respect for all religious teachers, and on a harmonious relationship between parents and children, teachers and pupils, and employers and employees.[19] It has been noted earlier that Buddhism is an agnostic faith and in that respect it is closer to humanism. Its message, therefore, is not antagonistic to secular principle. Though in the last year of his rule Ashoka did make Buddhism the state religion, he did not create a theocracy. He continued with his policy of religious tolerance. A scholar, Jawaid Quddus informs that despite the presence of religious animosity and sectarian bitterness that prevailed during Ashoka's time, he did not become prejudiced towards other faiths. Citing from a scholarly work, *Studies in Ancient India* by Provatansu Maiti, Quddus explains the religious policy of Ashoka as under:

1. All sects must dwell at all places so that they could know one another and develop tolerance for each other.
2. All sects must observe restraint of speech and purification of heart when they deal with each other.
3. The exaltation of one's own religion and condemnation of others' creeds is not permitted.
4. Different sects should study the scripture of other sects and develop concord among themselves.
5. All people must practise Ahimsa (non-violence) towards each other and towards animals.
6. Ashoka renounced the policy of conquest by the sword and urged people to adopt the policy of conquest by law.[20]

It may not be proper to conclude that Ashoka was a secularist in the strict sense of the term but the respect and openness he showed towards other faiths is similar to that of the Indian brand of secularism that is officially in vogue today.

On the issue of religion both Ashoka and Akbar had run into almost similar experiences. Both started as the firm believers of their ancestral faiths but later had to alter their religious beliefs albeit for different reasons. Jalaluddin Muhammad Akbar who ruled over a vast Mughal empire between 1556 and 1605 was a judicious and sagacious emperor. The mention of his name in connection with secularism is an imperative for he was perhaps the first ruler since Ashoka who not only implemented a very liberal religious policy but personally followed it. His religious policy was that of respect and tolerance of all religions.

Sources indicate that various factors were responsible for his change of heart from an orthodox Sunni Muslim to the originator of a very liberal and flexible faith. His father, Humayun, was a Sunni while his mother, guardian and others who mattered the most in the formative years of his rule were Shia. Additionally, he had a great respect for Sufism that gave him a much broader vision than the narrow restrictions of conventional faiths. Though an illiterate himself, Akbar was a keen seeker of truth and his hunger for knowledge and inquiry was insatiable.

His restlessness for finding out the religious truth made him build an *Ibadat Khana* (House of Worship) at Fatehpur Sikri in 1575. In this House of Worship scholars of all faiths, Islam, Hinduism, Buddhism, Jainism, Sikhism, Judaism, Christianity and even atheist intellectuals such as the Charvakas would discuss the issues of faith and transcendental questions. These debates, which would often turn acrimonious and even violent, however, made Akbar realize that despite the differences, all religions had many good principles that could help mankind. This realization forced him establish a new faith incorporating the humane contents of all the faiths. The new religion, *Din-e-Ilahi* (Divine Faith), nevertheless, was more a code of moral conduct than an assertive religion. It was believed to be an ethical order that prohibited lust, sensuality, slander and pride. These traits were considered sins. The virtues included piety, prudence, abstinence and kindness.[21] In the context, Akbar deserves all the praise for two reasons; first, despite being an absolute emperor he did not declare *Din-e-Ilahi* the official religion of his empire and second, he did not force anyone to embrace the new faith. As a result, the faith withered away after his death.

In 1562, Akbar took a major decision from the point of view of secularism and that was abolition of *jizya*, a tax that all non-Muslims were forced to pay in the so-called Islamic states. His firm beliefs in mysticism and humanism made him follow a policy of *Sulh-e-Kul* (peace to all) that helped Hindus and adherents of other religions to practise their faiths without any restrictions and seek employment to the coveted positions in the administration. As per a source, Akbar issued a written *firman* (command) that allowed the Christian missionaries to make willing converts.[22] In a nutshell, Akbar was a true precursor of the doctrine of secularism that became, in the modern age, a crucial value to be respected by a responsible democratic state. Amartya Sen observes: "Taking note of the religious diversity of his people, Akbar laid the foundations of secularism and religious neutrality of the state in a variety of ways; the secular constitution that India adopted in 1949, after independence from British rule, has many features already championed by Akbar in the 1590s. The shared elements include interpreting secularism as the requirement that the state be equidistant from different religions and must not treat any religion with special favour."[23]

It was after a gap of about two hundred years since the death of Akbar that the idea of secularism was ostensibly re-introduced in the administrative machinery by the colonial masters who had entered India as traders but gradually their business outfit, the East India Company, seized political power by various means such as fraud, intrigue, deception, violence, shrewdness and sagacity. To retain political control over a huge area and a heterogeneous populace the British officially declared religious neutrality as the working principle of their administration. In reality, it was not. The British only followed a policy of self-interest. It remained an invariable while the colonial masters adopted different stances in response to specific situations. To begin with they had no reason to side with the political aspirations of the two major religious communities, the Hindu and Muslim, for in their ambitious plan of gaining political control over the subcontinent both were enemies. The Company commanders did not betray an overtly anti-Muslim position even when they were fighting against Tipu Sultan because along with the Marathas, their other major ally was the Nizam.

The bloody events of 1857 forced the colonial masters to design an openly anti-Muslim policy for in their perception the Muslims were the real culprits. This continued for about a quarter of a century. With the rising wave of nationalism that swept across all sections of Indian political elite, the British could rightly foresee the imminent threat to the Raj. In order to weaken it they effectively implemented their notorious policy of *divide and rule* by patronizing the Muslim elite against the menace of the 'Hindu' Indian National Congress. The formation of the Muslim League in 1906 with the tacit support of the British ushered in an era of organized communalism in Indian politics. Three years later the idea of separate electorates on religious lines was firmly enshrined in the Morley-Minto Reforms. Jawaharlal Nehru's observation in the context that the idea of the separate electorates for the Muslims was synchronous with the inception of the Muslim League three years earlier was not without substance.[24]

The British master never lost the faith in the efficacy of their divisive policies that had created an atmosphere of distrust between the Hindus and Muslims and consequently divided the freedom struggle. Another decision of the Raj detrimental to national unity and secularism was the announcement of the Communal Award by the British Prime Minister, Ramsay MacDonald, in August 1932. The Award not only perpetuated the separate electorates for the Muslims but also extended it to other religious and ethnic groups such as the Sikhs, the Europeans, Indian Christians, Dalits and Anglo-Indians. Furthermore, it declared that since the two major religious communities, the Hindus and Muslims, were at loggerheads on most political issues, the Raj would, in future, introduce a political reform only if the two communities express their concurrence on it. This provided a communal party like the Muslim League tremendous power and from now onwards it could defeat every political move of the INC that was remotely aimed at national unity. These developments brutally broke the back of a unified nationalist movement and with it the idea of secularism too was put on the back burner. At the same time, the colonial masters also extended covert support to Hindu fascist outfits to check the 'secular' INC and the emergent challenge of the Communist movement. So the British claim that the Raj maintained complete neutrality in administrative matters was a sham.

It is surprising that though D.E. Smith acknowledges that in 1813 the British Parliament had established a 'legal connection between the Government of India and the Church of England'[25] and even until a year after the end of the British colonial rule, the Ecclesiastical Department, that had been in existence for long, 'continued to pay a large number of Christian chaplains and maintain Christian churches out of the public revenue of the country'[26], he asserts that the British administration 'was in general fair, impartial and secular.'[27] Needless to add that like most Western scholars, Smith too overlooks the infamous policy of *divide and rule* of the British administration and its obnoxious consequence, the communal riots. To put it plainly, communal violence is a striking gift of the British to the Indian subcontinent. The seed of distrust and hatred that the colonial rulers sowed in the Indian soil ultimately yielded the toxic fruit in the form of partition of the country.

Nonetheless, it must be admitted that the Indian nationalist movement itself was a spin-off of the colonial rule. The exposure of the elite classes to modern Western education and the tangible unification of the subcontinent thanks to railways and the telegraph emotionally bonded the Indians of different parts of the subcontinent whose elite could also communicate effectively with each other through the vehicle of English. Thus, it was the Indian elite class that set out on championing the nationalist cause. The inception of the Indian National Congress in 1885 was not exactly for throwing out the foreign rulers. In fact, the inspiration for establishing the INC was made available by a retired British civil servant, Allan Octavian Hume.

Gradually, the INC that, in the perception of the colonial rulers was to serve as a safety-valve to keep the extremist and violent sections of Indians opposed to imperialism under check, got itself transformed into a movement for independence. Though, ideologically the INC was a hotchpotch, the most prominent leaders were committed to liberal-democratic ideals that included secularism. In the first decade of the twentieth century a few leaders propounding extremist views with pronounced Hindu revivalist streak did become a significant force within the INC. Thereafter, when Britain was deeply involved in the First World War, the INC had launched a campaign for self-government that was popularly called the Home Rule movement. Nevertheless, the hold of the moderate leaders, with their abiding faith in constitutionalism, over the organization remained intact till Gandhi appeared on the political horizon and in a short while became the undisputed voice of the INC.

Though the INC never adopted a resolution explicitly declaring secularism as one of the ideals, it did pass a resolution in the Karachi Session (1931) stating: "Every citizen shall enjoy freedom of conscience and the right freely to profess and practise his religion subject to public order and morality."[28] Moreover, the ideal of secularism was applauded and proclaimed as one of the goals of the nationalist movement in the frequent statements and articles by the prominent leaders.

At this point it must be put on record that even Mohammad Ali Jinnah who started his political career in the INC was a staunch nationalist and was also committed to the ideal of secularism. It was precisely because of calling Jinnah a secularist L.K. Advani, the veteran leader of the Bharatiya Janata Party (BJP), had to step down from the post of party president and when another senior BJP leader Jaswant Singh published an extensive study of Jinnah's political career and concluded even more forcefully than Advani that Jinnah was indeed a secularist and nationalist, he was expelled from the party in late 2009 only to be readmitted in June 2010. Advani and Singh had to suffer humiliation not because they erred in the assessment of Jinnah's political ideas but because the dominance of the Hindu hawks over their party who blindly implement the diktats of the RSS.

Being a member of the Congress, Jinnah was as much a nationalist and secularist as any other prominent Congressman. Sarojini Naidu called him 'an ambassador of Hindu-Muslim unity' and M.C. Chagla recorded an anecdote that speaks volumes of Jinnah's integrity and patriotism. At the beginning of his legal practice, Jinnah was in the Chambers of Sir George Lowndes, a brilliant lawyer. The British government had asked Lowndes to give his legal opinion on a speech delivered by B.G. Tilak. The authorities were prosecuting Tilak for the speech in question. When Lowndes asked Jinnah "whether he had read the brief and what he thought of it", Jinnah snapped that "he had not touched the brief, and would not look at it, as he wanted to keep himself free to criticize the government for prosecuting a great patriot like Tilak."[29]

Another incident cited by Jaswant Singh underlines Jinnah's firm commitment to secularism. When Jinnah appeared before the Public Service Commission in 1913, the Chairman, Lord Islington, put a poser to him: "It has been represented to me that difficulties might arise if you put a Hindu in-charge of Mohammedan population. Do you think that a Hindu who got a few more marks than an educated and influential Mohammedan would make a better and more efficient administrator when he was in-charge of a population which was largely Mohammedan?" Jinnah's reply is significant: "I say that in that case you will be doing the greatest injustice to the Hindu...I do not see why a Hindu should not be in-charge of a district where the majority happens to be Mohammedan."[30]

It was unfortunate that Mohandas Karamchand Gandhi's association with the nationalist movement and his penchant for using Hindu idioms and similes in the nationalist discourse infuriated Jinnah so much that he decided to leave not only the Congress but India itself and set up house in England. It was only after the release of the Communal Award that the egoistic streak of Jinnah's personality forced him to become active politically as the all powerful leader of the Muslim League to settle his personal score with Gandhi. After 1932, though Jinnah remained as irreligious as he had always been, he turned Islam into a political ideology to defeat Indian nationalism and promote his notorious 'Two Nation' theory. It was one of those paradoxes of history that a truly nationalist and secular leader had to leave the nationalist movement, mainly because of ego clashes with Gandhi, and ended up as the *Qaid-e-Azam* of the Muslims in which capacity he would always have to share the major responsibility for dividing the subcontinent and creating Pakistan.

It is true that Gandhi was a devout, practising Hindu, he was impulsive, had reservations about modern scientific education and industrialism, was not committed to the parliamentary form of democracy and did not approve of urban-centric development but at the same time he was incapable of hating someone because of his religious affiliation. His religiosity was broad enough to accommodate the presence of other faiths. In fact, Gandhi had brought a new vision, a new discourse and a new methodology to give a new direction to the freedom struggle. His ideas and strategy were new for the INC as it was dominated by those who were staunchly committed to liberal ideas and constitutionalism. Gandhi pulled the rug of constitutionalism from under their feet as he questioned the legitimacy of the laws made by foreigners who had no legitimacy to subdue and rule others. Objectively speaking, Gandhi converted an elitist nationalist movement into a mass struggle.

It was creditable that Gandhi never concealed his obsession with Hinduism from anyone. On the contrary, he openly spoke about it going to the extent that he would have committed suicide had Hinduism not come to his rescue. He was openly a religious man, not a hypocrite. Despite all this he was liberal enough to respect the religious sensibilities of people of other faiths. He was the foremost promoter of Hindu-Muslim unity. It was the pluralistic character of Indian society that made him a firm believer in the ideal of secularism, not of the Western variety but the one that accommodates ground realities of Indian society. Gandhi, as early as 1924, had stated that it was unpatriotic even to bear in mind a dream of *Hindu Raj*. Thereafter, on the eve of independence, he further elaborated his perception of a secular state in India. He said: "The state should undoubtedly be secular. Everyone living in it should be entitled to profess his religion without let or hindrance, so long as the citizen obeyed the common law of the land. There would be no interference with missionary effort, but no mission could enjoy the patronage of the state."[31]

This version of secularism obviously differs from the Western paradigms of secularism that have been referred to above. Gandhi's definition of secularism comes closer to humanism with an emphasis on religious neutrality of the state. With such commitment to the ideal of secularism, Gandhi definitely guided the nationalist movement from 1920 until the independence of the country and finally laid down his life primarily for upholding the principle of secularism. It was almost his brand of secularism, barring complete neutrality of the state in matters of religion that got incorporated albeit mutedly, in various provisions of the Indian Constitution.

Pandit Jawaharlal Nehru was another stalwart of the INC who during the course of the nationalist movement emerged as the embodiment of modernity, scientific temper and secular outlook. As a matter of fact, Nehru, in matters of tastes and responses to Western education, culture and attitude towards religion was comparable to Jinnah (in his earlier avatar as a Congressman) except that he was more academically inclined and less egoistic. Under the influence of Gandhi he did alter his perspective and strategy about the course of nationalist movement but he never gave up the idea of putting India on the road to industrial progress. He is accurately regarded the architect of modern India. In many ways he was unlike Gandhi but on the issue of secularism or to be more precise, secular state they hardly differed. Nehru was a vehement critic of communalism, both Hindu and Muslim, and wanted it to be replaced by secularism.

Secularism, according to Nehru, "was not something *banishing religion from politics* but developing an outlook which was based on scientific and reasonable appreciation of modern conditions as well as laying stress on the economic factor so that religious differences would recede in the background and the economic bond could be stronger than even the national bond."[32] Here Nehru's commitment to socialism cannot be lost sight of as he is optimistic that in the course of time people are likely to develop class consciousness in place of religious one. Had he been alive he would have been extremely disappointed to see the conditions in today's India. Nehru was conscious of the religiosity of the Indian masses so, despite holding agnostic views personally, he clarified in 1961, what Indian secularism actually meant. He said that secularism did not mean opposition to religion; it rather implied, "a state which honours all faiths equally and gives them equal opportunities."[33] The notable point is that the Gandhi-Nehru perception of secularism is not anti-religion nor does it insist on absolute banishment of religion from politics.

III

The Constitution that came into force on January 26, 1950 did not include the term 'secular state'. The word secular got mentioned incidentally in Article 25 (2) (b) that while guaranteeing the freedom of conscience and the freedom of religion specifies "restrictions made by the state relating to any economic, financial, political or other *secular* activity which may be associated with religious practice but do not really appertain the freedom of conscience."[34] Despite the fact that the Constituent Assembly was almost entirely composed of the members of the Congress, a party which, during the course of the freedom struggle, had passed a resolution in its Karachi session in 1931 that "the state shall observe neutrality in regard to all religions", there was hardly any discussion on the issue of secularism within that august body.

Professor K.T. Shah, a member of the Constituent Assembly made sincere attempts twice to insert the word secular in the Constitution but his efforts were defeated on both occasions. In his second attempt he, in fact, wanted through an amendment, to add a new article to the draft of fundamental law of the land that was under making. His proposed article read in part: "The state in India being secular shall have no concern with any religion, creed or profession of faith; and shall observe an attitude of absolute neutrality in all matters relating to the religion of any class of its citizens or other persons in the Union."[35] Shah's contention in moving the amendment was to minimize the possibilities of communal clashes with which our freedom struggle was scarred in the first half of the 20th century and that ultimately led to the partition of the country that came together with disgusting violence and cruelty all in the name of religion. The amendment proposal, however, was defeated. It was only after a gap of 28 years that another amendment, viz. the 42nd Constitutional Amendment Act, 1976, inserted the word secular in the Preamble to the Constitution.

It must, however, be made clear that the Constitution that was in operation prior to the 42nd Amendment Act was secular in law and spirit because its secular character was reflected in various provisions, in particular those dealing with various kinds of rights. D.E. Smith's method of determining a secular state by identifying, in the constitution, an interrelated set of relationships between individual, religion and state is very scientific and here we must go along with it to underline the secular character of the Indian state. The set of the relationship implies three "components...freedom of religion, citizenship, and separation of state and religion."[36]

The significant point to be noted is that in Smith's concept of a secular state, religion is neither rejected nor is it ignored. Despite separating itself from religion, the state, Smith points out, accommodates religion by guaranteeing freedom of religion to the people. In a plural society such as India, which is obsessively religious as well, there was no other alternative before the Constituent Assembly to steer clear of including a specific article dealing with secularism and yet endow the Constitution with the spirit of religious neutrality. The secular state in India is primarily concerned with administering the relation between itself and the individual and by adopting an attitude of impartiality towards all religions. It is secured in the Constitution, exactly in tune with the first component of Smith's formula, by guaranteeing freedom of conscience and free profession, practice and propagation of religion.

Part III is perhaps the most significant segment of the Constitution because it guarantees almost all the essential rights that make a state democratic and *secular*. Among the existing six groups of rights that are enshrined in this segment of the Constitution, the fourth one, comprising Articles 25-28, deals with freedom of religion. Article 25 deals with the individual's freedom of religion. Article 25 (1) provides "Subject to public order, morality and health and to the provisions of this part, all persons are equally entitled to freedom of conscience and the right to profess, practise and propagate religion."[37] Firstly, the right is made available to *all persons* and not just to the citizens. Secondly, it reminds us the resolution of the Karachi session of INC, a part of which said: "Every citizen shall enjoy freedom of conscience and the right freely to profess and practise his religion subject to public order and morality."[38] The significant differences between the texts of Article 25 and the resolution passed in the Karachi session are, a) the text of the resolution intends to give the right only to the citizens and not to all persons and, b) the resolution makes no mention of the right to propagate religion. A section of the members of the Constituent Assembly did insist not to make mention of the right of propagation of religion for, in their opinion, it was implied in right to practise religion. Their opinion was also an outgrowth of the non-proselytizing character of Hinduism. It was, however, because of a small but vociferous group of Christian members that the right to propagate religion was finally made available.

The right of propagation of religion subsequently became contentious as a couple of state legislatures passed laws detrimental to its exercise. For instance, Madhya Pradesh and Odisha passed the laws that made it a crime to convert or making efforts to convert anyone by 'means of force fraud or allurement.' The Acts were challenged in the court by the Christian community. The Supreme Court in the *Stainislaus v State of Madhya Pradesh, 1977*, upheld the Acts of the states and rejected the plea of the Christian community completely on the grounds that a) though the right to propagate religion gives an individual the right to preach and publicize tenets of his religion but it does not include the right to convert another person; b) freedom of conscience means a person is free to choose his religion but it does not imply that he can be converted to another religion by way of 'force, fraud, inducement or allurement'; c) even if a religion believes in preaching as well as converting people of other faiths, the state, in accordance with the limitations imposed on the right to freedom of religion can stop such activity on grounds of 'public order, morality or health.'; d) if the right of conversion is made available to all religions it might lead to contravention of public order as every religious community would use 'force, fraud and inducement' to convert the maximum persons of other faiths. Thereafter, the state of Arunachal Pradesh passed the similar Act and that too was upheld by the Supreme Court. A Bill passed by the Gujarat legislature to prohibit conversion completely is awaiting President's assent.

The right to freedom of religion provided in the Indian Constitution is not absolute. In fact, very few rights could be.

Like most fundamental rights, right to freedom of religion is also subject to public order, morality, health and to other provisions of Part III. By imposing these restrictions the state aims at deterring the harmful practises, some of which such as *sati* and human sacrifice though banned, might keep recurring in the name of religious requirements. Another point that needs amplification is the distinction between freedom of conscience and the right to profess, practise and propagate religion. On account of the text of Article 25 (1) one may interpret that freedom of conscience too, like right to profess, practise and propagate religion, is subject to the restrictions mentioned at the beginning of the article. However, as Smith says, it is "simply a case of inaccurate drafting, and the courts have made it clear that the state can have no power over the conscience of the individual—this right is absolute."[39]

While dealing with the right to freedom of religion as guaranteed in the Constitution a tricky issue is that of defining religion. Who should have the authority to define a particular religion? The view that the relevant scriptures of a religion could be taken into consideration to determine its definition is fraught with predicaments. For instance, quite a few Hindu scriptures might be alluded to for the justification of the caste system or a couple of Quranic verses could be cited to give an explanation for the subordinate position of women in Islam. Nevertheless, a limitation on the exercise of the right to freedom of religion is that of '*other provisions of Part III.*' The practice of the caste system, therefore, shall violate Article 17 that abolishes and forbids untouchability while any attempt to assign a subordinate position to Muslim women shall amount a contravention of Article 14 that guarantees every person the right to equality.

If not the scriptures then whose authority is recognized in the context of definition of religion? It seems to be a nebulous area but Article 25 (2) empowers the courts to control any secular activity that may be linked with religious practice and to see that none of the fundamental rights enshrined in Part III is violated. By exercising this power the courts may curb the continuation of detestable practices in the garb of religion and can also contribute to the process of social reforms that has sadly remained incomplete. This particular clause has added a new dimension to the traditional equation between religion and state that has been widely appreciated. In this respect the observation of C.H. Alexandrowics deserves consideration: "The above clause constitutes in itself a revolution in the traditional conception of religion in India." He further adds it equals to "an extensive programme of disentanglement of religious and secular activities."[40]

Besides guaranteeing the right to freedom of religion to each individual the Constitution also provides for collective freedom to religious communities. Article 26 says: "Subject to public order, morality and health, every religious denomination or any section thereof shall have the right:

a) to establish and maintain institutions for religious and charitable purposes;
b) to manage its own affairs in matters of religion;
c) to own and acquire moveable and immoveable property; and
d) to administer such property in accordance with law."[41]

Here again the issue of the right of a religious denomination to manage its own affairs and the commitment of the state to bring about social reform might become contentious and it did in the case of *Tahir Saifuddin vs. Tyebbhai Moosaji.*[42] Syedna Tahir Saifuddin, the head priest of the Dawoodi Bohra community, had excommunicated a member of the community and this decision of the head priest was challenged in the Bombay High Court. While giving its verdict the Court, on account of the Bombay Prevention of the Excommunication Act of 1949, declared the excommunication orders void and rejected the contention of the Syedna that he was managing his own 'affairs in matters of religion.' The verdict of the Court *inter alia* pronounced that 'the religion is a matter of man's faith and belief, and is to be sharply distinguished from *religious practice...* religion has nothing whatever to do with the right of excommunication or expulsion.'[43]

In another case, *Venkataramana Deveru* v. *State of Mysore,* the validity of Article 26 was to be decided by the Supreme Court. The trustees of the Venkataramana temple, controlled by the Gowda Saraswath Brahman community refused entry of the untouchables on the strength of Article 26 (b) of the

Constitution. However, the Madras Temple Entry Authorization Act was in place and in the light of it the Supreme Court conceded that though the issue involved was a matter of religion, it brought about a compromise that allowed the entry of the untouchables while giving some leverage to the religious denomination to manage its own affairs.

The second parameter in the line of reasoning suggested by Smith to determine the secularity of a constitution is citizenship. There are many provisions in the Indian Constitution that govern the relationship between the state and an individual. The very first group of the fundamental rights is about the right to equality (Articles 14-18). Article 14 states: "The state shall not deny to any person equality before the law and the equal protection of the laws within the territory of India."[44] The point to be noted is that the Constitution guarantees the negative as well as positive concepts of equality to all persons and not just citizens.

The notion of *equality before law* may sound extremely judicious and impartial but it is still a negative concept of equality because it refuses to take into account the social background of an individual such as birth and faith and the economic realities like poverty and affluence. The concept is negative for it treats all individuals alike. In a perfectly equal society, 'equality before law' is a perfect concept. Since a perfectly equal society is a utopia, this notion proves to be a negative one. Nonetheless, the makers of the Indian Constitutions were not blind to the socio-economic realities of the land and, therefore, they added the positive notion of equality by inserting the expression *equal protection of the laws.* This notion means that among equals the law should be equal. However, if there are reasonable bases on which groups and classes exist in society then the legislatures are empowered to make laws differentiating between groups and classes and the courts will certainly take into account the socio-economic realities of the parties involved in a case and apply the appropriate law in the administration of justice.

Article 15 provides: "The state shall not discriminate against any citizen on grounds only of religion, race, caste, sex, place of birth or any of them."[45] Firstly, the Article is applicable to citizens only. Secondly, two words, viz. '*only*' prefixing grounds of religion, race, caste, sex, etc. and the mention of '*caste*' as a ground for non-discrimination need explanation. The word *only* implies that the state shall not discriminate against a religious community, say for example, Hindus only on ground of religion. The legislatures may take into considerations other grounds such as social-educational background, customs, etc. of different groups and communities for framing laws.

Therefore, a law such as the Hindu Marriage Act prohibits a Hindu to take more than one wife, whereas a Muslim under the Personal Law is allowed to have up to four wives. The situation *prima facie* appears to be discriminatory in favour of Muslims. This is also a politically contentious issue as the votaries of Hindu nationalism represented largely by the RSS, BJP and their affiliate organizations maintain that so long as there exist community civil laws in the country there cannot be true secularism in India. The truth is that the BJP was in power earlier too between 1998 and 2004 as the leading partner of the National Democratic Alliance (NDA). However, it did not invoke Article 44 of the Directive Principles of State Policy to implement a Uniform Civil Code across the country. The reason that is over and over again given by the Hindu Right is that it was after all a coalition government in which the BJP was not at liberty to implement its agenda. Now, the BJP is in power on its own. Yet, despite a promise in its manifesto, it is highly unlikely that the Modi *Sarkar* would legislate and implement a Uniform Civil Code. The reason is that ideologically the RSS, the real force behind the BJP government, is not eager to introduce a uniform civil code in India. Guru Golwalkar, who was the ideologue and the *Sarsanghchalak* of the RSS had stated once that anyone who would like to implement a uniform civil code in India was insane. For the RSS a Uniform Civil Code is a Western construct, whereas it actually intends to make India a Hindu *Rashtra* and implement the Laws of Manu.

The constitutionality of Article 15 (1) was, however, upheld by the Bombay High Court in the *State of Bombay* v. *Narasu Appa* (1952) on the ground that the socio-educational development of the Hindus and Muslims was different and the verdict *inter alia* pointed out, "one community might be prepared to accept and work social reform; another may not yet be prepared for it... The state may rightly decide to bring about social reform by stages, and the stages may be territorial or they may be community-wise."[46] It must further be added that the constitution merely puts up with the continuation of community civil laws till such time the state feels the inevitability of framing a Uniform Civil Code (Article 44).

The mention of the word *caste* in Article 15 (1) provides an opportunity to those who oppose the concept of affirmative action to criticize the reservations that are provided to the Scheduled Castes and the Scheduled Tribes in jobs, educational institutions and legislatures. Such a criticism is unfair firstly, because it smacks of ignorance about Indian socio-religious history. Indian history is replete with accounts of terrible discrimination in the name of caste. Huge sections of society were kept under subjugation and denied all indices of human existence by the force of religion actively supported by the state. The deprived sections are currently known as the Scheduled Castes and the Scheduled Tribes. The Constitution has justifiably provided them quotas in jobs, educational institutions and legislatures to uplift their lot to the level of other Indians.

Secondly, clause (4) of Article 15 provides: "Nothing in this article or clause (2) of the Article 29 shall prevent the state from making any special provisions for the advancement of any socially and educationally backward classes of citizens or for the Scheduled Castes and Scheduled Tribes."[47] In view of the clause not merely the reservations provided for the Scheduled Castes and Scheduled Tribes are perfectly constitutional but also the reservations extended to various Backward Classes by different state governments as per the recommendations of the Mandal Commission are justifiable. One who knows the history and sociology of Indian society may understand the significance of this kind of positive discrimination and probably shall not deride the concepts of equality and secularity enshrined in the Indian Constitution.

The principle of non-discrimination in public employment finds expression in Article 16. Clause (1) says: "There shall be equality of opportunity for all citizens in matters relating to public employment to any office under the state."[48] It represents the positive dimension of the right that guarantees equality of opportunity to all citizens regarding public employment. The negative side of the right that mentions grounds on which there shall be no discrimination gets expressed in Clause (2) of the article. It says: "No citizen shall, on grounds only of religion, race, caste, sex, descent, place of birth, residence or any of them, be ineligible for, or discriminated against in respect of any employment or office under the state."[49] Here too the presence of the word *only* leaves a room for the state to discriminate on any other *reasonable* ground that is not mentioned herein.

The significant point in the context of secularism is that the religion of a citizen cannot be a ground for denying him public employment. Nonetheless, there is an exception to the principle mentioned in clause (5) of the article that specifies: "Nothing in this article shall affect the operation of any law which provides that the incumbent of an office in connection with the affairs of any religious denominational institution or any members of the governing body thereof shall be a person professing a particular religion or belonging to a particular denomination."[50] The clause is applicable to certain government departments that look after religious affairs or control religious institutions. For instance, the commissioner and all other officials associated with a Hindu Religious Endowment Department cannot be non-Hindus. Similarly, all employees of the *Wakf* (Muslim Endowment) Department must be Muslims. This appears to be a reasonable exception considering the huge properties controlled by religious endowment departments in India and does not violate the Indian version of secularism.

The Indian citizens are also assured of equal treatment while seeking admission into public funded educational institutions. Article 29 (2) provides: "No citizen shall be denied admission into any educational institution maintained by the state or receiving aid out of the state funds on grounds only of religion, race, caste, language or any of them."[51] The makers of the Indian Constitution deserve all praise for getting rid of the concept of communal electorates and completely secularising political rights of the citizens. The damaging concept of communal electorates was first institutionalized by the colonial masters in the Morley-Minto Reforms of 1909 as a shrewd strategy to create a rift between the two major religious communities of India so that they should never join in a unified freedom struggle. The harmful notion of political representation based on religious affiliation remained intact in the Montague-Chelmsford Reforms Act of 1919 and in the Government of India Act of 1935 it was extended to almost all the religious minority communities of India. Though there were myriad factors that deterred the growth of a monolith-secular movement to fight for the independence of India from the foreign rule, the notion of communal electorates was perhaps the most damaging one. It is not merely from a secular point of view but also from a democratic perspective, the concept of communal electorates negates the principle of universal adult franchise, the corner-stone of a genuine democracy.

The founding fathers of the Constitution abandoned the principle of communal electorates in favour of secularizing the process of voting and representation. Among the relevant articles in the context the first one is Article 325 that states: "There shall be one general electoral roll for every territorial constituency for election to either House of Parliament or to the House or either House of the Legislature of a state and no person shall be ineligible for inclusion in any such roll or claim to be included in any special electoral roll for any such constituency on grounds only of religion, race, sex or any of them."[52] It was indeed a revolutionary step not only from the viewpoint of secularism but also from the perception of equality and human rights. The bulk of the Indian masses who had never tasted the fruits of democracy were, by this article, made the masters of their own destiny. More importantly the women, who have always been the worst exploited segment in any society of the world, were brought to the level of their male counterparts in matters of political rights.

The so-called 'advanced' and 'free' world comprising Western Europe and North America should address the poser to themselves—when did they make available equal political rights to their womenfolk? Did they do it simultaneously with the males or several years later after the adoption of their constitutions? For instance, Britain that seeks pride in claiming that it is the oldest democracy in the world by tracing the evolution of representative institutions in the country from Magna Carta of 1215, made the franchise available to women only in the 1920s. In the USA, the self-appointed harbinger of democracy and human rights in the contemporary world, the women got the right to vote only in 1920. In Switzerland, supposed to be a very advanced society, women got the right to vote only in 1971. Compared to these facts, the Constitution makers of India really did a great job. The only exception to the principle of political equality of the Indian citizens are the reservations provided to the Scheduled Castes and the Scheduled Tribes [Article 330 (1) and 332 (1)]. The reasons for making such an exception have already been examined above.

The third component of a secular state as per the prescription of Smith relates to 'separation of state and religion' that constitutes the core of the Western mode of secularism. In the Indian Constitution the right of an individual in matters of religion that is mainly protected by Article 25 has been further reinforced by Article 27 that provides: "No person shall be compelled to pay any taxes, the proceeds of which are specifically appropriated in payment of expenses for the promotion or maintenance of any particular religion or religious denomination."[53] It has been pointed out by the experts in constitutional law that the article does not completely prohibit collection of taxes for religion-related causes. It only prohibits levying of taxation for the assistance of a 'particular religion or religious denomination.' In other words, as Smith points out, "non-discriminatory taxes for the benefit of *all* religions would be perfectly constitutional."[54] It is because of the presence of a couple of such articles, the concept of 'separation of state and religion' gets undermined and the critics of the Indian Constitution seize the opportunity to cast aspersions on the secular character of the Indian state. Besides the lacuna that exists in Article 27, there is another Article 290A that substantiates the argument that the concept of secularism, which has been ultimately incorporated in the Constitution does not entirely prohibit linkages between state and religion. Article 290A is as follows:

> A sum of forty-six lakhs and fifty thousand rupees shall be charged on, and paid out of the state of Kerala every year to the Travancore

> Devaswom Fund; and a sum of thirteen lakhs and fifty thousand rupees shall be charged on, and paid out of, the Consolidated Fund of the state of Madras every year to the Devaswom Fund established in the state for the maintenance of Hindu temples and shrines in the territories transferred to the state on the first day of November, 1956, from the state of Travancore-Cochin.[55]

Though there is an historical justification[56] for the insertion of the above article, there are other provisions too that indicate state support to religious causes. For instance, clause (2) of Article 28 permits the educational institutions funded by the state, such as the Banaras Hindu University and the Aligarh Muslim University to impart religious instruction on the ground that they were originally established under endowments. Quite a few state governments allocate certain amounts for the benefit of different religious communities in their budgets. Besides, the Union government subsidizes various pilgrimages undertaken by Hindus as well as Muslims at the expense of the tax payers. The critics, therefore, attack these features of the basic law and religiously-loaded policies of the Union as well as the state governments to substantiate their contention that India is far from being a secular state.

Nonetheless, it must be underlined that the founding fathers of the Indian Constitution did make a sincere attempt to separate the realms of state and religion by prohibiting religious instructions in educational institutions controlled by the state or funded by the state. In the context Article 28, which contends with the issue in its three clauses is significant. According to clause (1) of the article: "No religious instruction shall be provided in any educational institution wholly maintained out of state funds."[56] The clause is self-explanatory. Religious instructions, in an educational institution that is entirely funded by the state, are prohibited. Clause (2) that has already been dealt with allows imparting of religious instructions in those educational institutions that have been originally established out of religious endowments. Clause (3) states: "No person attending any educational institution recognized by the state or receiving aid out of state funds shall be required to take part in any religious instruction that may be imparted in such institutions or to attend any religious worship that may be conducted in any premises attached thereto unless such person or, if such person is minor, his guardian has given his consent thereto."[57] Imparting of religious instructions is, therefore, possible in an educational institution established and controlled by a religious denomination provided it is not wholly funded by the state. True, these provisions do not correspond to the Western secular laws which prescribe a blanket ban on imparting religious education in public schools. But India is not a Western society; therefore, emulating Western laws in absolute terms is neither possible nor desirable.

IV

The post-Babri Masjid demolition scenario in the country is such that even the liberal intellectuals argue that Hinduism, because of its very ethos, i.e. flexibility, heterogeneous structure and eclectic character, can never espouse hatred against the adherents of other faiths. This may be true so far as Hinduism as a faith is concerned and the most famous practitioner of such a faith was Gandhi. However, when the same faith is converted into a movement to spread hatred against adherents of other faiths for political gains then it gets transformed, as Ashish Nandy explains, into an ideology.[58] Hence, it is Hinduism as an ideology that is openly in operation in political affairs for the last three decades and it has caused excessive damage to the ideal of secularism.

The forces of *Hindutva* have succeeded on quite a number of occasions to unite Hindus against the minorities particularly the Muslims for the control of political power. The persistent campaigns of misinformation and hatred against the Muslims begin in homes and carry on through schools and colleges. Such campaigns of misinformation and hatred against the Muslims make a member of the community in the eyes of an average Hindu "a person with extra territorial emotional affinities, if not an agent of Pakistan."[59] L.K. Advani's *rath yatra* mobilizing Hindus to build a temple dedicated to Lord Ram exactly at the site of a nearly five-hundred-year-old mosque in Ayodhya was probably the unrivalled mass campaign of hatred against the largest religious minority in the history of the country.

Communal violence was but a logical consequence of such a meticulously organized campaign. The post-Babri-demolition-Mumbai riots of 1992-93 ensured an unprecedented electoral victory for the BJP in the parliamentary elections that followed. Later, the anti-Muslim pogroms in Gujarat have made Narendra Modi, the BJP Chief Minister of the state and later the Prime Minister of the coutry, the darling of the Hindu Right. Such an unabashedly anti-Muslim agenda of the Hindu communal forces is the greatest threat to the idea of secularism.

At this point we must deliberate upon the poser: What happened to the ideal of secularism in independent India? Or why secularism is under siege in India? It must be, however, clarified without delay that the factors that laid siege to secularism did not get invented with the coming of the BJP into power on its own. They were always part of the political processes across party lines. It has been made obvious in the foregoing discussion that secularism was a much-publicized value of the nationalist movement. The Constituent Assembly that was overwhelmingly dominated by the Congress faithfully endorsed the spirit of the idea by accommodating it in the basic law of the land.

On the negative side, it was made plain that communalism or any demands emanating from communal politics would have no place in the democratic republic of India. Likewise the system of separate electorates for different religious denominations that was prevalent during the colonial period was abandoned. Imparting of religious instructions has been prohibited in all educational institutions that are fully funded by the state and most importantly no religion has been declared as the official religion of the state.

On the positive side all the rights, justiciable and non-justiciable, are made available to all irrespective of religious distinctions. Further, in addition to the guarantee of freedom of religion to individuals and religious communities, each cultural category of citizens was assured certain indispensable rights to preserve their culture, language and script. In short, the Constitution of India, as has been pointed out earlier, expresses the hopes and aspirations of the genuinely secular freedom fighters so that the successive generations of Indians must rise above narrow religious prejudices and jointly participate in political, social and economic developments of the country. Regretfully, it did not happen. What went wrong? Quite a few reasons have already got discursively mentioned above. Here a few more explanations may be brought into focus.

Firstly, the partition of the country and the creation of Pakistan as a Muslim state massively damaged the cause of secularism in independent India. It was an obvious victory of the votaries of the 'Two Nation Theory' and a setback to the secular leadership. The partition of the country also set off a chain of the worst sort of communal riots on both sides of the border. The refugees from west Punjab and east Bengal brought with them, besides the hatred of the Muslims, the gruesome stories of murder, arson, rape, loot and unspeakable violence. This severely vitiated the socio-political climate of the country and put the legitimate secularists such as Gandhi, Azad and Nehru of the INC and the leaders of the Left on the defensive.

Secondly, the assassination of Gandhi by a fanatic sympathizer of the RSS stunned the nation. The resultant ban on the activities of the RSS and the popular fury against the cohorts of Godse and supporters of the Hindu Right compelled the Hindu communalists to lie low for the time being. It was during this time that Nehru emerged as the rightful political heir of Gandhi and enjoyed unprecedented popularity across the country. It reinforced his position in the Congress and the Constituent Assembly. Consequently, the remarkable constitutional provisions dealing with the principle of secularism could find expression in the basic statute of independent India. In different circumstances, Nehru's advocacy for a secular polity would have been vetoed.

Pandit Nehru had always been trumpeted as an absolutely secular person and a friend of the Muslims by the drum beaters of the Congress. Nevertheless, the reality seems to be the opposite of what has been propagated until now. In a recent exposure of a classified report on the Hyderabad massacre of 1948, that has not been declassified by the government even after the lapse of more than 60 years, the most gruesome slaughter of the Muslims in independent India occurred under the premiership of Nehru. After the military takeover of

Hyderabad state, which is strangely referred to as 'police action', there were reports that the local Hindu fanatics in connivance with the Indian army unleashed a reign of killings and rapes of the Muslims to avenge the atrocities committed by the *Razakars.* In response the Nehru Government commissioned Prof. Pandit Sunderlal to submit a report after proper investigation. The report was submitted but was never made public because its findings were unpalatable to the government.

A few unauthenticated versions had always been in circulation outside India which quoted conservative figures of the Muslims killed in the revenge massacre. For instance, a much lower but still shocking estimate was reported by Professor Perry Anderson of UCLA. He writes: "When the Indian Army took over Hyderabad, massive Hindu pogroms against the Muslim population broke out, aided and abetted by its regulars. On learning something of them the figurehead Muslim Congressman in Delhi, Maulana Azad, then Minister of Education, prevailed on Nehru to let a team investigate. It reported that a conservative estimate between 27,000 and 40,000 Muslims had been slaughtered in the space of a few weeks after the Indian takeover."[60] The Nehru Government, of course, never admitted the occurrence of massacre. What was scandalous that Nehru brazenly announced that Indian victory in Hyderabad was achieved without a single communal incident! The famous historian William Dalrymple in his book, *The Age of Kali,* informs that the Sunderlal Report has been leaked and published abroad, and "estimates that as many as 200,000 Hyderabadi Muslims were slaughtered."[61] It was the largest and the most gruesome pogrom against the Muslims in independent India.

Another example of anti-Muslim bias from the Nehru era is about their economic exclusion. The loyalty of Indian Muslims is always questioned by the Hindu Right, the ruling political class and the bureaucracy. The bias started immediately after independence. The most prominent leader who gave expression to prejudice against the Muslims publicly was not a leader of the Hindu Mahasabha or a member of the RSS but Vallabhbhai Patel, the then Home Minister of India and a stalwart of the so-called secular Congress. "In a speech at Lucknow, in early

January 1948 he (Patel) reminded his audience that it was in that town that 'the formation of two-nation theory was laid.' For it was the UP intellectuals who had claimed that 'Muslims were a separate nation.' Now, for those who had chosen not to go to Pakistan, it was not enough to give 'mere declarations of loyalty to the Indian Union', they 'must give *practical proof* of their declarations."[62] So, here was the first Home Minister of free India demanding a *'practical proof'* of loyalty to the nation from the Muslims who decided on not to leave the land of their ancestors and many of them have been facing intra-community and inter-community social exclusion for centuries.

Patel did not stop at giving a vicious warning to the Muslims but embarked on a well-planned exclusion of Muslims from state institutions. Shortly after his Lucknow speech, the secretary of the Home Ministry wrote to all the secretaries to be vigilant about the few Muslims who might still be working under them because they could be potential spies of Pakistan. The letter clearly stated that the potential fifth-columnists, as the Muslim employees were being treated by Patel, posed a serious threat to national security because they might pass on secret information to Pakistan. The letter further cautioned: "It is obvious that they (Muslim employees) constitute a dangerous element in the fabric of administration; and it is essential that they should not be entrusted with any confidential or secret work or allowed to hold key posts."[63] So, the Indian State officially adopted an anti-Muslim policy right from the word go. It was ironical that such an obnoxious policy came into force when Pandit Nehru, supposed to be a truly secular man, was at the helm of affairs. What's more that this confidential circular was never rescinded by Nehru and continued to be in force until 1969.[64] The policy of excluding Muslims from public services started by Patel and willingly continued by Nehru, his daughter and the successive governments is firmly in place.

Thus, in reality, the idea of secularism did not have the genuine support of all the members of the Constituent Assembly nor of a sizable number of the members of the Congress. The fact is that the Congress has always been an umbrella group of adherents of all sorts of ideologies. For that reason, even the believers of *Hindutva*, such as Madan Mohan Malviya, Lala

Lajpat Rai, Shyama Prasad Mukherjee et al. were also members of the Congress. It was only after the enforcement of the Constitution Mukherjee left the Congress and established a Hindu party, the Bharatiya Jana Sangh. "It has also been alleged", informs Paul Brass, "that many of the politicians of the country who proclaim their adherence to secularism as a state ideology actually harbour Hindu communal sentiments."[65] What inference can we draw from such a discouraging state of affairs? Obviously, the principle of secularism got incorporated in the Constitution not with the unconditional and enthusiastic support of all the members of the Constituent Assembly but diffidently because of the towering presence of secular leaders like Nehru, Azad, Ambedkar and a few others. This also explains why the word secular or its derivatives did not get mentioned in the original text of the Constitution despite the valiant efforts of K.T. Shah.

Thirdly, we must also be conscious of the transformation of the Indian National Congress from a movement for the emancipation of the country into a political party, albeit defying Gandhi's advice in the aftermath of independence. Having got transformed into a political party, the Congress had to compete with its political opponents to capture political power. Thus, the compulsions of the competitive politics forced the Congress leaders to compromise on the principle of secularism. In a country of predominantly Hindu population the communal/casteist card always helps win elections. Moreover, as it has already been pointed out elsewhere, the elite never put forward the idea of secularism or at least its Indian version as the indigenous growth before the masses. It was always thought of as an imported 'liberal/modernist' idea. As a result it always remained a distant and nebulous concept in the consciousness of the masses.

Like the Muslim liberals, the Hindu secularists too failed in secularizing the teeming Hindu masses. Here lies the failure of Nehru as a mass-based leader that he never was. He was an intellectual and a visionary. His emergence as the most popular leader immediately after independence was primarily because, in the popular perception, he remained the legitimate political heir of Gandhi. A couple of years before his death he realized his failure in keeping majority communalism in check and wrote with much regret: "We talk about a secular state in India. It is perhaps not very easy even to find a good word in Hindi for 'secular'. Some people think it means something opposed to religion. That obviously is not correct." He further added: "Our constitution lays down that we are a secular state, but it must be admitted that this is not wholly reflected in our mass living and thinking. In a country like England, the state is...allied to one particular religion...Nevertheless, the state and the people there function in a largely secular way. Society, therefore, in England is more advanced in this respect than in India, even though our constitution may be, in this matter more advanced."[66]

These were the sorrowful words of an ageing public figure to whom secularism was never a political strategy to realize political goals but an article of faith. We tend to feel sorry for Nehru's melancholic tone that is distinct in the expression that transmits his sense of loss. Nevertheless, a closer reading of the statement may reveal that Nehru seems to find fault with the Indian masses rather than admitting his failure and the failure of his Congress colleagues in reinforcing the Indian secular traditions and informing the masses about the indigenousness of secularism so as to inspire them to rally behind the ideal. There may not be a 'good word in Hindi' for secularism but there is a 'good' and widely acceptable word for secularism in Urdu, Nehru's mother tongue. The word is *rawadari*, a term often used in Sufi literature to connote disregarding of religious differences in socio-political affairs.

The important point is that it was not because of the non-availability of a proper Hindi term for secularism which proved an impediment for the masses to embrace the ideal but it was the incapability and lack of confidence of Nehru and his secular colleagues to put the time-tested secular traditions of ancient and medieval India on the political agenda of the nationalist movement. Whenever they spoke about secularism they had a sense of guilt at the back of their minds that they were imposing a Western ideal on the people who had never been exposed to the implications of the ideal. They could have invoked the messages of Lord Mahavir, the Buddha, Ashoka, Akbar, Nanak,

Kabir, Tukaram and countless Sufis to bring home the principle of equality of all religions. Regretfully, they always expounded secularism in Western terms and the masses could never connect with the ideal precisely because of its *so-called* foreign origin.

Fourthly, the attitude of the political parties, in particular, that of the Congress towards Muslims forced them to remain perpetually obsessed with their minority status with a perception that they are surrounded by a hostile majority. The Congress leadership has always harped on the imminent threat to the minorities from the Hindu communal parties while projecting itself as the only protector of the lives and properties of the religious minorities. Thus, by creating a fear psychosis particularly in the minds of the Muslims, the Congress ensured that the community always votes to its candidates. In order to perfect this strategy, the Congress always sought the support of the most rabid communalists and the self-serving mullahs who, in turn, propel some of their stooges as the 'leaders' (read wholesale traders of Muslim votes) of the community. The Congress never made any honest attempt to reach out to the Muslim masses and involve them in the process of socio-economic advancement.

There is certainly a good deal of truth in the charge of the Hindu Right against the Congress that it has always treated the Muslims as their vote bank and for that reason kept the entire community embroiled in non-issues such as the Muslim character of Aligarh Muslim University, status of Urdu and Muslim Personal Law. The Congress has never made any sincere effort to address the real problems of the community such as poverty, illiteracy, unemployment, security of lives and property and so on. Consequently, the hold of the mullahs, all the way through their stooges masquerading as leaders, over the Muslim masses remained unyielding, which proved damaging for the process of secularization of the community. The Congress has, in fact, never allowed the secular leadership to take root and flourish among the Muslims.

Fifthly, the bureaucracy since independence has played havoc not only in respect with the interest of religious minorities but also with the overall socio-democratic development of the country. A free democratic and secular India required a different sort of civil service with a new mindset of transforming a superstition-ridden conventional society into a truly secular and democratic one. In order to create such administrative machinery a new set of service rules and conditions underlining accountability, transparency, impartiality and commitment to social justice was needed. It was not done. The bureaucracy that independent, democratic and secular India inherited from the colonial masters was allowed to continue almost unaltered with their stately privileges and vast powers with more or less no transparency or accountability. The upper class and the upper caste character of the civil services also remained intact.

In this backdrop we must consider the issue of discrimination against the minorities in general and the Muslims in particular in matters like policy implementation, recruitment to public services and most importantly their representation in the armed forces and police. "In some states, recruitment of the Muslims was stopped under ministerial orders on the ground that the Muslims were over-represented in the past. A UP Home Minister is on record having admitted this in the Assembly."[67] The process of discrimination against the Muslims began on the fervent advice of the bureaucracy immediately after independence. "Mahavir Tyagi, Union Minister of State for Defence admitted that at the time of partition the percentage of Muslims in the services was 32 and now it had gone down to two. Abul Hasan Nadvi also states that from 1946 to 1952, only three Muslims were taken in the Delhi police force. It is alleged that the Government of India had issued a circular to the effect that the Muslims should not be given key positions in the administration. It was issued when Sardar Patel was the Home Minister but was rescinded in 1969."[68] It means the anti-Muslim circular was very much in place throughout Nehru's premiership and five more years after that! So far as Patel is concerned no wonder he was the staunchest advocate of keeping the bureaucracy almost unaltered!

The consistent anti-Muslim policies of the Union and State Administrations resulted in Muslims being reduced to the most backward segment of Indian society. The Sachar Committee report that was tabled in Parliament on November 30, 2006, portrays a grim picture of the largest religious minority. The

Muslims lag behind almost all other segments of society in terms of most of the socio-economic and educational indices. Their educational index is dismal as only 56 per cent Muslims are literate while merely 3.6 per cent of them are graduates, the lowest among all the religious communities. Their share in central services is pegged at less than 3 per cent while in no state except Jammu & Kashmir do Muslims comprise more than 11 per cent of government servants. The most revealing statistics are from West Bengal where the Muslims constitute 25 per cent of the population, whereas their share in government jobs is only 4.2 per cent. The Leftist government led by the CPI (M), that is in power in that state for more than three decades and being a harbinger of secularism and the rights of the minorities has to make an explanation on this count. The other statistics are similarly appalling. For instance, 94.9 per cent of the Muslims living below the poverty line don't get the food grains. In rural India, 60.2 per cent of Muslims don't own land and only 1 per cent own hand pumps or tube wells. These are alarming findings indeed and it is equally true that immediate corrective measures are badly needed. The crucial point is that such an administrative bias against the largest religious minority has led to its alienation from socio-economic and political processes and consequently it falls prey to the machinations of the mullahs.

Lastly, the Hindu communal organizations and political parties have been playing an extremely vicious game of dividing Indian society along communal lines. The RSS, the fountainhead of the ideology of the Hindu Right defines that "four categories of people are enemies of India: Indian followers of foreign religions such as Islam and Christianity; Communists and their sympathizers; Westernized members of the Indian intelligentsia; and foreign powers."[67] Now, if such an ideology of hatred is the source of inspiration for the ruling party and some other political groups in India then how can the principle of secularism become a 'substantive political commitment'?

Presently, we are passing through the most difficult phase of independent India because the people committed to make India a genuine democratic, secular and progressive nation are totally demoralized because of the ascendancy of the Hindu

Right during the last couple of decades and with the formation of the BJP government at the Centre and in many states. The secular character of the Indian State is in serious trouble. In the light of this it is appropriate to say that secularism in India is indeed under siege and there is an urgent need to revisit secular credentials of Indian State. Almost every day the persons holding power and having affiliations to various organizations that jointly go by the name Sangh Parivar are either making provocative statements or actually attempting to Hinduize India. For those who cherish the values that are enshrined in our constitution such as liberty, equality, fraternity, justice and secularism, the current political scenario is extremely depressing.

Though the votaries of the Hindutva and the Islamic supremacists have always opposed secularism, the ideal has been under attack more intensely for about three decades not only by the communal fanatics but also by the liberal intellectuals who are not even remotely connected with communal politics. Scholars such as T.N. Madan, Ashish Nandy, Partha Chatterjee and others who contributed to the valuable book, *Secularism and Its Critics*, edited by Rajeev Bhargava argued that the ideal of secularism is a foreign construct and since it is imported from the West it could not take root in Indian soil. Such an oft-repeated attack on secularism for being an imported notion is disingenuous criticism to say the least. Objectively speaking almost all the constituent values of the Constitution of India are of Western origin. Nationalism, democracy, socialism, rule of law, parliament, the executive, bureaucracy and judiciary—all these ideals and institutions the mode in which they have been incorporated in the Constitution are of Western origin. Then why single out secularism?

Moreover, we must not lose sight of the Indian version of secularism which is different from the Western mode of secularism which is mostly identified with the core principle of separation of State and Church. However, this Caesar and God dichotomy can be traced to the teachings of Christ and it is mentioned in the Holy Bible. So who decides what is Western? The teachings of Christ belong to West Asia not to the West. We can only concede that Thomas Jefferson lifted the sentence from the Holy Bible and erected a wall between the state and Church and for that reason this brand of secularism came to be identified with the West. Indian secularism does not erect a wall between the State and religion; it recognizes the role of religion even in the public domain. Abolition of untouchability, Article 290A providing that the funds required for the upkeep of the South Indian temples should be charged upon the consolidated fund of Kerala, banning of slaughter of milch animals, in particular, cows and calves and a few other provisions of the Constitution are testimony to the fact that Indian secularism does not completely banish religion to the private sphere. This version of secularism is indigenous and compatible with social realities of our country. It is unfortunate that even this mode of secularism is gasping for its survival because of the assaults of communal forces of various hues.

Conclusion

By way of conclusion, I can only reiterate that the Indian version of secularism is barely similar to the Western concept of secularism. The secular idea that was expressed in the Indian Constitution and keeps recurring in the political discourse is largely indigenous that underlines the importance of religion in Indian society. It does not ignore, let alone condemn, the institution of religion; it only stipulates symmetric treatment of all religions in socio-economic and political affairs of the country. It is, therefore the responsibility of the secular parties and their leaders as well as the intelligentsia to present the ideal of secularism as a home-grown value of socio-political interaction. The earlier they do it the better.

Although I realize that secularism is too significant a subject to be left with the politicians and state, I do not completely discount the role of the political leaders and the state in secularization of a society like India. The leaders have the might of the party organizations at their disposal. If they are sincerely committed to the idea of secularism they can make use of the organizational force to make the masses aware of the Indian version of secularism.

The state has a far deeper penetration and larger reach in society than any other institution. Above all, it has the power to keep the social affairs on the right track. I must, however, immediately clarify that I am not suggesting that the state should use coercion to make people secular. Nonetheless, the state must protect its constitution and see to it that all its agencies, the legislature, executive (including bureaucracy) and judiciary, respect and put into practice the core principles of the basic law of the land. Secularism is one of those principles. For instance, there are certain issues such as saffronization of education, administrative bias against religious minorities, the dismal representation of minorities in bureaucracy, armed forces and police, discriminative practices of banks and other financial institutions vis-a-vis minority customers, frequent occurrences of communal violence targeting non-Hindus, in particular, the Muslims and a horde of other problems that can be effectively dealt with the accountable agencies manned by the conscientious people of a secular state.

Likewise, I strongly feel that secular intellectuals have so far shunned their moral responsibility of secularizing the masses and for that reason are usually written off as arm-chair intellectuals. The tag is not without justification. They must play a proactive role in disseminating secular ideas among the common people who are basically peace-loving and law-abiding but for want of proper guidance might fall prey to the politics of hatred propelled by the communal parties and organizations of different hues. I realize that it is not expected from an academician or a theorist to become a campaigner of secularism and frequently participate in picketing and demonstrations but they can at least subtly influence those with whom they regularly come in contact. What course of action are they supposed to adopt? I leave it to their ingenuity and imagination.

The role of media, print as well as electronic, is crucial in strengthening the democratic-secular character of the Indian state. We cannot rule out the existence of counter-views in a democracy that attaches equal importance to free speech. However, in the name of free speech a newspaper, a television channel or a film maker cannot defy the constitutional principles and the penal laws of the country. In all democratic states they have to function within the framework of the law. Therefore, if a newspaper or a television channel intentionally sets in motion a campaign of misinformation and hatred against any segment of society it is guilty of transgressing the limits of free speech. Furthermore, being part of a liberal-modern-democratic-secular polity, the media is expected to promote rational ideas and scientific temperament. Considering its influence and reach it should not help strengthen (save in creative works) superstitions, myths, feints and false notions among the unsuspecting masses.

The secularists, in particular those who are agnostics or atheists, must be cautious while expressing their views on religion. In a democracy, as a non-believer secularist is entitled to be an agnostic or an atheist, a believer secularist is also equally at liberty to profess and practice her/his religion. The Indian version of secularism does not deride, condemn or assail the institution of religion. On the contrary, it insists on symmetric treatment of all religions. Anyone who has a cursory knowledge of Indian society will endorse this mode of secularism because it is realistic considering the stupendous role religion plays in the lives of Indians.

In India we cannot wish away religion. Religion, to the common man is the hope for a better tomorrow. For that reason an atheist or an agnostic, unless she/he has a better alternative to offer for balancing out her/his afflictions, has no right to snatch from her/him the last straw that facilitates her/him psychologically to swim through the turbulent ocean of life. I must caution the readers that I am not suggesting that the common people should be left alone to languish in the cesspool of superstition and fantasy but only trying to make a point that the humanistic contents present in almost all religions should not be dispensed with. Then, what does it mean to be a secularist in India? It means to be sensitive about the religious beliefs of others so long as they do not violate the law of the land; it means not to be a religious supremacist; it also means to be peace-loving and law-abiding.

We must also reformulate faith in our liberal spiritual wisdom. We may perhaps be at an advantage if the non-state groups help promote the humanitarian and syncretic traditions of our country. I tend to believe that it was because of the unmitigated influence of the Bhakti movement and Sufism that there was barely any communal violence during the medieval period of Indian history. Unlike Nandy, I am not putting across an argument from an anti-modernist point of view; it is only a reaffirmation in the efficacy of our conventional wisdom.

Most importantly, we must have a rethink about our educational system. It must be underscored that the focus of education in contemporary India is absolutely on the professional and the so-called job-oriented courses. Consequently, the liberal education has almost been discarded. Ideally speaking, acquisition of knowledge should not have linkages with someone's competence to earn money. Business is the right area for accomplishing this purpose. Regretfully, in independent India the successive governments have been promoting non-academic courses at the cost of liberal education. The state agencies as well as private sector feel it is redundant to invest in liberal education. They fail to comprehend that in the long run it shall only be the value-based liberal education that is most likely to help maintain peace and harmony in society that are the preconditions for all development, economic or scientific.

In the current educational system in India most universities have divided various disciplines of knowledge in water-tight compartments and claim that it is necessary for specialization. The end result is that an Indian doctor or engineer hardly knows anything about her/his society, philosophical traditions, literary masterpieces and the ethos of the people she/he is surrounded by. Similarly, a postgraduate in the humanities or social sciences does not know even the basic scientific knowledge that is expected from an educated person. Therefore, educational reforms might help produce conscientious human beings rather than self-centred robots.

NOTES

1. I refer to *Bhakti* and Sufi traditions that were quite effectual in breaking the shackles of religious orthodoxy.
2. Quoted by Jean Bauberot in his insightful article, 'The Two Thresholds of Laicization', in Rajeev Bhargava (ed.), *Secularism and Its Critics*, Oxford University Press, New Delhi, 1998, p. 95.
3. Cited from Valerian Rodrigues (ed.), *The Essential Writings of B.R.*

Ambedkar, Oxford University Press, New Delhi, Third Impression, 2006, pp. 177-178.

4. Mathew, 22: 21, *The New Testament*, The Gideons International, 1982, p. 44.
5. Sunday *Times of India*, Mumbai, May 23, 2010, p. 21.
6. Ephesians, 1:21-22, *The New Testament*, op. cit., p. 353.
7. *The Meaning of the Glorious Quran*, II: 256, translated by Muhammad Marmaduke Pickthall, Idara Isha'at-e-Diniyat, New Delhi, 2006, p. 57.

   Ibid., CIX: 6, p. 452.
8. W.T. Jones, *Masters of Political Thought*, Vol. 2, George G. Harrap & Co. Ltd., London, 1967, p. 50.
9. *Encyclopaedia of Religion and Ethics*, Vol. IX, p. 347.
10. Ibid., p. 347.
11. Holyoake, G.J., *The Origin and Nature of Secularism*, Watts and Co., London, 1896, p. 51.
12. *Encyclopaedia of Religion and Ethics*, op. cit., p. 349.
13. See Moin Shakir's article, 'M.N. Roy's Concept of Secular State', in V.K. Sinha (ed.), *Secularism in India*, Bombay, 1968.
14. D.E. Smith, *India as a Secular State*, Oxford University Press, Bombay, 1963, p. 22.
15. Amartya Sen, *The Idea of Justice*, Allen Lane, Penguin Books, India, 2009, p. 37.
16. "The Edicts of King Asoka: An English Rendering" by Ven. S. Dhammika.
17. Ibid.
18. Romila Thapar, *Ashoka*, Microsoft Encarta Encyclopaedia, 2001.
19. http://www.truthindia.com.
20. Roy Choudhury, Manik Lal, *The Din-i-Ilahi or, The Religion of Akbar*, Oriental Reprint, New Delhi, 3rd ed., 1997.
21. Krishnamurti, R., *Akbar: The Religious Aspect*, Faculty of Arts, Maharaja Sayajirao University of Baroda, 1961, p. 83.
22. Amartya Sen, op. cit., p. 37.
23. Jawaharlal Nehru, *Discovery of India*, 1956, p. 385.
24. D.E. Smith, op. cit., p. 68.
25. Ibid., p. 83.
26. Ibid., p. 68.
27. Cited from Ibid., p. 102.
28. M.C. Chagla, *Roses in December*, Bharatiya Vidya Bhavan, Mumbai, 1973, p. 41.
29. Jaswant Singh, *Jinnah, India-Partition-Independence*, Rupa & Co, New Delhi, 2009, pp. 72-73.

30. Cited from C.N.K. Bose, *Selections From Gandhi*, 2nd edition, Ahmedabad, 1971, p. 293.
31. G.N. Sarma and Moin Shakir, *Politics and Society*, Parimal Prakashan, Aurangabad, 1976, p. 242.
32. Ibid.
33. Quoted by D.E. Smith, op. cit., p. 101.
34. Ibid., p. 102.
35. *The Constitution of India*, Professional Book Publishers, Delhi, 2010, p. 12.
36. Quoted by D.E. Smith, op. cit., p. 102.
37. Ibid., pp. 103-4.
38. Quoted by Smith, Ibid., p. 108.
39. *The Constitution of India*, op. cit., p. 13.
40. Cited from Smith, op. cit., p. 110.
41. Ibid.
42. *The Constitution of India*, op. cit., p. 5.
43. Ibid., p. 6.
44. D. E. Smith, op. cit, p. 116.
45. *The Constitution of India*, op. cit., p. 6.
46. Ibid.
47. Ibid.
48. Ibid., p. 7.
49. Ibid., p. 13.
50. Ibid., p. 137.
51. Ibid., p. 13.
52. D.E. Smith, op. cit., p. 129.
53. *The Constitution of India*, op. cit., pp. 122-23.
54. Prior to 1949, the maharajas of the two neighbouring princely states of Travancore and Cochin had committed the huge annual state grants to various Hindu temples. At the time of their merger in the Union of India, a Covenant was entered into by the rulers of the two states, and the responsibility to perpetuate the grants for the upkeep of the temples got transferred to the Government of India. Thereafter, the reorganization of the states created the state of Kerala in 1956 and consequently the financial obligation was mainly transferred to Kerala with the then state of Madras bearing a part of it.
55. *The Constitution of India*, op. cit., p. 13.
56. Ibid.
57. See Ashis Nandy's Article in Bhargava, op. cit., pp. 320ff.
58. Narendra Bhardwaj quoted in Moin Shakir, *Muslims in Free India*, op. cit., p. 92.

59. Quoted by Swaminathan S. Anklesaria Aiyar in his article, 'Declassify Report on the 1948 Hyderabad Massacre', Sunday *Times of India*, November 25, 2012.
60. Quoted by Swaminathan S. Anklesaria Aiyar, Ibid.
61. Guha, Ramchandra, *India After Gandhi: The History of the World's Largest Democracy*, Macmillan, Picador India, New Delhi, 2007, p. 366.
62. Ibid.
63. See Moin Shakir, *Muslims in Free India*, Kalamkar Prakashan, New Delhi, wherein he quoted from *Link* issue of November 9, 1969 and Y.B. Chavan's statement in the Lok Sabha reported in *Times of India*, November 29, 1969.
64. Paul R. Brass, *The Politics of India Since Independence*, 2nd ed., Cambridge University Press, New Delhi, 1999, pp. 192-93.
65. Quoted by T.N. Madan in his essay included in Bhargava, op. cit., pp. 311-12.
66. Quoted in Moin Shakir, *Muslims in Free India*, Kalamkar Prakashan, New Delhi, 1972, p. 12.

2

Reimagining Secularism: State, Religion and Principled Distance*

Rajeev Bhargava

In an article, 'Giving Secularism its Due'[1], I introduced a distinction between ethical and political secularism. Ethical secularism means something like a comprehensive normative perspective by which to lead an individual or collective life or both. Here secularism is a well-reasoned but partly speculative perspective on how best to lead one's life, here and now, in this world on the assumption that all ends pursued by humans pertain only to this world and this time.

Politico-moral secularism or political secularism for short, outlined a perspective on what earthly restraint, coercive or non-coercive, that can be placed in the pursuit of the good life, regardless of whether one is an ethical secularist or not, something on which both secularists and the religious might both agree. Indeed it might be an object of consensus among different kinds of secular and religious believers. One of the objectives of that paper was to show that unlike what many of

---

* See also Bhargava, Rajeev. 1998. *Secularism and Its Critics*, Oxford University Press, New Delhi, 2004, Inclusion and Exclusion in South Asia: The Role of Religion. Background paper for Human Development Report, UNDP; Rajeev Bhargava, Political Secularism in Dryzek, Honnig and Phillips (eds.), *A Handbook of Political Theory*, Oxford Unversity Press, 2006; Rajeev Bhargava, India's Secular Constitution in Hasan, Sridharan, Sudarshan (eds.) *India's Living Constitution: Ideas, Practices, Controversies*, Oxford University Press, New Delhi, 2002.

us hitherto believed, political secularism neither entails nor presupposes ethical secularism.

The paper also clarified the distinction between the process of secularization studied widely by sociological theorists and political secularism, then largely neglected by political theorists. I had argued that political secularism is frequently needed precisely in those societies where either people belonging to multiple religions or religious believers and philosophical secularists or all of them coexist or are engaged in prolonged conflicts. A society that is already fully secularized wouldn't *need* a secular state because it would, in some form, already have it. Political secularism, I argued is needed precisely in those conditions where complete secularization is impossible, unavailable as an option or undesirable.

Secularization refers to a social process that gets underway and remains in motion largely but not wholly independent of intentional human action. Secularization was not launched as a programme of collective action. It has occurred, if, where and when it has, largely because of the unintended consequences of human action. Indeed, in Europe, it appears to have happened as a result of changes within religion, induced by religious people out of very religious motives. Secularism, on the other hand, is a collective normative project. It sets out a plan of desirable collective action. It is probable that the more successful its realization the more secularization there is but to some extent secularization can occur even without secularism, perhaps despite its failure.

The 1994 article spoke of the challenge faced by secularism in India. But well before its crisis in India, secular states and the doctrine underpinning them had begun to come under strain elsewhere. Secularism was severely jolted with the establishment in Iran of the first modern theocracy, rejected partly because of the perception that it was a Western idea. By the late 1980s similar Islamic political movements had emerged in Egypt, Sudan, Algeria, Tunisia, Ethiopia, Nigeria, Chad, Senegal, Turkey, Afghanistan, Pakistan, and even Bangladesh[2]. Movements challenging secular states were hardly restricted to Muslim societies. Protestant movements decrying secularism emerged in Kenya, Guatemala, and the Philippines. Protestant fundamentalism became a force in American politics. Singhalese Buddhist nationalists in Sri Lanka, practitioners of religious ultra-orthodoxy in Israel, and diasporic communities in Canada and Britain all began to question the separation of state and religion.[3]

In short, Western conceptions of political secularism do not appear to have travelled all that well in other societies. More importantly, such conceptions and the secular states they underpin are coming under strain even in Europe, where, till recently, they were believed to be firmly entrenched and secure. Why so? It is true that the substantive secularization of European societies has brought about the extensive secularization of European states; regardless of their religious affiliation, citizens have a large basket of civil and political rights unheard of in religion-centred states, past or present. Nevertheless, two problems remain.

First, migration from former colonies and intensified globalization have thrown together in Western public spaces Christian, Islamic, and pre-Christian faiths such as Hinduism[4]. The cumulative result is unprecedented religious diversity, the weakening of the public monopoly of single religions, and the generation of mutual suspicion, distrust, hostility, and conflict. This is evident in Germany and Britain but was dramatically highlighted by the headscarf issue in France, the cartoon affair in Denmark and the murder of filmmaker Theo Van Gogh in the Netherlands shortly after the release of his controversial film about Islamic culture.[5] Second, despite substantial secularization, in some European states inequities resulting from the formal establishment of the dominant religion have done little to bolster better intercommunity relations or to reduce religious discrimination. With the deepening of religious diversity, the religious biases of European states have become increasingly visible. European states have continued to privilege Christianity in one form or another. They have publicly funded religious schools, maintained clerical salaries and real estate holdings of Christian churches, facilitated the control by churches of cemeteries, and trained the clergy. In short, there has been no impartiality within the domain of religion, and despite formal "equality" this privileging of Christianity continues to have a far-reaching impact on the rest of society[6]. Even the widespread belief regarding the existence of a secular European public sphere is based largely on a myth. As a result, the formal or informal establishment of a single religion, even the weaker variety of establishment, continues to be part of the problem.

This challenge to secularism has come not only from politicians, civil society groups and clerics but also from academics. Critics have argued that the conceptual and normative structure of secularism is itself terribly defective. There is something wrong with the ideal itself. Secularism has been linked to a flawed modernization, the repressive structures of the nation state, to the indefensible conception of science and rationality and to an excessive individualism. It has been charged for trivializing faith and being insensitive to religious believers. Its failure to be impartial and universal is linked to its Christian biases.

I agree that secular states are in crisis, that the problems of secularism are real and go deep. However, it is the contention of this paper that secularism is not irredeemable, that while many of its conceptions are flawed, one can still reimagine, redefine and rescue it. This is crucial because there is still no alternative to secularism on the horizon. Under present conditions it continues to be badly needed.

The criticism of secularism, I argue, looks indefeasible only because it has focused on a few doctrinal versions of Western secularism. I argue that it is time we shifted focus away from doctrines and towards the constitutional provisions and normative practices of a wide variety of states, including the best practices of non-Western states such as India. Once we do so, we will begin to see secularism differently and might realize that we need not an alternative to but an alternative conception of secularism. Identifying a defensible alternative conception is not always easy. It can be done only if we make two crucial moves. First, leave the standard church-state models and focus instead on secularism as a response to religious diversity. Second, as already mentioned above, pay more attention to normative practices rather than to existing doctrinal formulations. Allow me to elaborate these points.

Most societies today are characterized by religious diversity. The pressing question before us, then, is how is this diversity, and the problems that accompanies it, to be handled? What does religious diversity mean? It means both diversity *of* religion and diversity *within* religion. Diversity of religion exists in a society when it has a populace professing faith in, say, Christian, Jewish, or Islamic ideals. Diversity within religion may be of two kinds. The first might be called horizontal diversity, which exists when a religion is internally differentiated. For example, different confessions, denominations, and sects within Christianity and Islam. Religions are characterized, however, by another kind of diversity, which may be called vertical diversity. Here, people of the same religion may engage in diverse practices that are hierarchically arranged and might include certain kinds of practices that other co-religionists are excluded from. For example, caste-ridden Hinduism makes a distinction between pure and impure practices, and, women or Dalits may not be allowed entry into the inner sanctum of temples and in many cases even into the precincts of an upper caste temple. This example already brings home a point that I ought to have made at the very outset of this discussion. Every form of diversity, including religious diversity, is enmeshed in power relations. It further follows that inherent in religiously diverse societies is the possibility of both interreligious and intra-religious domination—a broad term that encompasses discrimination, marginalization, oppression, exclusions, and the reproduction of hierarchy. (Two other forms of domination are also possible: the domination by the religious of the non-religious and the domination of the religious by the non-religious).

This shift allows me to conceive secularism as a response to a deeply distorted form of sociability within the domain of religion, as a normative stance that seeks to facilitate better social relations within and across religious groups. Secularism in this view is not against religiosity per se but is opposed to institutionalized religious domination. Allow me to draw an analogy with one of the Karl Marx's better known ideas. Marx had claimed that in order for production of material goods to take place, humans must enter into relations with one another—production relations. He further claimed that such production frequently takes place within structures of exploitation and dominance. His entire project might be viewed as an attempt to emancipate the production process from distorted human relations. Likewise, one might view the production of symbolic goods as requiring certain relations of production. However, the production of most symbolic goods including religious goods almost always takes place under the conditions of domination within and between religions. Secularism might then be viewed as an attempt to emancipate the production of symbolic goods, values and services from inter-and intra-religious domination. That's what I mean when I say that secularism is not against religiosity but fiercely opposes institutionalized religious domination. To rescue secularism requires a profound reconceptualization of what secularism means.

A second equally crucial move to reimagine secularism is this: a set of distinctions must be drawn and kept in mind to retrieve a defensible secularism. First, we need to distinguish between the entire complex of practices and institutional arrangements that either connect religion to or disconnect religion from the state and a subset of these practices and arrangements that embody norms — that is, an implicit sense of how states and religions *should* relate to one another. Whereas the former include the normative and the non-normative and operate at the entire *practical* level, the latter operate only at the *normative* level. Second, these norms are then articulated in representations and ad hoc, unstable reflections found in statements of politicians, laws enacted by legislators, executive decisions, judicial pronouncements, and constitutional articles. These articulations operate at the *discursive* level. Finally, the normative conceptions implicit in these practices and either subtly or explicitly articulated in the legal and political discourse are then posited as a normative ideal that is sometimes expressed as ideology and doctrine and that occasionally becomes an object of theoretical enquiry, thus operating at both the *doctrinal* and the *theoretical* levels. The distinction between a comprehensive practical and the exclusively normative level is important because identifying secularism with any particular practice or institutional arrangement that relates religion and the state will not do. True, secularism needs to be institutionally grounded, but to distinguish secular from religion-centred states and, even more important, to articulate a critical, normative secularism, the distinction between the normative and the non-normative is crucial.

More to the point, I argue that secular norms conceived at the doctrinal and the theoretical levels are by now highly restricted and inadequate. This has happened because these levels are colonized by mainstream, Western doctrines and theories of secularism. Reimagining secularism is virtually impossible unless we reduce our reliance on these formulations. These doctrines and theories have become part of the problem, hurdles to properly examining the issues at stake. Wittgenstein's warning that the hold of a particular picture is so strong that it prevents, even occludes, awareness of other conceptions of reality is apt here. We are so seized by one or two conceptions that we simply cannot notice other conceptions that have been pushed into the background. Once we shift away from currently dominant models and focus on the normative practices of a broader range of Western states beyond the more familiar ones, indeed also on non-Western states, we shall see that better forms of secular states and much more defensible versions of secularisms are available. And although in some contexts, minimally decent religion-centered states may be adequate, by and large, they will not do, because they, too, are as much a part of the problem as are some secular states.

So we need to move away from these doctrinal formulations of political secularism and unearth different versions found in the best practices of many states and in their judicial pronouncements and constitutional articles. Focusing on normative practices and constitutional articles and refashioning secularism will help us displace a worn-out ideal and shift the norm, bringing it closer to how people wish to lead their lives, rather than how they should lead their lives in accordance with a more or less redundant ideal. Once we shift away from these currently dominant models and focus on the normative practices of Western and non-Western states, we shall see that better forms of secular state and more defensible versions of secularism are available.

Models of Secularism

Which existing models am I talking about? Mainly there are two: the French and the American. In addition, there is a third found in the rest of Western Europe. Let me critically examine each of these models.

The Idealized French Model

The idealized French conception holds that the state must be separated from religion while retaining the power to interfere in it. However, religion is divested of any power to intervene in matters of the state. In short, separation means *one-sided exclusion.* For example, in March 2004, the French Assembly and the Senate introduced a new law signed by the President Jacques Chirac. The first article of the new law says 'In public primary, secondary, and high schools, the wearing of signs or dress with which the students manifest ostentatiously a religious affiliation is prohibited. Due to this, 47 Muslim and 3 Sikh students who did not follow the new rules were expelled from their school.[7] Clearly, the French state is less sensitive to the autonomy of religious associations, can brand them as dangerous and monitor them.[2] But religions have no such influence on the state. This one-sided exclusionary attitude continues a long standing move in France, after Catholic dominance in French public schools was replaced with a philosophically secular outlook. Since then, religious instruction has been abandoned. Organized prayer is forbidden and students cannot make a pledge that refers to God. The French exclude religious symbols and discourses from the public sphere. French public institutions have no prayer or reference to God.[8] Over time, states that follow this conception also develop a hierarchy between the secular and the religious and may perpetuate the non-religious domination of the religious. This happens even more so when, to promote more rigorous non-religious conceptions of positive freedoms and substantive equalities, states cross minimal thresholds of morality, formal equality, and decency.

States governed by this conception typically have a single, robust conception of the good life that translates into deep scepticism about the truth claims and value of religion and about its public role and capacity to prevent forms of oppression and domination. Typically, this secularism does not understand the believer's life as it is lived from the inside. It misses out on perhaps the most significant feature of most religions: that they encourage their members to choose to live a disciplined, restricted, rule-bound, and desire-abnegating life. To be sure, even such an anti-religious stance may help states to deal with cases of intra-religious domination where some members of a religious community dominate members of their own religion, as occurs with anti-clericalism in France. But often their relative blindness to religion makes states driven by such conceptions insensitive to religious freedoms, particularly to the religious freedoms of minorities. As a result, states may even, wittingly or unwittingly, perpetuate interreligious domination.

Many segments in virtually every society, on the right but particularly on the left, are tempted to follow the anti-pluralist French model, largely because they have bought into the view that religion—in Europe, more specifically Islam—is a "problem" and that its solution requires the coercive power of the state. Such an approach would be detrimental to interfaith relations particularly because while strongly interfering with non-Christian faiths, it leaves the formal or informal establishment of a single Christian religion untouched. A striking example is the accommodation of majority Catholics in public schools. School cafeterias serve fish for those Catholics who abstain from meat, but no such provision exists for those students who eat only *halal* meat. Catholic Chaplains in France operate in approximately half of French public secondary schools. French prisons and hospitals also have chaplains. Other exceptions to the secular laws exist in the region of Alsace-Mosselle and overseas colonies. The French state and local government have owned and funded the maintenance of the grand majority of the 45,000 of the Catholic churches, half of the Protestant churches and about 10 per cent of synagogues.[9] The French state also pays about 80 per cent of the budget including the salary of teachers in Catholic schools that follow the national curriculum and to be open to students of all faiths.[10] Jocelyne Cesari stresses that 'the collective dimension of Islam was confined to the intimate space of the residences, the hearths, the provided places at hotels, or the backs of the shops.'[11]

It is evident that attempts to further intervene in religions is likely to meet with resistance not only from Muslims but from non-Muslims as well. Moreover, any reliance on the heavy-handed and one-sided French model is likely to exacerbate problems. In addition, a remedy normatively unsuitable for European states will be rejected outright elsewhere. Indeed, states that have drawn inspiration from this model—for example, communist states such as China and the Kemalist state in Turkey—have a very poor record of protecting religious freedoms or sustaining intra- and interreligious equality.

The Idealized American Model

The idealized American self-understanding interprets separation to mean *mutual exclusion.* Neither the state nor religion is meant to interfere in the domain of the other. This mutual exclusion is held to be necessary to resolve conflicts between different Christian denominations, to grant some measure of equality between them, and—most crucially—to provide individuals the freedom to set up and maintain their own religious associations. The protection of religious liberties more generally is viewed as the raison de'tre of this model. This strict or "perfect separation," as James Madison has termed it, must take place at each of the three distinct levels of ends, institutions and personnel, and law and public policy. The first two levels make the state non-theocratic and disestablish religion. The third level ensures that the state has neither a positive nor a negative relationship with religion. On the positive side, for example, there should be no policy of granting aid, even non-preferentially, to religious institutions. On the negative side, it is not within the scope of state activity to interfere in religious matters even when some of the values professed by the state, such as equality, are violated within the religious domain. Consider President Barack Obama's helplessness in the face of the recent threat in America to publicly burn the Quran. As Leonard W. Levy[12] puts it, Congress simply has no power to legislate on any matter pertaining to religion.[13]

This non-interference is justified on the grounds that religion is a privileged, private (i.e. non-state) matter, and if something is amiss within this private domain, it can be mended only by those who have a right to do so within this sphere. This view, according to its proponents, is what religious freedom means. Thus the freedom that justifies mutual exclusion is negative liberty and is closely enmeshed with the privatization of religion. However, privatization here means non-officialization. American political secularism does not promote secularization in two of three senses mentioned above. It encourages a vibrant presence of religion in the non-state, public domain and does little to discourage religious beliefs or practices.

This model of secularism encourages the state to passively respect religion. Since any intervention is tantamount to control, the only way to respect religion is to leave it alone. Idealized American secularism, then, has some resources to fight interreligious domination (e.g. it necessitates the disestablishment of the dominant religion) but few resources to wage a struggle against deeper, more structural aspects of this domination. The state's hands off approach binds it to not facilitate freedoms or equality *within* religions. The American state may have worked out other strategies to minimize such dominations. However, states that lack its more conciliatory history or that possess religions that do not easily allow the option to exit would perpetuate religion-related domination in following the American model. Moreover, by interpreting separation as exclusion, this model of secularism betrays its own sectarianism; it can live comfortably with liberal, Protestantized, individualized, and privatized religions, but it has fewer resources to cope with religions that mandate greater public or political presence or that have a strong communal orientation. This group insensitivity makes it virtually impossible to accommodate community-specific rights, such as the right of religious communities to set up and maintain their own educational institutions, and therefore virtually impossible to more robustly protect the rights of religious minorities.

Furthermore, as a product of the Protestant ethic, American secularism's greatest drawback is its universal pretension. It presupposes a Christian civilization, something easily forgotten because over time this civilization has silently slid into the background. Christianity allows this self-limitation, and much of the world innocently mistakes this somewhat cunning self-denial for Christianity's disappearance.[14] But if this is so, this "inherently dogmatic" secularism cannot coexist innocently with other religions.[15] Given the enormous power of the state, it must try to shape and transform other religions—a clear instance of illegitimate influence. Thus, despite all its claims of leaving religions alone and granting religions liberty, this secularism is inhospitable to non-liberal, non-Protestant believers.[16] It can become inhospitable to non-believers as well. In March 2000, Michael Newdow, an atheist filed a law suit pleading that the daily recitation of the pledge of allegiance that included the phrase one nation under God harmed his daughter and violated the establishment clause of the first amendments. Though he lost in the district court, he won the case in the court of appeals. But both houses of legislature reaffirmed the words "under God" with a heavy majority endorsing strong religious expression in American public life.[17] This is widely seen as a virtual affirmation of the establishment of Christianity. If so, and whenever it happens, prospects of inter-religious discrimination loom large. Indeed, an excessive focus on religious freedom from the state may enhance inter-religious domination. As I say this, I am conscious that this is not an empirical claim about American society or politics. Instead I am suggesting that if such a model is followed elsewhere it may neither protect people from some forms of inter-religious domination nor from intra-religious domination.

The current theoretical formulations of this model—represented, for example, by philosophical liberalism—only exacerbate these problems. Thus liberal secularist theories enjoin the citizen to support only those coercive state laws for which there is public justification. If others are expected to follow a law based on terms that they do not understand and for reasons they cannot endorse, the principle of equal respect is violated—so the reasoning goes.[18] Coercive principles must be as justifiable to others as they are to us and therefore must be based on terms that all citizens can accept on the grounds of their common reason.

Because a religious rationale is a paradigmatic case of a basis for conduct that other citizens have good reasons to reject, it does not count as public justification; thus a law grounded solely in a religious rationale must never be enacted. In short, purely religious convictions or commitments have no role to play in democratic and pluralist polities. This requirement that religious reasons be excluded from liberal-democratic politics is offensive to religious persons who, like others, wish to support their favoured political commitments according to their conscience.[20] If people believe that their politics must be consistent with their morality as derived from religion, why should they be discouraged or stigmatized for grounding their politics in religious convictions? By asking the religious to exercise restraint and exclude theological reasons from their justification for a coercive law, liberal secularism forces them to act against their conscience and, in so doing, violates its own principle of equal respect. Indeed, the demand that restraint be exercised is counterproductive because exclusion from the larger public sphere forces the religious to form their own narrow public where resentment and prejudice will flourish.[21] This response would lead not only to the freezing of identities but also to the building of unbreachable walls between religious and non-religious citizens. Therefore, "engagement with religious people is typically better than shunning them"[22]

Furthermore, these theories of secularism rely excessively on a rationalist conception of reason that imposes unfair limits on the manner in which issues are to be brought into the public domain. Some issues are constitutively emotive; others become emotive because they are articulated by people who are not always trained to be rational in the way that secularists mandate.[23] Overall, the model of moral reasoning typical of such secularisms is context-insensitive, theoreticist, and absolutist (or non-comparative), enjoining us to think in terms of this or that since it is too heavily reliant on monolithic ideas or values considered to be true, superior, or wholly non-negotiable. In sum, both French and American versions developed in the context of a single-religion society and as a way to solve the problems of one religion, namely Christianity. They were not designed to deal with deep religious diversity. Both the idealized French and American versions of secularism understand separation as exclusion and make individualistically conceived values—individual liberty, or equality between individuals, or both—the grounds for separation. Overall, it would not be wrong to say that they force upon followers of secularism a choice between active hostility and benign indifference to religion. Because of its diversity-resistant and individualistic character, these two models have become part of the problem.

Western Secularism in European Societies

Neither of these two models adequately captures the models of secularism actually in play in European societies. Most European states follow neither the French nor the American model. Virtually all European states have a stable regime of individual rights that includes the right to religious liberty. None could have managed to install this regime without having attacked the power and privilege of their churches in the past, a stridency that would not have been possible without some degree of state-church separation. Yet, unlike in France, there is no lingering hostility towards religion in other European state structures. In Europe initial hostility was followed by active support. Virtually all European states have developed an institutional arrangement that grants some privilege or public recognition to their church. Indeed, some still have an established church, a privileged arrangement that goes well beyond recognition. Tariq Modood[24] finds the combination of separation of church and state and support for religion compatible with secularism; he calls it "moderate secularism."

Such is the context in which non-Christian migrants to Europe, the majority of whom are Muslims, have been arriving, settling, and making claims that relate to the place of religious identity in the public sphere. But it is precisely here that a sense of a crisis of secularism can be found. Since the advent of large-scale non-Christian migration, moderate secularism has had a precarious life in Europe.

Europe's political secularism is currently destabilized. Europe cannot just go on with the same moderate secularism and properly face this destabilization. Modood hopes that the historical compromises between church and state will be extended to other religions, particularly to Islam. However, the multiculturalization of this secularism is neither easy nor sufficient. It is not easy because it presupposes massive change in the cultural background. Institutional adjustment is bound to be difficult because an internal link exists between the collective secular self-understanding of European societies and deeply problematic institutional arrangements. Quite plainly, current European institutions are deeply biased. They have accommodated Christians but will not be able to accommodate Muslims. They are not sufficient because simple accommodation without some accompanying "hostility" or critical questioning may not work for all Muslim citizens. For instance, many Muslim women might welcome hostility to some customs that have come to be associated with their religion.

Why are institutional adjustments difficult to achieve? Using a broad brush, we might say that European secularisms arose in predominantly single-religion societies. Issues of radical individual freedom and citizenship equality arose in European societies *after* religious homogenization. The birth of confessional states was accompanied by the massive expulsion of subject communities whose faith differed from the religion of the ruler. Such states eventually found some place for toleration in their moral space, but as is well known, toleration was consistent with deep inequalities and with a humiliating, marginalized, and virtually invisible existence. The liberal democratization and the consequent secularization of many European states has helped citizens with non-Christian faiths to acquire most formal rights. But such a scheme of rights neither embodies a regime of interreligious equality nor effectively prevents religion-based discrimination and exclusion. Indeed, it masks majoritarian, ethno-religious biases.

The new reality of deepening religious diversity has brought the religious biases of European states into increasingly sharper relief.[25] Despite all changes, European states have continued to privilege Christianity in one form or another. They have publicly funded religious schools, maintained the real estate of churches and clerical salaries, facilitated church control of cemeteries, and trained the clergy. In short, there has been no impartiality within the domain of religion, and despite formal equality, this lack of impartiality continues to have a far-reaching impact on the rest of society.

Thus these biases are evident in different kinds of difficulties faced by Muslims. For example, in Britain one-third of all primary school students are educated by religious communities, yet applications for state funding by Muslims are frequently turned down. Veit Bader[26] informs us that there are currently only 5 Muslim schools, compared to 2,000 run by Roman Catholics and 4,700 run by the Church of England. Similar problems persist in other European countries. In both France and Germany not a single school run by Muslims is subsidized by the state. This bias is also manifest in the failure of many Western European states to deal with the issue of headscarves (most notably France), in unheeded demands by Muslims to build mosques and therefore to properly practise their own faith (Germany and Italy), in discrimination against ritual slaughter (Germany), and in unheeded demands by Muslims for proper burial grounds of their own (Denmark, among others). Given that in recent times Islamophobia has gripped the imagination of several Western societies—as exemplified by the cartoon controversy in Denmark and by the minarets issue in Switzerland—it is very likely that their Muslim citizens will continue to face disadvantages due only to membership in their religious community.

Removing the biases of European states will not be easy because of resistance from the right, institutional resilience, and differences between Christianity and Islam, not to mention between Christianity and non-Semitic religions such as Hinduism. Moderate secularism will be severely tested. Indeed, the test has already begun, which is why talk of strain or even crisis is justified.

So far I have been talking as though the initiative lies squarely with only one agent, the European state (and its supporters), and as though Muslims will respond enthusiastically to any initiative from this reformed (i.e. multiculturalized) state. But this view is too sanguine about the self-understanding of Muslims and about their current condition in Europe. It underestimates their alienation and ghettoization. Only with a better and deeper understanding of Muslims in different parts of Europe can we learn about what should and should not be accommodated and about what currently can and cannot be accommodated. Indeed, only in a more relaxed atmosphere can a plurality of voices—the more vulnerable voices—emerge and be better heard, a change that will have a huge bearing on our collective judgment of what should and should not be accommodated. (As of now, we hear two dominant voices: that of the ultra-orthodox Muslim and that of the lapsed Muslim, a convert to radical secularism.) These voices may necessitate not just accommodation but also more active state intervention either to foster or to suppress some hitherto unnoticed beliefs and practices of Muslims. It is entirely possible that the state may not only have to support some religious practices but also have to inhibit others. European states may be only too happy to abort some Muslim practices, but such intervention would entail a massive shift in their conception of secularism—from first separate—and then only support religion to first separate and then—sometimes support, sometimes inhibit religion, what I call *principled distance.* In short, they may have to set aside their moderate stance of accommodating, rather than being hostile to, religion. Currently, the practice of most European states is to offer little official support, to provide no accommodation, and with few exceptions, to stay indifferent to massive societal intolerance. What might be required is more support of some religions, less support of others, and active interference in societal intolerance—that is, an attempt by the state to tackle both inter- and intrareligious domination.

In sum, extending moderate (i.e. accommodative) secularism to Muslims, under existing conditions, will be very difficult, for it presupposes massive shifts in background cultural conditions for which Europe may not yet be prepared. It would not be too off the mark to say that not appreciating deep religious and cultural diversity is one of the central failures of modern Europe. To my knowledge, overcoming this issue is a bigger challenge than any other. Even the conceptual resources for such change appear to be missing. In any case, moderate secularism's accommodation will not be sufficient because the modern (i.e. democratic) state must have the legitimacy to also negatively intervene in some socio-religious practices, if only to protect the interests of vulnerable internal minorities. This in part entails abandoning moderate secularism. To respond to the challenge of deep diversity, Europe might be better off with an altogether different conception of secularism.

What I have said above needs some qualification, for it ignores two facts. What I have said above needs some qualification, for it ignores two facts. First, it neglects the informal politics of state and non-state actors, where interesting changes might be occurring. Second, it does not take into account the existence of the European Constitution, which is very different from the constitutions of individual European states. I acknowledge the importance of both. These factors could make a substantial difference. But difficulties block progress in these sites too. First, nothing prevents individual states from ignoring the European Constitution. Will France, Belgium, or Italy listen to the EU if it declared the banning of the burqa to be unconstitutional? Second, moderate secularism stands in the way of nurturing norms of principled distance embedded in the informal politics of state and non-state actors.

I believe then that the doctrinal, ideological, and theoretical formulations of Western secularism have become highly restricted and inadequate, as too have the formal politics and laws inspired by these doctrines and ideologies. A reimagination of secularism is virtually impossible unless we reduce our reliance on these formal practices and formulations, including the French and the American models of exclusionary separation of church and state as well as the formal, institutional political practices of most European states. If we continue to remain in the grip of these formulations and practices, we will simply not notice other conceptions that have probably been pushed into the background. Once we shift away from these alternate perspectives and start to focus on the normative informal practices of a broader range of Western and non-Western states, we shall see that better forms of secular state and much more defensible versions of secularism are available.

The Indian Model of Secularism

Can a version of secularism be found that is sensitive simultaneously to the moral integrity of both liberal and non-liberal religious ways of living, as well as able to address religious or religion-based oppression and exclusions—one that goes beyond liberal, libertarian, and republican theories? Although theoretically less developed, another model of secularism exists, one not generated exclusively in the West, that meets the needs of societies with deep religious diversity and also complies with the principles of freedom and equality. This model meets the secularist objection to non-secular states and the religious objection to some forms of secular state. To identify it, we must consider the *normative* and *discursive* levels and look at some of the developing normative practices of the French, British, and even American states. Take the example of the public funding of faith-based schools. Officially, American secularism does not sanction public financing of religion. Yet public funding of religion exists—albeit without proper assessment of the dilemmas of recognition and cooperation. Likewise, in practice, the French state not only directly and indirectly funds Roman Catholic schools but also tries to accommodate even Muslim minorities. In the Netherlands, at least until recently, forty-six Muslim schools were directly funded by the state. However, the best place to find this version of secularism is within the best inter-communal practice in the subcontinent of India and in the country's Constitution appropriately interpreted. In India the existence of deep religious diversity has ensured a conceptual response to problems not only within religions but also between them. Without taking it as a blueprint, the West must examine the Indian conception in the hopes of learning from it.

Several features of Indian secularism can be identified that distinguish it from other variants. First, multiple religions are not extras added on as an afterthought but were present at Indian secularism's starting point as part of its foundation. Indian secularism is inextricably tied to deep religious diversity. Second, this form of secularism has a commitment to multiple values, namely liberty, equality and fraternity—not conceived narrowly as pertaining to individuals but interpreted broadly to cover the relative autonomy of religious communities and their equality of status in society—as well as other more basic values such as peace, toleration and mutual respect between communities. It has a place not only for the right of individuals to profess their religious beliefs but also for the right of religious communities to establish and maintain educational institutions crucial for the survival and sustenance of their distinctive religious traditions.

The acceptance of community-specific rights brings me to the third feature of Indian secularism. Because it was born in a deeply multireligious society, it is concerned as much with interreligious domination as it is with intrareligious domination. Whereas the two Western conceptions of secularism have provided benefits to minorities only incidentally (Jews benefited in some European countries such as France not because their special needs and demands were met but because of a change in the general climate of the society), under the Indian conception even community-specific political rights (through political reservations for religious minorities) were almost granted during the drafting of the Constitution but were withheld in the last instance only for contextual reasons. In fact, it is arguable that a conceptual space is still available for these rights within the Indian Constitution.

Fourth, Indian secularism does not erect a wall of separation between religion and state. There are boundaries, of course, but they are porous. This situation allows the state to intervene in religions in order to help or hinder them without the impulse to control or destroy them. This intervention can include granting aid to educational institutions of religious communities on a non-preferential basis and interfering in socioreligious institutions that deny equal dignity and status to members of their own religion or to those of others—for example, the ban on untouchability and the obligation to allow everyone, irrespective of their caste, to enter Hindu temples, as well as, potentially, other actions to correct gender inequalities. In short, Indian secularism interprets separation to mean not strict exclusion or strict neutrality but what I call *principled distance*, which is poles apart from one-sided exclusion, mutual exclusion, strict neutrality, and equidistance.

Fifth, Indian secularism is not entirely averse to the public character of religions. Although the state is not identified with a particular religion or with religion more generally, official and therefore public recognition is granted to religious communities. The model admits a distinction between de-publicization and de-politicization, as well as between different kinds of de-politicization. Because it is not hostile to the public presence of religion, it does not aim to de-publicize it. It accepts the importance of one form of de-politicization of religion. Sixth, this model shows that in responding to religion, we do not have to choose between active hostility and passive indifference or between disrespectful hostility and respectful indifference. We can combine the two, permitting the necessary hostility as long as there is also active respect. The state may intervene to inhibit some practices as long as it shows respect for other practices of the religious community and does so by publicly lending support to them. Seventh, by not fixing its commitment from the start exclusively to individual or community values and by not marking rigid boundaries between the public and the private, India's constitutional secularism allows decisions on these matters to be made either within the open dynamics of democratic politics or by contextual reasoning in the courts. Eighth, one might say that Indian political secularism shows a marked preference for morally grounded secularization in each sense mentioned above. There is no process out there which cannot be brought partially under human (democratic) control. Nor must an attempt be made for a blanket, morally insensitive restriction, privatization or decline of religion. Ninth, it opens up the possibility of different societies working out their own secularisms. In short, it opens out the possibility of multiple secularisms. Tenth, it breaks out of the rigid interpretative grid that divides our social world into the Western modern and the traditional, indigenous non-Western. Indian secularism is modern but departs significantly from mainstream conceptions of Western secularism. Finally, the commitment to multiple values and principled distance means that the state tries to balance different, ambiguous, but equally important values. This makes its secular ideal more like a contextual, ethically sensitive, politically negotiated arrangement—which it really is—rather than a scientific doctrine conjured by ideologues and merely implemented by political agents.

A somewhat forced, formulaic articulation of Indian secularism goes something like this. The state must keep a principled distance from all public or private and individual-oriented or community-oriented religious institutions for the sake of the equally significant—and sometimes conflicting—values of peace, worldly goods, dignity, liberty, equality and fraternity in all its complicated individualistic and non-individualistic versions. Indian secularism, then, is an ethically sensitive, negotiated settlement between diverse groups and divergent values. This model thus embodies what I call *contextual secularism.*

Let us elaborate on two features of the Indian model: principled distance and contextual secularism.

Principled Distance

The idea of principled distance unpacks the metaphor of separation differently. It accepts a disconnection between state and religion at the level of ends and institutions but does not make a fetish of it at the level of policy and law; this distinguishes it from all other models of secularism, moral and amoral, that disconnect state and religion at this level. It accepts that humans have an interest in relating to something beyond themselves, including gods or God, and that this manifests itself as individual belief and feeling as well as social practice in the public domain. It also accepts that religion is a cumulative tradition[27] as well as a source of people's identities. But it insists that even if it turns out that God exists and that one religion is true and others false, this will not give the "true" doctrine or religion the right to force itself down the throats of others who do not believe it. The moral obligation to ensure the equal distribution of liberties and other valuable resources would prevent discrimination.

At the same time, a secularism based on principled distance accepts that although religion may not have special public significance antecedently written into and defining the very character of the state or the nation, it does not follow that religion has no public significance at all. A second idea distinguishes it from strict neutrality, which dictates that the state must help or hinder all religions to an equal degree and in the same manner; if it intervenes in one religion, it must also do so in others. This makes principled distance rest upon a distinction explicitly drawn by the American philosopher Ronald Dworkin[28] between equal treatment and treating everyone as an equal. The principle of equal treatment in the relevant political sense requires that the state treat all citizens equally in the relevant respect—for example, in the distribution of a resource of opportunity. In contrast, the principle of treating people as equals entails that every person or group is treated with equal concern and respect. This second principle may sometimes require equal treatment —say, equal distribution of resources—but it may also occasionally dictate unequal preferential treatment. Treating people or groups as equals is entirely consistent with differential treatment. This idea is the second ingredient in what I have called principled distance.

When I say that principled distance allows for both engagement with or disengagement from and do so by allowing differential treatment, what kind of treatment do I have in mind? First, religious groups have sought exemptions when states have intervened in religious practices by promulgating laws designed to apply neutrally across society. This demand for non-interference is made on the grounds either that the law requires them to do things not permitted by their religion or that it prevents them from doing things mandated by their religion. For example, Sikhs demand exemptions from mandatory helmet laws and from police dress codes to accommodate religiously required turbans. Muslim women and girls demand that the state not interfere in the religious requirement that they wear the chador. Rightly or wrongly, religiously grounded personal laws may be exempted. Elsewhere, Jews and Muslims seek exemptions from Sunday closing laws on the grounds that such closing is not required by their religion. Principled distance allows a practice that is banned or regulated in the majority culture to be permitted in the minority culture because of the distinctive status and meaning it has for the minority culture's members. For the mainstream conception of secularism, this variability is a problem because of a simple and somewhat absolutist morality that attributes overwhelming importance to one value— particularly to equal treatment, equal liberty, or equality of individual citizenship. Religious groups may demand that the state refrain from interference in their practices, but they may equally demand that the state interfere in such a way as to give them special assistance so that they are able to secure what other groups are routinely able to acquire by virtue of their social dominance in the political community. The state may grant authority to religious officials to perform legally binding marriages or to have their own rules for or methods of obtaining a divorce. Principled distance allows the possibility of such policies on the grounds that holding people accountable to a law to which they have not consented might be unfair. Furthermore, it does not discourage public justification—that is, justification based on reasons endorsable by all. Indeed, it encourages people to pursue public justification. However, if the attempt to arrive at public justification fails, it enjoins religiously minded citizens to support coercive laws that, although based purely on religious reasons, are consistent with freedom and equality.[29]

However, principled distance is not just a recipe for differential treatment in the form of special exemptions. It may even require state intervention and moreover, in some religions more than in others, considering the historical and social condition of all relevant religions. To take first examples of positive engagement, some holidays of all majority and minority religions are granted national status. Subsidies are provided to schools run by all religious communities. Minority religions are granted a constitutional right to establish and maintain their educational institutions. Limited funding is available to Muslims for *Hajj*. But state engagement can also take a negative interventionist form. For the promotion of a particular value constitutive of secularism, some religion, relative to other religions, may require more interference from the state. For example, suppose that the value to be advanced is social equality. This requires in part undermining caste and gender hierarchies. Thus there is a constitutional ban on untouchability, Hindu temples were thrown open to all, particularly to former untouchables should they choose to enter them. Child marriage was banned among Hindus and a right to divorce was introduced.

Contextual Secularism

A context-sensitive secularism, one based on the idea of principled distance, is what I term contextual secularism. It is contextual not only because the precise form and content of secularism will vary from one context to another and from place to place but also because it embodies a certain model of contextual moral reasoning. It is a multivalue doctrine. To accept its multivalue nature is to acknowledge that its constitutive values do not always sit easily with one another. On the contrary, they are frequently in conflict.

Some degree of internal discord, and therefore a fair amount of instability, is an integral part of contextual secularism. For this reason, it forever requires fresh interpretations, contextual judgments, and attempts at reconciliation and compromise. No general a priori rule of resolving these conflicts exists, no easy lexical order, no pre-existing hierarchy among values or laws that enables us to decide that, no matter what the context, a particular value must override everything else. Almost everything, then, is a matter of situational thinking and contextual reasoning. Whether one value will override or be reconcilable with another cannot be decided beforehand. Each time the matter will present itself differently and will be differently resolved. If this is true, the practice of secularism requires a different model of moral reasoning than the one that straightjackets our moral understanding in the form of well-delineated and explicitly stated rules.[30] This contextual secularism recognizes that conflicts between individual rights and group rights, or between equality and liberty, or between liberty and the satisfaction of basic needs cannot always be adjudicated by recourse to some general and abstract principle. Rather, they can be settled only case by case and may require a fine balancing of competing claims. The eventual outcome may not be wholly satisfactory to either claimant but may still be reasonably satisfactory to both. *Multi-value* doctrines such as secularism encourage accommodation—not the giving up of one value for the sake of another but their reconciliation and possible harmonization so that apparently incompatible concepts and values may operate without changes to their basic content.

This endeavour to make concepts, viewpoints, and values work simultaneously does not amount to a morally objectionable compromise. This is so because nothing of importance is being given up for the sake of something less significant, something without value or even with negative value. Rather, what is pursued is a mutually agreed-upon middle way that combines elements from two or more equally valuable entities. The roots of such attempts at reconciliation and accommodation lie in a lack of dogmatism, in a willingness to experiment—to think at different levels and in separate spheres—and in a readiness to make and accept decisions on a provisional basis. The pursuit of this middle way captures a way of thinking characterized by the following dictum: "Why look at things in terms of this or that, why not try to have both this and that?"[31] This way of thinking recognizes that, although we may currently be unable to secure the best of both values and may therefore be forced to settle for a watered-down version of each, we must continue to have an abiding commitment to searching for a transcendence of this second-best condition.

It is frequently argued that Indian secularism is contradictory because it tries to bring together individual and community rights and that those articles in the Indian Constitution that have a bearing on the secular nature of the Indian state are deeply conflictual and at best ambiguous.[32]

This characterization, however, misrecognizes a virtue as a vice. In my view, the attempt to bring together seemingly incompatible values is a great strength of Indian secularism. Indian secularism is an ethically sensitive negotiated settlement between diverse groups and divergent values. When it is not treated as such it turns either into a dead formula or into a facade for political manoeuvres.

Two other serious objections are frequently raised against this model. First, it assumes that the state has the capacity to impartially arbitrate among conflicting religious groups. But is any state ever impartial towards all religious or between religious and the secular? Are not structural biases present in every state? Second, the notion of principled distance is found to be problematic. It is claimed that it is far too pragmatic in the crude opportunistic sense, the assumption here being that any negotiation or compromise is morally wrong. In what follows I shall try to counter these objections.

It is not my claim that the state has no biases. Indeed a commitment to certain goals makes the state bend in the direction of those objectives. Only those who have a gods-eye view of impartiality or neutrality expect the state not to have any biases. Since I believe that all humans and human made entities are laden with some interest or values, I reject a gods-eye view of impartiality, an absolutist impartiality from nowhere.[33] Yet, the state can embody a set of minimal values that all citizens, if they were to use their powers of reason and empathy, can agree on and without which a decent, egalitarian social life is impossible . For instance, they can all agree not to subordinate themselves to each other and to live their lives in accordance with conceptions of the good they have worked out with each other's help, though without undue influence. More importantly, a state not only embodies a set of professed values but reflects the overall cultural ethos within which it is located. This ethos may or may not be made of multicultural strands of equal weight or strength. For example, if a state is situated within a lively Christian tradition, it is, if it is examined close enough, likely to reflect the character of that tradition. The more important issue then is what the state does once it begins to recognize its own cultural and religious leanings—those which are not stated and have even been disavowed but are nonetheless present in its institutions and practices. An example would help. In India a very large and significant number of people either call themselves Hindu or are taken to be so. Though not entirely, the ethos of many of India's social and political institutions is saturated, it might be reasonably claimed, by one or the other strand of 'Hinduism'. So, regardless of our evaluative judgment, it would not be entirely incorrect to say that these institutions are somewhat Hinduized or wear a Hindu look. Yet, India also has Muslims, Christians, Parsis, Buddhists, Jains, Sikhs, atheists and people with many other not so easily definable outlooks. Sections of Hindus may find their practices disagreeable, morally discomforting, or just downright strange but they tolerate them. They may collectively have the power to interfere in them, even banish them, but they refrain from doing so. Of course, legally they have no other option. These religious communities have rights not to be interfered with in their religious and cultural practices. But the minorities will not be able to effectively exercise their rights, if Hindus do not possess the capacity for other-related self-restraint. Most Hindus do as a matter of fact exercise such restraint. But is this sufficient for a morally justified coexistence between Hindus and minority communities? Suppose then that community-specific rights of minorities are respected but Hindu self-assertion becomes more pronounced. Let us say they build new temples around every corner, ensure that these are mightier in size than mosques and churches, fund new radio and television channels that stream Hindu teachings and no other, introduce textbooks that speak largely of and glorify Hindu gods and goddesses, change national and state symbols in order to make them explicitly and exclusively Hindu and so on. What would its impact be on the psyche of the minorities? Most likely, it will increase their sense of social and cultural alienation. It will force them to feel left out of many public domains. It might even lower their self-esteem. Alternatively, Hindus can show some self-related self-restraint, so as not to show off, to not always wear their own religion and culture on the sleeve, to not always advertise their wares, as it were. Indeed, to persistently announce in public than you are the boss in your own country might be a definitive sign of deep rooted insecurities and anxieties, one that is both potentially damaging to others and to oneself. Abandoning this self-related self-restraint might then adversely affect everyone, destroy the very fabric of contemporary Indian society.

A second, related objection can be answered by spelling out what kind of state I have in mind when I speak of 'the state'. I am certainly not talking here about an authoritarian, centralized state. I take it for granted that the state is democratic not only in the sense that its own institutions are so but also in the other sense that it is continually nourished by a democratic ethos. A state with democratic institutions can be impartial to some degree, if at least some politicians behave as statespersons, some judges scrupulously make decisions that are legally sound and wise and so on. But for its biases to be revealed and rectified, in short for a state to act in a properly secular and democratic manner, it is imperative that there be a free and vibrant press, committed social activists and an alert citizenry. An impartial and secular state is dependent on multiple agents both within its structure and outside it. There is no way to ensure that the first act of the state on a relevant issue be properly and unmistakably secular. However if the state is understood as multiple agent-dependent, then overtime it can shed most of its significant biases for one religion and emerge instead as secular and impartial. A frequently asked question is who decides what is right and properly secular and my answer always is: a relatively correct and endorsable decision cannot be taken without the involvement of all relevant agents including those who are directly and adversely affected by the decision. All decisions in a democratic state are taken over a time and invariably involve a large number and different kinds of agents. So must the case be with decisions of the state that are expected to be appropriately secular. They take time and must involve a number of agents if they are to arrive at sound and endorsable decision. Indeed, such decisions involving multiple agents do take a long time even if it turns out that they are mistaken as is attested by the French hijab issue which was sparked off in 1989 and resolved by law fifteen years later, in 2004.

On principled distance, all I have to say is this: I have used the term distance to distinguish my account from a separationist reading of political secularism. On the latter view, separation of state and religion means somewhat strict and wholly unambiguous exclusion of religion from the state at each of the three levels mentioned above. As indicated earlier, this interpretation of separation I find neither desirable nor possible. Distance is a less extreme mode of relation. Keeping a distance from something does not prevent one from relating to it in multiple ways. It implies only that there is neither identity nor closeness. The rest is left unspecified, opening a terrain of multiple possibilities. It allows for flexibility when it is desperately needed and therefore, for change in perspective and practice when the situation demands. But it is precisely this openness and flexibility that has led some critics to the mistaken conclusion that virtually any mode of relation between state and religion is permissible. Does this not allow anything and everything to barge in? Does it not introduce an ad hocism or opportunism that is conceptually defeating and morally outrageous? Thus, it is alleged that this model of secularism allows for state involvement in or detachment from religion grounded purely in reasons of say vote-bank politics or appeasing the tantrums of particular religious groups. But then it is precisely to block such interpretation that the term 'principled' so crucial in the phrase "principled distance" is used. Every action of the state in relation to all religious communities must be grounded in, supported by and justified in terms of principles or values. Given this, it would be preposterous to think of principled distance as a purely tactical and opportunistic policy adopted for self-aggrandisement, for purely political and financial consideration. Principled distance is *not* opportunistic distance. Furthermore, the not so visible plurality of principles can hardly be overemphasized. Multiple values always come into play in the process of any decision-making. I am committed to value pluralism and therefore to a potential conflict of values. There are very few instances where a single value applies unambiguously. Most human situations are saturated with multiple and competing values and therefore any decision requires a sensitive interpretation, negotiation and balancing of all relevant values. I consider it wrong if any one value was to unreflectively and unambiguously override other values relevant to the situation, almost as wrong as taking a decision grounded in pure considerations of wealth or power despite the need to take into account human values.

All compromises are not wrong or despicable. If something of value is sacrificed for the sake of pure consideration of self-interest say in the pursuit of power, wealth or fame, then clearly the compromise is morally dubious but if one begins with the recognition that multiple values are at stake, then provided one sets issues of self-interest aside, any negotiation or balancing among values is entirely appropriate from a moral point of view.

Indeed such negotiations are morally required. My entire contextualist, morally sensitive approach to secularism as principled distance will lose its distinctiveness and individuality, if it is viewed in any way that is Machiavellian.

Thus, the decision arrived by a defensible secular state must be viewed as a practical judgment, a result of an elaborate public reasoning with citizens over a long period of time. By its very nature it is not final but provisional and revisable. It just happens to be the best possible answer to a problem, under the circumstances, at that point of time, which retrospectively may even be understood as part of a long, continuing series of similar morally sensitive practical judgments.

Conclusion

Political secularism must be viewed as part of critical social secularism, indeed, as a self-critical social perspective against not religion or faith but against institutionalized religious domination. Indeed, as part of a family of perspectives against four types of domination: interreligious, intra-religious, domination of religious by secular, and domination of secular by religious. We also need to give up the binary opposition between the secular and the religious. A new, refashioned conception of secularism must not see a necessary opposition between the secular and the religious. On the contrary, it must encourage a way of conceiving a world inhabited by both religious and nonreligious people. Second, we should jettison seeing political secularism as a mere strategy, even as an institutional strategy. Third, secularism should sever its ties with amoral secular states. This means coming to realize that, somewhat paradoxically, secularism is against some secular states. Fourth, the state cannot avoid having or endorsing a policy toward religion or religious organizations. Religion plays an important part in the lives of many people, and religious institutions function in this world like purely secular institutions. So, separation cannot mean the exclusion of religion from the domain of the state. Separation of church and state should also not be interpreted as absolute or strict neutrality. No state can possibly help or hinder all religions in the same manner and to the same degree. The state may interfere with religion and refrain from such interference, depending entirely on which of these promotes the values of freedom and equality or undermines interreligious and intra-religious dominations. Thus, we must rethink disconnection or separation talk instead in terms of principled distance. Furthermore, values of freedom and equality must be interpreted both as rights of individuals and, wherever required, as rights of communities. Community rights are particularly important if religious groups are vulnerable or, because of their small number, have relatively little power to influence the process of decision making.

To conclude, secularism must be neither servile nor hostile to religion. It must manifest an attitude of neither blind deference nor indifference but of critical respect toward all religions. Secularism that professes principled distance and is sensitive to multiple values cannot avoid making contextual judgments. Contextual judgments allow for ethically sensitive balancing and compromise.

If secularism is to survive as a transcultural normative perspective, it must be de-Christianized, de-Westernized, de-privatized, and de-individualized. In saying so, I do not mean that it must wholly sever its links with Christianity or the West, but its ties with them must be loosened. It should be able to accommodate other civilizations and community-based rights. Only with this form of secularism and a state nourished by it can deep religious diversity be managed.

NOTES

1. See Rajeev Bhargava, 'Giving Secularism its Due', *Economic and Political Weekly*, Vol. 29, No. 28, July 9, 1994.
2. David, Westerlund, *Questioning the Secular State*, Hurst & Company, London, 1996; Gilles, Kepel, *The Revenge of God: The Resurgence of Islam, Christianity, and Judaism in the Modern World*, Pennsylvania State University Press, Pennsylvania, 1994; I. Ahmed, *The Concept of an Islamic State: An Analysis of the Ideological Controversy in Pakistan*, Frances Pinter, London, 1987; Mohsin, Amena, "National Security and the Minorities: The Bangladesh Case", in D.L. Sheth and Gurpreet Mahajan (eds.). *Minority Identities and the Nation-State*, Oxford University Press, New Delhi, 1999.

3. Mark Juergensmeyer, *New Cold War? Religious Nationalism Confronts the Secular State,* University of California Press, California, 1994.
4. Bryan S. Turner, "Cosmopolitan Virtue: On Religion in a Global Age," *European Journal of Social Theory* 4.2 (2001), pp. 131–52.
5. John Bowen, *Why the French Don't Like Headscarves: Islam, the State and Public Space,* Princeton University Press, Princeton, 2007; Ian Buruma, *Murder in Amsterdam: The Death of Theo van Gogh and the Limits of Tolerance,* Penguin, London, 2006; Jane Freedman, "Secularism as a Barrier to Integration? The French Dilemma," *International Migration* 42.3 (August 2004): 5–27; Christine R. Barker, "Church and State: Lessons from Germany?" *The Political Quarterly* 75.2 (2004): 168–76; and Tariq Modood, Anna Triandafyllidou, and Ricard Zapata-Barrero (eds.), *Multiculturalism, Muslims and Citizenship: A European Approach* Routledge, London, 2006.
6. J. Klausen, *The Islamic Challenge: Politics and Religion in Western Europe,* Oxford University Press, 2005.
7. Ibid., p. 108.
8. Ibid., p. 108-9.
9. Ibid. p. 109.
10. Ibid.
11. Ibid.
12. Leonard W. Levy, 1994. *The Establishment Clause: Religion and the First Amendment,* University of North Carolina Press, Chapel Hill, 1994.
13. Philip Hamburger, *Separation of Church and State,* Harvard University Press, Cambridge, 2002.
14. William E. Connolly, *Why I Am Not a Secularist,* University of Minnesota Press, Minneapolis, 1999.
15. John Keane, 'Secularism', *The Political Quarterly,* Blackwell Publishers, Oxford, 2000, p. 14; T.N. Madan, 'Secularism in its Place', in Bhargava (ed)., *Secularism and Its Critics.* Oxford University Press, New Delhi, 1998, p. 298.
16. Philip Hamburger, op. cit., pp. 193-251.
17. A. Kuru, op. cit., pp. 42-45. .
18. Paul Weithman, *Religion and Contemporary Liberalism,* University of Notre Dame Press, Notre Dame, 1997, p. 6.
19. Charles Larmore, *The Morals of Modernity,* Cambridge University Press, Cambridge, 1996, p. 137.
20. Michael J. Sandel, 'Freedom of Conscience or Freedom of Choice', in Terry Eastland (ed.) *Religious Liberty in the Supreme Court,*

Erdmans Publishing Company, Cambridge/Michigan, 1993.

21. Jeff Spinner-Halev, *Surviving Diversity: Religion and Democratic Citizenship*, Johns Hopkins University Press, Baltimore, 2000, pp. 150-56.
22. Ibid., p. 155.
23. Connolly, op. cit., p. 27.
24. *'Is there a Crisis of Secularism in Europe'*, SSRC website 24-8-2011 (http://blogs.ssrc.org/tif/2011/08/24/is-there-a-crisis-of-secularism-in-western-europe/).
25. Klausen, op. cit., 2005.
26. Veit Bader, Secularism or Democracy?, Amsterdam University Press, 2007.
27. Wilfred Cantwell Smith, *The Meaning and End of Religion*. First Fortress Press, Minneapolis, 1991, pp. 154-69.
28. Ronald Dworkin (ed.), Liberalism, in Stuart Hampshire, *Public and Private Morality*, Cambridge University Press, Cambridge, 1978, p. 125.
29. Christopher J. Eberle, *Religious Conviction in Liberal Politics*, Cambridge University Press, Cambridge, 2002.
30. Charles Taylor, 'Justice After Virtue' in John Horton and Susan Mendus (ed.), *After MacIntyre*, Polity Press, 1994.
31. Granville Austin, *The Indian Constitution: Cornerstone of a Nation*, Oxford University Press, New Delhi, 1972.
32. Stanley J. Tambiah, 'Crisis of Secularism in India', in Bhargava, *Secularism and Its Critics*, Oxford University Press, New Delhi, 1998, pp. 445-53.
33. See Rajeev Bhargava, Giving Secularism its Due, *Economic and Political Weekly*, Vol. 29, No. 28, July 9, 1994.

3

Secularism, Secularization and Human Rights

Ram Puniyani

Introduction

The last two decades have seen the rise of new paradigms in the arena of political discourse. The accepted terminologies got challenged and new ones got rooted in the popular psyche. The established norms, secularism, democracy got challenged by the politics of Hindu right. The talk of the Hindu nation, *Hindutva* came to the fore. The concept of duties started getting more prominence. The compromising practices of ruling party were distorted to put doubts on the very concept of the gains of India's freedom movement, the ones related to secular democracy.

What does secularism mean, is it is Western, or is it modern? Is it alien to Indian values? Secularism as a social phenomenon emerged with the rise of industrial society. From the 17th century discoveries of science were challenging deeply held beliefs and faiths, which were an integral part of the broad canvas of religion. The application of these technologies and rise of industrial societies necessitated the change in social equilibrium, which was then prevalent. The earlier society where agriculture was the dominant production activity and 'feudal' mode of production was prevalent; the major sectors of society were tied to land as poor peasants. Demands of newly developing industries required the peasants to be freed from land. What tied them to land was the feudal social structure and the concomitant ideological constructs, which were again part of the religion in the broad sense of the term. The clergy (Church is the most organized form of the same but a similar role is played by Brahmins, and Mullahs also) supplemented the feudal structure, 'kingdoms' and fulfilled the need to ensure firm implementation of the ideology, which supplemented the feudal production norms. This was the time when social life revolved around the dictates of the clergy.

Industrialization

With the onset of the industrialization process, the earlier ideological chains proved to be obstacles to the emerging industrial society. It is in this realm that one has to understand the loosening hold of clergy and some religious traditions in social life. One has to understand the social norms developing around modern rationality, ideas from science, i.e. the beginning of 'age of reason', in contrast to 'age of faith'. The former having its roots in science and technology and latter in the clergy's interpretation of the word of God, clergy's imposition of ideologies in the name of religion, clergy's use of emotions of people for smoothening the exploitative social system of feudalism. Historically this process first occurred in clear form in the West, where the above phenomenon manifested itself in the struggle between church and the state. Church stood for the declining social force of feudal lords, stood for age of faith, while the emerging "nation state" (vis-à-vis kingdom) stood for 'age of reason', for the industrialization process based on science and technology, concretizing newer social relations (industrialists and the workers) in the process. This process which was called 'Enlightenment' and is a part of the secularization process began as a radical rationalist critique of some facets of religion, especially those pertaining to the mediation between people and God by the clergy. This process assumed the undisguised role of displacing aspects of religion and faith (manufactured by clergy) to the private lives of people, freeing the social life from the constraints of orthodoxy and obscurantism towards the emerging realms of modernity.

Secularism

Thus secularism is a product of social movement of the

industrial bourgeoisie and landless peasants, manifested initially (in the West) as Renaissance and Enlightenment, being the expression of man's urge to live life of his own, independent of the domination by Church, which was the prevalent feature of medieval society. Starting from this premise, secularism assumed a socio-historical context in the mid-19th century, shaped by circumstances and philosophy of the time. Secularism was based on the values, which recognized the contribution of science as a major source of knowledge and considered technological progress, social amelioration and human welfare as the goals of life. The goals of life shifted to this world (secular, profane) from the other world (sacred). With crumbling of dogmas and supernaturalism under the wheels of science and reason, the repository of dogmas, the clergy took a back seat and modern secular democratic states began to occupy the 'drivers' seats. Secular ethos is not concerned about the other world (leaving them as a merry hunting ground for the custodians of dogmas, the clergy). In a sense secularism is the policy of the modern nation-state, it is the philosophy of the secularization process. A process through which man becomes a free person from his earlier domination by the blind faiths imposed on the society by the clergy to ensure the smooth running of kingdoms, which require divine legitimacy, conferred on them by clergy, to continue their crass exploitation of the peasantry, which is the main source of their wealth. Secularization introduces instrumental values, rational procedures and technological methods, which bring along urbanization, pragmatism, profanity, pluralism and mutual respect. The secularization process brings in the ideas that all value systems are a product of historical circumstances, without any claims of finality. As a part of the package, science replaces supernatural explanation of things with those in terms of natural laws and an intellectual attitude in which reality is accounted from the worldly mode of thinking.

Colonization

Those nations, which industrialized initially, went out to colonize other countries, especially in Asia, Africa and South America. India was colonized mainly by the British, small portions by Portuguese and French. The British 'plunder project' aimed at taking away the raw materials from here and creating markets for their goods. In order to do these, they set up new ventures here in agrarian, commercial and industrial arenas. In these, Indians first acted as subordinates but soon took to modern technologies and with this a new class of merchants, bankers, landlords, industrialists, plantation owners and brokers came into being. Introduction of English education in 1835 was meant to produce a class of clerks and administrators. This changing social dynamics laid the foundation of the new phenomenon of 'nationalism'. In a very elementary form this changed scenario formed the backdrop for the rise of different reform movements and new associations and unions of economic, social and political nature on the Western pattern. In due course, the intelligentsia started demanding widening of franchise, simultaneous examinations for administrative services and Indianization of services. And in this demand, emerging industrialists supported them adding their own demands for increased facilities for industrialization in India. A spirit of Indian consciousness started emerging for the first time and this was due to a combination of various factors like material demands of newly emerging classes (professionals, businessmen, industrialists).

Modern education, communication (railways, telegraphs, free press), hatred for British racial arrogance, economic exploitation, weaknesses of judiciary were the initial features of British rule. The process unleashed by the British was pregnant with contradictory features. Free press created a strong impetus for the rise of national consciousness. This led to the formation of many local regional associations aimed at voicing the grievances of the emerging elite and projecting their vision of 'nation'. Some of these associations were, the Bombay Association, Madras Natives Association, Pune Sarvajanik Sabha and Madras Mahajan Sabha. The major meeting of these associations started taking place and the one such which took place in Calcutta in 1883 was the precursor of the formation of the INC (Indian National Congress) in 1885.

India: Nation in the Making

The Indian National Congress expressed the ambitions of these associations and rising classes and asked for holding of the Indian civil service exam in India, more facilities for the industry and commerce and land reforms. The basic principles of INC (Indian National Congress) were eradication of race, creed and provincial prejudices, and encouragement of natives in the political process.

In reaction to this Sir Syed and Raja Sheo Prasad of Kashi formed the United India Patriotic Association (August 1888). The aim of this association was to convey to the British that all communities and aristocracies are not with Congress, to convey the views of Hindu and Muslim organizations to the British Parliament and to strengthen the rule of the British in India, to wean away people from Congress. Many people associated with this association were later to be part of the Muslim League and Hindu Mahasabha. The mix of these processes and secular organization being thrown up was described by Surendranath Banerjea and Lokmanya Tilak as '*India is a nation in the making*' meaning thereby that it is a representation of common interests of Indian people vis-a-vis the colonial power. At this time reformers like Rammohan Roy were asking for abolition of abominable practices like Sati. Phule at this time called for modern education and women's education. Pandita Ramabai took up the cause of women's education. Phule also laid the foundation of a Non-Brahmin movement aimed against the social power of zamindar-Brahmin nexus. Later Ambedkar was to pick up the threads of this movement and struggle for the rights of the untouchables

Communalism

Rise of communalism has been a very complex process. Colonial policies generated the growth and economic domination of merchant-moneylenders (by and large Hindus). Hindus could take maximum advantage of modern education and accordingly, a place in the bureaucracy. Post-1857 anti-Muslim bias of the British gave a slight edge to Hindus, who took to modern enterprises/professions with great keenness.

British historians used the categories Hindu, Muslim, and Brahmin. Indian historians picked up only two of these categories, Hindu and Muslim. Indian leadership used religious consciousness to inculcate 'modern nationalism amongst the people, e.g. Ram Rajya, Khilafat. This resulted in two processes: (a) arousal of nationalism (b) arousal of communalism. We will shortly see that communalism arose due to the politics of Muslim feudal lords, Hindu zamindars and British policy of divide and rule.

The secularization of society though slow, its political reflection in the freedom struggle and the national movement was dominantly secular, though communal (Muslim and Hindu) nationalisms also came up in the wake as a reaction to the growth of secular nationalism. Initially, the secularization process got reflected in movements of Jotiba Phule, Savitribai Phule and other radical reformers. Secular nationalism was finding expression in the politics of Gandhi and Nehru while Muslim communalism found expression in the politics of the Muslim League and Hindu communalism was manifested in the Hindu Mahasabha and RSS. Some of the Hindu nationalists were part of the Indian National Congress as well. The social base of Muslim communal nationalism was Muslim zamindars and moneylenders; similarly, Hindu communal nationalism had its base in Brahmin, Bania (caste level), Hindu zamindars and moneylenders (at class level). Secular nationalism was rooted amongst the nascent industrialists, newer professionals and vast sections of peasantry and the low castes. It was the aspirations of these classes, which gave strength to the freedom struggle and were translated in the foundation of the Indian State and its constitution. Thus secularism as a principle of this society was not an artificial graft but a result of the struggles of the rising industrial class and the section of the peasantry and Dalits.

Secularism: Western or Modern

To see secularism as a principle of the Christian West is a very simplistic way of looking at social phenomenon. It is true that for a brief while the church possessed state power and controlled it, kings of Europe were subordinate to it for some time and then they revolted against the authority of the church to set them free. As pointed out above, secularism is an outcome of the secularization process, which is a comprehensive term for the changes in social values with the advent of industrialization and accompanying social relations, introduction of science, technology and rationalist thinking in society. Secularism in that sense is a marker of modernity, overcoming of feudal relationships and value system and thereby is a battle cry of newer social classes interested in overthrowing the feudal relationships and the accompanying baggage of constraining ideologies which find their vehicle in the religious clergy. It is the political expression of democratic values, Liberty, Equality and Fraternity. So secularism is a must for India. As it has entered the modern era with the introduction of industrialization and accompanying rationalism the logical values are those of secularism. Those propagating the above myth are the sections of society who stand to lose in the liberal ethos which are an accompaniment of secularism, those are the social elements who hold to religious nationalism in contrast to modern, secular democratic nationalism. No country can be a stagnant pool and with dynamic changes in society in the progressive direction secularism comes in as an outcome of struggle of rising industrialists, poor peasants, workers and women against the obscurantist, dogmatic values and the feudal social system and further provides the base for enhancement of struggles of the exploited and subalterns.

During the freedom movement the major political tendencies which came up were due to two main group of classes, one the rising one due to industrialization and education and two the declining classes, the landlord and associated clerical one. From the former came up the political streams of Indian national Congress, revolutionaries of the type of Bhagat Singh and Dr. Bhimrao Baba Saheb Ambedkar. While from the declining classes and declining ideologies came up the Muslim League, Hindu Mahasabha and RSS.

Table: Introduction of Education: Industrialization: Changes in Social Values, Relationships

Rising Classes	*Declining Classes*
1. Rise of new classes of businessmen-industrialists, workers, educated classes.	1. Decline of landlords, kings and section of clergy associated with them.
2. These Groups form Associations, Bombay Association, Madras Mahajan Sabha, etc.	2. This groups looks at new changes with fear and suspicion.
3. Their political expression in the form of Indian National Congress.	3. Fearful of the rise of new classes and INC, they form United India Patriotic Association (UIPA) to Promote loyalty to the British
4. In due course other political streams expressing the values of this group come up, Hindustan Socialist Republican Association, (Bhagat Singh and Friends), Republican Party of India	4. UIPA gave rise to Hindu Mahasabha, Muslim League. Later RSS came up as an ideology inspired by leaders of the Hindu Mahasabha.
5. This stream was conceptualizing for India as 'a nation in the making'.	5. Muslim League held that they were a Muslim nation since the advent of Mohammad bin Kasim. Hindu Mahasabha/ RSS held that they were a Hindu nation since times immemorial.
6. This group held the values of liberty and equality. Equal rights to people of all religions, castes and both genders.	6. Ideology was based on hierarchy of caste and gender, as sanctified by all the organized religions, clergy.
7. Participated in freedom movement and process of social change.	7. Totally aloof from the freedom movement and opposed to social change.

During the freedom struggle itself, secularism was emerging as the most dominant principle of the 'Nation in the making',

India. The leaders of the Indian National Congress, Gandhi, Maulana Abul Kalam Azad, Nehru and others were deeply committed to the ideal of secularism though its expression was very different for all of them. It is not to be denied that some of the Hindu nationalists also joined the Congress and some other leaders in the Congress had ideologies coloured by communalism of different hues, but it is undoubted that Congress did represent secular ideology to a large extent.

The Constituent Assembly debates clearly reveal that it reflected the national aspirations of the time. Secularism does not suppress religion. Secularism as a principle is the outcome of the deeper social process called secularization. As seen above with change in the material conditions, with change in social relations of production, with introduction of science and technology, society comes to a newer equilibrium in which the hold of religion especially as mediated through the mediation of clergy changes in the society. It is important for us to understand that religion is a collation of multiple components like institutional, ritualistic experiential, doctrinal, mythical and ethical ones.

The social dynamics was very complex. The process of secularization/industrialization was going on at a slow pace, not completed. At this stage, though the constitution was secular, state apparatus: bureaucracy, judiciary, army and police, was infiltrated by Hindu communal elements. The Congress Government, though predominantly secular, had many leaders in important positions that were influenced by Hindu communal ideology. This resulted in a social development, which was mixed; on the one hand, secularism thrived and on the other, communalism though remained dormant, was never dead. With social changes during the late 1970s and early 80s communalism got a strong boost and it started attacking secularism in a big way. Its expression surfaced first through the policies of Indira and Rajiv, but in due course the Ram Janam Bhumi was taken up by the BJP and during the course of this secularism came under severe attack.

Freedom Movement

India won freedom under the aegis of the secular democratic

movement led by the Indian National Congress, with the leadership of people like Mahatma Gandhi and Jawaharlal Nehru and Maulana Abul Kalam Azad. Secularism was the guiding principle of the anti-colonial struggle and it thereby succeeded in mobilizing vast sections of this plural society. It was recognized as an essential element of the platform for multi-religious, multi-caste, poly-ethnic population of the subcontinent, as an instrument for unity of the people at large. It did act as a vehicle for transmitting the common aspirations of colonially oppressed people into a broad, powerful movement targeted at achieving independence from the clutches of colonial masters.

The different strata of society, which were the main bulwark of this movement, were modern, i.e. industrial bourgeoisie, urban proletariat, poor peasants, Shudras and modern intelligentsia. This core was able to mobilize sections of the other population. After Independence, the Constituent Assembly was formed which framed the constitution, which was diverse in nature, and represented the aspirations of the majority of population. The constitution thus framed after prolonged debates made different provisions, which formed the base of secular practice. These secular provisions of the Indian constitution are:

(i) State by itself shall not espouse or establish or practise any religion,
(ii) Public revenues will not be used to promote any religion.
(iii) The state shall have the power to regulate any economic financial or other secular activity associated with religious practice (Article 25(2) (9) of constitution).
(iv) Every individual person will have an equal right to freedom of conscience and religion.

Thus, "ours is a secular state which has no particular religion of its own and must observe neutrality and equality in respect of all religions prevalent in the country. The state cannot discriminate between one religion and the other, or between their respective followers—regardless of their numerical strength in the country. At the same time the constitution guarantees to individuals and groups/sections of citizens the fundamental right to religious freedom in all its facets. Thus, secularism, equality of religions and neutrality of state to various religions within the constitutional limits are the basic features and part and parcel of unalterable basic structure of the constitution of India." (Mahmood, 1996, 1) Jawaharlal Nehru explained it thus "What it means is that it is a state which honours all faiths equally and gives them equal opportunities; that as a state, it does not allow itself to be attached to one faith or religion, which then becomes the state religion... In a country like India, no real nationalism can be built up except on the basis of secularity...narrow religious nationalisms are a relic of the past age and no longer relevant today" (Nehru, 1961)

Thus, though the constitution makers had not used the word secularism in the explicit fashion, Indian constitution was standing on the firm foundations of secular principles. Indira Gandhi merely added a descriptive word for something, which was already ingrained in the constitution. The spokesmen of Hindu Right taking advantage of the fact that the word was added during the much-dreaded 'emergency' are trying to throw mud on the very concept of secularism, which is anathema to their political interests.

Hindu Right Wing

The rise of Hindu right wing, RSS combine, with BJP as its political wing and Vishwa Hindu Parishad as the wing operating directly in the name of religion and roping in Mahants and Sadhus, came up to challenge the basic notions of the Indian constitution from 1980s. The process of its rise was very assertive with large sections of affluent middle class supporting it in the face of rising assertion of Dalits and women in the society. It managed to externalize the internal goals, by deflecting the whole aggression against minorities, Muslims and then Christians. It went on growing in intensity assuming horrendous proportions after the Babri Masjid demolition. The riots of Mumbai, burning of Pastor Stains in 1998, coming to power of BJP at centre and trying to review the constitution as per the agenda of RSS were the major setbacks to the secular values of the nation. These also halted the progress of the nation in a serious way with adverse effects of globalization being presented as shining India. The Gujarat carnage may be the biggest blot on the plural and democratic values of India and Gujarat by now has become a sort of Hindu Rashtra in one state, where the rights of minorities have received a severe blow, where they have been reduced to second class citizens. With this the human rights of weaker sections of society, Dalits, Adivasis and women have also taken a severe beating. The Hindu right talks of Hindu Rashtra and wants the Indian constitution to be based on the values of Indian holy books. With the global phenomenon of terrorism the demonization of Muslim minority in India is more or less complete and their human rights in severe jeopardy. One realizes that during this phase many a neighboring countries have also faced an onslaught on the prospect of their path to democracy. Wherever the religion based politics, politics deriving its legitimacy from religious identity came to the fore the trampling on human rights was very much there. This politics tough will be talking of one or other religion, the women's rights of that community and the rights of weaker sections belonging to that community have taken a backseat.

Table: Showing the Differences Between Hindu Rahtra and Secular Democratic India

Hindu Rashtra	*Secular Democratic India*
This concept began as the goal of RSS and Hindu Mahasabha, which were not part of the freedom struggle.	This concept evolved as a part of the freedom struggle led by the Indian National Congress. Revolutionaries like Bhagat Singh, and of the streams led by Babasaheb Ambedkar stood for this.
Supporters of this concept in the earlier period were Brahmins, Banias, zamindars and now the this gets support from uppercaste and upper-middle class Hindu elite.	Supporters: Vast mass of poor peasants, workers , dalits, and sections of industrialists

Concept crystallized by ideologues of Hindutva: Savarkar, Golwalkar, etc.	Concept enshrined in Indian constituition which was formed by Constituent Assembly: fairly representative of Indian people.
This nationalism is based on race, religeon and hatred of 'others' on the grounds of race or religion.	Based on recognition of pluralism and geopolitical diversities.
Inherent special status to elite	Based on formal equality of all.
Strengthens 'status quo' based on caste, gender and class.	Provision of liberal space to struggle for the rights of the oppressed.
In this society to be guided by Hindu clergy (Mahants, Acharyas).	Social life to evolve through mutual interaction of people and communities.
Impose monolithic values and culture on society.	Space for plurality. Respect for diversity.
Franchise to be controlled as per the dictates of the elite, the 'self appointed' leaders of 'Hindu society' i.e. by the leaders of the Sangh Parivar.	Universal franchise. Everybody has the voting power. All equal in the eyes of law, irrespective of caste, class and gender.
Brahminical norms, elite Sanskritised values to be the 'official', 'mainstream' laws.	Indian Constituition to guide social and political life.
Everybody has to accept 'Hindu' (Brahminical culture).	Communities free to pursue their own culture.
Concept close to Mussolini's Italy, Hitler's Germany, Khoemeini's Iran and Taliban's Afghanistan.	Aspires to be a Democracy, Values of Liberty, Equality and Fraternity for all. Nurtures liberal space.
Hindu elite and co-opted 'other' elite will dominate and dictate terms.	Possibility of everybody constituting the political process.

Human Rights

Concept of human rights begins with the rise of democracies. The feudal societies had a neat division between rights and duties. The landlords, kings had the right on tribute and free labor, while the peasants and deprived sections had the apportionment of duties for them. Duty to give tax, duty to serve the landlords, kings. Men had the right over women, while women had the duties towards their husbands, fathers or sons. The concept of Liberty, Equality and Fraternity (community) brought in the era of formal equinity between all the citizens. Even the concept of citizenship begins with democratic society and accompanying social transformation.

With the rise of religion based nationalism, the assertion of Taliban in Afghanistan, Zia-ul-Haq in Pakistan and Hindutva in India the notion of rights is being sidetracked and major emphasis is on the duties. One had witnessed similar processes in the US with the rise of Christian fundamentalism, and in Germany with the rise of race-based politics of Fascism. Under the pressure of this politics gender and caste/class hierarchy is asserted in the newer language. Since the society began as unequal one, some of the sections like Dalits and women began with a big disadvantage. Social subjugation and gender subjugation were the starting point. The constitution makers kept the provision of affirmative, protective clauses for these so that century old disadvantages are done way with and there is a march from formal equality to substantive equality. With the rise of Hindutva in India the opposition to reservation is manly to retain the social hierarchies. The Hindutva is also opposed to equality in a subtle way.

Women and Hindu Right

The coming to power of these groups affects the rights of women as well. It can very well be gleaned from the interview given by Mridula Sinha, the chief of BJP Mahila Morcha, spelt it out very well.

In an interview to *Savvy*, April 1994, she states that (1) a woman should not work outside the home unless her family is financially very deprived. (2) I gave dowry and received dowry.

(3) I oppose women's liberation, as it is another name for 'loose morals'. (4) We oppose equal rights for both sexes. (5) There is nothing wrong with domestic violence against women: very often it is women's fault. We advise women to try and adjust, as her not adjusting creates the problem. (6) Women's future lies in perpetuating the present, because nowhere else are women worshipped as we are in India. (7) For us women's liberation means liberation from atrocities. It does not mean they should be relieved of their duties as wives and mothers. One of the past presidents of Mahila Morcha, Vijaya Raje Scindia, led a group of women in a protest march against 'anti-sati' legislation, asserting that, 'It is the fundamental right of Hindu women to commit *sati* (burning of a woman on the funeral pyre of her husband), as it is in preservation of our past glory and culture'. Nearly 20,000 *kar sevikas* helped the *kar sevaks* who went to demolish the *masjid*, by cooking and cleaning for them. During demolition of the masjid, Uma Bharati and Sadhavi Rithamhara exhorted their male 'brethren' to participate in demolition.

Wherever Hindu right wing groups are dominant, they will try to impose a dress code on women, will oppose Valentine's Day and try to create problems if a Hindu girl marries a Muslim boy.

Dalits and Hindutva

BJP has couched its views and attitudes towards Dalits in a very clever way. It will not criticize Dalits, but when faced with their movements, demands and cultural upsurge it will start beating the drum of abolishing reservations and upholding merit. This was perfected as an art when the Mandal Commission recommendations were implemented and later when BSP began a verbal tirade against the symbolism projected by SP. To counter Mandal, it did not want to be visible in opposing it. So it did not support the upper caste Hindu students' self-immolation, etc., but to side track the issue it began its Rath Yatra and later withdrew its support from the V.P. Singh government leading to its fall (1990). Similarly, when faced with Mayawati's Periyar Mela-anti-upper caste pronouncements its 'supplicated face' Vajpayee, attacked the proposed extension of reservations to non-Hindu Dalits and by demanding a review of the reservation policy.

While Dalit reformers have always stood for opposing the *Manusmriti*, Dr. Ambedkar burnt it; the ideologues of Hindutva have always upheld it. They have devised the clever ideology of integral humanism, which argues that every society has a balanced integral whole and any change of equations will put it in a crisis. The argument is to uphold the caste equations as they prevail. The scriptures and practices of Brahminical Hindu religion do ask for Shudra Dharma, holy duty of Dalits, to serve the upper castes, Stree Dharma, to serve the lord and master: husband or the male relative controlling her life.

Minorities

The Indian Constitution being secular gives the right to freedom of conscience and religion and it is also duty bound to preserve the composite culture of the country. Article 15 ensures that there is no discrimination on the grounds of religion. Article 29(1) gives the right to preserve language, script and culture. Article 30(1) gives the right to establish and run educational and other institutions; while Article 30(2) ensures that there should be no discrimination against minority institutions. Also Article 25 gives the freedom of conscience, free profession, propagation and practice of one's religion.

Rights of Minorities under the Constitution of India

Article 29(1): "Any section of the citizens residing in the territory of India or any part thereof having a distinct language, script or culture of its own, shall have the right to conserve the same."

Article 29(1): "No citizen shall be denied admission into any educational institution maintained by the state or receiving aid out of the state funds on grounds only of religion, race, caste, language or any of them."

Article 30(1): "All minorities whether based on religion or language, shall have the right to establish and administer educational institutions of their choice."

These provisions ensure that minorities are able to lead their lives in full security. Most of these are endorsed by United Nations Commissions, to which India is a signatory. Irrespective of this the communalization of state apparatus and direct assault of RSS affiliates has resulted in a situation where the minorities are slipping rapidly into the status of second class citizens. While this is the overt plight of Muslims/Christians in Gujarat, other states are gradually slipping into such a situation.

Conclusion

Secularism is an inalienable part of democracy. The modern transformation to democracy essentially stands for the abolition of structural hierarchy of caste and gender and its replacement by formal equality. The democratic state in turn gives a liberal space which can be the ground for transforming the formal equality towards substantive equality.

The religious right wing abolishes secular values, in the garb of 'minority problem' and its core agenda is to bring back the feudal caste and gender based structural hierarchies. While the minorities get the boot in the apparent way with the attack on secular values, the core victims of this are the deprived sections of society, whose rights get suppressed. In current times it is an attempt to abolish the liberal democratic space by rousing the hysteria of religious sentiments and use this suppression of democratic values to perpetuate the pre-modern status quo of caste and gender hierarchy. Human rights are essentially a concept which can go along only with democracy, which in turn can only be secular. So in the Indian context the opposition to secularism is basically an attack on the human rights of workers, women, Dalits and minorities, with religious minorities bearing a direct brunt of violence, intimidation and also being relegated to being second class citizens.

BIBLIOGRAPHY

1. Asghar Ali Engineer, "Some Thoughts on Pluralist Model of Nation Building", Minorities in India, Conference Papers, Rajiv Gandhi Institute for Contemporary Studies (RGISS), 1996.
2. Ashwini K. Ray, "Constitution Reform", *Economic & Political Weekly*, March 18, 2000.
3. Fali S. Nariman, "The Constitution of a Review", *Asian Age*, May 2, 3 and 4, 2000.

4. Imtiaz Ahamd, 'Indian Minorities', *Minorities in India*, RGISS, 1996.
5. Iqbal A. Ansari, *Readings on Minorities: Perspectives and Documents*, Institute of Objective Studies, New Delhi, 1996.
6. Rudolf Heredia, *Secularism and Secularization: Towards Secular India*, Vol. 1, No. 3, 1995.
7. S.P. Sathe, *Secularism and Supreme Court of India*, The Lawyers Collective, August, 1996.
8. Satish Saberwal, "Constitutional Ideas and Political Practices", *Economic & Political Weekly*, March 11, 2000.
9. Shiver Larry, *Conception of Secularization in Empirical Research in Sociological Perspectives*, Pelican 1971, Thompson and Tunstall.
10. Subhash Kashyap, *Indian Constitution*, National Book Trust, New Delhi, 1995.
11. Suhas Palashikar, "Why We Must Oppose Review of Constitution", *Economic & Political Weekly*, April 2000.
12. Upendra Baxi, "Kar Seva of Indian Constitution", *Economic & Political Weekly*, March 11, 2000.
13. Upendra Baxi, The Struggle for Redefinition of Secularism in India, in Heredia and Mathais (eds.) *Secularism and Liberation*, Indian Social Institute, 1995.

4

Confronting Communal-Fascism@ Bolshevik.com

Murzban Jal

> Confusion is the beginning of wisdom.
>
> Plato, *Memo*

> All revolutions perfected the state machine instead of smashing it.
>
> Karl Marx, *Eighteenth Brumaire of Louis Bonaparte.*

> The day European industry and science are united with Hindu dharma, man will be god.
>
> Bankim Chandra Chattopadhyay

Un-clarity and Dramaturgy

"It is not entirely clear", so Charles Taylor said, "what is meant by secularism".[1] Seems quite absurd does it not? For the rational mind there ought to be no confusion on secularism especially when one is witness to what is happening to nations like Iran and Pakistan when they have placed anti-secularism and theological messianism at the basis of their political ideology. There should also be no confusion to what is happening to India post May 2014 when the Bharatiya Janata Party (BJP)—the neoconservative political arm of the fascist Rashtriya Swayamsevak Sangh (RSS)—came to power, especially when it is busy declaring India to be a "Hindu Rashtra" and promoting the politics of beef and yoga and challenging the politics of Constitutional Democracy.

And yet there seems to be confusion. Why is this so? Why

should there be no confusion and yet why is there confusion? Would this confusion lead to wisdom? And what is the nature of this un-clarity? One needs to answer these questions. What I am saying is that this un-clarity is not because the idea of secularism is problematic, not because it is an idea shrouded in mystery and fantasy. Instead it is because this idea is seen as rooted in the history of the emergence of capitalism in Western Europe and by and large hegemonized by liberal democracy. That this same idea that early liberalism advocated against feudalism (especially against European feudalism's idea of a theocratic state) has been severely abused by both liberal democrats and right-wing elites is quite another question. It must be stated that this abuse of secularism is not merely a phenomenon that is national which propelled the BJP to come to power. Instead this abuse of secularism is tied down inexorably to the crisis of capitalism, the legitimacy of the bourgeois state and the consequent abuse of humanity that is essential global.

This essay is on the rethinking of the idea of secularism. But this essay which is reworking the classical theories of secularism is based on the reworking of Revolutionary Marxism itself. We begin with a confession in this double reworking: of secularism and Revolutionary Marxism. Bolshevik.com is actually a construct, almost a form of fiction. Yet, this fiction is simultaneously very real. This fiction that is at the same time very real, we are grafting in Marx and Engels' theme of the specter that they had evoked in the *Manifesto of the Communist Party*. In the *Manifesto*, Marx and Engels talk of the spectre of communism that is haunting the powers of old Europe. This spectre is actually non-existent. In actuality it is the proletariat that has risen against the elites of Europe. What the elites in the form of the popes and the czars, French ministers and German police spies have done is shouted that the insurrectionist proletariat is actually this terrible and uncanny spectre. What Marx and Engels did was create a new genre of dramaturgy where the idea of fiction that is simultaneously real enters the scene of scientific discourse. Bolshevik.com as both dramaturgy and science now deals with the question of secularism. It also studies how anti-secularists are gaining ground not only in India, but large parts of South and West Asia.

The leitmotiv of this essay would seem somewhat strange. According to this motif, Marx was not a secularist as one has hitherto imagined—i.e. not a liberal democratic secularist—but was a revolutionary historicist and humanist who was critical of what I call "secularism as we know it", or to be precise the liberal democratic version of secularism. What I have done is involve a terrain shift in the study of secularism from three perspectives:

(1) that the politics of secularism in India has its own independent and autonomous history determined by the concrete class struggles in South Asia, that cannot be reduced to the West European versions of social formations (especially the question of "class") and secularism,

(2) that secularism in India is continuously tied down to the issues of caste and class, and,

(3) that there is a rigorous difference between "secularism as we know it", or rather liberal democratic secularism and Marx's idea of the "secular".

I shall begin with a quote from Slavoj Žižek. According to Žižek (he is quoting Gilles Deleuze here): "If you're trapped in the dream of the other, you're fucked".[2] What I am claiming is that both the dreams of the liberals and the fascists are the dreams of the other, the other who is not merely the other (the "humanistic other" of Marx's *Economic and Philosophic Manuscripts of 1844*), but the "other as hell" (to recall Jean-Paul Sartre) the "hellish other" who now appears as the "big other" and the "symbolic order" (as Jacques Lacan had put it). What I am also claiming is that because one has not been able to differentiate the liberal view of secularism (as the mere separation of religion and state) from the continent of knowledge that Marx opened (the continent of knowledge of understanding history as insurrection), one is blunting the politics of anti-fascism in India. This essay claims that one cannot rely on liberal politics in confronting fascism, nor can one rely on the liberal view of secularism in confronting fascism. What I am thus claiming is that if one takes the liberal view and shuts one's eyes to Marx's contribution to the development of the science of politics, then one is not exactly contributing to the cause of the anti-fascist movement.

Besides this, I am saying that it is in this new Marxist space discovered (one can call this the "New Physics" of the social sciences) that one links Marx's original idea of the Asiatic mode of production to the question of secularism. One then links the question of secularism to the social structure of Indian society and thus to the caste question which is inexorably bound to the idea of the Asiatic mode of production and the form of semi-feudal capitalism that emerged from this Asiatic mode. It must be noted that this idea of "semi-feudal capitalism" is Lenin's idea which I am placing at the centre of this narrative of secularism and the struggle against fascism. Since secularism in India is now linked to the Asiatic form of semi-feudal capitalism and caste, one then links Marx's idea of the secular with the programme of the annihilation of caste combined with the Marxist idea of annihilation of capitalism. Remember that Marx calls caste the "solid foundation of Oriental despotism."[3] And since caste is based on the ideas of graded inequality and division of labourers (motifs that B.R. Ambedkar consistently exposed) that actively repress liberty, equality and fraternity; the programme of the annihilation of caste is placed at the centre of radical secular politics.

The question that one may ask is: "But what is caste, how can one scientifically define it and how is it related to the question of secularism in India?" Following Ambedkar one defines caste as an "enclosed class"[4], even a gang or a clique.[5] And since we are dealing with the idea of an enclosed class, Marx's theory of alienation combined with his theory of the Asiatic mode of production are relevant here. Caste is to be understood as a parasitical clan-class system with a deeply hierarchical social order (based on endogamous communities) and a bureaucracy that defends this hierarchical social order. But this bureaucratic enclosed-estranged clan system based on privileges and the totem of purity and the taboo of pollution have also the sub-systems of racism that the RSS has perfected, combined with a deeply neurotic and psychotic cultural disorder embedded within its ideological cranium. The Indian fascists would perfect this caste-based form of racism and the psychotic cultural system emerging thereon.

It must be noted that the relation between class and caste is a very deep one in India. As Ambedkar said that one has to understand the genesis of caste and consequently to "determine what was the class that first made itself into a caste, for class and caste, so to say, are next door neighbours, and it is only a span that separates the two."[6] The following question is pertinent here: "What is the class that raised this 'enclosure' around itself?"[7]

Besides grounding the discussion in the issues of caste and the Asiatic mode of production, there are certain methodological guidelines where we develop new terms and conditions to understand an authentic "people's secularism". This essay deals with the question of secularism as rooted in the strain and stress between the idea of "secularism in general" and the emergence of communal-fascism, not to forget the conflict between "secularism from above" (which we articulate as the liberal democratic idea of secularism usually imported from the West) and "secularism from below" (or the lived ideologies and cultures of the popular classes of India). Based on this latter conflict this essay makes a distinction between liberal secularism and radical secularism. This distinction is based on the conflict between Brahmanical rationalization and the radical secularist Dalit Bahujan programme of the annihilation of caste and capitalism. It claims that while liberal secularism deals with the rationalization of capitalist governance in India, radical secularism deals with the historization and humanization of society, the annihilation of caste, tied down to semi-feudal capitalism (to borrow Lenin's term once again) and the programme of people's democracy that propagates political, social and economic democracy. Radical secularism is thus about the direct conflict not only with communal-fascism, but also with caste, capitalism and imperialism.

Three Ideas of Secularism, Theological Messianism and New Humanism

There are three ideas of secularism:

(1) The commonsensical (in the Gramscian sense), where secularism implies the political narrative which involves

democracy in the everyday life-world. This commonsensical narrative confronts caste and communalism at the pre-conceptual, pre-theoretical levels. This is the everyday idea of secularism as used by the popular classes of India. Secularism here implies fraternity and promotes the ideas of equality and citizenship.

(2) The liberal democratic idea which itself has a number of parts: the separation of state and religion, the privatization of faith, the equality of all religions and the spirit of tolerance; and

(3) The Marxist idea of secularism which talks of the historization and humanization of society and the transcendence (*Aufhebung*) of religion and the state, along with the complete transcendence of class society itself.

In contrast to these three ideas of secularism is the idea of anti-secularism which conservatives and neo-cons have mobilized all over the world. For them the separation of religion and the state is an error since it creates an amoral state, if not a totally immoral state, a state that is devoid of all moral values. For the anti-secularists (whether the RSS, the Iranian Shiite elites, or the Taliban), only religion can provide a framework for a moral worldview. The conservatives and neo-cons then talk of the *politicization of religion* and *theologization of politics*. These writers of anti-secular manifestos and the ideologists of the "return to religion" then deal with a philosophical anti-humanism. Secularism is taboo here, whether in Saudi Arabia, Pakistan or Iran. Consider how anti-secularism and anti-humanism work in this framework. Note how the theme of alienation is central to the framework—but an idealist-theological alienation, i.e. an alienation of the individual from an imagined and fantasized God. Note for this theological anti-secular version, the politics of secularism emerges when the individual is alienated from this phantasmatic God. Note also this anti-humanist thesis where the entire humanist tradition of the Renaissance is put in the hermeneutics of suspicion. According to this conservative and reactionary reading, it is the Renaissance which creates what is called *Westoxication*, where one, as if, forgets a form of transcendental truth (as Truth) and gives birth to the human, in fact alienated humanity, a form of Adam who has sinned and is bereft of all forms of spirituality and transcendentalism. Consider this anti-secularist, anti-humanist narrative:

> Westoxication began when man arrogantly claimed the status of *Haqq* for himself and in the West this claim, knowingly and unknowingly, became the foundation of all ideologies, views, rules, institutions and norms.......Notwithstanding the roots of Westoxication in Greek philosophy with its 2500 years of history, its specific and predominant form has emerged with the Renaissance. With the appearance of Westoxication, the old form of history is abolished and a new man is born who is no longer submissive to the *Haqq* (Truth, right, authentic). He forgets the *Haqq* so that he can replace Him to expropriate the earth and the heavens....The freedom of religious beliefs in the Declaration of Human Rights means alienation from religion; it means leaving the individuals to their own devices so that they may do whatever they want with religion in their lives and have any religion they want....Modern man sees his own image in the mirror of *Haqq*, has entered into a covenant with himself. Therefore it is inevitable and natural that such a man would turn his back to religion and cover up his act with claims to nationalism, internationalism, liberalism, collectivism and individualism...That Kant has put aside the category of existence (*vajud*) and emphasized knowledge, reducing philosophy to epistemology was not merely an accident resulting from personal observations; rather it was necessitated by the unfolding of the history of metaphysics... ...The Islamic revolution must summon a return to the beginnings and a renewal of the Covenant. This renewal of the Covenant requires that we (Iranians) break the Covenant to which we acquiesced in Westoxication. If we break away from this Convent with Westoxication it will be remembered in the world and would undermine the current Covenant. We take refuge in God and ask Him for assistance on our renewed Covenant, a Covenant which constitutes the future of mankind.[8]

Now, note what happens. It is humanity as humanity that is condemned by the anti-secularist. One must note that the author of the above passage is the philosophical mentor of the last president of the Islamic Republic of Iran, Mahmoud Ahmadinejad. One must also note that Ahmadinejad is someone said to be of Jewish descent. Very strangely this messianic politician of Jewish descent (Ahmadinejad) denies the genocide of the Jews by the Nazis, thus denies the Nazi holocaust. One must also note that the philosophical mentor of the author of the above passage (Riza Davari-Ardakani) is Martin Heidegger whose sympathy for Nazism is now well recorded. It seems that anti-secularism finally culminates in Auschwitz. It seems that the road for the anti-secularists is paved by fascism. The project of the anti-Enlightenment is central to anti-secularism.

Now what happens is that we have a very strong anti-Enlightenment shared code between the Indian conservatives along with the neo-cons and the Iranian Shiite elites. In contrast to this anti-humanism one posits the discourse of what the young Marx called the philosophy of the "the human essence" (*das menschliche Wesen*). Note that the very discourse of secularism shifts with Marx's humanism.

It must be noted that for Marx, by "secular" is meant "worldly" (*weltliche*). And this narrative of secularism is double fold, which has within its cranium the two worlds of the bourgeoisie and the proletariat. What we find thus is that two types of the secular appear: the bourgeois and the proletarian types of secularism. To understand this, a brief genealogy of the term "secular" is necessary. We shall go into this genealogy in the next section of the essay. The question shall remain is that because the word "secular" appears on the scene of history from its Latinized context—it is *Saeculum*, implying century or age, or profane time, as distinct from theological time—must one believe that it is purely of European import, the view held by not only Ashis Nandy, T.N. Madan and Partha Chatterjee; but also by Mahmoud Ahmadinejad, the Indian neo-cons and the Islamic right all who swear by anti-secularism?

Instead of the separation of religion and the state (the theme of liberal secularism) let us see the humanist idea of secularism. Marxist secularism as radical secularism is going to the roots of humanity itself. This *das menschliche Wesen* defines the real possibilities of human rights because it postulates not anything but the human essence as its fundamental ontological core. Authentic human rights can be possible only when *das menschliche Wesen* is sighted. We see from the above quote of Davari that primordial Being in the Heideggerean sense (the estranged God the male "Him" who is wrathful, the one who curses and punishes) necessarily extinguishes the human essence. In his *What is Philosophy?* Davari-Ardakani in true Heideggerean style says that:

> Human essence lies in his "nobodyness" and nothingness. He has no real existence and essence. His essence lies in annihilation.[9]

This is the basis of the contemporary Iranian-Islamic version of anti-secularism. What the anti-secularist camp says is that it is not *humanity as humanity* that is important, but a form of primordial Being ("God", or "Nation") that exists *over* and *above* humanity that is important. Now in contrast to this discourse of the annihilation of humanism is Marxist philosophy. But to understand this Marxist philosophy it is necessary to understand Ludwig Feuerbach's humanism. Consider Marx's reading of Feuerbach:

> In these writings (*Philosophie der Zukunft* and *Wesen des Glaubens*) you have provided—I don't know whether intentionally—a philosophical basis for socialism and the Communists have immediately understood them in that way. The unity of human with human, which is based on the real differences between humans, the concept of the human species brought from the heaven of abstraction to the real earth—what is this but the concept of *society*![10]

That is why I am insisting on demarcating the three ideas of secularism. I am also insisting that Marxism is not liberal secularism, and because of the rise of the global right-wing, Marxism does not have to relapse into the defence of the liberal variation of secularism. Our idea of the secular is thus not on the preservation of the secular state, but on the transcendence of the state itself (whether liberal democratic or fascist).

The Genealogy of the Idea of the Secular and the Limits of Liberal Secularism

I begin here with the genealogy of the idea of the secular. This genealogy is conceptual in the Hegelian sense. For Hegel the concept (*Begriff*) has to grasp the essence of the object under investigation. Armed with the Hegelian *dialectics of the concept* that grasps the essence of the idea of the secular, I proceed to analyse its genealogy.

As we noted above, "secular" as the Latin *Saeculum* implies "age", "epoch", "century", and "profane time". It is, to recall Taylor, "the time of ordinary succession, which the human race lives through between the Fall and the Parousia."[11] Whether the term secular is itself a "Christian term" (as Taylor suggests)[12] or whether only the separation thesis (separation of church and government) emerges in a Christian context is something to be analysed. I shall restrict this idea to liberal secularism, and not to "secularism as such". As should be noted, the idea of secularism is an overdetermined term (i.e. complexly structured, unevenly determined) and therefore having multiple meanings. To restrict it to Western Europe and the experiences of European people could be a bad idea.

One should be able to differentiate the generic idea of secularism from the particular modes, as well as learn how to differentiate the two particular modes (the liberal and the Marxist). "Secularism as such" implies how humanity deals with religion, while liberal secularism deals with the separation of religion and the state and Marxist secularism deals with the historization and humanization of religion and politics. One should not collapse Marxist secularism into the liberal democratic narrative. Marx's *On the Jewish Question* is a text based on this difference: the liberal one and the revolutionary one. The revolutionary's attitude to religion is different from that of the liberal.

However, it is in the liberal democratic narrative (the narrative that is central to liberal democracy), that religion does not vanish, but as the Biblical "Fall" stands at the centre of liberal democracy. The separation of religion from the state, that liberal secularism talks of, is in actuality the mimesis of the Biblical separation of heaven from earth. We get the startling conclusion when liberal democracy in the separation thesis mimics the Biblical narrative: humanity (civil society) is consequently sinful and suffering. Sinful civil society thus needs the disciplining state in order to redeem itself.

The following opposition is made: God/humanity, sacred/profane, church/government, state/civil society. What liberal secularism did not notice that the "separation" thesis is in actuality the thesis of the emergence of capitalism freed from feudal restrictions based on human alienation, a point that the theological right-wing are able to exploit. "*Separation*" actually means *alienation*. The irony is that liberal democracy and liberal secularism in attempting to construct a secular society, mimics literally the old Biblical split of the heavens and the earth, the split and estrangement that begins with Eve's original sin and the consequently Fall of all humanity.

Now there are two versions of the Christian Fall in Europe: (1) sinful humanity has fallen and the rule of the theologians will redeem humanity from original sin. This was the Catholic theological rule in the times of feudalism in Europe, and (2) the Protestant separation of the sacred and the profane, where the separation of powers, the equality of all religious dominations along with religious tolerance and freedom is central.

What happens is that liberal democracy in the times of ascending capitalism perfected the Protestant separation of the sacred and the profane. But in the times of imperialism, the ruling elites in the form of the fascists of Europe rebelled against the secular project of the Enlightenment. This rebellion was against the separation of God from earth. Bereft of God, the earth had turned even more sinful. This God/humanity separation could simply not work. What the fascists did was to transform this separation and alienation of God/humanity into the cult of the fascist superman where the fascist is seen as the new God-man. The Nazi flirtation with the philosophy of Friedrich Nietzsche has to be seen in this light. To put in a nutshell, the fascist rebellion against secularism is simultaneously a rebellion against the Fall. In India, the Hindutva right-wing borrows from this Christian background of the Fall, where the Biblical story is transformed into a new narrative where the "Hindu Fall" is sutured into the discourse of the "Imaginary Fall" as spelt out as Islamic invasions. This Imaginary Fall becomes the master narrative in the Hindu right.

If in the Christian world, the Fall signifies the alienation of humanity from God, where the individual in the era of ascending capitalism stands before this Absolute God and in the era of fascism and imperialism becomes this strange God-man; in Hindu cosmology there is strictly no Fall, but the slaughter of primeval 'man' and the birth of the hierarchical

Hindu God (Brahma) who divides humanity into four castes. In the Hindu order, caste is the balancing force of the universal cosmic order. And this is why the Hindu right-wing is essentially casteist and anti-secularist. If in European fascism, this God-man rebels against the Fall and the consequent separation of powers; in the Hindu cosmic order the fascist superman (as the imaginary Hindu God-man) rebels against monotheism (Christianity and Islam) and the modern liberal order. The Hindu rightist sees monotheism, especially Christianity and Islam, as suppressing pagan celebration. He also sees the modern democratic state (built on the ideas of the separation of powers and the rights of humanity) as the enemy of the Hindu god-man and the principle of caste stratification. In the Hindu pagan order, both the moral law and the cosmic order are based on caste-stratification. One must also note that Nazism learnt from Indian mythology and the Vedic idea of the warrior-priest was central to the Nazi imagination as the ideal Teutonic warrior in perpetual war with the godless communists.

Radical Secularism as Seeking the Human and the Profane

But besides this separation thesis of secularism (which fascism has really been able to exploit), there is a much larger world that one needs to explore. This is what the much larger world, the humanist world devoid of fetishes, looks like:

> In the same way atheism being the supersession (*Aufhebung*) of God, is the advent of theoretical humanism, and communism as the supersession (*Aufhebung*) of private property, is the vindication of real human life (*wirklichen menschlichen Lebens*) as humanity's possession and thus the advent of practical humanism, or atheism is humanism mediated with itself through the supersession of religion, while communism is humanism mediated with itself through the supersession of private property. Only through the supersession of this mediation (*Aufhebung dieser Vermittlung*)—which is itself, however, a necessary premise—does positively self-deriving humanism, *positive* humanism come into being.[13]

And it is with this "positively self-deriving humanism", or "*positive* humanism" that one is thus able to rescue secularism from both the theological fundamentalists and the liberal democrats. It must be recognized that both while riding the horse of caste-supremacy are also riding the horse of Western capitalism and its ideologies emanating thereon. But it is not merely the fascists and the liberal democrats that are perched on the backs of Western capitalism and the borrowing from the baggage of Eurocentric thinking (whether it is Savarkar, Golwalkar, Jinnah, or Nehru and Gandhi). The Indian Left (what I call the "Established Left) completely forgot that for Marx, Asian histories have an autonomous history of their own and could not be reduced to the history of Europe. None of them could conceptualize the Asiatic mode of production and the caste-clan system in India based in this Asiatic mode of production. They could not understand that caste has a life longer than they imagined and that the programme of the annihilation of caste has to be the sine qua non on the project of secularism.

All the above schools of political thought fell prey to the liberal secular idea of the separation of religion and the state, because they became prey to Eurocentric understandings of history and society. They could not understand that caste is the solid foundation of Indian society even today and capitalism and parliamentary democracy have not been able to dislodge caste. They could not fathom that caste is an estranged and elite created order with their anti-democratic enclosed systems that can coexist with modern capitalism, especially in the epoch of late imperialism in permanent crisis.

What Marxist secularism (as radical secularism) has to do is to move away from the liberal fetish of the state (in the thesis of the separation of religion and the state). After all, for Marx (whether it is the *Eighteenth Brumaire of Louis Bonaparte, Civil War in France* or his 1871 letter to L. Kugelmann) the state has to be smashed. One cannot take the state mechanism and use it for secular purposes. After all, the state is a war machine, to be precise the "national war engine of capital against labour".[14]

What one thus does is moves away from the site of the separation thesis and proceeds to the site of the "profane" and the "secular". And it is the ideas of the "profane" and the "world" which rescue secularism from the theological fundamentalists and the liberal democrats. Firstly by "profane" one means the "non-sacred", "irreligious", "non-theological" all which necessarily involve the process of deritualization that Walter Benjamin and Peter Berger talk of. Secondly by the "world" (in the narrative of secularism) one means the real material world. But this "world" itself has two worlds within it (as we noted above): the world of the bourgeoisie and the proletariat. Radical secularism will involve the struggle between the bourgeoisie and the proletariat, the caste-bureaucratic enclosed class system (tied down inexorably with Monsieur Moneybags) and the Indian multitude.

Radical secularism (as "positively self-deriving humanism", as "*positive* humanism") will have to struggle against not only fascism, whether the European one or the Indic-Brahmanical type, but also against liberal democracy. Liberal democracy is not the opponent of fascism. It is fascism's breeding ground. Bolshevik.com goes directly into this breeding ground. It takes the spectral, yet human form of the spectre of communism that haunts not only the powers of old Europe, but of the entire world and unleashes a direct attack on the mythopoetics of Indian fascism.

After all, both the authoritarian state and the mythopoetics of fascism emerge from concrete political economies and social conditions. One has to confront these material conditions, rather than give sermons on the importance or non-importance of not so much religions, but the importance of the political elites.

Fascism's Traumatic Fantasies

Clearly what we have seen is that Marx's historical materialism takes a completely different route to the question of secularism, and is not bogged down with platitudes of liberalism and the separation thesis. In this sense, traditional studies on secularism (whether done by Rajeev Bhargava or Ashis Nandy) mime the liberal democratic project. For them the only question is: "Do you believe in the separation thesis?"

What we on the other hand involve is an entire epistemic break from the liberal view of secularism. It must be noted that fascism loves liberalism (though it professes hatred towards liberalism), just as the liberals love the fascists (though they shout sometimes at the fascists in parliament). It is this intertwinement of liberalism and fascism, this libidinal lust for one another that unfortunately has not been understood. If, however liberalism has failed to understand fascism, it is the Established Left that also has largely not been able to understand it. This is due to the economist understanding of fascism. It was the classical Comintern understanding of fascism as the "dictatorship of finance capital" made famous by Dmitriov that is almost totally insufficient, if not totally off the mark. Why the masses give consent to finance capital has never been theorized by the Established Left.

Instead we understand fascism as a mass movement (recognized by Arthur Rosenberg) where a form of "nationalist-psychosis" is created, a psychosis that grips the masses. Finance capital one must remember is elitist, whilst fascism is plebian in form and content. What I am doing is involving the ideological and political superstructure and involving thus a historicist and humanist reading of fascism. Fascism after all involves the needs and aspirations of people. Yet these needs appear in censored and duplicated form (if one is to recall Freud's *Interpretation of Dreams*). They appear as a fantasy, but again as censored and duplicated fantasy. We call fascism the "innermost traumatic fantasies" and "innermost disavowed fantasies" phrases that we are borrowing from Žižek.[15] What the Indian fascists did was that they transformed the Gandhian form of melancholia into a form of hysteria.

What I am claiming is that liberal secularism could never deal with this form of hysteria produced by fascism. I call this liberal secularism *impotence in action* (to recall Engels from a different context).[16] Since liberal secularism is so tied down to the process of capital accumulation and private property, it can never go beyond these boundaries. What it does is that it merely mimes these economic structures. To separate religion from the public life-world (that emerged in Western Europe in the 18th century) implies only the removing of the fetters of the advancing forces of production. In this way I will say that the great studies on secularism, especially found in the work of Rajeev Bhargava, *Secularism and its Critics*, can only be totally bourgeois.

In contrast to this liberal form of secularism, one needs to evoke thinkers like Walter Benjamin who brings in the idea of the intertwinement of civilization and barbarism.[17] One also needs to say that much more lies behind liberalism and fascism than what is ordinarily thought. What Marx calls the "estranged mind"[18] (as the production of the barbaric) is almost not recognized in studies in liberalism and communalism. When Marx says that one is "moving in the realm of estrangement"[19], I now claim that this realm of estrangement rules over political discourses in India.

In actual social life what this estrangement creates is a feeling of terror as well as feeling of necrophilia, a love of death. Traditional studies and discourses on secularism almost leaves this untouched. Fascism creates a subject, but this subject becomes an estranged subject that actively represses all traces of critical subjectivity. And if fascism represses critical subjectivity, liberalism involves what Žižek calls a *Denkverbot,* a total probation against thinking. And in this prohibition against thinking, one also involves a political dependency on the bourgeoisie and political elites.

What Marxism has to do is to fight liberalism and fascism at the same time. This revolution has to be permanent. And to understand this one must recognize the fact that one needs to move beyond liberalism in order to fight communal-fascism. Liberalism lives on alienated humanity, on the Western created petty bourgeoisie. Marxism needs what Paulo Friere calls after Lukács a "critical intervention" and thus a de-schooling of society, de-schooling the production of the barbaric-estranged mind. If fascism is about trauma and necrophilia, Marxism is about biophilia. If capitalism is about alienation and anxiety, Marxism is about humanity as humanity—or what Marx calls the recovery of the human essence from the sites of alienation and class dehumanization.

On "Communist Secularism"

If Marxism, especially Leninism, spelt out the difference between nationalism of the oppressed and the nationalism of the oppressor along with another difference, namely the difference between just and unjust wars; we say that there is a difference between the religion of the oppressed and the oppressor. Unfortunately what a certain form of Marxism did (inspired by a form of socialist messianic theology) was that it lambasted religion in the abstract. We know of Dühring, the messianic socialist who thought that blasting religion from the face of the world would emancipate humanity. We also know that Engels in his *Anti-Dühring* critiqued Dühring as an abstract idealist and utopian socialist. The Marxist idea of secularism (in contrast to the West European rendering of secularism that is tied down to the bourgeois revolutions—the English one of 1640 and the French Revolution of 1789—and the experience of the rising bourgeoisie) is totally different from the hegemonic rendering of secularism. Imitating this version of secularism would be imitating the European bourgeoisie.

But this search for something new in the Marxist idea of secularism, should not lead us to cultural relativism, something that Ashis Nandy has largely been promoting. It by no way implies that the 'East' is something different from the 'West'. Instead it talks of a multi-linear theory of history where concrete analysis of concrete conditions replaces abstract and metaphysical theorization. Nor is this Revolutionary Marxist rendering of secularism to be confused with the subaltern project initiated by Ranjit Guha. While critiquing the nationalist and the Established Left's rendering of secularism (as the mere separation of religion and the state), Revolutionary Marxism does not relapse to the subaltern project, whether as found in Guha's *Elementary Aspects of Peasant Insurgency in Colonial India* or Gayatri Chakravorty Spivak who I would call after Vivek Chibber as a "parachuted subaltern".[20]

And since we are claiming that we are not borrowing the East vs. West ideology and also since we as dialectical and historical materialists talk of concrete analysis of concrete conditions, our analysis follows the logic of understanding non-Western societies from a non-Eurocenrtic point of view. However let it be known that this method ought not to be understood with the method of Guha, Spivak, et al. Here I would agree with Chibber that subaltern studies carries out the faulty methodology of postcolonial studies and poststructuralism, where they abolish the notion of class and the idea of universals, besides celebrating the logic of difference (or *différance*, as

Derrida spelt it) besides propagating their much hyped ideology of "anti-foundationalism". If one follows this logic to its logical culmination, one meets with the alarming conclusion that secularism is a discourse or even a type of meta-narrative whose time seems to have ended. And also since subaltern studies (of Guha and Spivak) decries against meta-narratives (whether they be of "class" or "nation" they seem to be following the postmodern logic heralded by Lyotard), their criticism of secularism happens to echo right-wing politics.

What subaltern studies did was that it transformed everything into phantasmagorical abstractions. They would never have concrete analysis of concrete conditions. They would, of course, claim that they are concrete—that nationalism is a "way of seeing"[21], thereby reducing objectivity to pure subjectivity. So if thinkers like Rajeev Bhargava follow the Nehruvian line where industry as the "temples of modern India" would usher in secular and rationalist society, we have the subalterns who do exactly the opposite.

So what we need is a certain methodological guideline where we develop new terms and conditions to understand an authentic "people's secularism" or "communist secularism". What we reiterate is that there is a difference between "bourgeois secularism" and "communist secularism". We thus contextualize the question of secularism in India as rooted in the conflict between "secularism from above" and "secularism from below". What 'secularism from above" does is that either appeals to a form of Kantian moral law (the hyper-imagination of understanding humanity as the kingdom of ends and never as a means) or borrows from the history of Western Europe a borrowing that becomes merely academic. What this form of academic secularism does is that it merely utters a little of European history—that it was first used in 1648 in the thirty years war in Europe where Church property was transferred to the princes, or that George Holyoake in 1851 used the idea of secularism as an ideology of progress and development.

If theologians thought that humanity is an "abstract being squatting outside the world"[22], liberalism would never be able to counter this phantasmagoria. The liberals would create a liberal democratic state as the perfection of the state machinery that is distinct from civil society. But, as we noted earlier, what they would also do is that they would be miming the Biblical dualism of earth and heaven. Civil society is the mundane earth, while the state is Christian heaven. What capitalism and liberal democracy do is that they perfect Christian ontology. They do not negate it. What liberal secularism does is that it purges Christianity from feudal paganism.

For Marx, at least in his celebrated essay, 'On the Jewish Question', *the secular state is the true Christian state.* Thus just as religion is "the recognition of humanity in a roundabout way through an intermediary", so too the state is an intermediary between humans.[23] The modern bourgeois state appears as Christ, the *intermediary* to whom humanity transfers the burden of his divinity, all his religious constraint".[24] Both religion and the state function in a "roundabout route".[25] Thus what secularism does is that it does not transcend religion—instead it perfects it:

> Religion is precisely the recognition of humanity in a roundabout way, through an intermediary. The state is the intermediary between one human and another human's freedom. Just as Christ is the intermediary to whom humanity transfers all his divinity, all his *religious constraint*, so the state is the intermediary to whom humanity transfers all his non-divinity and all his *human unconstraint.*[26]

Both religion and the state are *alienated machines* "divorced from the real individuals and collective interests".[27] And it is to these two sites of alienated machines that Marx turns his attention to. Marx's communist secularism is predicated on the critique of alienated machines.

Alienated Machines

First, for Marx, the term "secular" is not above the radical politics of suspicion. One could call Marx's critique (after Paul Ricoeur) a "hermeneutics of suspicion". However since I do not intend Marxism to be reduced to the academics of hermeneutics and since I intend to be involved in radical politics, I am calling this *the radical politics of suspicion.* For Marx, the "secular" implies the "world". And, as we all very well know, this "world" is divided into the worlds of the bourgeoisie and the proletariat. Second, Marx is not overawed by the phantasmagoria of religion, nor gripped by the liberal discourse of secularism. Instead he intends to go into both this mystery of the phantasmagoria of religion and what he calls the "secular conflict" between civil society and the state:

> This secular conflict, to which the Jewish question ultimately reduces itself, the relation between the political state and its preconditions, whether these are material elements, such as private property, etc., or spiritual elements, such as culture or religion, the conflict between the general interest and private interest, the schism between the political state and civil society—*these secular antitheses Bauer allows to persist, whereas he conducts a polemic against their religious expression* (emphasis are mine. M.J.).[28]

For Marx we have at least two renderings of the "secular"—the first is the liberal democratic one which involves the separation of the state and religion, while the second is involved with the humanizing part of secularism. This second part then deals with the process of de-ritualization. In the first part (the liberal democratic part) Marx talks of three "secular divisions.... between the political state and civil society".[29] And this is where liberal democracy mimes the Biblical narrative. The state takes the form of universality, albeit like in theology, a form of spurious universality; whilst civil society is like the sinful earth of the *Bible*, wherein reigns pure particularism[30]:

> In the state....humanity is the imaginary member of an illusory sovereignty, is deprived of his real individual life and endowed with unreal universality.[31]

And it is to this "unreal universality", in fact as *alienated universality*, that Marx aims his revolutionary attack:

> The members of the political state are religious owing to the dualism between individual life and species life (*Gattungsleben*), between the life of civil society and political life. They are religious because humanity treats the political life of the state, an *area beyond their real individuality*, as if it were their true life. They are religious insofar as religion here is the spirit of civil society, expressing the *separation and remoteness of human from human.* (Both emphases are mine). Political democracy is Christian since in it humanity, not merely one human but every human, ranks as *sovereign*, as

> the highest being, but it is the human in his uncivilized, unsocial form, the human in his fortuitous existence, the human just as he is, the human as he has been corrupted by the whole organization of our society, who has lost himself, been alienated, and handed over to the rule of inhuman conditions and elements—in short, the human who is not yet a *real* species-being. That which is a creation of fantasy, a dream, a postulate of Christianity, i.e., the sovereignty of humanity—but humanity as an alien being different from the real human—becomes, in democracy, tangible reality, present existence, and secular principle.[32]

For the liberal, who thought that Marx too would be following the liberal secular line of reasoning, the above passage would come as nothing but a shock. Marx was a materialist. For him the real object of investigation was important and not some normative device. For him, the great wall of separation between religion and the state was nothing but an expression of both the rising bourgeoisie (in confrontation with the feudals) as well as an expression of alienation. Note his statement in the above passage: "humanity treats the political life of the state, an *area beyond their real individuality*, as if it were their true life". Note also what he calls "the spirit of civil society" which is nothing but the expression of "the *separation and remoteness of human from human*".

What we need to do in the reading of secularism, is to bind this question with history and the class struggle. One does not read the question of secularism as an abstract ideal. Unfortunately a large part of the parliamentary left in India refuses to read Marx historically, refuses to engage with the class struggle, but intends to work with a priori moralizing formulae. They are thus the Kantians of Indian politics.

Two Renderings of the Fall and the Fascist Response

For Marx, the Biblical Fall stands central to his critique of feudalism and capitalism. In the feudal state, there is no separation of religion and the state. The pope is a hidden reagent of God to take care of sinning humanity. But for Marx in 'On the Jewish Question' the feudal state (the so-called "Christian state") is not the true Christian state. The true Christian state is the liberal democratic state that *separates* civil society from the state, religion from politics, the individual from the general and appears as Spirit (*Geist*). And this separation and the miraculous appearance of *Geist* (as we said earlier) is the mimesis of the principles of estrangement and the Biblical separation of the earth from heaven.

Thus the state is like heaven, the realm of spurious universality, or what Marx calls "fantasy"[33], while civil society is the realm of false or alienated individuality, the egotism of alienated, corrupted and debased humanity. This state of fantasy creates what Freud called the "oceanic feeling of oneness"—the feeling of being a "Hindu", even a Hindutvavadi armed like Don Quixote attacking windmills.

It is important to understand this genealogy of secularism and to link it with the sections of metamorphosis of commodities and the fetish character of commodity production (in *Capital*, Vol. I). Remember the concepts "magic", "theological niceties", "metaphysics", "transcendent", "necromancy" and "irrational" stand central to Marx's way of theorization.[34] What we get from this reading is that capitalism (and the ontology of the commodity) do not negate theology and the story of ghosts. Nor does capitalism negate ritual. Instead both theology and ritual enter the discourse of commodity production. What liberal capitalism does is that it negates religion (as Catholicism) only to posit it once again (as Protestantism).

In the Hindu life world, there is strictly speaking from the Christian point of view no Fall. There is instead what one calls the "Great Sacrifice" sketched as the "rites of humanity" and the birth of the great cosmic order. In this narrative, the primeval or *Ur*-man (*Purusa*) is sacrificed and slaughtered and from this slaughtered humanity is born the archaic system of caste society. It is this caste-stratified society which serves as the balancing force of the cosmos.

Consequently, if in Christianity, the separation of earth and heaven balances the cosmos since the 'Fall', in Hinduism it is the caste system that becomes the balancing force. This is the secular rendering of the two renderings of the Fall. But then comes the crisis of capitalism and the fascists' rebellion against both the Fall and the separation of religion and the state. In European fascism imagination, since religion and the state were separated, that communists, trade unionists and Jews could take over society. The fascist pseudo-rebellion then waged war against this separation thesis and the liberal democratic state. The fascist as God-man appeared on earth to redeem Germany, Italy and the entire 'Aryanized' Europe against the Jewish conspiracy.

But for the Indian fascists, though they learnt a lot from their European parents, the Fall of Indian civilization (rather "Hindu civilization" as they imagine it) was brought by the Christians and Muslims, who with their monotheistic theology seek to suppress Hindu paganism. Indian fascism then takes the form of what one calls after Žižek as "fantasmatic spectrality" and the rebellion against "monotheistic repression of pagan enjoyment".[35] This imagined "Hindu civilization" had to rebel against the Christians and Muslims and those who appeased them like the liberals and the communists. For the Indian fascists, monotheism brings in the Law (i.e. law with a capital "L", thus Law). The Law was made by Moses. Moses is the vanguard of repressed societies. He is the prophet of repression itself.

But what happens to the Indian fascists is a strange reversal of fortune. The Indian fascists imagine that they are the pagan celebrators of particularities. But this New Pagan takes on the repressed role of traditional monotheism that it itself wanted to critique. For late capitalism needs a totalitarian mono-politics of the authoritarian type and thus a repressed monotheistic-like state with the Law it itself wanted to repress. Indian fascism creates a form of mythopoetics, a spectral-fantasmatic history of an imagined traumatic event. If the Biblical narrative located this "Original Sin" as *Original Trauma* in Eve's radical disobedience to God named Monsieur Jehovah, the Indian fascists located this in the breaking of the caste system, the advent of Islam in India and the rise of communism.

What Revolutionary Marxism has to do is to locate these two primordial fantasies and traumatic events—the two types of the Fall (the monotheistic and the pagan Hindu one)—which has the manifold characters, *Purusa*, Jehovah, Eve and Moses playing the puppet-masters in this tragicomedy of the rise of fascism in India. What we now see is that secularism needs an entire new script. Revolutionary Marxism as communist secularism cannot work in the liberal narrative. It has to encounter the spectral-fantasmatic history of fascism.

And when one moves into this new terrain, one finds a doorway on which is written the following: "The monotheism of the Jew, is therefore, in reality the polytheism of many needs, a polytheism which makes even the lavatory an object of divine law".[36]

The State as Lavatory

What one needs to do in our understanding of communist secularism, the spectral-fantasmatic history of fascism and its fetishistic attachment to religion, is to shift our focus from temples to lavatories. What needs to be done is to locate liberal secularism and the bourgeois state in the problematic of alienation and the consequent process of metamorphosis of commodities. In *Capital* we see how humans are changed into things, or commodities to be precise. Now what we need to do is relate this metamorphosis of humans into things—commodities with Žižek's idea of the digestive system[37], but a digestive system gone totally wrong, where, in the production of commodities one has actually a process of shitting. What we are doing is placing the idea of shitting, an idea that is repressed from our clean-bourgeois thought. Read the opening pages of *Capital* and witness how people shit commodities. Not only do people under capitalism shit commodities, they worship them. Recall Marx recalling Shakespeare;

> Gold, yellow, glittering, precious gold!
> Thus much of this will make black white, foul fair,
> Wrong right, base noble, old young, coward valiant.
> .....What this, you gods? Why, this
> Will lug your priests and servants from your sides;
> Pluck stout men's pillows from below their heads:
> This yellow slave
> Will knit and break religions, bless the accurs'd,
> Make the hoar leprosy ador'd, place thieves,
> And give them title, knee and approbation
> With senators on the bench: this is it,
> ..... Come, damned earth,
> Thou common whore of mankind.[38]

Marx also says that the accumulation of capital is actually an accumulation of whores and shit. But this whoredom that capitalism begets is a duplicate and fake form of enjoyment. To become a capitalist, one has to hoard where one initially has to suppress all enjoyments. Consequently the "hoarder, therefore", as Marx suggests, "makes a sacrifice of the lusts of the flesh to his gold fetish".[39] The hoarder now "acts in earnest up to the gospel of abstention".[40] We have now what Žižek calls "the rise of 'dead nature'".[41] That is why we say after Marx: "Accumulate, accumulate! That is Moses and the prophets!"[42], and relate this with the process of accumulation of capital with the process of shitting. Marx's statement then becomes: "Shit, shit, this is the essence of both bourgeois political economy and fascist political theology".

This is how we read Marx's monotheism of the Jew which becomes the polytheism of many needs thereby making the lavatory an object of divine law. In *Capital*, Marx says that, "modern society, which soon after its birth, pulled Plutus by the hair of his head from the bowels of the earth, greets gold as its Holy Grail, as the glittering incarnation of the very principle of its own life".[43] In order to understand this let us see that what modern capitalism did was not merely create a pure form of universal abstraction (money), as it imagined it, but created an abstraction with the manifold particularities (different commodities: soaps, junk food, guns and bombs) within it. What we are stressing on is that these forms of spurious particularities (e.g.: soaps, junk food, guns and bombs—the paganism of commodity production) and spurious universality (money as the monotheism of the capitalist Moses) become two forms of surpluses: "excremental excess" and "traumatic excess".[44]

The relation between liberal democracy and fascism is the relation between the shitter and the lavatory. Just as the shitter needs a lavatory, liberal democracy needs fascism. And since the parliamentary left in India refused to confront what Žižek calls "the Real of today's capitalism"[45], we are left with the shitter and the lavatory To confront this purgatory of capitalism, Revolutionary Marxism creates Bolshevik.com wherein re-writes its dramaturgy for world revolutionaries. Bolshevik.com does not cry over the primal losses—of the end of the Soviet era for the parliamentary left, or of welfare capitalism for the Nehruvians. It refuses to engage in nostalgia.

Instead it questions the logic of capital flows that is inherently related to psychotic flows, not to forget the flows of the "excremental excess". It claims that capital flows creates the reified-economic base of capitalism combined with the deluded mind that the fascists pick on. The point is not to recall the old liberal idea of the welfare state as the already mentioned "illusory community"—the incarnation as the modernist Christ[46]. What Bolshevik.com does is that it understands capitalism in its rising epoch and its violent, imperialist stage. It understands the violence of imperialism and fascism as the perfection of what Adorno called the "totally administered society", wherein reigns the completely neurotic, narcissistic and psychotic personality. This neurotic and psychotic characteristics of fascism undermines secularism through the routes of parliamentary democracy and liberal secularism. Consider Meera Nanda who grasps this slippery characteristic of liberalism:

> The question that interests me in this electoral route to faith-based governance is how this counterrevolution is actually accomplished, or to put it differently, how the spirit of secularism gets subverted, without any formal abrogation of secular laws. Unless we understand the ideological mechanism of this sacralization of politics, we will not be able to combat the ongoing coups against secularism under nominally secular democracies. As a student of the history and philosophy of science, I have been watching with concern how modern science itself—perhaps the single most powerful force for secularization—is being re-coded as sacred, either as affirming the Bible or the Vedas, or as 'lower knowledge' of 'dead matter', in need of spiritualization.[47]

The fascist as the complete psychotic is always in complete denial. If you ask the fascist if the Holocaust was their creation, they will deny it. If you ask them if the Babri mosque was demolished by them in a state-sponsored barbaric act, they will deny it. If you ask them if the 2002 anti-Muslim genocide in Gujarat happened, they will deny it. They will deny that they are barbarians only to state that they are cannibals.

But if you ask the fascist leader if he is a cannibal he will say: *I am not a cannibal, in fact they are no cannibals in my fascist party. I ate the last one just last night.*[48] Just look outside your window and you will see various fascists: little fascists, big fascists, etc. The liberal wants to transform the already fascistic state mechanism into a liberal one. The parliamentary left agrees with the liberal. Both are obsessed with the state. They imagine that the state is "the 'realization of the idea' or the Kingdom of God on earth, translated into philosophical terms, the sphere in which eternal truth and justice should be realized".[49] They forget Marx, who had said that it is no longer the case:

> ...as before, to transfer the bureaucratic-military machine from one hand to another, but to smash it, and this is the preliminary condition of every real people's revolution....[50]

It is as simple as that. One should stop worshiping lavatories and all the excremental excesses caught up in it. But then would the lovers of shit allow this?

NOTES AND REFERENCES

1. Charles Taylor, 'Modes of Secularism', in *Secularism and its Critics*, ed. Rajeev Bhargava (New Delhi: Oxford University Press, 2014), p. 31.
2. Slavoj Žižek, *Event. A Philosophical Journey through a Concept* (London: Melville House, 2014), p. 74.
3. Karl Marx, 'The British Rule in India', in *On Colonialism* (Moscow: Progress Publishers, 1976), p. 40.
4. B.R. Ambedkar, 'Castes in India', in *The Essential Writings of B.R. Ambedkar*, ed. Valerian Rodrigues (New Delhi: Oxford University Press, 2008), p. 253.
5. B.R. Ambedkar, 'Annihilation of Caste', in Ibid., p. 268.
6. Ibid.
7. Ibid.
8. Riza Davari-Ardakani, *Falsafih Chist?* [What is Philosophy?] (Tehran: Anjum-I Islami-I Hikmat va Falsafih-I Iran, 1980), *Inqilab-i Islami va Vaz'-I Kununi 'Alam* [*The Islamic Revolution and the Current Conditions of the World*] (Tehran: Markaz-e Farhangi-I 'Alame Tabatabai, 1982), Quoted in Farazin Vahadat, 'Post-revolutionary Islamic Discourses on Modernity in Iran: Expansion and Contraction of Human Subjectivity', in *International Journal of Middle East Studies*, Vol. 35, Nov. 2003,

No. 4, pp. 605, 608, 610.

9. Riza Davari-Ardakani, *Falsafih Chist?* Quoted in Farazin Vahadat, 'Post-revolutionary Islamic Discourses on Modernity in Iran: Expansion and Contraction of Human Subjectivity', p. 607.
10. Karl Marx, 'To Ludwig Feuerbach in Bruckberg, Paris, August, 1844', in *Marx. Engels. Collected Works.* Vol. 3 (Moscow: Progress Publishers, 1975), 354.
11. Charles Taylor, op. cit., p. 32.
12. Ibid., p. 31.
13. Karl Marx, *Economic and Philosophic Manuscripts of 1844* (Moscow: Progress Publishers, 1982), p. 142.
14. Karl Marx, 'Civil War in France', in *Marx. Engels. Selected Works* (Moscow: Progress Publishers, 1975), p. 286.
15. See Slavoj Žižek, *Event. A Philosophical Journey Through a Concept* (Brooklyn. London: Melville House, 2014) , p. 16.
16. Frederick Engels, 'Ludwig Feuerbach and the End of Classical German Philosophy', in *Marx. Engels. Selected Works* (Moscow: Progress Publishers, 1975), p. 600.
17. Walter Benjamin, 'Theses on the Philosophy of History', in *Illuminations,* trans Harry Zohn (Glasgow: Fontana/Collins, 1979), p. 258.
18. Karl Marx, *Economic and Philosophic Manuscripts of 1844*, p. 97.
19. Ibid.
20. Vivek Chibber, *Postcolonial Theory and the Spectre of Capital* (New Delhi: Navayana, 2013), p. 8.
21. See Dipesh Chakrabarty, *Provincializing Europe. Political Thought and Historical Difference* (Princeton and Oxford: Princeton University Press, 2000), p. 149.
22. Karl Marx, 'A Contribution to the Critique of Hegel's Philosophy of Right. Introduction', in *Karl Marx. Early Writings,* trans. Rodney Livingstone (London: Penguin Books, 1992), p. 244.
23. Karl Marx, 'On the Jewish Question', in *Marx. Engels. Collected Works,* Vol. 3 (Moscow: Progress Publishers, 1975), p. 152
24. Ibid.
25. Ibid.
26. Ibid.
27. Karl Marx and Frederick Engels, *The German Ideology* (Moscow: Progress Publishers, 1975), p. 52.
28. Karl Marx, 'On the Jewish Question', p. 152.
29. Ibid., p. 154.
30. Ibid.
31. Ibid.

32. Ibid., p. 159.
33. Ibid.
34. See Karl Marx, *Capital,* Vol. I (Moscow: Progress Publishers, 83), pp. 76-87.
35. Slavoj Žižek, *The Fragile Absolute—or, Why is the Christian Legacy Worth Fighting For?* (London: Verso, 2000), p. 63.
36. Karl Marx, 'On the Jewish Question', p, 172.
37. Slavoj Žižek, *The Sublime Object of Ideology* (London: Verso, 1989), p. XIII.
38. See Karl Marx, *Capital,* Vol. I, p. 132, n.
39. Ibid., p. 133.
40. Ibid.
41. Slavoj Žižek, op.cit.
42. Karl Marx, *Capital,* Vol. III, p. 558.
43. Karl Marx, *Capital,* Vol. I, pp. 132-3.
44. Slavoj Žižek, *The Plague of Fantasies* (London: Verso, 1998), p. 5.
45. Slavoj Žižek, *The Fragile Absolute,* p. 60.
46. Karl Marx, 'On the Jewish Question', p. 152.
47. Meera Nanda, 'Intellectual Treason', in *Seminar,* 2005.
48. This take on the fascist cannibal who is in a state of denial is from Žižek recalling Eric Santner in *The Fragile Absolute,* p. 63.
49. Frederick Engels, 'Introduction to the Civil War in France', in *Marx. Engels. Selected Works* (Moscow: Progress Publishers, 1975), p. 258.
50. Karl Marx, 'To L. Kugelmann in Hanover, London, April, 12, 1871', in *Marx. Engels. Selected Works* (Moscow: Progress Publishers, 1975), p. 670.

5

Contents and Discontents of Indian Secularism

Anand Teltumbde

"Secularism is the religion of humanity; ... It is a protest against theological oppression, against ecclesiastical tyranny, against being the serf, subject or slave of any phantom, or of the priest of any phantom."

— Robert Green Ingersoll

The ideology of secularism emerged from the conflict between religious faith and human reason, which surfaced in the late middle ages. Historically, it is linked to two major interrelated processes in Europe. One, some theological developments within Protestantism that legitimated scientific investigations as a search for laws of nature that God had instituted, which gradually lent internal autonomy and legitimacy to the practitioners of scientific research without consideration of God. Two, the dominance achieved by Enlightenment rationalism in European thought from the 17th century onwards. This change began in Europe at the end of the thirty years' war[1] when the church properties started being transferred to the exclusive control of the princes. The role of church was again dampened during the French Revolution. On October 10, 1789, Charles Maurice de Talleyrand (1754–1838) had announced to the French National Assembly that the vast properties of the Church be put at the disposal of the state in exchange for salaries.[2]

The terms secular and secularization "came into use in European languages at the Peace of Westphalia in 1648, where it was used to describe the transfer of territories previously under ecclesiastical control to the dominion of lay political authorities."[3] The word "saecularis" in ecclesiastical Latin, meant the world, the profane, the base, the lowly in opposition to the church that symbolized lofty ideals, the godly, the sacred, the otherworldly and selflessness.[4] It did not mean freedom from "relegere" or independence from church neither did it mean independence from sects. The term 'secularism' was first coined in 1851 in England[5] by a social reformer named George Jacob Holyoake, to describe "a form of opinion relating to the duty if this life which substituted the piety of useful for the usefulness of piety."[6] In his journal Holyoake criticized Christianity and suggested that it should be replaced by a belief system based on reason and science. Holyoake called this new theory Secularism and inspired foundation of Secular Societies in Britain. Holyoake believed that the government should work for the benefit of the working classes and poor based upon their needs in the here and now rather than any needs they might have for a future life or for their souls. Even in his usage, secularism did not explicitly mean opposition to religion but implicitly it surely meant disdain for religions.[7] Holyoake's secularism was imbued with materialism, when he enunciated the first principle of secularism as "Theology works by "spiritual" means, Secularism by material means."[8] He certainly insisted that state should be primarily concerned with the material well-being of its people and should not have anything to do with religion. Following it, in the West, secularism stood for the separating wall between the politics and the religion and the orientation to concern with the material well-being of the people.

In India, secularism came to mean 'sarva dhrama samabhav', i.e. treating all religions with equal respect by the state. Paradoxically, this doctrine has been borrowed from the ancient text (*Upanishads*) that is associated with India's dominant religion, Hinduism. Its protagonists argue that the Western conception of secularism was not applicable to India and since religion constitutes the pivot of the lives of millions, it cannot be ignored by the state. Considering the extent of diversity of India, they tend to take it as a uniquely successful model of secularism. The empirical evidence however, problematize this consideration on several counts. Rather, the current spectacle of majority communalism threatening the integrity of India is largely attributed to peculiar conceptions of secularism observed both by right wing and liberal political parties, accusing the other of not being *secular* as per their own terms. The reality is that any conception of secularism other than as the separating wall between religion and politics, which is its established meaning in the West, necessarily creates unending arguments about secularism while the misuse of religion in politics go unabated. While India never tires claiming herself as a secular country, neither her Constitution nor her practice reflects separation of religion from politics.

This paper argues that contrary to the scholarly claims that the Western conception of secularism was not applicable to India, the unique religious demography of India with presence of all major religions and innumerable other creeds and sects; and the bitter experience of communal strife during the past seven decades establishes the need to adopt the true conception of secularism. It is also argued that the skilful avoidance of 'secularism' in the Constitution on the basis of so-called uniqueness of India were deliberate intrigues of the post-colonial ruling classes to preserve religion as the potential weapon to divide people as they were in preservation of caste in the Constitution.

Colonial Legacy

India, with its racial, ethnic, religious, linguistic, and cultural diversity, is a unique country. Moreover, India is the birthplace of major religions. Broadly, she constitutes along with Iran a region, Indo-Persian region, one of the two broad regions that produced Hinduism, Zoroastrianism and Buddhism through the Aryan race, the other being the Palestine-Arabia region that produced Hebraism, Christianity, and Islam through the Semitic race. Indian subcontinent is particularly remarkable, not only as a birthplace of religions, but also as a meeting-place and arena of conflict for all these major religions of the world. Owing to its extraordinarily rich natural endowment, people from other regions have been coming here from ancient times and getting assimilated with the local population giving India its multi-cultural, multi-racial, multi-ethnic, and multi-religious character. Brahmanism, the precursor of what came to be known as Hinduism, with its characteristic caste structure and system of rituals had hegemonic sway over the subcontinent, which despite the dominating spells of rebellious systems of thoughts like Jainism and Buddhism for centuries had remained undisturbed. Later, from the medieval times, with the advent of Islam and Christianity, the religions of rulers, many native people, initially mostly belonging to the lower castes, converted to these religions and in course of time, with the conversion of the people from the upper castes, acquired the caste hierarchy. If one takes a broad look at the society all these religions, races and cultures lived amicably in the subcontinent without any significant conflict. The idea of secularism entered India during the colonial rule but remained subdued under the pressure of colonial logic. The state feigned to distance itself from religious affairs but had given itself leeway to intervene in a calibrated manner whenever necessary. This mode eulogized by the protagonists as the model of secularism for India has informed much of the post-colonial state policy, as in most other spheres.

When the East India Company developed colonial aspirations, it adopted a conciliatory attitude towards the local elites belonging to two major communities, Hindus and Muslims. It manifested into a policy of religious neutrality. The company officials were also particularly careful not to be seen as promoting their own religion, Christianity. Warren Hastings, the first Governor General of Bengal wrote that he believed that the duty of the British was "to protect their [Indian] persons from wrong and to leave their religious need to the Being who has so long endured it and who will in his own time inform it".[9] It was a pragmatic response to the reality of trying to control millions of Indian subjects with the help of a few European and mainly *sepoy* army. In 1662, the company ordered that there would not be compulsory conversions, interference with Indian religious prejudices and killing of cows in 'Hindu Areas'.[10] This long-standing policy of non-interference was eventually codified in Section I of Bengal Regulation III of 1793 and later included in the Company's Charter of 1813 and became known as the Company's 'compact' with Indian people

Although the British policy was officially one of "religious neutrality", there were "various kinds of involvements of the East India Company in religious affairs that produced a somewhat confused interpretation of this simple phrase"[11]. There is ample evidence that the company involved in Hindu festivals and management of temples in the 1780s and even before it. It continued the prevailing traditions of royal maintenance of endowments to religious temples and shrines. The company attempted to cement local loyalties by confirming the tax-exempt status of such endowments, collecting pilgrim taxes for upkeep of shrines and their priests, giving police support and showing mark of respect such as firing salutes at the major festivals.[12] One of the indulgences of the company in religious matters, that would have far reaching consequences, was the colonial construction of separate personal laws for Indian communities. It began codification of Hindu and Muslim laws in 1772, and continued it through the next century, with emphasis on certain textual sources as the authentic sources of the law and custom of Hindus and Muslims. In the process, the company administration sought the assistance of Hindu and Muslim religious elites to understand the law, inevitably leading to the "Brahmanization and Islamization" of customary laws.[13] For example, British Orientalist scholar William Jones translated key texts such as the *Al Sirjjiyah* in 1792 as the Mohammedan Law of Inheritance; and *Manusmriti* in 1794 as the Institute of Hindu Law, or the Ordinances of Manu. In short, British colonial administrators reduced centuries of vigorous development of ethical, religious, and social systems in the subcontinent to fit their own preconceived notions of what Muslim and Hindu law should be. Similar policies were pursued through the colonial courts. In 1774 a Supreme Court was established in India, which was granted jurisdiction over natives in 1781, but Hindus and Muslims were given the right to follow native custom and law in personal matters such as inheritance, marriage, and succession.[14] The confusion about the scope of native and personal laws is clearly reflected in its conflation of religion and custom, thereby creating the legal fiction that Hindu and Muslim laws were derived from their respective scriptures, and that Hindus and Muslims were homogeneous communities following uniform laws.[15] It made personal and religious laws synonymous. The colonial process of codification rendered an over-determined religious identity of native population.

Although there were several reasons for the 1857 conflagration[16] but in popular imagination it was simplified to the colonial interference with the religious customs and traditions of the natives by both, Hindus as well as Muslims. Religious idiom played a major role in binding them together. Both communities made gross use of religion to mobilize people against the British rule.[17] The impact of the mutiny was so severe that it had shaken the colonial establishment to its core. It became extra cautious in dealing with religious matters. The British Crown assumed reins of power in India vide the Royal proclamation on November 1, 1858. It became very particular about maintaining their religious neutrality. Recognizing that one of the causes of the Mutiny had been the fear that the British intended to make all Indians Christians, Queen Victoria proclaimed that although "firmly relying ourselves upon the truth of Christianity and acknowledging with gratitude the solace of religion, we disclaim alike the right and the desire to impose our convictions on any other subjects."[18] However, to say that this neutrality and equidistance, in some sense implied a 'secular' approach would be thoroughly mistaken both from the perspective of the liberal framework within which secularism had developed in the West as also in terms of how it was materialized and staged in colonial India. Peter Robb (2002) aptly points out that:

> After all [...] secular values were quite weakly advanced both by the colonial state—In practice the state offered religious neutrality and mutual toleration. The British, for all the heated rhetoric of some missionaries, soldiers and officials, mostly took great care to avoid attacking religious sentiment. Often they gave succour to religion, respecting Brahman dietary arrangements, or giving semi-clandestine support to mosques and temples, or promoting the political identities and interests of castes and religions.[19]

Post-1857, the passive tactics of neutrality was succeeded by active strategy of conscious control of Indian population. Following the dictum, "you cannot control what you cannot measure", the colonial rulers resorted to measure everything Indian. A battery of British anthropologists, sociologists, and statisticians, was commissioned for the purpose. The anthropologists began to take all kinds of anthropometric measurements of people to categorize them into ethnic groups and to deepen their ethnic identities. The sociologists mapped their social structure, and documented their customs and traditions in order to reinforce these identities. The statisticians and demographers began counting their numbers per caste and use other sociological parameters. They all expectedly induced identity consciousness and concretize their division into castes and communities. What was an amorphous life-world of local people of the subcontinent was thus administratively defined in terms of pan Indian hierarchies. The developments in transport and communication technologies played a major role in this construction. A significant step was taken in instituting equality before law by enacting uniform codes of civil and criminal law but the personal law was continued to be governed by the respective religious laws as recognized and interpreted by the courts. In civil matters of Hindus, they relied on a *pandit*, and on a *maulavi* to settle issues concerning Muslims. They wanted this space for intervention as it allowed them to calibrate reforms in society.[20] The Madras Hindu Religious Endowments Act (1927) and the Child Marriage Restraint Act (1929) were examples of this. The reason why personal law was not brought within the scope of a uniform civil code was the reluctance of the colonial state to risk public resentment as it was intimately linked to religious doctrine and practice. The British emphasized the communitarian composition of the subcontinent right from the beginning. These conscious strategies did exacerbate the pre-existing rifts in Hindu-Muslim communities.

Attitude of the Native Elite

The colonial encounter produced two streams of reactions among the native elites: one section impressed by Western liberalism was best represented by Keshab Chandra Sen, a social reformer who attempted to incorporate Christian theology within the framework of Hindu thought. He had said in one of his speeches delivered in 1870 in London that your [British] philosophy is ours, 'we are one in thought', 'we are also intellectually united'[21]; the other section wanted to go back to the civilisational ethos of India best represented by Aurobindo as he articulated in *Bande Mataram*.[22] Whereas the ideology of the former had a low anti-British content, the latter was not (contrary to commonplace notion) necessarily anti-British. In a country like India, the elites aspiring for the 'civilizational ethos', becomes their supremacist expression, simply because the so called civilization itself is fractured. The lower strata did not necessarily share what the elites think as their civilisational ethos. The colonial rule favoured the first school, which not only supported the religious neutrality of the colonial state but also sought its intervention in religious reforms as part of the modernizing project of the country. In essence, their religious modernity provided impetus to individual freedoms by curtailing the public sphere of religion. Religion became a private concern and could not compel the community to behave in a unilinear/uniform way. The political role of the religion was marginalised as a result of religious modernity.

These two streams became pronounced after the constitution of the Indian National Congress by the western educated elite. Largely inspired by British liberalism, for quite some time it held a view (against the nationalist radicals) of relying on the Empire and merely seeking certain constitutional reforms from within its framework.[23] There was an imperative need to conduct as a unified body in negotiations with the British and hence initially it functioned purely as secular class organization without any religious divide. However, when the time for actualization of such reforms arrived, the communitarian divide began to surface. The demographic asymmetry between the Muslims and Hindus in many regions brought the demand for separate electorates or nominations for Muslims to the fore. Muslim leaders like Sir Syed Ahmed Khan had argued that the principle of one man, one vote was not suited to India, because it led to Hindu majority domination and was unfair to the Muslims and demanded separate electorates for Muslims. The Congress opposed it as based on religion and community and focused on the logic of individualism, representation and individuality and favoured joint electorates in opposition to the separate electorate. The colonial logic of course favoured the communal divide and released Morley-Minto reforms vide the Indian Councils Act in 1909 Act, which granted separate electorates for Muslims. The Congress initially opposed it but then reconciled accepting separate electorates for the minorities at its Lucknow session in 1916. Initially meant for the Muslim minority provinces, the separate electorate became an all India feature. Moreover, it provided for three-fourth of the members of the community to block any legislation that they felt harmful for the entire religious community.[24]

The two streams, mainly among the Hindu members of the Congress came to be known as Extremists and the Moderates. Although they differed on the issue of whether the Indian nation should be based on Western modernity or 'civilizational' ethos of India, there was no essential difference in their outlook with regard to the nature of the future state. There was general realization moreover that considering the religious diversity of the country no single religious identity could help it give a truly national character, which led to a compromise towards 'secularism'. It was a compromise out of practical considerations to profess inter-communal tolerance rather than taking a strongly secularist line." In order to increase national solidarity and reinforce a sense of a common anti-colonial grievance, the Congress had maintained a strategy of absorbing the different religious communities into the Indian polity rather than demanding a uniform, secular adherence to the concept of the nation."[25]

Paradoxically, the very factors necessitating the politics of secular nationalism laid the basis for particularistic religious communalism. While professing commitment to secularism, a succession of Congress leaders kept resorting to popular Hindu religious symbols as a strategy for mass-mobilization.[26] It started much before Gandhi came on the scene and transformed the Congress as a mass movement massively deploying religious idiom and symbols. There was no conflict or contradiction with the Congress when organizations like Hindu Mahasabha came into being openly promoting Hindu interests. It is generally recorded that the foundation of Hindu Mahasabha in 1915 was in response to the founding of the Muslim League in 1906 in Dhaka and the subsequent Morley-Minto Reforms of 1909 that granted communal representation to the Muslims. But this is erroneous. A brief history of the Hindu Mahasabha is that Hindu Sabhas had sprung up in Lahore in 1882, much before the birth of the Indian National Congress. These sabhas were established in almost each district of the Punjab by 1906. On the foundation of these Hindu Sabhas, Lala Lajpat Rai, Lal Chand and Shadi Lal founded the Punjab Hindu Sabha in 1909.[27] The Hindu Mahasabha was founded much later in 1914 in Amritsar with its headquarters in Hardwar, where it held its first session in 1915. From the very beginning, it was dominated by the upper class Hindu gentry. It picked up momentum among the Hindus on account of the Lucknow Pact, the Mopla atrocities on Hindus in Malabar, the Multan and Kohat riots by the Pathan fanatics. Amongst its early leaders were Pandit Madan Mohan Malaviya and Lala Lajpat Rai, who was the pivot for its precursor Hindu Sabhas in Punjab. Malaviya campaigned for Hindu political unity, for the education and economic development of Hindus as well as for the reconversion of Muslims to Hinduism. Indeed, several Congress leaders until 1930s continued to participate in the annual sessions of the Mahasabha. Although the Congress overtly wore its secular posture, in its behaviour it remained pre-dominantly a Hindu organization. Interestingly, the extremist sections of the Congress, represented by Lal, Bal, Pal (Lala Lajpat Rai, Bal Gangadhar Tilak and Bipin Chandra Pal) appear particularly active in this. The important proponents of the Extremist school espoused Hindu culture as the fount of the Indian nationhood. Lala Lajpat Rai, as stated above, was actively involved in organizing Hindu Sabhas in Punjab and later Hindu Mahasabha. He was also a leader of the Arya Samaj, whose dominant mission was *shuddhi* (reconversion of Muslims and Christians into Hinduism).[28] The partition, generally attributed to intransigence of Jinha, was actually announced openly for the first time by Lala Lajpat Rai, who was then the president of the Hindu Mahasabha in his newspaper *The Tribune* in 1925. Lokmanya Tilak basically belonged to the Chitpawan linage in Pune which revolted against the British to regain its lost kingdom in *Peshwai* (rule of Peshawas). Tilak is credited as the fountainhead of the idea of Hindutva, developed later formally by V.D. Savarkar. He had constructed the "Aryan theory of race", claiming a white racial stock for upper caste Indians and accepted *Veda*s as their core literature. Tilak was also the first to try and unite a large section of the masses around Brahmanical leadership with celebration of Ganesh festival to wean away the popular participation of lower caste people in the Muharram festival, under the influence of Sufi saints.[29] Later Tilak went on to launch celebration of birth anniversary (jayanti) of Shivaji, not as a national hero but as one who broke the Mughal hold on western India and opened the way for rampage of Maratha armies through much of India. They had as such a subtle anti-Muslim slant. Tilakites' projection of Swami Ramdas, a Brahmin, as Shivaji's guru, reflected reestablishment of the Brahminical hegemony. Tilak's nationalism thus had strong undercurrents of Brahmanical supremacy and hatred of Muslims.

Another Congress leader in the extremist triad along with Rai and Tilak, Bipin Chandra Pal (1858-1932) also believed that Hinduism is the fundamental core of Indian nationhood. He had observed: "The Indian Muslims are first Muslims, then Indians. According to the Muslim leaders like Syed Amir Ali, if the foreign Islamic countries invade India, the duties of the Indian Muslims will be to help those Muslim invaders against India, because 'Muslim identity' is more important to them."[30] Anandita Bajpai quotes Pal writing on the anniversary of the partition of Bengal: "In thy waters, Holy Mother, are mixed the two streams of Aryan and Semitic culture [...] both the Hindus and the Mahomedans have a common inheritance in art and civilisation [...] resonant with the minstrelsy of two great world-cultures.". In this seemingly exemplary construction of a Hindu-Muslim composite syncretic identity, Bajpai perceptively finds communal insinuation. She observes, "Here the Aryan culture is equated as the 'original' Indian one (essentially Hindu), whereas Islam is equated with a Semitic culture, indicating that it was indeed an 'Other', that bore an affiliation to the Middle

East rather than 'belonging' to the Indian subcontinent."[31] Even the moderates also were not behind in their Hindu projection. Madan Mohan Malaviya, a moderate member of the Congress, very close to Gandhi, who was the president of the Indian National Congress in the year 1909 and 1918, was also a vociferous proponent of the philosophy of *Bhagavad Gita*.[32]

While many Congress leaders thus tried mobilizing the Hindu masses by using religious idiom, their 'Hindu' still excluded the Untouchables, who constituted almost one-sixth of their population. It was only after the Lucknow Pact, wherein the relative numbers of Hindu and Muslim population came in discussion, the upper caste Congress leaders realized the importance of the Untouchables and commissioned their agents to work among them[33]. These religious overtures of the Congress leaders were distinctly upper castes and alienating to Muslims.

The constant references to *Bharatvarsha* for India, the term with religious overtone, were not a naive engagement of the nationalist leaders, but rather a statement, associating the country with its first Hindu king, Bharat, after which it was named and from whose story, the epics unfold. Ayesha Jalal observes, "[a] definition of the Indian nation fashioned on ideas of territoriality, found in ancient Hindu texts and popular mythology, was not seen to compromise Congress' secularism."[34] More than anyone, Gandhi, used Hindu religion to mobilize the masses. His entire persona cast into Hindu saintliness, the epithet 'mahatma' and the ideals of *ram rajya* everything had an unmistakable tinge of Hindu religion. He would often describe himself as orthodox (sanatan) Hindu. He also emphasized the inseparability of religion and politics and the superiority of the former over the latter. He wrote "those who say that religion has nothing to do with politics do not know what religion means."[35] He also said that politics separated from religion and religion detached from politics is meaningless. Later, in the 1940s, when he said that religion or denominational religion should be kept separate from politics and religion should be treated as private[36], he clarified that it was to limit the role of the state to secular welfare and not letting it interfere with the religious life of the people.[37] He had not shunned his idiom of Hinduism even in 1947, when he wrote

"My Hinduism teaches me to respect all religions. In this lies the secret of Ramarajya."[38] Nevertheless, this Gandhian conception of secularism—respect for or equal treatment of or equidistance from all religions—supposedly coming from the Hindu religion is what informed the Constitutional secularism.

This excessive Hindu symbolism of the Congress leaders led to the growing insecurity among the Muslims who apprehended that an independent India might not have adequate place for them. The emergence of the All India Muslim League in 1906, that would later advance the claim for a separate nation for the Muslims, helped feed into the construction of a dichotomous narrativization of the movement itself, whereby all associated with the Muslim League implied a politics of communalism, whereas that associated with the Congress was secular nationalism.

Secularism in the Constitution

Britain, dilapidated in the Second World War, and alarmed by the increasingly militant national struggle in India, decided to withdraw from India and ordained formation of a Constituent Assembly (CA) with the membership indirectly elected by the provincial assemblies, which were formed in 1946 with the limited franchise that represented just 28 per cent of the population. The Congress had an overwhelming majority in assemblies which was naturally carried in the CA. In order to allay such fears in its opponents, it showed strategic magnanimity in getting notable people from other parties into the CA. However, most crucial decisions were either taken by the Congress or influenced by it. Nehru presented the objective resolution which would provide a framework for the draft Constitution. Numerous subcommittees that were formed to decide on crucial issues were headed by the Congress members and their decisions thereafter had to be vetted by the Advisory Committee which comprised most Congress leaders. The make-up of the CA reflected the reality of what groups wield power in India, then as well as now. An analysis of membership in the most important advisory committees of the CA found that 6.5 per cent were SCs, whereas Brahmins made up 45.7 per cent.[39] As such, the Congress had ensured that the decisions of the CA shall eventually be its own. There was a rift in the Congress between the so-called liberals headed by Prime Minister Jawaharlal Nehru and Hindu nationalists supported by home minister Vallabhbhai Patel. When Pakistan was created as an Islamic state, some Hindus argued that the Indian Constitution should also be based on Hindu culture. However, gradually liberal and generally progressive ideas were accepted as the expedient solution in the circumstances prevailing then. The deaths of both Gandhi and Patel, particularly the latter, during the drafting of the Constitution strengthened the 'secularist' camp.

The Constitution, eulogized as one of the finest constitutions, was skilfully drafted assimilating many good provisions of other Constitutions but as it stands, much of its operative structure was lifted verbatim from the colonial constitution of 1935.[40] As such, the Indian Constitution has imbibed the governance ethos of the colonial regime including its infamous tactic of "divide and rule". The colonial state was characteristically unsecular, treating citizens differently in the eyes of the law, notwithstanding its professed policy of neutrality towards religions. One can distinctly see a similar stance in the post-colonial regime. The regime not only inherited the infamous colonial policy of 'divide and rule', it has rather excelled over it. One can easily see the divisive nature of the Constitution in two ways: (i) Incorporating different codes for different religions; and (ii) mirroring the structure of the caste-based Hindu society, the first with the pretext of the commitment to a pluralistic society, and second, for instituting affirmative action policies (reservations, etc.) in favour of certain backward castes. This necessarily violated the fundamental principle of secularism.

India's claim to be a secular country is solely based on its Constitution which ostensibly does not have any religion for its state. The Constitution of India has at least a dozen of its provisions imparting 'secular' character to the Indian state:

1. The term secular was added to the Preamble of the Constitution by the 42nd Constitutional Amendment Act of 1976.

2. The Preamble secures to all citizens of India liberty of belief, faith and worship.
3. The state shall not deny to any person equality before the law or equal protection of the laws (Article 14).
4. The state shall not discriminate against any citizen on the ground of religion (Article 15).
5. Equality of opportunity for all citizens in matters of public employment (Article 16).
6. All persons are equally entitled to freedom of conscience and the right to freely profess, practise and propagate any religion (Article 25).
7. Every religious denomination or any of its section shall have the right to manage its religious affairs (Article 26).
8. No person shall be compelled to pay any taxes for the promotion of a particular religion (Article 27).
9. No religious instructions shall be provided in any educational institution maintained by the state (Article 28).
10. Any section of the citizens shall have the right to conserve its distinct language, script or culture (Article 290).
11. All minorities shall have the right to establish and administer educational institutions of their choice (Article 30).
12. The state shall endeavour to secure for all the citizens a Uniform Civil Code (Article 44).

The concept of secularism adopted in the Constitution is quite different from its established conception in the West. The constitution guarantees freedom of religion as a fundamental right to all citizens. On the face of it, this appears to be as secular as any other constitution. However, unlike the first amendment of the American constitution, which specifically prohibits the making of any law 'respecting an establishment of religion, or prohibiting the free exercise thereof' and or the Australian Constitution which has similar provisions for the separation of state and religion, the Indian Constitution does not have any such "non-establishment" clause erecting a "wall of separation" between state and religion, and no space for the French doctrine of *lacite*.[41] Religion has no substantive role to play in the affairs of the state, but there is no ban on allowing it a ceremonial role in state functions and official events. Conversely, the state is not at all prevented by law from playing a role in the affairs of religion and has, in fact, always held a pivotal position in this area of social life. As a matter of fact, the Constitution did not contain the word 'secular' till it was introduced in the preamble in 1976 by the 42nd amendment. Copland points out that the term 'secular' was deliberately omitted by Nehru, who understood what true secularism was, and did not want it included in the Constitution.[42] The Indian Constitution digresses from the principles of secularism, not only in ways of separating state and religion, but also in its equal treatment of citizens. The Constitution provided for the state intervention into religion with an alibi to carry out reform in the society. But looking back no such reform was actually carried out except for the Sati Prevention Act, aimed to abolish the practice of burning a Hindu widow on the pyre with her husband, came into effect only in 1987, i.e. forty years after independence, in the wake of national indignation over the burning of a 17-year-old Roop Kanwar on her husband's pyre in Rajasthan. Clearly, reform was not the priority of those who drafted the Indian Constitution and made the laws.

As regards religious freedom, the Preamble to the Constitution speaks of securing the people of India, inter alia, "liberty of thought, expression, belief, faith and worship" and the chapter on Fundamental Rights guarantees them freedom of conscience and the right to "profess, practise and propagate" religion—clarifying that this right is not absolute and can be restricted by the state in the interest of public order, morality, health, and other provisions of the Constitution. At the same time, all religious communities and every "denomination thereof" are guaranteed freedom to manage their own affairs in religion, acquire and manage property and establish institutions for religious and charitable purposes.[43] The Constitution, however, makes it specifically clear that these guarantees for religious freedom will not preclude the state from introducing social reforms by law or from "regulating or restricting any economic, financial, political or other secular activity which may be associated with religious practice."[44]

Though the Constitution does not specify any "preferred

or privileged" religion, it has some special religion-based provisions relating to the majority community. For instance, it declares that "untouchability"—an age-old practice associated with Hindu religion—is abolished and its practice in any form is prohibited. [Article 17] On the other hand, the chapter on Directive Principles of State Policy under the Constitution directs the state to protect by law the holy cow (without, of course, a reference to the Hindu reverence for it [Article 48]. Moreover, certain denominational Hindu temples in two South Indian states—Kerala and Tamil Nadu—must, by a constitutional dictate, receive prescribed subsidies from public funds. [Article 290-A] There is no provision in the Constitution directing the state to remain neutral to religious issues; nor does it specifically ask the state to cooperate with the religious communities in respect to their faith affairs. With regard to secularism, the mandate is only for non-discrimination between people on religious grounds. The silence of the Constitution on secularism is taken as tacit approval for state intervention in religious affairs of all communities, and all organs of the state—legislature, executive and judiciary—have accordingly been taking active interest in such affairs in a way that may be inconceivable under a truly secular political set up.

Post-Colonial State

The political class skilfully preserved castes and religious identities in the Constitution as potential weapons to be used to divide people to their advantage. It created a mirage of socialist, democratic, republican India during the anti-colonial struggle and pasted it as the motto of the Constitution but actually they continued with the same colonial strategies with added zeal and an advantage of being an insider. In the early decades after independence, the Congress did not have any significant rival in politics but in its anxiety to fortify its hegemony, it tried to carve out a congenial class of rich farmers in rural India. While it worked to some degree for the Congress, it gave rise to regional parties making electoral politics increasingly competitive. Here came the importance of castes and religion as both represented collectivity of votes which could be manoeuvred far more cheaply than if they were independent individual votes. Even a small bunch of votes could make or unmake a victory in the first-past-the-post type of election system, the adoption of which was itself not without a strategy. Every political party competitively indulged in wooing castes and religious communities. Many parties sprang up purely on the basis of caste and religious identities and they enjoyed legitimacy of Indian secularism. Blatant abuse of religious symbols in politics became so commonplace that it may be awkward to think of them being violative of law. The character of politics is inevitably reflected in the character of the state. Majority of people manning the state apparatus naturally belong to the majority religion, who without any potent constitutional arrester openly bring in their religious prejudices to bear on state functions to the detriment of minorities.

The constitutional state in India is popularly assumed to comprise three independent wings: legislature, executive and judiciary, as a mechanism of internal checks and balances. In theory itself this assumption did not hold: the elected representatives of people head the executive as ministers as well as sit in parliament/legislative assemblies as law makers. In practice, they are indistinguishable. The professional bureaucracy separated from politicians could have exercised some amount of check but it was not to be. Being based on the colonial model, it inherited the colonial ethos that basically separated it from the masses and integrated with the political masters. The resultant nexus not only helped both, politicians and bureaucracy, expropriate state resources with impunity for their self-aggrandizement but also turned the state undemocratic in consequence. Secularism as the correlate of democracy became necessary casualty. Judiciary was the only wing that had a semblance of separation from this unholy combine, as it was in the colonial times, which therefore served to provide much needed legitimacy to the state.

The state in India is supposed to present itself as a neutral entity by recognizing all religions and their social practices. However in practice, religious rituals, often with a preference for the Hindu, form a part of public functions held under the auspices of the state.[45] It is commonplace to see the government offices including police stations adorned with the pictures of (sometimes statuettes) Hindu gods and goddesses. Every state function starts with lighting of five lamps in the Hindu tradition and singing some hymn from the Hindu religion. The schools run or supported by the state begin with some prayer to a Hindu god or goddess. It is not unusual to find a quasi Hindu temple in state-run educational institutions such as IITs. Even the judiciary is not immune to this overt Hindu ritualism. Three years ago, one activist, Raju Solanki, of the Council for Social Justice, an Ahmedabad-based organization, had filed a case in the Gujarat High Court against its chief justice and other judges for violating the provisions of secularism in the Indian Constitution by having a Hindu ritual performed for laying the foundation stone for the new building of the High Court. He had attached photographs of the function in testimony, which showed a Hindu priest performing *yagna* and the chief justice of the high court among other judges sitting as hosts. The Gujarat High Court did not deny the facts but dismissed the petition as frivolous and slapped a fine of Rs. 20,000 on Solanki. He had challenged this verdict in the Supreme Court but even it upheld the High Court judgement, justifying that it was a custom and not any religious ritual.

The constitutional ambiguity necessarily reflects in judicial acrobatics while dealing with religious matters. While it easily dismisses complaints against observance of rites of a particular religion by the state functionary, and the judicial officials at that, as frivolous, it can willingly entertain issues like whether Ram was born at the spot as claimed by the Hindus or what is essential and non-essential in a religious practice, perhaps following the true legacy of the colonial regime. The decision whether a particular practice is essential to a religion or not is obviously difficult because sometimes practices, religious and secular, are inextricably mixed up, and 'what is religion to one is superstition to another'. But the courts have decided such matters going into the doctrines of that religion. Sometime, these interpretations have been progressive as in the case of the appointment of a non-Brahman priest in Kerala to perform ritual worship the Supreme Court[46] had rejected the claim of the Brahmans and upheld the appointment saying:

> Any custom or usage irrespective of even any proof of their existence in pre-constitutional days cannot be countenanced as a source of law to claim any rights when it is found to violate human rights, dignity, social equality and the specific mandate of the Constitution and law made by Parliament. No usage which is found to be pernicious and considered to be in derogation of the law of the land or opposed to public policy or social decency can be accepted or upheld by courts in the country.[47]

There were many such judgements, with questionable interpretation of scriptural sources or objective assessment of the religious customs but certainly alluding to the progressive stance of the judiciary. In a case, the Supreme Court would bring in the Constitutional provision on the Fundamental Duty of the citizens dismissing the community view and caution people against treating 'superstition' as religion[48] and "to develop scientific temper, humanism and spirit of inquiry and reform."[49] However, in other cases such as challenging the laws against the killing of cows on the basis of religious freedom and freedom of vocation and profession, the courts have invariably upheld the laws saying that "ours being a secular state is not relevant" in judging an administrative action taken under such a law.[50] The courts obviously face a dilemma in following conflicting provisions of the Constitution in regard to secularism. For instance, in one of the judgements, it said, "The Constitution has not erected a strict wall of separation between the church and the state. We have grave doubts whether the expression "secular state" as it denotes a definite pattern of relationship can with propriety be applied to India... There are provisions in our Constitution, which make one hesitate to characterize our state as secular... Secularism in the context of our Constitution means only an attitude of live and help live." (AIR, 1974: 1434). This fluidity in the Constitutional provisions has enabled propaganda by the majoritarian communal party to accuse the state of pseudo-secularism and inflame the hatred for the religious minorities.

Several states have enacted legislation to prevent conversion by force, fraud or allurement making such conversion a punishable offence. Such statutes are constitutionally valid because forcible conversions impinge on the 'freedom of conscience' guaranteed to all the citizens of the country alike. In a decision which has been very heavily criticized both by scholars and the media across the country, the Supreme Court has construed the word 'propagate' very narrowly. According to the Court the right to propagate was not a right to convert another person to one's own religion, but only to transmit or spread one's religion by an exposition of its tenets. The Constitution envisages homogeneity to be brought about in respect of all aspects of Civil Law applicable to all Indians and Article 44 says that 'the state shall endeavour to secure for the citizens a uniform civil code throughout the territory of India'. Nevertheless, the state's right of regulation has not been exercised in respect of personal laws of religious communities relating to marriage, divorce, adoption and inheritance or succession although laws relating to marriage, inheritance and adoption can hardly be said to be an intrinsic part of religion. The reluctance of the state is not a question of Constitutional power but political expediency. To a large extent uniformity in civil law has already been brought about within the different faiths. The British sought to introduce uniformity in civil laws as a measure of administrative convenience, and succeeded to a large extent. Thus, there was the Muslim Law (Shariat) Application Act, 1937, the Parsi Marriage and Divorce Act, 1936, the Christian Marriage Act, 1872 and the Indian Divorce Act, 1869. The Shariat Act removed the differences between the different sects of Muslims such as the Khojas and Kutchi Memons of Gujarat and the Malsan Muslims with regard *inter alia* to inheritance. Under strict Hanafi Law, there was no provision enabling a Muslim woman to obtain a decree dissolving her marriage on the failure of the husband to maintain her or on his deserting her or maltreating her and it was the absence of such a provision entailing (according to the Legislature) 'unspeakable misery in innumerable Muslim women' that was responsible for the Dissolution of the Muslim Marriages Act, 1939. The Christian Marriage Act similarly applies equally to the various sects of all Christians. After independence, this process of uniformity in personal laws was continued. Till the 1950s, Hindus in different regions and belonging to different sects had different personal laws and practices. These were brought under one umbrella by the Hindu Code Bills which made the various personal laws uniformly applicable to all Hindus. For example, new concepts such as monogamy, divorce and inheritance by females were introduced despite vociferous opposition by the Hindu Marriage Act, 1955 and the Hindu Succession Act, 1956 respectively. Therefore at present, the laws relating to succession, marriages, and adoption are governed by the personal laws of the different faiths. All other aspects of personal Civil Law are covered by statutes which apply to all Indians irrespective of their faith. Unfortunately the effort to secure a uniform civil code has taken on a communal hue. It is resisted by the minority religious communities as it is seen as an attempt by Hindu fundamentalists to take away their cultural identity and survival. The distrust is heightened by the insistence of the Hindu fundamentalists on a uniform code to eliminate so-called 'special privileges' to 'pampered minorities'.

In a leading case, the Supreme Court of India stated that secularism is "more than a passive attitude of religious tolerance; it is a positive concept of equal treatment of all religions," asserting at the same time that "when the state allows citizens to profess and practise religion it does not either explicitly or impliedly allow them to introduce religion into non-religious and secular activities of the state."[51] The idea that *Hindutva* was much more than merely a religious ideology once got active support from the country's apex court, but, as it evoked public outcry, the court had to issue a supplementary decision that its ruling did not mean to dilute the Indian concept of secularism.[52] The Constitution , it is argued, does not say or even remotely suggest that religion is to be the foundation or source of state law. Parliament and state legislatures are empowered to make laws in the areas of personal status, family relations and religious endowments, shrine management and organization of inland and overseas pilgrimages, without saying that these are to be drawn on religious sources. But in practice, religious tenets are usually kept in mind while enacting such laws. Legislative enactments and administrative regulations in these areas—both those of the pre-Constitution era since retained and those enacted later—contain provisions based on religious sources..

As the religion and state are not separated, there is no differentiation between the state functionaries and private people in the society. This naturally gives an edge to the majority community to hegemonies the state sphere. There is no arresting their religious practice in state affair. Entire bureaucracy and particularly police display open communal bias. It is a fact that the state has systematically demonized Muslims among people. In any terrorist act, the police liberally round up innocent Muslim boys and incarcerate them in jails for years without any evidence. There is too much prejudice against them in every state.

Conclusion

Much is made of India's uniqueness in denying applicability of progressive principles taken as coming from the West, to the sole detriment of people. The argument is not applied while adopting capitalism or neoliberalism which admittedly are the credo of the imperialist West. It should be clear that this 'uniqueness' argument is a spurious argument and is only used to keep the masses of people in bondage. The Indian ruling classes typically used this alibi avoiding secularism being incorporated in the Constitution.[53] The version of their 'secularism' is nothing but the continuance of the colonial policy with regard to religion as in many other matters. Religion and castes were proven masterly weapons in the colonial arsenal of governance, which the ruling classes would not easily let go of. Both were skilfully preserved in the Constitution while projecting the state to be 'secular' (non-religious) and against castes. The havoc these ruling class intrigues unleashed on the Indian people is legion. The upsurge of the right wing Sangh Parivar and its political outfit Bharatiya Janata Party to power, blatantly professing Hindu nationalism and proclaiming India as the *Hindu rashtra*, well under the Constitution, is solely attributable to these intrigues. While the minorities are systematically castigated as 'the other' of the religious majority and reduced to the status of second class citizenship, the scholarly quibble over the Indian version of secularism continues unabated. It is time we understood that the only meaning of the term secularism is to have a separating wall between politics and religion and the only conclusion it entails is that India is not a secular country.

It is important to understand that the post-colonial ruling classes are basically continuing the colonial policies vis-a-vis the masses. The issue of secularism is sacrificed at the altar of the sterile debate over what is true secularism, giving rise to accusation of communalism and pseudo-secularism by the rival camps. It may be important to note that at every significant node in the process of BJP's rise, the misdoing of the Congress has been responsible. It may even be traced to the colonial rule that left behind much of its foundation. For instance, the record of correspondence at the India Office, London, showed in the case of the Ramjanmabhumi issue that the British had erected a fence to separate the Babri Masjid and Ram chabutra in Ayodhya, allowing the inner court to be used by Muslims and the outer court by Hindus in 1859 as part of the infrastructure for their two nation theory. It is adequately noted that the BJP's rise was basically facilitated by the wrong moves by Rajiv Gandhi in handling the Shah Bano case and opening the locks of the Ram Lalla temple. It is also clear that its growth is catalyzed by the neoliberal paradigm which is known to have promoted fundamentalism and right wing ideologies all over the world. The West and elsewhere where secularism operated as a firewall between religion and politics, these tendencies could not surface in a menacing manner as in the countries which had manipulated secularism to leave space for mixing religion with politics. India being the ideal example of the latter, it naturally finds its resonance.

The argument of the protagonists of the Indian version of secularism that it was "practically impossible to strictly separate every religious from every non-religious practice" only gave rise to the truncated concept of secularism, which is what we have. It leaves spaces for politics to selectively exploit secularism and in process helps the majority community create its antithetical Frankenstein. The question whether it was possible to separate religion form the state could well be answered in the affirmative if one understands that secularism is necessarily a conscious attitude which is innately alien to the popular ethos but still needs to be effectualized with the conviction that religious influence on politics would render it retrogressive and therefore undesirable. Secularism is a conscious choice of the polity and needs to be implemented consciously. Any religion at the level of masses, reduces to other worldliness that naturally alienates man from man; promotes irrationality; becomes an identity marker, all of which is potentially injurious to heterogeneous polity. If the state proposes to promote a scientific attitude in people, as the Constitution mandates it, it ought to negate religion. Both, religious beliefs and the scientific attitude cannot coexist. Because it is not possible to wish away religion from people's lives, it should be confined to people's private affairs and should be prevented to enter politics.

NOTES AND REFERENCES

1. The Thirty Years' War was a series of wars in Central Europe between 1618 and 1648. It was one of the longest, most destructive conflicts in European history, which began when the Holy Roman Emperor Ferdinand II of Bohemia attempted to curtail the religious activities of his subjects, sparking rebellion among Protestants. The war came to involve the major powers of Europe, with Sweden, France, Spain and Austria all waging campaigns primarily on German soil. It ended with a Treaty of Westphalia, the first truly European settlement in history, which helped to end the age of religious wars. The greatest achievement of these wars was elimination of the role of religion in European politics. Lee, Stephen J., *The Thirty Years War*, Routledge, New York, 2001, also, Wilson, Peter H., *Europe's Tragedy: A New History of the Thirty Years War*, Penguin Books, London, 2009.
2. Greenbaum, Louis S., *Talleyrand, Statesman Priest: The Agent-General of the Clergy and the Church of France at the End of the Old Regime*, Catholic University of America Press, Washington, DC, 1970.
3. Eliade, Mircea (ed.), *The Encyclopaedia of Religion*, Macmillan, New York, Vol. 13, 1987, p. 159.
4. Nunn, H.P.V., *An Introduction to Ecclesiastical Latin*, Cambridge University Press, Cambridge, 1927 (2013), p. 137.
5. Madan T.N, Secularism in Its Place, *The Journal of Asian Studies*, Vol. 46, No. 4 (November 1987), pp. 747-759.
6. Holyoake, George Jacob, *English Secularism: A Confession of Belief*, The Open Court Publishing Company, Chicago, 1896 (digitial

version), p. 60.
7. Holyoake said, "Religious moralism is a term I might use, since it binds a man to humanity, which religion does not." Ibid., p. 80.
8. Ibid., p. 38.
9. Wild, A., *The East India Company: Trade and Vonquest from 1600*, HarperCollins, London, 1999, p. 162.
10. Mayhew, A., Christianity and Government in India, Faber & Gwyer, London, 1929, p. 39.
11. Smith, D.E. "India as a Secular State" in Rajeev Bhargava (ed.), *Secularism and Its Criticism*, Oxford University Press, Delhi, 1999, p. 189.
12. Penelope, Carson, *The East India Company and Religion, 1698-1858*, Boydell Press, New York, 2012, p. 15.
13. Agnes, Flavia. *Law and Gender Inequality: The Politics of Women's Rights in India*, Oxford University Press, New Delhi, 1999, p. 44.
14. An-Na'îm, Abdullahi Ahmad, *Islam and the Secular State: Negotiating the Future of Shari'a*, Harvard University Press, Cambridge, 2008, p. 149.
15. Agnes, op. cit., 1999, p. 43.
16. Srivastava, M.P., *The Indian Mutiny, 1857*, Chugh, Allahabad, 1979, p. 24.
17. Ray, Rajat Kanta, *The Felt Community: Commonalty and Mentality before the Emergence of Indian Nationalism*, Oxford University Press, New Delhi, 2003, pp. 354-355.
18. Neill, Stephen, *A History of Christianity in India: 1707-1858*, Cambridge University Press, Cambridge, 1985, p. 472.
19. Robb, Peter, *A History of India*, Palgrave, New York, 2002, pp. 300-301.
20. Anand, Anchal, The Curious Case of Indian Secularism. Available at *mercury.ethz.ch/service engine/Files/ISN/152307/.../ Chapter+7-1.pdf. Last accessed on 04 July 2015.*
21. Desikachar, S.V. (ed) *Readings in the Constitutional History of India*, Oxford University Press, Delhi, 1983, p. 303 cited in Himanshu Roy, Western Secularism and Colonial Legacy in India, *Economic and Political Weekly*, January 14, 2006, pp. 158-165.
22. Ibid.
23. Kulke, Hermann and Dietmar Rothermund, *A History of India*, Routledge, New York, 2004, p. 260.
24. Himanshu Roy, op. cit.
25. Morey, Peter and Alex Tickell (eds.), *Alternative Indias: Writing, Nation and Communalism*, Rodopi, Amsterdam, 2005, p. xvi.
26. Jalal, A., *Democracy and Authoritarianism in South Asia*, Cambridge

University Press, Cambridge 1995, p. 25.

27. Bapu, Prabhu, *Hindu Mahasabha in Colonial North India, 1915-1930: Constructing Nation and History*, Routledge, New York, 2013, p. 17.
28. Berglund, Henrik, Religion and Nationalism: Politics of BJP, *Economic and Political Weekly*, Vol. 39, No. 10 (March 6, 2004), pp. 1064-1070.
29. Morey, Peter and Alex Tickell, op. cit., p. 14.
30. Pal, Bipin Chandra, 'Rashtraniti', *Bijaya*, 1319 Bangabda. Available at http://eminentpeopleonislam.blogspot.in/2013/08/bipin-chandra-pal-1858-1932.html. Last accessed: 02.07.2015.
31. Bajpai, Anandita, Imagining a 'Secular' India: Roots, Offshoots and Future Trajectories of the Secularism Debate in India, Südasien-Chronik - South Asia Chronicle 2/2012, Available at *edoc.hu-berlin.de/suedasien/band-2/189/PDF/189.pdf. Last accessed 04 July 2015.*
32. Mahajan, Vidya Dhar and Savitri Mahajan, *Constitutional History of India, Including the Nationalist Movement* (6th edition), S. Chand, Delhi, 1971.
33. Mendelsohn, Oliver, and Marika Vicziany, *The Untouchables: Subordination, Poverty, and the State in Modern India,* Cambridge University Press, Cambridge, 1998, p. 28.
34. Jalal, A., op. cit., p. 26.
35. Gandhi, M.K., *An Autobiography or The Story of My Experiments with Truth,* (1929), Navjivan Publishing House, Ahmedabad, 1940, p. 383.
36. Mallick, Md. Ayub, Contextualizing the Concept of Secularism in India, *International Journal of Humanities and Social Science Invention*, www.ijhssi.org, Vol. 2, Issue 5 , May 2013, pp. 39-45.
37. The actual quote is: "If I were a dictator, religion and state would be separate. I swear by my religion. I will die for it. But it is my personal affair. The state has nothing to do with it. The state would look after your secular welfare, health, communications, foreign relations, currency and so on, but not your or my religion. That is everybody's personal concern!" See, Iyer, Raghavan ed., *The Moral and Political Writings of Mahatma Gandhi.* Vol. 1: *Civilization, Politics, and Religion.* Oxford: Clarendon Press, 1986, p. 395.
38. *Harijan*, October 19, 1947.
39. Jaffrelot, Christophe, *India's Silent Revolution*, Hurst & Co. London, 2008, citing research by G. Austin in *The Indian Constitution*, Appendix III.
40. Copland, Ian, "What's in a name? India's tryst with secularism,"

Commonwealth & Comparative Politics 48, No. 2, (April 2010), p. 1.

41. Principle of laïcité, is the principle of French secularity stipulating absence of religious involvement in government affairs as well as absence of government involvement in religious affairs. French secularism has a long history but its current version is based on the 1905 French Law on the Separation of the Churches and the State.
42. Copland, Ian, op. cit.
43. *S.R. Bommai v. Union of India* (1994) 3 SCC 1. Article 26.
44. Article 25 (2).
45. Panikkar, K.N., Introduction. In Panikkar K.N. (ed.), *Communalism in India*, Manohar Publications, New Delhi 1991, p. 10.
46. N. Adithyan v. Travancore Devaswom Board & Ors. (2002 8 SCC 106).
47. See more at: http://indiatogether.org/combatlaw/vol3/issue4/flipflop.htm#sthash.IjOTFATl.dpuf. Last accessed on 04 July 2015.
48. *Durgah Committee v. Syed Hussain* AIR 1961 SC 1402.
49. Constitution of India 1950, Article 51-A (h).
50. State of West Bengal v Ashutosh Lahiri AIR 1995 SC 464.
51. *SR Bommai v. Union of India* (1994) 3 SCC 1.
52. See the multiple so-called "Hindutva judgments" and the clarification ruling, all reported in the 1996 volume of *Supreme Court Cases*.
53. The inclusion of secularism in the preamble, paradoxically during the state of emergency, does not mean anything because the preamble merely spells a vision and does not constitute an operative part of the Constitution. As a matter of fact, the entire preamble stands as a crude joke on the Indian people.

6

Discourses on Nationalism and Question of Secular State

K. Srinivasulu

With the rise of the Hindutva as a major politico-ideological influence in Indian politics and the expansion of the BJP and *sangh parivar* in the civil and political society arenas as an organizational expression of the Hindutva and the BJP's coming to power at the Centre and in the states during the 1990s has brought the secular credentials of the Indian state into question. The understanding of Indian politics in the last couple of decades, dominated as it is by electoral analysis, has inclined to view political change in terms of party competition, shifts in social bases and regime change. As a result, the underlying paradigm shift marked by the political rise of the BJP has largely been ignored or underplayed. Thus there is a hiatus in the understanding of the electoral and larger social and political processes of Indian politics. The discussion on the electoral and political processes has largely been framed unrelated to ideological shift brought about by the BJP.

This paper seeks to examine the deeper shifts underlying Indian electoral politics and regime change by focusing on the changing conceptual relations characterizing the paradigm shift in Indian politics. This is sought to be attempted by problematising the assumed conceptual relationship between nationalism and secularism in the dominant historiography of Indian nationalism and theorization of Indian state.

This presentation seeks to make sense of the politico-ideological change marked by the ascendancy of the BJP in terms of conflict between different notions of India, nationalism and secularism being two important axes on which the idea of India is premised. Thus the political contestation between the Congress and the BJP in a significant sense is an ideological conflict between the dominant secular nationalism and Hindutva nationalism.

The argument is presented as follows:

Firstly, it attempts to go beyond the dominant political analysis cantered around electoral politics to map the nature of discursive contestations underlying the political change in India; Secondly, it discusses the nature of nationalism in India in comparison to the Western trajectory of nationalism. Thirdly, it maps the trajectory of the dominant frame of secular nationalism and examines its internal weaknesses and limitations. Lastly, the challenge of the Hindutva nationalist project to the secular nationalism is examined to show how the former's expansion is related to the limitations of the latter.

I

In the existing analyses of Indian politics, in comparison to BJP's electoral spread, its ideological contestation that sought to put mainstream dominant nationalism of the Congress on the defensive is paid less attention. The BJP's ideological expansion is two-pronged. It consists of an aggressively negative ideological campaign against the Congress at the national level and the attack on secular regional parties in different regional theatres on the one hand and the positive emphasis on the Hindutva as cultural nationalism that is projected to be in the true spirit of India's historical ethos on the other hand. By implication the dominant nationalism becomes an ideological trend that is not in tune with the Indian indigeneity but is seen as a derivative of the western provenance. Further it also presumes that Hinduism is inherently a plural cultural tradition that is diverse, tolerant and accommodative. Secularism and tolerance is thus assumed to be part of India's past but not alien to its ethos. What has been circulated and propagated as secularism is alien and unreflective of the Indian tradition. The characterization of Congress nationalism as 'pseudo-secularism' follows from the above position is a clear instance of the undermining and even rejection of nationalism-secularism combine implicit in Congress' political stand as historically a transplant and unsuitable to India as a nation.

The contestation and the debate on secularism deep down is related to the question of nationalism. The contention of this paper is that the deeper processes informing the political change are related to contestation on nationalism.

In the politics of India in the post-Emergency period and especially in the last couple of decades, the political contestation has assumed a significant politico-ideological character. Political analysts have sought to understand these developments in terms of electoral contestation between the Congress, BJP and different regional parties that dominate specific regional political theatres. The view of Indian politics seen through the prism of party competition is only a surface view.

But what is lost sight of are the deeper processes involving significant ideological contestation between different visions of India with the questions of the idea of India, nation/nationalism, the nature of socio-economic and political transformation being central to them.

Since the 1990s, India's political history, despite fuzziness, can be said to revolve around contestations between three visions of India as a nation. They are:

1. The declining vision of the Congress drawn from the nationalist legacy that claims to building a modern, secular and just India;
2. Rise and expansion of Hindutva agenda; and,
3. The Dalit-Bahujan vision of India drawing on the resources of anti-caste movements and the thought of Phule and Ambedkar.

II

Historically the emergence and growth of nationalism as the basis of the formation of nations and nation-states is closely related to the development of capitalism. This is evident from the history of nationalism in western Europe. Nationalism can be defined as the socio-political and cultural-ideological complex that paves the way for the formation of a nation. A nation can theoretically be defined as a historically evolved community formed on the basis of a common language and cultural identity within a territorial boundary for a stable market and organized political power. Nation-state was the political framework that was historically required by the emergent bourgeoisie to claim a territory as its own to create and to organize the state power and to control the economy and market.

The path of capitalist development and of nation-states has witnessed a wide range of variations. Despite the empirical diversity, it is theoretically possible to identify two distinct models of development of nationalism: namely, the 'classical' and 'belated' models.

In the classical model, it is the capitalist class that assumed the lead role in organization of the modern market and process of capital accumulation, its cultural and ideological hegemony on the principles of bourgeois rationality through the medium of a common language within a nation-state political space. The Western European experience with the nation-state formation is the basis of charactering the 'classical path' of development of nationalism.

Critical to the idea of a nation is the emergence of what Benedict Anderson calls a sense of 'imagined community' (Anderson 1983). In Anderson's view, the development of capitalism and the process of urbanization and individualization resulted in the dissolution of the old face-to-face groups. On the debris of this old society emerged new identity of nation defined as an imagined community where "the members of even the smallest nation will never know most of their fellow-members, meet them, or even hear of them, yet in the minds of each lives the image of their communion." (Anderson 1983:15).

The act of imagining is crucial for the national formations. The means through which this becomes possible are provided by print capitalism. The growth of print capitalism, according to Anderson, created conditions for the emergence of "a new way of linking fraternity, power and time meaningfully together." (Anderson 1983: 40). The role of print capitalism in creating "languages of power", with certain dialects playing a dominant part in communication through printing is to be noted. The possibility created by print capitalism of "growing number of people to think about themselves, and to relate themselves to others, in profoundly new ways" (Anderson 1983: 40) was the basis on which people could imagine themselves as a community that forms the basis of crystallization of nationality identity.

Europe thus witnessed an "explosive, interaction between a system of production and productive relations (capitalism), a technology of communications (print), and the fatality of human linguistic diversity" (Anderson 1983: 46) resulting in the nation-state formation.

The process of formation of the nation has been problematic in the belated capitalist countries like India. The nation formation in India has to be understood against the backdrop of colonial rule, historical regional diversity and cultural complexity. The uneven and retarded development of capitalism largely due to the fact of colonialism has impacted on the nation formation in India. The relative structural weakness of the bourgeoisie here rendered it inadequate to accomplish a thorough going economic and social transformation. As a result, the economy remained unevenly developed with the classes of earlier modes of production still remaining dominant.

The weak structural position of the bourgeois class is evident in its lack of initiative and leadership in the civil society. Because of its organic weakness in the civil society, the class failed to organize the bourgeois cultural and intellectual hegemony and leaves the ideological and cultural space to pre-capitalist ideologies making it amorphous without a critical organizing principle.

The bourgeois weakness in the organization of consent and hegemony in civil society had its impact on the formation of national consciousness. This could be seen the inability of the Indian nationalist movement to bring about any deep ideological transformation. Despite the nationalist movement being a modern progressive movement the uncritical and profuse use of Hindu dharmic and caste ideologies and Gandhian moralism in the nationalist discourse was largely because of the incomplete character of bourgeois hegemony.

Against the above background we have to understand the nation-state formation and the unfolding ideological and political contestations in contemporary India.

III

Both the secular nationalism of the Congress and the Hindutva nationalism posit the sense of nation on to the past. All nationalist projects attempt to politically and ideologically use history to construct and reconstruct the past to give themselves a sense of historical rootedness and authenticity. This is despite the fact that the idea of nation is hardly three centuries old and the fact that except territorially being under a certain ruling dynasty, objectively there was hardly any possibility of there being an idea of Bharat or India.

This myth of historical rootedness of nationalism from ancient times is best expressed by Jawaharlal Nehru, the most articulate representative of Congress nationalism, in his *Discovery of India* as follows[1]:

> Though outwardly there was diversity and infinite variety among our people, everywhere there was that tremendous impress of oneness, which had held all of us together for ages past, whatever political fate or misfortune had fallen us. [p. 38]

His exuberance becomes evident when he says,

> The unity of India was no longer merely an intellectual conception for me; it was an emotional experience which overpowered me. [p. 38]

The link with the past becomes emphatic when he states,

> and yet have been *throughout these ages distinctively Indians*, with the same national heritage and same set of moral and mental qualities. [p. 40]

Nehru falls short of concretely defining/negotiating with the same national heritage, oneness, same set of moral and mental qualities, and emotional experience. The unity is an assumption while diversity has been a fact of history.

The ambiguity in Nehru's *Discovery of India*'s past—in fact becomes the strength of Hindutva nationalism.

In the context of critical historical scholarship on India, the above views of Nehru can only be said to constitute a myth that is sought to be constructed to serve the purpose of Congress-led nationalist movement. Nehru's inability to concretely define and demonstrate and negotiate with the "tremendous impress of oneness", and "the same national heritage and same set of moral and mental qualities" is more than his personal failure, demonstrates the limitations of the Congress nationalist project to identify and state clearly the historical faultlines in Indian society. The reluctance to ask and find solutions to the fundamental question of, for instance, caste as the dividing factor forms the foundational weakness of dominant nationalist project.

The nation-building and state-building project in Nehru is assumed to be consequent upon the process of modernity. With the transition of India from tradition to modernity, the power and importance of caste and religion, the two significant pre-modern identities and institutions, would weaken and gradually recede from the public domain with secular citizen identity assuming pre-eminence. The developmentalist solution to the caste question has proved to be a misdiagnosis of the issue for, with the process of development the caste instead of losing its importance has gained potency.

If the internal weaknesses of the Congress nationalist movement to emerge as the hegemonic project leaving large sectors of society and culture uninfluenced is one factor then its inability to pursue the social question within the so-called Hindu society and the use, sometimes cynical, of religion and caste for electoral gains has only shown its ideological and political weaknesses and limitations. The Congress' hegemonic secularism from above with its compromises of all sorts and playing with religious identities dictated by the compulsions of power politics has strengthened the existing social divides and furthered their reproduction through electoral strategies and rhetoric and policy initiatives.

The failures and weaknesses on the part of the Congress which ruled India uninterruptedly for three decades has to be seen as creating the basis for the rise and consolidation of the Hindutva forces.

IV

Hindutva Nationalist Project

When Nehru's conception of nationalism emphasized the territorial and geographical characteristics in the definition of India as a nation, the Hindutva premised its notion of India as a nation on the religious cultural factors. If the politics of Nehru's nationalism is to project a secular inclusive India, then the Hindutva project aims at creating a *Hindurastra* or a Hindu nation. Thus what is important to note is the rejection of the territorial-political conception of Indian nation and attempt to replace it by a definition of India in terms of cultural nationalism. In other words, the emptiness implicit in Nehru's notion of nationalism and its ambiguity is sought to be filled by Hindutva in the name of cultural nationalism.

V.D. Savarkar, the foremost theoretician of Hindutva, defined Hindutva in terms of concepts of *Pitrubhoomi* (Fatherland) and *Punyabhooomi* (Holy land). Upon this view, only those for whom India is both *Pitrubhoomi* and *Punyabhooomi* can be considered for full-fledged citizenship of Indian nation. A large proportion of population in India does not consider India as their *Punyabhooomi* for given their religious faith they have their holy lands outside India. For instance, the Muslims and Christians consider Mecca and the Vatican as their holy places. Therefore, they do not fulfil an important criterion on account of their faith to claim entitlement to full citizenship.

It is needless to state, since only Hindus consider India as both their *Pitrubhoomi* and *Punyabhoomi,* they alone can be the proper citizens of an imagined *Hindurastra.* By projecting an imagined homogeneous community of Hindus, the Hindutva nationalism attempts to underplay the seriousness of the internal differences among the so-called Hindus in terms of sects and divisions and hierarchy based on caste. By bringing this conceptual apparatus into the definition of nationalism and citizenship the *Hindutva* not only camouflages the internal divisions and caste-based exclusions within Hinduism but also constructs the other and legitimizes and exercises its politics of exclusion vis-a-vis the Muslims. In the same token it also treats the Muslims and even the Christians as a uniform monolithic community ignoring the denominational, sect and caste differences among them which is far from the truth.

The theory of Hindutva that informs the notion of Hindurashtra conflicts with and constitutes the subversion of the basic values of Indian constitution like secularism, democracy, republicanism promising justice, liberty, equality and promotion of fraternity. The assertion that India has been a Hindu nation from times immemorial is aimed at appealing to the primordial emotions of patriotism.

This fabricated view of Hindu nation supported by the notion of Hindus and Muslims being monolithic entities denies the internal differences in these communities and difference, diversity and pluralism that characterized the history of India. By essentialising the Hindu identity it seeks to imagine India as a nation in exclusive Hindu terms. This exclusionary Hindu imagination of India, the basis of Hindu majoritarian consolidation, excludes the minorities and thereby seeks to disempower them. This is the essence of the 'hate minorities' stance of the sangh parivaar.

Thus the Hindutva cannot simply be understood in terms of nationalism—secularism—communalism grand narrative that dominated the mainstream historiography. Upon this view, communalism becomes a negation of secularism and Hindutva a variant of communalism. This viewpoint would grossly undermine the dangerous portents of the Hindutva as a nation-state project. We need to look at the attempts of the BJP in power to translate its state agenda into concrete reality may not be comprehensively but consciously. Realization of the original idea of Hindurastra in its totality is an impossibility as the sangh parvaar is well aware of.

The BJP coming to power in 1999 was seen as an opportunity to lay the foundations for the Hindutva political project. The series of initiatives despite the compulsions and limitations of coalitional politics of NDA like the changes in the education and pedagogic practices show the regime's long-term project. But what is of significance to note is that the constitution and its core secular principle, on which they swear to form and run the government, is seen as a major obstacle to the pursuance of the Hindutva agenda. The review of the constitution during NDA I was a move to test the reactions and their strength.

Two strategies could be identified in the politics of the BJP and sangh parivar. One was the frontal attack on the basis of Indian polity. The review of the constitution was indicative of it.

Second strategy is to pursue the agenda of delegitimizing and debunking the ideas, values and institutions that have long been seen as symbolic and reflective of the secular spirit of the constitution and introduce changes often surreptitiously that go to rationalize the Hindutva discourse. Unlike in the earlier tenure this time around the BJP seems to exercise patience and caution that is reflective of its confidence partly emanating from its secure position at the centre.

The central plank of BJP's political agenda has been development, corruption free India, youth power, etc. all these are argued to be the means of making India a strong nation-state. The comparison with China which has become a fashion among the intellectuals and political class alike is orchestrated to enthuse the popular mood for the pursuance of the social and economic agenda. On the surface there is not much difference between the Congress regime and the BJP for both talk about economic reforms and all that goes with it.

One needs to go slightly deeper to see the difference which is serious and marked. First difference pertains to the emphasis on making India a strong nation-state echoing rashtra. The projection of Modi as the development icon, none comparable to him in the Congress or any other party in terms of ability and resolve, was one of the central planks the BJP in the 2014 elections. The focus on the persona of Modi is sought to be built through appropriation and depoliticization of the known icons of the nationalist movement. The projection of Sardar Patel, later of Gandhi, demonstrates this strategy of selective appropriation by divesting them of their politics, values and message reflected in their active and intense political life. Thus Sardar Patel, despite his staunch anti-communal stance becomes just a symbol of resolution and determination (iron man) and Gandhi, despite him being the symbol of India's diversity, pluralism, tolerance and harmonious coexistence, gets projected only as a symbol of cleanliness. These two icons of the nationalist movement are projected as the victims of the Congress under the Nehru-Gandhi dynasty. The BJP through its remember Patel slogan and *swachch* Bharat campaign apparently aiming to restore them and give them their place has sought to coopt them into the Hindutva pantheon.

Once this goes well and becomes acceptable in the popular psyche, this itself could become a major justification for the initiatives, policies and rhetoric that could smoothen the path towards the grander agenda. It must be stated that the BJP in the present political conjecture cannot pursue the classical Hindutva agenda of establishing *Hindurashtra* literally and openly. For in large part that agenda is anachronistic and unacceptable both domestically and internationally. The pursuance of the Hindutva agenda of Hindu majoritarianism has and could continue to have challenges from the civil society and the subaltern lower caste society. So the strategy is one of gaining legitimacy and making itself acceptable or at least not be seen as intolerable.

REFERENCES

1. Anderson, Benedict, *Imagined Communities: Reflections on the Origins and Spread of Nationalism*, Verso, 2006.
2. Nehru, Jawaharlal, *Discovery of India*, Penguin, 2008.
3. Noorani, A.G., *Savarkar and Hindutva*, Leftword, 2002.

7

The Roots of Secularism in the Indian Tradition

Zeenat Shaukat Ali

Introduction

Throughout human history, religion and politics have entertained the most intimate of connections as systems of authority regulating individuals and society. It has at times been called an "unholy alliance". A cogent analysis unravels the nature of the "connection, disconnection, and attempted reconnection between religion and politics". Notwithstanding the fact that the two are independent through the process of secularization, secularism itself, in India, seems challenged today.

The Present Relevance of Vasudhaiva Kutumbakam

Vasdhaiva Kutambakum, a key concept for peaceful coexistence embodying pluralism, diversity and secularism within its structure, can bring about transformation on the future socio-political-cultural landscape of India and subsequently on the rest of the world. Considered as an integral ,distinctive part of the Indian Vedic Tradition, *Vasdhaiva Kutambakum* or the whole world is a family is quintessentially a universal vision that sees the whole of the human species as comprising one family.

The phrase is mentioned as *Maha Upanishad (Chapter 6, Verse 72-73)* emanates from the words *"vasudha" meaning earth; "eva" meaning "indeed is" and "Kutumbakam"* meaning family[2]. In addition, the text, *Hitopadesha, ruling out any form of discrimination*, further elaborates, *"Udaracharitanam tu vasudhaiva kutumbakam*", meaning " To say, 'This is my own relative and that is a stranger'—is the reasoning of the narrow-minded; for the noble hearts, however, the entire earth is but one family" spells pluralism, egalitarianism and human rights.[3]

It unveils the secular fabric and religious milieu of Indian syncretism with a view to explore the underpinnings of harmony within. *Besides encompassing peace, harmony and inclusiveness among the societies, it also addresses "a truth that in one way or another the whole world has to live by some rules like a family, set by an enlightened transcendent source"*. A similar concept is to be found in *Sangam (300-100 BCE) Tamil Purananuru poem (Yaadhum Oore, Yaavarum Kelir)* meaning, "every country is my own and all the people are my kinsmen", universalizes the notion.[4]

> "To us all towns are one, all men our kin,
> Life's good comes not from others' gifts, nor ill,
> Man's pains and pain's relief are from within,
> *Death's no new thing..."*[5]

The Gandhian philosophy of non-violence finds its inspiration from this concept of Vasudhaiva Kutumbakam. To quote Dr N Radhakrishnan, former director of the Gandhi Smriti and Darshan Samiti, "The Gandhian vision of holistic development and respect for all forms of life; non-violent conflict resolution embedded in the acceptance of nonviolence both as a creed and strategy; were an extension of the ancient Indian concept of Vasudhaiva Kutumbakam."[6]

The Hon'ble President of India Shri Pranab Mukherjee emphasized the importance of values for the youth and said Indians are fortunate to have learnt from the ancestors the principle of Vasudhaiva Kutumbakam while addressing the Overseas Youth of Indian origin.[7]

Shri Narendra Modi, Hon'ble Prime Minister of India used *Vasudhaiva Kutumbakam*, in an interview to a Japanese reporter, adding that "Commitment to peace is ingrained in the DNA of Indian society. This commitment is far above international treaties or processes."[8] He also "opened his historic United Nations General Assembly address with a tribute to India's ancient civilizational traditions, telling a packed Assembly hall of delegates that India's philosophy, which was not an ideology, was the *Vasudhaiva Kutumbakam,* or world family, and this has guided the nation since Vedic times."[9]

Yet, despite the course of *Vasudhaiva Kutumbakam* presently, there is a tendency towards a national identity based on "uniformity" or "unity without diversity". Although *Vasudhaiva Kutumbakam* entails social inclusion signifying a coalescing and fusing force of it seems missing today.Is there a global trend seeping into local politics where majoritarianism and exclusion are engulfing minority identities? Or is the ideal of India with the secular, diverse pluralist ideal under siege?

Sarva Dharma Sambhava or Embodiment of Respect and Equality of All Religions

Another Vedic concept, *Sarva Dharma Sambhava* or all religions are equal, symbolizing religious equality, is one of the central tenets of *secularism in India.* Mahatma Gandhi, used it first in September 1930 in his communications to his followers to quell divisions that had begun to develop between Hindus and Muslims towards the end of the British Raj.[10] The concept of *Sarva Dharma Sambhava* was also embraced by Ramakrishna and Vivekenanda.[11]

It is one of the key tenets of *secularism in India,* wherein there is not a separation of church and state, but an attempt by the state with respect towards all religions.[12]

Sarva Dharma Sambhava confers a wisdom contained in the *Isa Upanishad.* In India it personifies that the entire human race and all religions need to work for the "ennoblement" of every other human.[13] Hence, "the wise man, who realizes all beings as not distinct from his own Self and his own Self as the Self of all beings, does not by virtue of that perception hate anyone. Hence love and not hatred shall be the basis of the Vedic Rashtra."[14]

The roots of *Sarva Dharma Sambhava* can be traced in the wisdom imparted by the *Neeti Saara* or *Neeti Shastra,* a popular collection of morals written by Baddena, a Telugu poet, emphasizing ethical norms. Among its humane secular norms some are the following: "Listen to the complete essence of *dharma* (right action) and contemplate on it. Do not do unto others what one would not like others to do unto oneself." "Righteousness prevails and not unrighteousness. Truth prevails and not untruth. Patience prevails and not anger. God prevails and not demons".[15] This advice is extended to all citizens including leaders. The *karma* theory widely accepted in India held that the wrong doers would incur demerits in the next round of births.

It is interesting to note that "*Dharma* in the political and economic contexts becomes a commitment to social justice. It mandates the creation of the conditions necessary to help all people to develop and attain optimum quality of life. *Dharma* ....This also includes the sacred duty to fight against the forces of injustice, oppression and exploitation."[16]

The practice of secularism is age-old in India. In keeping with the canon, Chanakya (also known as Kautilya) insisted that the ruler should be a model of good conduct to his subjects.[17] Protection to ethnic groups can be seen in the laws of the time. In the 3rd century B.C., Alexander reached the borders of India; this even gave rise to a socio-political ferment. Although Alexander abruptly returned to Macedonia, Chanakya "inspired Chandragupta (a warrior) to establish the Mauryan State in eastern India........and by decree they protected the many ethnic groups..."[18]

The Vedas are "by nature a pluralistic vision that accommodates a variety of spiritual quests and manifestations". Many writers and historians, have said that there was no greater monarch than Ashoka in history. Ashoka who became the ruler of the Mauryan empire was personally a Buddhist but extended his protection to Brahmins and Jains. In his royal edicts engraved on stone he declared that he had undertaken welfare measures for the common people. In his realm, roads were laid, trees planted, water sources created, rest houses constructed for travellers, and hospitals for human beings, animals and birds were set up. He extended his patronage even to the tribals who lived in the forests. More than this he was available to the common people most part of the day and night. Could he be more secular?[19]

Emperor Akbar's *Din-i-Ilahi* spelt secularism where all religions were respected and studied. Maharaja Ranjit Singh of the Sikh empire of the first half of the 19th century successfully established a secular rule in the Punjab. This secular rule allowed members of all races and religions to be respected and to participate without discrimination in Ranjit Singh's darbar and he had Sikh, Muslim and Hindu representatives heading the darbar.[20] Ranjit Singh also extensively funded education, religion, and arts of different religions and languages.[21]

In India, the Bhakti and Sufi movements bound people in a close spiritual partnership. The writings of Ramananda and Kabir, Ramdas, Dadu, Tukaram and Tulsidas, Nanak and Chaitanya and Sufis like Chishti, Baba Farid and Jami to name a few, are illustrious representatives of this philosophy.

The great religions speak in different languages and dialects to seek the Unseen. We may choose diverse paths but the ways for all their winding roads have a single direction. The living faiths of mankind are different paths to the same goal, different ways to the supreme mountain whose summit is the divine reality.[22]

Secularism Within the Constitutional Framework of India

George Holyoake's 1896 publication *English Secularism* defines secularism as: Secularism is a code of duty pertaining to this life, founded on considerations purely human, and intended mainly for those who find theology indefinite or inadequate, unreliable or unbelievable. Its essential principles are three: (1) The improvement of this life by material means. (2) That science is the available Providence of man. (3) That it is good to do good. Whether there be other good or not, the good of the present life is good, and it is good to seek that good.[23]

On the other hand, in India, seminal patterns and principles of secularism with religious and cultural plurality, have been an integral part of the Indian tradition from time immemorial and embedded in the Indian Constitution. The Indian Constitution (1950) has not seen any contradiction of belief in religions and secularism.

However, apart from the definition of secularism given above or provided in books and dictionaries, or that secularism in the West evolved over time due to technological, industrial and scientific development conditioned by moral and rational considerations and the rights of the individual and of groups to which he or she belongs, the concept in which the word secularism is used in the Indian Constitution is different from similar concepts elsewhere.

Although India did and continues to have a population where two thirds belong to the Hindu community, it did not, like Nepal, declare itself to be a Hindu state. This by itself reflects the first evidence of a secular attitude of the state. The rights of different groups have been guaranteed by the Constitution to protect minority groups do not suffer under the dominance of the majority community. All religions have flourished in India from ancient times: Ekam Sat Bahuda Voranti or " The Real is one; sages call it by various names "is a well known dictum.

Hence, the spirit of secularism in the Indian Constitution acknowledged respect for all religions and the presence of an interrelated set of certain elements such as freedom of religion, citizenship rights, equality of people before the law, respect for individuals, irrespective of faith, caste or creed. Moreover, a secular state meant one that protected all religions equally and did not uphold any religion as the state religion. A separate and distinct right of religion was provided in Articles 25-28. Any discrimination in public spaces on the basis of religion or the like was prohibited by the Constitution.

The framers of the Constitution were very clear in their minds when they erected the right to religion to be a fundamental right. Mr. M. Ananthasayanam Ayyangar, during the Constituent Assembly Debates said "we are pledged to make the state a secular one. I do not by the word secular mean, that we do not believe in religion, and that we have nothing to do with it in our day-to-day life. It only means that the state cannot aid one religion or give preference to one religion against another."[24]

India has been declared a secular state by its written Constitution. Despite a deeply religious and a basically traditional society, absence of a state religion and separation of state and religion in central areas of governance and politics has been a remarkable achievement. Mr. Chester Bowles said one of the greatest achievements of Pandit Jawaharlal Nehru, India's enlightened and visionary first Prime Minister, was the creation "of a secular state in which 45 million Muslims who chose not to go to Pakistan could live peacefully and worship as they please"[25]

Although the word secular was not included at the commencement of the Constitution, the Constitution's (Forty-Second Amendment) Act in 1976 introduced the specific term "secular" in the Preamble. Thus what was implicit in the Constitution was made explicit by the Amendment by way of abundant caution.

Throughout the freedom struggle, secularism was seen emerging as a leading principle. Leaders of the Indian National Congress, Mahatma Gandhi, Maulana Abul Kalam Azad, Jawaharlal Nehru and others were deeply committed to the ideal of secularism, though each articulated it in a different manner. The social dynamics in post independent India were very complex. Unlike in the West, where secularism came mainly out of the conflict between the Church and the State, secularism in India was conceived as a system that sustained religious and cultural pluralism.

In breaking down the barriers of religion, class and caste, the successors to the founding fathers in the Congress Party officially adopted the concept of a secular nation-state as India's path to political modernity and national integration, secularism was ultimately enshrined in the Indian Constitution. It reflects the way of life adopted by Indian citizens for themselves after independence. In fact every civilization has also been a mirror of way of life as well as reflecting the movement of the human spirit.

Until the 1980s, secularism was recognized as one of the primary principles of Indian democracy whereby the nation would accomplish a maturity through the democratic processes. Furthermore the augmentation of modern, scientific education took India to new heights.

It has its fault lines and conflicts, but the character has survived for centuries—whoever came here got absorbed into the larger whole. The phrase unity in diversity, often used by Jawaharlal Nehru, was no cliché—it summed up the ethos of the nation. Despite provocations and crises, that ethos has survived.

Mahatma Gandhi has rightly said: "I swear by my religion, I will die for it. But it is my personal affair. The state has nothing to do with it. The state would look after your secular welfare, health, communications, foreign relations, currency and so on, but not your or my religion. That is everybody's personal concern." *Sarva Dharma Sambhav* has to operate at the personal as well as the social level, while *Dharma Nirpekshata* or secularism continues to be the state policy.

In India, some scholars believe this is due to "reflection on the inadequacies and weaknesses of secular practice in India" secularism "has neither lived up to its principles nor adopted innovative modes of communication to reach out to the people." Several others hold that the concept of secularism is , "borrowed from the West" is itself "flawed and irrelevant in Indian conditions," since it is not rooted in Indian social, cultural or political experience. According to them, this rootlessness has adversely affected its vibrancy and acceptability. Therefore they believe that "secularism has no chance of survival and is doomed to an eventual and inevitable death, unless it is reconceptualized. Hence the plea in recent times is to 'rethink' and 'redefine' secularism."[26]

Freedom of Religion: An Era of Crisis and Challenge

It is not so much a question of defending or preserving the existing norm of secularism in Indian polity, as the requirement to construct a strong secular polity in the nation. Ultimately only the idyllic model of building a secular democratic nation can transform the mindset of the unfortunate ascendance of the negative forces of divisive religion based policies leading to discordance.

Despite the right to religious freedom granted by the Indian Constitution at least 200 people from 57 families, mostly slum dwellers, were reportedly re-converted to Hinduism at a ceremony organized by Dharma Jagran in the cantonment area of Agra on December 8, 2014. Muslims have alleged that these conversions were "forcible" as they were offered inducements like BPL and ration cards. The *Dharma Jagran* has stated by 25th December, a few lakhs more Indian citizens will undergo conversion. Despite the Hon'ble Prime Minister, Shri Narendra

Modi clearly stating that the focus must be on the plank of development and governance asserting that nobody was allowed to deviate from the core agenda, one of the Members of Parliament from his party said the "ghar wapasi' was an ongoing process and will continue to happen.[27]

In organizing *ghar vapsi* programmes is the belief that Indian Muslims and Christians were once targets of forcible conversion by missionaries and *madrassas*. Recently conversions have become a politically charged issue on the ground by raising issues like *love jihad*.

Although "freedom to convert or be converted whatever the inducement offered surely remains an important democratic freedom. Yet fear of conversion has long gripped mainstream political parties...Anti-conversion laws were passed in Odisha, Madhya Pradesh and Andhra Pradesh as far back as 1967, 1968 and 1978 respectively. Recently anti-conversion laws have been passed in Chhattisgarh (2000), Gujarat (2003), Himachal Pradesh (2006) and Rajasthan (2008), three of them being BJP initiatives."[28]

Charges regarding conversions by missionaries seem naive if majority communities organizations complacently resort to the same. "The ghastly burning to death of Australian missionary Graham Staines, allegedly because he was converting locals to Christianity, resulted in a life term for the accused but at the time the Supreme Court also inveighed rather controversially against 'forcible' conversion". If one section" has the right to proselytize and convert then surely other faiths and organizations do as well. There can be no such thing as 'good conversions' and 'bad conversions', just as there is no 'good' and 'bad' terrorism."[29]

Shri Sitaram Yechury said that forced conversions had inclinations "of transforming the secular, democratic Indian republic into their version of a rabidly intolerant fascist nation", while Anand Sharma attributed such conversions to the "agenda" of divisive, communal forces. However Parliamentary Affairs Minister M. Venkaiah Naidu held that "conversion and reconversion, if forced, is wrong". He said, "There should be no conversion either through force or inducement..."[30]

A circular dated December 9, 2014 was issued by the

Ministry of Human Development Resources marking December 25th, Christmas Day as "Good Governance Day to celebrate the birthday of Shri Atal Bihari Vajpayee, former Prime Minister of India and birth anniversary of Madan Mohan Malaviya. It asks schools to 'ensure activity participation of your students' in a declamation contest, quiz contest, film screening and "innovative programmes...." forcing children to attend school on Christmas day, was later reversed. It nonetheless injured the sensibilities of the Christian community.[31]

Similarly, the issues in education relating to the scientific temper, the rewriting of history, caste and gender hierarchy, the question relating to the preference of study with regard to language, need to concentrate on genuine scholarship and objective study.

Conclusion: The Quest for A Pluralistic Vision

The Father of our Nation, Mahatma Gandhi once posed an important and interesting question: *Why is culture perceived—and sometimes deeply felt—as a source of division, instead of a path to dialogue and human solidarity?* He asked, *Why is the fear of the 'other' an easy platform for those whose simplistic philosophy implies a world of mutually exclusive identities? Why has multiculturalism failed and xenophobia risen in some societies? Why are anti-immigration policies receiving, here and there, increased political support?*

Prejudice, racism, hate speeches, forcible conversions are antithetical to the humanitarian, the nature of its spiritual values and compassionate concepts of *Vasdhaiva Kutambakum, Sarva Dharma Sambhava, Ekam Sat Bahuda Voranti The Real is one; sages call it by various names and "Loka samasta sukhina bhavantu"* (Let the entire world be happy). Yet they seem to abound.

In his famous speech in 1893 in Chicago at the Parliament of World Religions, Swami Vivekananda said: "I am proud to belong to a religion which has taught the world both tolerance and universal acceptance.... We believe not only in universal toleration, but we accept all religions as true. I will quote to you, brethren, a few lines from a hymn which I remember to have repeated from my earliest boyhood, which is every day repeated by millions of human beings: "As the different streams having their sources in different places all mingle their water in the sea, so, O Lord, the different paths which men take through different tendencies, various though they appear, crooked or straight, all lead to Thee."[32]

He continued: "Sectarianism, bigotry, and its horrible descendant, fanaticism, have long possessed this beautiful earth. They have filled the earth with violence, drenched it often with human blood, destroyed civilization and sent whole nations to despair. Had it not been for these horrible demons, human society would be far more advanced than it is now. But their time is come; and I fervently hope that the bell that tolled this morning in honour of this convention may be the death-knell of all fanaticism, of all persecutions with the sword or with the pen, and of all uncharitable feelings between persons wending their way to the same goal."[33]

Swami Vivekananda's final address , at the Last Parliament of World's Religion, Chicago, has been immortalized. He concluded his speech saying, "Much has been said of the common ground of religious unity. I am not going just now to venture my own theory. But if any one here hopes that this unity will come by the triumph of any one of the religions and the destruction of the others, to him I say, "Brother, yours is an impossible hope." *Do I wish that the Christian would become Hindu? God forbid. Do I wish that the Hindu or Buddhist would become Christian? God forbid.*[34]

"The seed is put in the ground, and earth and air and water are placed around it. Does the seed become the earth, or the air, or the water? No. It becomes a plant... Similar is the case with religion.... If the Parliament of Religions has shown anything to the world, it is this: It has proved to the world that holiness, purity and charity are not the exclusive possessions of any church in the world, and that every system has produced men and women of the most exalted character. In the face of this evidence, if anybody dreams of the exclusive survival of his own religion and the destruction of the others, I pity him from the bottom of my heart, and point out to him that upon the banner of every religion will soon be written in spite of resistance: "Help and not fight," "Assimilation and not Destruction," "Harmony and Peace and not Dissension."[35]

The savage murder by the Taliban of 132 children at an Army School in Peshawar, Pakistan, spraying them with machine gun fire on December 16, 2014, as an act of vengeance in retaliation to an army offensive in the area of North Wazirstan and Khyber siege, are a blot on Islam's civilizational values for peaceful coexistence. They have twisted the interpretation of a religion based on the norms of peace.[36]

For all those discrediting secular paradigms and *misinterpretation and mis*using religion including Muslims, to justify sinister agendas need to read the motto that decorates the gate of the United Nations (building) Entrance 51, would make constructive reading . The motto is an aphorism of Saadi Shirazi calling for the breaking of all barriers and was quoted by President Obama in a meeting with Iranian leaders. Many of his poems greatly impacted India, and had influence throughout Central Asia.

> Human beings are members of a whole,
> In creation of one essence and soul.
> If one member is afflicted with pain,
> Other members uneasy will remain.
> If you've no sympathy for human pain,
> The name of human you cannot retain![37]

Factors popularizing communalism and communal politics or violence have little to do with enlightenment, spirituality and values that all religions teach, and more to do with mass mobilization and populism. These affect the age-old synergetic fibre of the country and need to be arrested. The norms of secularism, pluralism and social cohesion embedded in *Vasdhaiva Kutambakum or the whole world is a family, Sarva Dharma Sambhava or respect for all religions, Ekam Sat Bahuda Voranti The Real is one; sages call it by various names and "Loka samasta sukhina bhavantu.* Let the entire world be happy both in letter and spirit' need to be adopted in letter and spirit.

NOTES AND REFERENCES

1a. HarperCollins Publishers New York, *Religion*, 2014; Hart, George L. and Hank Heifetz (2001), *The Four Hundred Songs of War and Wisdom: An Anthology of Poems from.* New York: Columbia

University Press, p. 16; Encyclopædia Britannica (India) (2000), *Students' Britannica India,* Volumes 1-5. *Maha Upanishad VI.71-73; Hitopadesha-1.3.71 (12th century CE); "Vasudhaiva Kutumbakam" (The Earth is a Family).*

1b. Pratap, Vijay, Ritu Priya and Thomas Wallgren, "Pursuing the Democratic Dream", *Vasudhaiva Kutumbakam:* An Alliance for Comprehensive Democracy. Forum for Dialogues on Comprehensive Democracy, Courtesy: Coalition for Environment and Development, Designed and maintained by CAPITAL Creations, New Delhi.

1c. United Nations Universal Declaration of Human Rights 1948 , United Nations (UN), copy @ lexmerca-toria.org, Copyright © 1949 United Nations (UN), lexmercatoria.org , p. 2

1. HarperCollins Publishers New York, *Religion*, 2014; Hart, George L. and Hank Heifetz (2001), *The Four Hundred Songs of War and Wisdom: An Anthology of Poems from Classical Tamil; The Purananuru*, Columbia University Press, New York, p. 16; Encyclopædia Britannica (India) (2000). *Students' Britannica India*, Volumes 1-5. *Maha Upanishad VI.71-73 ; Hitopadesha - 1.3.71 (12th century CE); "Vasudhaiva Kutumbakam" (The Earth is a Family).*
2. The above verse is also found in *Hitopadesha - 1.3.71* (*12th century CE*). And is also found *V.3.37 of Panchatantra* (*3rd century BCE*).
3. *Purananuru*, Hart, George L. (2014) and Hank Heifetz (2001). *The Four Hundred Songs of War and Wisdom: An Anthology of Poems from Classical Tamil; The Purananuru*, Columbia University Press, New York, belonging to the *Sangam period.* It is dated between the first century BCE and the fifth century CE.*

* Purananuru is a Tamil poetic work in the *Emmuttokai*, one of the eighteen melkanakku noolgal. It is a treatise on kingship: what a king should be, how he should act, how he should treat his subjects and how he should show his generosity. Sangam Collection is classified into *Patile Gmlkanakku* and *Patinenkilkanakku* and each classification has eighteen collections, as an anthology of Tamil literature.

Purananuru is one of the eight books in the secular anthology of *Sangam literature*, namely *Ettuthokai.* The secular anthology is entirely unique in Indian literature, which nearly all religious texts during this era *Purananuru* contains 400 poems of varying lengths in the *Akaval* meter. More than 150 poets wrote the poems. It is not known when or who collected these poems into these anthologies.

Purananuru is a source of information on the political and social history of pre-historic Tamil Nadu. There is information on the various rulers who ruled the Tamil country before and during the Sangam era.

5. *Kaniyan Pungundranar*, Purananuru–192 (Translated by G.U. Pope, 1906)
6. Radhakrishnan, Dr. N., "Gandhi in the Globalised Context", Site Gandhi Institute Bombay Savodaya Mandal and Gandhi Research Foundation, New Delhi, orginal Source: www.transna tional.org.
7. Speech by the President of India Shri Pranab Mukherjee at the Eleventh Convocation of Symbiosis International University, Pune, Maharashtra, September 26, 2014.
8. Prime Minister Shri Narendra Modi's special lecture at the University of the Sacred Heart, Tokyo, September 2, 2014, Author: Admin.
9. During his address to the UN General Assembly on September 27, 2014, the Hon'ble Prime Minister of India Shri Narendra Modi asked the World leaders to adopt, June 21, as International Yoga Day which was approved by the 193-member UN General Assembly and a resolution establishing June 21 as 'International Day of *Yoga*'.
10. Smith, Donald E. (2011). *India as a Secular State.* Princeton University Press.
11. Long, Jeffrey (2012). "The Politicization of Hinduism and the Hinduization of Politics: Contrasting Hindu Nationalism with the Transformative Visions of Swami Vivekenanda and Mahatma Gandhi". In Ricci, Gabriel R., *Politics in Theology.*
12. Larson, Gerald James (2001). *Religion and Personal Law in Secular India: A Call to Judgment*, Indiana University Press.
13. *Dharma Rajya - Veda*, veda.wikidot.com/dharma-rajya.
14. Weber, Albrecht, *The History of Indian Literature* (1878) 1878:103, "The Isha Upanishad is significant for its description of the nature of the "*Supreme Being*", exhibiting *monism* or a form of *monotheism*, referred to as *Isha* "Lord". It describes this being as "unembodied, omniscient, beyond reproach, without veins, pure and uncontaminated" (verse 8), one who "moves and does not move', who is 'far away, but very near as well'" and who "although fixed in His abode is swifter than the mind" (verses 4 & 5)". OMIT

    Easwaran, Eknath, *The Upanishads*, translated for the modern readers, Nilgiri Press, 1987, p. 205.

    "The first verse of the text has been cited as of particular importance to Vedanta or to Hinduism as a whole. Mohandas Karamchand Gandhi thought so highly of it that he remarked, "If all the Upanishads and all the other scriptures happened all of a sudden to be reduced to ashes, and if only the first verse in the Ishopanishad were left in the memory of the Hindus, Hinduism would live for ever."

15. Baddena (1220-1280? AD) is the composer of the most famous *Sumathi Satakam* as well as Niti Sastra. Complete details about his origin are not known. But, he was believed to be a Chola prince and was called Bhadra Bhupala. He was a Samanta Raju (vassal) under the Kakateeya Rudrama Devi (reign: 1262-1296 AD) during the 13th century.
16. Swami Agnivesh, *Secularism and the World View,* Workshop on State and Secularism, November 25-26, 2008, Tuesday and Wednesday, Venue: Asia-Europe Foundation, 31 Heng Mui Keng Terrace, Singapore 119595, organized by East Asian Institute, Singapore; Sponsored by Asia Europe Foundation and the Lee Foundation.
17. Brass, Paul R., "Indian Secularism in Practice" *Indian Journal of Secularism,* Vol. 9, No. 1, January-March 2006, pp. 115-132.
18. Venugopal, C.N., "Polity, Religion and Secularism in India: A Study of Interrelationships", *Politics and Religion,* Jawaharlal Nehru University, New Delhi, UDK 316.74:2 (540), • *Politologie Des Religions* • No. 1/2013, Vol. VII, 2012, pp. 21-40.
19. Ibid.
20. Sheikh, Majid, Destruction of Schools as Leitner Saw Them. *Dawn.* Retrieved June 4, 2013.
21. Lapidus, Ira M., "The Separation of State and Religion in the Development of Early Islamic Society", *International Journal of Middle East Studies* 6 (4), October 1975, pp. 363-385.
22. The (Radhakrishnan) Report of the University Education Commission (December 1948-August 1949), Vol. I, pp. 258-259
23. Holyoake, George J., *English Secularism,* Vol. 1, The Open Court Publishing Company, Chicago, 1896.
24. *C.A.D.*, Vol. VII, Lok Sabha Secretariat, pp. 881-882.
25. Bowles, Chester, *Indian Journal of Political Science* XLVIII 2 (April-June 1987), p. 222.
26. Pannikar, K.N., "Secularism Under Seige", *The Hindu,* Opinion, Wednesday, March 31, 2004,
27. *The Asian Age,* December 17, 2014, p. 1.
28. *The Times of India,* Converting Hypocrisy: The Right to Convert is a Religious Freedom and Applies to all Religions, Edit Page,

December 11, 2014, p. 11.

29. Ibid.
30. *The Indian Express,* Opposition Targets Government over Conversion in Agra: 'Bid to impose Hindutva agenda', Express News Service, New Delhi, *Religions,* December 11, 2014, p. 11-30.
31. *The Times of India,* December 13, 2014, p.19.
32. Swami Vivekananda, Address (September 11, 1893) , Parliament of Religions, Art Institute of Chicago as part of the World's Columbian Exposition, Chicago, Illinois, 1893 (11-27 b September).
33. Ibid.
34. Swami Vivekananda, Final Session Parliament of World's Religion, (September 27, 1893).
35. Swami Vivekananda, Address at the Final Session (27 September 1893) , Parliament of Religions, *Art Institute of Chicago* as part of the *World's Columbian Exposition,* Chicago, Illinois, 1893 (11-27 September) Parliament of World's Religion, Chicago, Swami Vivekananda, has been immortalized.
36. *The Asian Age,* Mumbai, Wednesday 17, 2014, p. 1.
37. Shirazi, Saadi, From Gulistan , Chapter 1, story 10. His poem 'Bani Adam' Inscribed on United Nations Building Entrance 51, Saturday, September 17, 2011.

8

Breaking the Siege: A Few Tentative Suggestions

Subhash Gatade

I

Leading journalist and political analyst Pranoy Guha Thakurta gave a piece of his mind while giving a talk on 'Media and Modi' organized by JSM in Delhi. Frankly admitting that as the situation exists today in the country one does not see a ray of hope and the coming years would be difficult for the common people. He underlined the fact that a country with a size of India cannot be forever run in such a manner despite a compliant media. Underlining the diversity of the country he mentioned that although voices of resistance are not to be seen on the horizons right now but it should not be construed as an ultimate victory of the rich and the mighty. According to him the present juncture should be seen as '*Bhor Se Pahale ka Ghana Andhera*' (darkness before morning).

All the voices who are for sanity and equity in Indian politics would agree with broad contours of Mr Thakurta's argument. It is true that the ascendance of rightwing forces led by Hindutva Supremacists has definitely put the future of secular democracy here in jeopardy—a colossal task undertaken by the builders of Modern India, which remains unmatched at least in this part of South Asia. As of now it is difficult to map its future trajectory but it would not be incorrect to say that it would be a version of (what Prime Minister Nehru used to call) 'Hindu Pakistan' if they are not stopped in their tracks. Today when we are facing a new low in our journey it needs to be remembered that while opposing all sorts of communalism—be it of the majority or the minority type—Nehru could foresee how communalism of the majority presents itself as nationalism in a multi-religious country and can one day overwhelm the state.

II

As far as the 'change in fortunes' of the Hindutva supremacists is concerned it is noticeable that they have travelled from the margins to the centrestage of Indian politics. There was a time when they were an object of ridicule because of their opposition to the anti-colonial struggle at the time of independence and their participation in the assassination of Mahatma Gandhi, but that period is over.

Their journey from margins to centre could be attributed to broadly three factors:

1. Better organizing capacity and strategising exhibited by them in post-independence period.
2. Cultural-civilizational makeup of our society.
3. Failure of the secular forces to sustain momentum after independence.

You will notice that I have not specifically mentioned capitalism in general or neoliberal capitalism in particular which supposedly has played a role in its ascendance to, of course it does find mention in the related discussion.

III

At this juncture one would not like to detain oneself with the first two aspects, namely organizing strategems by the Hindutva Supremacists and our societal makeup—which have been widely commented upon and discussed but would like to focus on ourselves—people/formations like us and to engage in deep introspection—about our theoretical understanding of the challenge and our practice. It is puzzling for me how and why the momentum was lost after independence, how we facilitated its silent emergence by vacating/not taking up tasks which needed to be taken up.

One way to do it is to move away from standard questions and their pet answers to an arena less probed and investigated. Perhaps it is time to raise questions which were never raised before or did not receive the attention they really deserved.

I have three broad queries in my mind, one concerns genesis of Hindutva Supremacist politics, the other relates to the way secular politics evolved in this country and the third one concerns what is known as 'minority communalism'. A related question is why despite the correctness of their understanding the seculars never seem to be on the offensive despite history providing enough opportunities before them about the anti-human nature of Hindutva politics vindicating the maxim 'The best lack all conviction and the worst are full of passionate intensity.'

1. Genesis of Hindutva Politics

A question has always baffled me about why Maharashtra—which prides itself on the great legacy of Phule, Ambedkar Shahu Maharaj and many other social revolutionaries, where the population of minorities has never crossed the ten per cent mark, and where they were never politically dominant, could metamorphose into a region which saw not only emergence of many leading Hindutva ideologues—ranging from Savarkar, Hedgewar and Golwalkar—and their organizations but a strong base as well as popular legitimacy. Why and how an organization called RSS or the whole idea of Hindutva has received a legitimacy which is not witnessed outside. And this query appears contrary to how we have viewed the politics of Hindutva. The general practice has been to see the idea and politics of Hindutva in the form of religious imaginaries.

For its proponents, it is the way to correct 'historial wrongs' supposedly committed by 'aggressors' of various hues against the 'Hindu Nation' which according to them has been in existence since time immemorial. It does not need recounting how this strange mix of mythology and history which is fed to the gullible followers unfolds itself before us with dangerous implications.

The dominant antidote to this exclusivist idea, rubbishes the 'us' versus 'them' rationale provided to justify its actions, denies any such continuous strife on the basis of religion amongst people, talks of emergence of composite heritage and the flourishing of many syncretic traditions, etc. It is no surprise that the explosive manifestations of communal conflict are presented here as a handiwork of a 'few bad apples' within the communities which need to be weeded out or quarantined.

Perhaps it is high time to revisit this prevalent understanding as it not only appears incomplete but also seems to miss the target.

Would it be proper to say that Hindutva is rather an extension of the ongoing Brahminical project of hegemonizing and homogenizing of Indian society and in fact could be seen as part of Brahminical counterrevolution against the *Shudras-Atishudras* who had witnessed loosening of the social bondages and restrictions under the twin impact of policies promulgated by the colonial regime coupled with the path-breaking movements led by the social revolutionaries.

How does one relate to the emergence of the *weltanshauung* (world view) of Hindutva with the struggles against Brahminism pioneered by the likes of Savitribai and Jyotiba Phule and the ongoing efforts of many stalwarts of the movement—ranging from the leaders of the Satyashodhak Samaj to the *Bahishkrit Hitakarini Sabha*, Independent Labour Party or for that matter the Republican Party of India and the path-breaking role played by the legendary son of the oppressed Dr. Ambedkar?

To put it the other way we need to address what Dilip Menon calls 'the general reluctance to engage with what is arguably an intimate relation between the discourses of caste, secularism and communalism.' He adds :

The inner violence within Hinduism explains to a considerable extent the violence directed outwards against Muslims once we concede that the former is historically prior. The question needs to be: how has the deployment of violence against an internal other (defined primarily in terms of inherent inequality), the Dalit, come to be transformed at certain conjectures into one of aggression against an external other (defined primarily in terms of inherent difference), the Muslim? Is communalism a deflection of the central issue of violence and inegalitarianism in Indian society? (See p. 2, *The Blindness of Insight*, Navayana 2006).

2. Debating Secularism

Coming to secularism, as we look back, it clearly indicates the lack of a social foundation for secularism. During any conflict situation involving different communities it becomes more evident. The question arises why more than sixty years after we embarked on a secular path, it has remained so weak.

Perhaps it needs to be mentioned that there is still confusion/lack of consensus within the broader secular movement about what constitutes 'secularism'—should we see it as 'Sarv Dharm Sambhav' as popularized by Gandhi and his band of seculars or should we look at it as 'separation of religion and politics'? In fact within the left also a confusion exists. Absence of clarity gets reflected in the strange formulation one witnessed after demolition of the Babri mosque when a section of mainstream left tried to 'appropriate Rama in its own way' by dividing Ram into Real Ram and Phoney Ram

For various reasons serious thought could not be given to the whole process of secularization (a process by which sectors of society and culture are removed from the domination of religious institutions and symbols'—Peter Berger) in a country like India and we remained focussed on maintaining/ strengthening secularity of the state in a society which was not secular but was based on exclusions of various kinds—be it based on caste, gender, ethnicities, etc. It is possible that most of us broadly concurred with the prevalent understanding then made popular by scholars like Peter Berger (*The Sacred Canopy*, 1967) which argued that why the decline of religion was inevitable in modern industrial society. As an aside it can be mentioned how this understanding flows out of what Meera Nanda calls: '[E]nlightenment project which believed that as men and women begin to understand the underlying order of nature without involving God, they will learn to outgrow their faith in God.' (*The God Market*, p. 178)

One knows that the Indian Constitution is based on this classical view of secularization.

Our confidence in the rationalization of work process,

removing all scope of divine intervention or magical action or the unfolding reality of 'emancipation of the state from the sway of religious rationales for economic activity, law and politics which is universal characteristics of all modernizing states (Nanda, p. 179) led us to a situation where the whole world of culture and society has left the field open to various status quoist, reactionary interventions, be it from the religious formations or from the likes of RSS/Jamaat which further helped desecularize society. It was a manifestation of the situation within the society where one witnesses emphasis of the progressive/transformative movements on political-economic struggles and their neglect of intervention in the social-cultural arena.

One discovers that forces like RSS/Jamaat-e-Islami or other status quoist or reactionary organizations have been very clear about their 'anti-secular' agenda which they tried to bolster through intervention in culture in a strategic manner. They tried to enhance their 'religious viewpoint' by institutionalizing it through a number of affiliated organizations. Be it the formation of schools or hospitals or organizations catering to diverse sections of society they tried to fashion society in their own image. It is not for nothing that RSS describes itself not as 'organization in society' but 'organization of society' (*Samaj me Sangathan nahin, Samaj ka Sangathan*). Prof. K.N. Pannikar writes that RSS's educational work started in the 1940s itself and today they have 70,000 schools—from Ekal Vidyalayas to Saraswati Shishu Mandir—spread all over the country. These activities have helped them 'in transforming the cultural consciousness of the people from the secular to the religious' (*History as a Site of Struggle*, Three Essays Collective, p. 169) According to him:

> This is a qualitatively different effort from that of the secular forces who mainly focus on cultural intervention, the impact of which is limited and transient. The difference between cultural intervention and intervention in culture distinguishes the cultural engagement of the communal and the secular and their relative success.

If we take a closer look at the functioning of Jamaat-e-Islami, we can find similar processes unfolding before there.

Secondly, the secular movement, has always emphasized what Harsh Mander has described in his article (Learning from

Ambedkar, http://kafila.org/2014/08/23/learning-from-babasaheb-harsh-mander/#more-23461) 'an image of India which has been 'through most of its long history, a diverse, pluralist and tolerant civilization—the land of Buddha, Kabir and Nanak, of Ashoka, Akbar and Gandhi' as a counter to a narrow, intolerant, exclusivist, monolithic interpretation of Indian culture done by the Hindutva right, which Romila Thapar describes 'as the right-wing Semitization of Hinduism'. It has celebrated the existing culture here which has provided space and freedom for every major faith to flourish, where 'persecuted faiths have received refuge' and 'where heterodox and sceptical traditions thrived alongside spiritual and mystical traditions'.

Basing itself on this understanding it has tried to interrogate, question and challenge Hindutva Supremacist forces. But this understanding as anyone can notice seems to be a partial description of our society which invisibilizes the stark reality of caste—the hierarchial division of society—an integral part of the Indian social fabric based on the age-old doctrine of exclusion legitimized and sanctified by the Brahminical ideology. This sociological blindness towards such an age-old structure has impacted its task of secularization.

Thirdly, secularism was envisaged broadly in terms of an extension of anti-communal struggle which left many a 'fraternal' struggles outside its purview. If secularism could be broadly construed (to quote Charles Taylor) as 'emptying of religion from autonomous social spaces' movements whose direct/indirect impact was on similar lines, were never considered as an essential part of the movement. For example, anti-caste or Dalit movement, movement against patriarchy and gender-based oppression, people's science movement, rationalist movement or movement of the exploited and oppressed for dignity and rights, definitely bear the potential of limiting the role of religion in statecraft as well as society, but there was no attempt to broaden the constituency of 'secular movement' or integrate them in a larger framework.

Perhaps it is opportune here to quote Ajay Gudavarthy and Nissim Mannathukkaren (The Politics of Secular Sectarianism, *EPW*, December 6, 2014) wherein they discuss how a society based on caste hierarchies and absence of secular spaces facilitated the emergence of Hindutva politics.

A society suffused with caste hierarchies and culture (or caste privilege itself (masquerading as merit) and the lack of secular spaces, have prepared the ground for the rapid incursion of Hindutva—modified now to incorporate the oppressed castes without dismantling the hierarchy, and modified also to make it a majoritarian ideology tied now with the economic one of neoliberalism. The failure of the Left in building secular identities, even in their traditional strongholds, is a colossal one. This failure is worsened further by the domination of the upper castes and the exclusion of the marginalized, the Dalits, Adivasis and Muslims in the communist movement as in West Bengal (though Kerala does much better, especially with regard to the OBCs). Prabhat Patnaik (2013) calls this exclusion an "extraordinary phenomenon".

Put it otherwise the ascendance of anti-secular/communal politics could be seen as a result of the new low which one witnesses in struggles waged by the exploited and the oppressed which constitute the vast majority of the population. And intensification of struggles to dismantle class, caste, gender, religion-based oppressions, searching for and forging commonality among them is the need of the hour.

3. What is Our Understanding of Minority Communalism?

One knows that when it comes to the situation of minorities especially Muslims—the biggest religious minority here—we find ourselves in a particular bind. While we are aware that a large section of the community faces deprivation, dispossession, pauperization—brought in by the nature of socio-economic development followed here which gets accentuated because of the prejudice/bias prevalent against them in all the organs of the state and 'civil society'. Thanks to the report of the Sachar Committee, many of the myths perpetuated by the majoritarian forces like 'appeasement of Muslims' lie shattered and their 'majority going for Madrasa education' stand exposed. We also know that the Kundu Committee formed to undertake the 'post Sachar evaluation' that though a start has been made in 'addressing development deficits of the community, government interventions have not quite matched in scale the large numbers of the marginalized.'

There have been thousands of riots in post-independence times, where they have been at the receiving end of administrative apathy and connivance and the combined might of the majoritarian forces. None of the real planners/ masterminds of the riots have been caught or people leading riots have been arrested and despite reports by various judicial commissions rarely one notices prosecution of anyone from the administrative side or people supposed to maintain law and order for their complicity in the pogroms. And as rightly expressed by Paul R. Brass, there have developed what he terms as 'institutionalized riot systems' which are in a position to engineer riot at any moment.

We are also becoming aware—post 2002 riots—how the state has slowly abdicated the role of providing relief and rehabilitation to riot-affected people and victims of communal violence and the vacuum has been filled by different community organizations. And this one witnessed not only in Gujarat but even in a state like Assam—ruled by the Congress consecutively for three terms—when there was violence in BTAD areas. According to a journalist most of the relief camps set up for the internally displaced people were run either by Jamaat-e-Islami or Jamiat-Ulema-i-Hind making the victims and other affected people more amenable to their agendas.

As upholders of the idea of secularism and fighters against communalism it definitely becomes our bounden duty to not only to protect minorities in such a grim situation and support them in their struggle for justice. But what does one think about the community leadership—the dominant politics there—which is undemocratic to say the least.

In fact, one can cite many examples which go to show the growing disjunction between the leadership and the Muslim masses which is neither ready to take up issues of internal divisions, asymmetries nor does it want to move beyond 'community interests' while taking highly problematic stands on various issues of concern, e.g. neither has it bothered to take up the issue of rights of Muslim women nor has it ever acknowledged the issue of discrimination based on caste in the community. Despite the existence of a nascent *Pasmanda* (backward) Muslim movement in the community it is yet to acknowledge its significance. Much on the lines of Pakistan, which happens to be the only country in the world which has declared 'Ahmadiyas/Qadianis' as unIslamic, one witnesses similar forces on the ascendance in the community here as well.

It has also exhibited its myopic nature by not coming clean on anti-human actions undertaken by Islamist groups/ formations elsewhere. Be it the activities of Boko Haram or for that matter the war crimes committed by Jamat-e-Islami in neighbouring Bangladesh during its war of liberation, it has either maintained ambivalence or went out unashamedly supporting them, e.g. recently when one Sunni scholar—grandson of Ali of Nadwa—called upon the Sunnis of India to join the Jihad undertaken by Baghdadi in Iraq and Syria, who declared establishment of Islamic Khalifat, there were no voices of condemnation here.

One feels that it is high time that we move beyond the bind in which we find ourselves on various 'sensitive' sounding issues. While we should fight against deprivations of the Muslim masses, we should not remain silent over depradations of its leadership. Our fight against targeting of Muslims in general, and Muslim youth in particular, should not mean that we remain silent when some Popular Front issues diktats to Muslim women to wear this or that dress or has no qualms in attacking a Professor and cutting his hand just for the fact that the question he put in a question paper 'hurt their sentiments'.

The fact of the matter is that despite claiming that we are opposed to all sorts of communalism the secular movement/ we have remained focussed on majority communalism leading us to a ridiculous situation where we objectively sided with leaders of the community which was opposed to granting any right to the oppressed/marginalized within the community. Perhaps we approached the religious minorities as 'homogeneous' denying any internal fissures within. It also helped our adversaries winning over a vacillating section within the secular movement for our 'silence' towards 'minority communalism'.

A related point—which is not less troubling—is how do

we view minorities? Whether for us they are merely victims who basically need protection or are equal citizens of the republic who need equal rights and opportunities in every field. Secular leaders like to describe their success in terms of 'absence of any riot' under them or 'controlling them in a short period' but when it comes to human development indices of the minorities they are at the margins only. It is really ironic to mention that the Left in power has also not been able to break this 'record'.

It is true that the Left in power or outside has played an important role in defence of minorities. West Bengal, where Left ruled for more than three decades can be considered a classic example but coming to all round development of minorities picture seems to be far from satisfactory. The report presented by the Sachar Commision underlined it very sharply. The question arises whether 'mainstream left' also looks at 'Minorities' as victims only—who basically need protection—and not as equal citizens.

IV

After a flurry of random questions around the theme, it would be opportune to discuss the general ambience in which we are discussing this 'siege'.

A few pertinent facts are worth emphasizing. We are living in a period where:

- Spurt in religious violence everywhere and less tolerance towards people belonging to other faiths.

  One can refer to the UN report which came out in the year 2007—where Ms Asma Jahangir acted as special rapporteur, for more details.
- This region of South Asia has also seen an upsurge/ascendance of majoritarian/authoritarian/exclusivist formations/movements in recent decades. In fact it is really a strange coincidence that while we are debating ascendance of the Hindutva Right here, the situation in this part of South Asia looks very similar where majoritarian forces owing allegiance to a particular

religion or ethnicity seem to be on the upswing. Mynamar, Sri Lanka, Maldives, Pakistan, you name a country and find democratic forces being pushed to the margins and majoritarian voices gaining a new voice and strength.

Not very many people would have imagined that people claiming themselves followers of Buddha—who is considered an apostle of non-violence—would metamorphose into perpetrators of tremendous human rights violations in Mynamar. It was only last year that the *Guardian* had done a special story on the Burmese monk Wirathu—called 'Bin Laden of Burma'—who with his 2,500 follower monks has become a dreaded name in the country, instigating Buddhist fanatics to attack Muslims. The plight of Rohingya Muslims has become a cause of international concern. The military in Mynamar has provided tacit support to him or others of his ilk.

Or, come to Sri Lanka, two months back the Bondu Bala Sena(BBS) started by Buddhist monks had reached headlines for attacking Muslims and causing loss of property and human lives. Since the suppression of the Tamil militancy the Sinhala extremist forces—which has enough sprinkling of Buddhist monks—with due connivance of the Rajpakshe government has discovered 'new enemies'. If Muslims are target number one, Christians and Hindus are not far behind.

Or reach neighbouring Pakistan where you find Islamist forces trying to play havoc with the lives of 'others'. It is true that because of a strong tradition of secular movement, the situation is still under control in Bangledesh but Pakistan seems to be bursting at its seams where various fanatic groups with their violenct acts against the 'others'—ranging from the Ahmadiyas, Shias, Hazaras, Hindus, etc.—have created a situation of implosion.

What is noticeable in this picture is the perpetrator community changes as you cross the national borders. In Burma, Buddhists seem to be the perpetrators and Muslims seem to be at the receiving end, in Bangladesh there is reversal of roles and likewise in other countries of the region.

It is disturbing to note in such a volatile situation one type of fanaticism feeds on the other. Buddhist extremists in

Mynamar strengthen Islamists in Bangladesh and they further add strength to the Hindutva supremacists here. If the first half of the 20th century this area has been witness to anti-colonial struggles which had strengthened each others emancipatory aspirations, in the first quarter of the 21st century we have all been witness to explosion of majoritarian movements trying to put the achievements of democracy and secularism on the backburner.

The latest in the series is Wirathu's trip to Sri Lanka at the invitation of BBS, the 'grand welcome' he received there and this despite the fact that minority groups in Sri Lanka and human rights organizations had pressurized President Rajpakshe to deny him an invite. Leaders of BBS have proposed to turn this part of South Asia into a 'peace zone' against 'menace of Muslims' and are said to be intending to interact with Hindutva groups especially RSS over this proposal.

But how does one comprehend the dialectic between democracy and majoritarianism and its relationship with capitalism in general and neoliberalism in particular?

V

What is a *sine qua non* of democracy? It is the understanding that minority voices will be allowed to flourish and they will not be bulldozed. At the apparent level majoritarianism—rule by majority—sounds very similar to democracy but it essentially stands democracy on its head. For real democracy to thrive, it is essential that ideas and principles of secularism are at its core. The idea that there will be a clear separation between state and religion and there won't be any discrimination on the basis of religion has to be its guiding principle. Majoritarianism thus clearly defeats democracy in idea as well as practice.While democracy's metamorphosis into majoritarianism is a real danger, under rule of capital—especially its present phase of neoliberalism—another lurking danger is its evolution into what can be called as plutocracy—government by the rich.

Recently two interesting books have come out discussing 21st century capitalism. The one by Thomas Picketty's *Capitalism in the 21st Century*—which demonstrates convincingly that the

20th century exhibited a secular tendency toward continuous and widening inequality—has been received well here also. It discusses increasingly disproportionate concentration of income at the top, and the widening inequality that goes along with it, is integral to the system and a consequence of "the central contradiction of capitalism," (*Capital*, 571). Piketty's core theoretical concept is expressed in the formula 'r>g', where 'r' represents the return on capital/INVESTMENT, and 'g' the rate of growth of the economy.

Much like Piketty's contribution, a major study of democracy in America has also received almost as much attention in the West. It confirms our suspicions that oligarchy has replaced democracy. The authors found that "policies supported by economic elites and business interest groups were far more likely to become law than those they opposed.... [T]he preferences of the middle class made essentially no difference to a bill's fate".

The study *Testing Theories of American Politics: Elites, Interest Groups, and Average Citizens* by Martin Gilens (Princeton) and Benjamin Page (Northwestern)—which entirely undermine the notion that America is a democracy—and carries wider significance has not received attention here..(http://www.counterpunch.org/2014/05/02/apolitical-economy-democracy-and-dynasty/)

"Majority rule" accounts, construed numerically or by any "median voter" criterion, are found to be a "nearly total failure." Controlling for the preferences of economic elites and business-oriented interest groups, the preferences of the average citizen have a "near-zero, statistically non-significant impact upon public policy."

The preferences of economic elites have a "far more independent impact upon policy change than the preferences of average citizens do." This does not mean that ordinary citizens never get what they want by way of policy. Sometimes they do, but only when their preferences are the same as those of the economic elite...

"[M]ajorities of the American public actually have little influence over the policies our government adopts... [I]f policymaking is dominated by powerful business organizations and a small number of affluent Americans, then America's claims to being a democratic society are seriously threatened."

(http://www.counterpunch.org/2014/05/02/apolitical-economy-democracy-and-dynasty/)

According to the authors their results are 'troubling news for advocates of "populistic" democracy.' "When a majority of citizens disagrees with economic elites and/or with organized interests, they generally lose...even when fairly large majorities of Americans favour policy change, they generally do not get it."

In such an unfolding situation, where we are faced with this danger of democracy metamorphosing into majoritarianism and democracy becoming oligarchy with the highly undemocratic, violent Indian society—which glorifies violence against the oppressed and legitimizes, sanctifies inequality in very many ways acting as a backdrop question arises—the same question which Comrade Lenin had asked in a very different context 'What is to be Done'?

VI

There could be many such questions which demand answers. For example, till date not much attention has been paid to the parallel growth of nationalism and communalism in this part of South Asia. One also needs to revisit the anti-colonial struggle more critically, as one discovers that although it was fought invoking the idea of the nascent nation, at every crucial step, it tried to silence the voices of the oppressed already present here.

There is a Sanskrit Subhashitam which says *Wade wade jayate Tatwabodha* (As the debate progresses, we can reach a better understanding). One sincerely hopes that we will emerge from the meeting with new clarity, new resolve and new enthusiasm to fight demons of the present.

These are really dark times. But we should never forget that humanity has faced darker times than we have been witness to today. And despite occasional setbacks it has always moved ahead, surged ahead.

Today in these gloomy times news coming in from Tunisia —where the Islamist regime was defeated by a secular combination, or the perseverance of Bangladesh—where seculars are engaged in the life and death struggle with the communalists, with they having an upper hand today, definitely acts as a breath of fresh air.

Everybody would agree that there is much to learn from these victories.

9

Crony Secularism, Dialogue and Sacrifice: A Study of Kandhamal Violence, Odisha

Arun K. Patnaik and Rajesh Bag

Adversity is the mother of progress.

– M.K. Gandhi

Bure din hamare uttam shikshak hain. (Bad days are our excellent teachers)

— a Hindi proverb

Introduction

Crony secularism refers to a process of manipulation of the state power by elites while promoting secularism. It believes in relying on the state machineries to transform a conservative society as a secular one. Our case study demonstrates this. Crony secularism also relies on a political coalition of elites from different religious communities to carry out a secular programme. Whenever religious disputes grow, crony secularism resorts to legal machineries to settle these disputes. Because of severity of violence and the necessity of immediate restoration of social harmony, crony secularism uses peace committees to carry dialogue with two or more disputant parties. But these dialogues are ad hoc in nature, devoid of public participation and are marked by non-involvement of political party leaders of state or national level eminence. Crony secularism thus keeps religious communities out of the purview of dialogue. By overcoming crony secularism and fundamentalism, there emerges a story of dialogue with a direct participation of communities with the hope for a good society.

I

Learning from the Enemy

R.M. Lohia suggests that Hindu mythologies may be read progressively for moral and methodological lessons for contemporary purposes.[1] Lohia's progressive strategy has significant implications for secularism.[2] While a progressive (critical but respectful) interpretation of religion may connect with social imaginary and thereby reshape popular imagination, a negative/reactive strategy of secular intellectuals against *all* mythologies may alienate social imaginary of the popular from secular thinking and may ultimately help in the expansion of the extreme right-wing tendencies. Following Lohia's spirit of enquiry, we may recall an interesting dialogue between Lord Ram and his brother Lakshman in the last sections of Lankakanda of the Ramayana. Ravan is lying in pain on his death bed. Then, Ram advises Lakshman to meet Ravan in order to learn the art of governance from him. Lakshman is taken aback. Being fairly surprised by Ram's suggestion, he politely asks a question: what is there to learn from Ravan, 'our enemy'? Then Ram replies that there is something to learn from Ravan's wisdom, his art of governance and his devotion to Lord Shiva. It would be useful for the future rulers of Ayodhya.

The Ramayana gives us a very important moral lesson: learn from the strength of enemies while opposing them.[3] We are afraid that secular forces share Lakshman's unwillingness to learn from their combating enemies, whereas the Hindu right shows a Ram-like mindset in following this education technique. *The Hindu right deliberately forgets Ram's sacrifices to build the Kingdom, lest it should sacrifice some of its claims for rebuilding modern India.* But it follows Ram's technique of learning from the strength of enemies, especially socialist forces. It compromised with its old slogan of Akhanda Bharat by learning from the socialist slogan of Vananchal for the formation of small states. (Patnaik, 2011: 19-22) Since 1985, it has learned a two-line struggle—law and politics—to pursue its war for a temple in Ayodhya whereas secularism relied on the path of law alone to settle the Ayodhya dispute. The Hindu right gave up its sole reliance on law courts after 1985. (Patnaik and Mudiam, 2014b: 376) After every war against Christians, it asks for dialogue on conversion. After the killing of Graham Staines in Odisha, the RSS chief and also the then Prime Minister Atal Bihari Vajpayee called for dialogue on conversion.[4] The Hindu right has thus absorbed the old Marxist technique of combining dialogue with war. Similarly, it believes in penetrating social imaginary of subalterns by using folklores, folk-theatres, and religious common sense in a fundamentalist format. (Narayan, 2009; Froerer, 2007) It no longer believes in talking to the subalterns 'from outside'. All this turn around came most probably during the anti-emergency experiments and thereafter with which it was too deeply involved. This has enormously helped it in breaking its Lakshman-like isolationism (or non-dialogic mood). By connecting with enemies on the one hand and social imaginary of Hindu masses on the other hand since the Emergency period (1975-77), it has gained ascendancy in public imagination as never before.[5] Secular forces are left behind its methodological innovations. Secularists still assume that the Hindu right has grown leaps and bounds due to a sort of Goebblesian propaganda by its organizations and the corporate media. This assumption flatly ignores 'the mass character of the Hindu right, a point Antonio Gramsci and William Reich remind us to see in European fascism. Secular forces are rather fond of characterizing tribal, Dalit and OBC supporters of the RSS as 'foot soldiers' of the Hindu right.[6] This means that ordinary followers of the Hindu right are considered having empty minds guided by their commanders. Secular forces thus assume that secularism must penetrate mass psychology from outside. Here, secularism lost its war as its strategy bypasses social imaginary of the popular. To win this war, the secular forces must learn from Lord Ram's advice to Lakshman and overcome their Lakshman-like isolationism from both enemies and social imaginary of the popular with or without the Hindu right.

Crony Secularism

Secularism in India is in a crisis as it is trapped within a crony mentality. It may be useful to define what is meant by crony secularism. As the word "crony" has been discovered in the contemporary economic processes, it may be pertinent to recall crony capitalism. Crony capitalism refers to a process where the state routinely seeks out favours from the private sector individuals or businesses, and in exchange for political support, the state extends favours in the form of monopoly access to certain markets, preferred access to sales to government, special access to those in power and so on.

So also, crony secularism takes a grip in a society where the secular state extends political, administrative and judicial favours to the elites within religious communities on cultural issues. Crony capitalism encourages free riders in the economy in the name of "free market". Crony secularism encourages "free riders" in religious/cultural matters in the name of religious freedom or secularism. One of the outcomes of crony capitalism is the erosion of freedom in the market leading to the emergence of monopoly interests, whereas one of the outcomes of crony secularism is the erosion of secularism, giving rise to the entrenchment of fundamentalist forces. In both cases, the state fails to apply itself as a regulator/mediator.

In the context of secularism, the state fails to follow its own doctrines enshrined in the Constitution. For example, the state compromises with forms of intra-religious domination or inter-religious domination by way of patronizing elites from among all religious communities. Its complicity is rather suicidal for secularism.

Crony capitalism is believed to arise when political cronyism first rises and then gradually grips the economic world. Crony secularism also arises due to political cronyism which initially seeks out favours from religious communities for votes, by gradually doling out favours in the form of patronage system: a sort of "let them do whatever they want", thereby encouraging free riders' instincts in the cultural sphere. When democracy is reduced to a mere voting mechanism, when secular politicians have to seek voting favours with unfulfilled promises, then political cronyism spills over the field of religion/culture. Let us add here. It would be a mistake to think that crony secularism is a policy of the nation-state only. Many international players and non-state players try to enjoy a free rider's economy and culture. Its international character must be kept in mind. Just as global financial capital has set up crony capitalism in the name of free market, so also it has aided crony secularism in the form of several benefits such as (some) NGO services and (some) foreign trips for intellectuals and a few material gifts for the popular elements, thereby leading to a degeneration of cultural/religious values in the name of secularism.

Ambedkar, Weak Democracy and Crony Secularism

India's weak democracy and crony secularism are deeply connected. It is in this context, one is reminded of Ambedkar's forewarning. Ambedkar proposes a three-fold classification of democracy. First, there is a distinction between social and political democracy. This distinction is well-known. But he also proposes two more distinctions which are less known for reasons stated below.

Second, political democracy should establish another distinction between 'mechanism' and 'value system'. Democracy should not be reduced to a mere "mechanism" and that it should also be seen as a "value system" within which its mechanisms must operate. This implies that democracy should not be merely identified with the mechanisms like the periodic elections, the rotation of power, a competitive party system, and so on. It should preserve its value system such as human rights, issue of autonomy, secularism and so on. If democracy is obsessively concerned with its organizational mechanisms as in India, then it would bring its own downfall. In India today, all those who celebrate the deepening of democracy tend to forget Ambedkar's hypothesis. Ironically, the same forces are deeply worried about the future of secularism. They do not see connections between their celebration and their worry. The balance between democracy as mechanism and democracy as value system as proposed by Ambedkar is already lost in their intellectual projects. This is a huge paradox of democracy in

India. If democracy is already 'deepened', why should democracy be deeply worried about the survival of its elementary values like secularism? In other words, by implication, democracy has collapsed within 'vote bank' politics. Secular politics represents left-wing vote bank politics, whereas communal politics represents right-wing vote bank politics. Both contribute to the weakening of democracy in different ways. Today's communalism ironically celebrates electoral democracy.

Third, Ambedkar proposes another distinction in democracy: democracy as appeasement and democracy as settlement of grievances.[7] He argues that democracy should not be seen as a policy of appeasement of elites in the name of religious communities. Rather it should be seen as a policy of 'settlement' of popular 'grievances'. If democracy becomes a policy of appeasement, it would actually appease elites from religious communities and then produce 'Hitlers' from among them. There lies a danger to democracy in India. Ambedkar was deeply worried about the consequences of the Congress's policy of appeasement of Muslims and argues that it would initially produce Hitlers from among Muslim elites. This tendency in turn adversely affects Hindus who would sooner or later produce Hitlers from among their elites. So a policy of appeasement and its adverse impact would not be confined within one religious community. There lies the danger to India's secularism. The rise of Hitlers across all religious spectrums would hamper the interests of subalterns across the board. Any threat to political secularism is thus simultaneously a threat to subaltern's causes. This proposal of Ambedkar is also lost to us as most intellectuals are caught with one or another policy of appeasement and try to forget Ambedkar's inconvenient hypothesis. However, as we recall Ambedkar's forewarnings as above, we get jittery feelings as if he is still around us in 2015! For several historical reasons, democracy in India today is not in a position to dispel his misgivings.

As stated before by Ambedkar, a weak democracy creates conditions of a weak secularism or what may be called 'crony secularism'. The following conditions of crony secularism have persisted in India since independence. Let us sum up its features.

There are six features of crony secularism as follows:

1. It relies on the state power for promotion of secularism. It believes in secular elites to control state power through democratic or coercive means. It follows a policy of appeasement of elite interests and supports them in the name of religious communities.
2. The Constitution of India envisages 'building of political secularism' in India since 1950 through the imperative of reforms vide Article 25.[8] Following Charles Taylor, this reform strategy may be called a 'reform master narrative'. (Taylor, 2007: 773-776) As a part of its reform narrative, the Constitutional Order of 1950 was introduced. But this law is contradictory. On the one hand, it recognizes subaltern castes within the Hindu fold but does not recognize subaltern castes within Muslims and Christians for the constitutionally guaranteed reservation policy. Revised constitutional understanding since 1990 (after the inclusion of Buddhist Dalits) reinforces the Hindutva agenda of excluding 'non-Indic religions'. On the other hand, constitutional law follows an appeasement policy. It assumes that 'non-Indic' minorities are egalitarian and are free from caste practices. It thus hides caste within them. By doing so, the Indian Constitution keeps elites from Muslims and Christians happy by assuming that their religions are free from caste domination and thereby offers signals to victims of caste discrimination within 'Indic' religions to migrate to so-called egalitarian religions. No wonder, the biggest votaries of this contradictory and inconsistent constitutional law today are the Hindutva forces who are sharply opposed to the extension of reservation benefits to subaltern castes within 'non-Indic' religions. For, their 'ghar wapsi' programme could be carried out through the material allurement of reservation policy. The Hindutva parties also follow a 'pseudo-secular' reservation policy, if we may use their own vocabulary against them. What is initially meant for appeasing elites from Indian Islam and Indian Christianity by the secular camp is now ironically

being used to corner them by the anti-secular camp.

3. This policy of appeasement of non-Indic religions has another major implication from the subaltern's vantage point. The constitutional law assumes that Hindus must sacrifice for their 'subaltern' interests on account of caste and also compromise with proselytizing religions in safeguarding their right to propagation.[9] Muslims and Christians need not reform/sacrifice anything in order to build secularism in India. By excluding Muslims and Christians from a 'reform master narrative', the secular Indian constitution adopts a patronizing attitude towards these religions in India. Such a law could not appeal to 'social imaginary' of subalterns from among Muslims and Christians on secular grounds.[10] By now, they have experienced alienation due to this law and have started demanding scrapping the discriminatory 'Constitutional Order, 1950' which has created a crisis for secularism.
4. Religious communities are made passive observers in the secularization process or even during its crisis and wait to be manipulated for their votes by using fear psychosis prevalent among them. The manipulation of fear of the *Other* for votes is a common feature of both secular and fundamentalist camps.
5. Faced with the crisis of secularism, it relies more on the state machinery to settle religious disputes: police, judiciary and army. Peace committees with different community leaders are formed but dialogue is ad hoc and conflict resolution is through indirect means under an administrative driven process rather than politics and community-driven process.
6. Where secular politics shies away from 'direct conflict resolution' and all conflicts are referred to law courts for decades, it creates a void in social imaginary of people who get politically connected with religious fundamentalism at appropriate times.

II

Crony Secularism in Bamunigaon

The events in Bamunigaon propelled a series of anti-Christian riots across Kandhamal district in 2007. Swamy Lakshmananda (Swamiji) of the VHP was widely perceived to have provoked communal riots in the district in 2007. Eight months later, the Maoist squad took revenge on Swamiji for his alleged role in 2007 by killing him and four other associates in his ashram in August 2008. The Maoists were widely seen to have acted on behalf of Christians in this attack. So his killing in turn led to a major series of attacks on tribal and Dalit Christians across the district as well elsewhere in the state. Though communal massacres of 2008 bypassed Bamunigaon, it affected people of the village and made them very tense. The Bamunigaon events, as we shall show below, are thus at the root of the spiralling conflicts in Kandhamal witnessed during 2007 and 2008.

Bamunigaon is the Panchayat headquarter with 7 villages and 4 hamlets under the Bamunigaon Panchayat. It has also a police station with an Inspector in charge with the jurisdiction over eight Gram Panchayats. On the south eastern side of the village the Eastern ghats are located and on its western border lies a thick forest hill. These hills provided shelter to Odias and Dalit Christians respectively during the riots of 2007. Over a period of time, the village has emerged as a market hub. The Bamunigaon Panchayat has a network of villages bordering the districts of Gajapati, Ganjam and Rayagada in Odisha. It is located at a longer distance from the district headquarter Phulbani than from Brahmapura, a prominent town in the East coast. It is connected with the Block headquarter at Daringibadi by a road distance of 40 kms. But it takes three and a half hours by bus to reach the village as the road is not easily motorable.

Bamunigaon is an administrative and market hub. It has several administrative offices like a police station, government primary school and High School, Arts College, Primary Health Centre, Veterinary office, State Bank of India branch, Post Office branch, Panchayat Office and Revenue Inspector Office. Owing to the location of several administrative offices, people from the nearby eight Panchayats also come to the village. It organizes one of the weekly Hata (market) held every Monday. It has become a market hub due to this weekly market since 1981.[11] Villagers from nearly eight Gram Panchayats of Daringibadi Block and two Gram Panchayats from Gajapati and Ganjam districts solely depend on it for buying and selling of materials, livestock, forest and agricultural products. While every week 5 to 7 thousand visitors come here, during festival times 15 to 20 thousand people visit the market.

The upper and middle caste businessmen basically sell household items, dress and other consumer goods but purchase forest and agricultural goods. The livestock business is done by the Christian Panas.[12] People from nearly 87 villages solely depend on the weekly market to purchase food items and usable materials. For Panas and Kandhas, the weekly Hata not only provides an opportunity to buy and sell but it also gives space for social interaction with friends and relatives.[13] It gives an opportunity to bridge friendship. It also gives an opportunity to get information about relatives or friends. When there were no telephones, people used to depend on the Hata to know about their daughters married in other Panchayats. People used to come to the market and pass on messages from friends and relatives. When communal riots happened its market life got severely affected. It was closed for nearly three years, affecting livelihood options and social communication for all occupational groups belonging to different religions. This brought tacit pressure on communities to think of reconciliation. We shall return to this later.

The social profile of the village is as follows. The village (old and new Bastis) as a whole has a population of around 3008 men and women with a total of 609 families.[14] Basically the old Bamunigaon consists of three Sahis (street). They are known as Odia Sahi, Pana Sahi and Kandha Sahi. People from the old Sahi depend on the forest resources such as fire wood, leaves and other forest products for their sustenance. In a total of 151 households in the Odia Sahi, most families are from the OBC category. The households of the street are distributed as follows: Paika (peasant warrior caste, 30), Sundhi (toddy tapper,

25), Gouda (milkman, 5), Kumbhar (potter, 5), Bindhani (Lohar, 5) and Telli (oil pressurer, 20). A few upper caste families also reside here. Odia communities (henceforth 'Odias') are Hindus.[15] The Pana (broom and rope weaving or drummer) Sahi is adjacent to the Odia Sahi and has about 53 families. They are all Christians. And the Kandha Sahi is adjacent to the Pana Sahi and has about 15 families. At present, a few more Sahis have come up due to the settlement of trading communities in the village. These Sahis are Batappali Sahi with Panas, Bazar Sahi with business communities and Basudevpur Sahi with the retired SC/ST employees. Along with the main roads, business communities reside with their shops. The recently migrated business communities belong to the caste Hindus particularly the Komatis (Telugu Vyasya), Tellis, Sundhis and few Brahmins. In 1982 there was one cloth store and two grocery shops in this village. Owing to the recent migration, the present market establishment has expanded twenty times more. The business communities basically belong to Kumuti, Sundhi, Telli and a few Brahmin castes.[16] The conflict in Bamunigaon in 2007 is about issues pertaining to people from two Sahis: the Odia Sahi and the Pana Sahi. But it involved everybody else from other Sahis. It shut down the weekly Hata for a long three years. It ruined every body's life and livelihood options. So also, in the conflict resolution process people from these two Sahis were thus mainly involved.

Secularization of Social Imaginary: Social Discrimination from High to Moderation

If we look at the social relations between the Pana Christians and the Odia Sahi's middle castes, we may find them historically evolving from high to low discrimination after 1985. After 1985, periodic solidarities between religious communities developed while pursuing festive activities. The visible forms of social discrimination began to decline.[17] Panas are mostly agricultural workers and the Odia Sahi people are mainly landowners. Panas are mostly employed during paddy plantation and harvesting by the Odia castes for a wage and in other seasons of the year, Panas are engaged as sweepers and drummers during the marriage time, festival time and household functions of the Odia

Sahi people.[18] However, four to five Pana families own agricultural lands to the extent of 2 acres and the rest are landless labourers. In the Odia Sahi, 25 families own land up to 2 acres and other traditional castes work as wage labour, petty traders, seasonal migrants and so on. There are only medium, small and marginal farmers in this village.[19] Odia Sahi families do prepare and sell Lia (fried paddy), Muan (Odia sweet made from jaggery and fried paddy) and other traditional sweets during the Siva Ratri (night long Jagar for Lord Siva) and Christmas festivals. While these traditional economic exchanges continue in the village, many new forms of exchange between caste communities have been introduced since the 1990s.

Visible forms of discrimination are still practised but are gradually being reduced. Before the 1990s, the Panas were looked down upon as low caste people.[20] They would not come nearer Veranada (porch) of the Odia Sahi houses.[21] They would collect dead cows from Odia Sahi families for food or burial. The Pana women were subjected to humiliation near the village ponds. They were told to stay away from the Odia women at a distance and could access the village pond only after the Odia women finished their baths and washing of clothes. Sometimes, at the sight of Pana women, they would mock, "Have Pana Brahmanianis come here or not?"[22] Both Paika men and women claimed superiority over Panas openly and humiliated them publicly even without any provocation. Even, Panas were disliked to ride on bicycles by the Paika youth.[23] They used to encourage Kandhas more than Panas in social proximity. Up to the 1990s, Panas used to wash their glasses after drinking tea in the village tea stalls and keep the clean glass upside down so that residual water would touch the ground and the glass would be deemed as pure.[24]

From the early 1990s, the visible forms of discrimination began to decline gradually for several reasons. After the introduction of social play during festival times in the 1990s, youth from both Sahis began showing social solidarity. The Pana youth participated in social dramas in the village festivals actively and contributed to their success. As a result, they became talking points of the village. The Pana youth were not asked to wash their tea glasses. Their mocking and public humiliation began to decline.[25] When the self-help group schemes were introduced for women's empowerment in the village, it exposed both Odia Sahi women and Pana women to the Banking sector.[26] They used to go together to the government offices and banks and stand in the queues before the Bank counters. This enabled them to interact with each other more. So the old caste prejudices began to decline. Mocking references at the village pond became less visible now. A Pana cycling his way was no more mocked. Panas began to get invitations to attend marriage feasts in the Odia Sahi as per rules and norms. They used to eat at the end. But they were welcome now. Waste food was not thrown at them anymore. Now they were welcome to sit on the verandahs of the Odia Sahi families for discussions.[27]

However, when positive interactions between two religious and caste communities became clear year after year, the year 2003 witnessed the rising hatred at Panas, their social mobility and greater visibility. According to both Panas and Odia Sahi elders, this happened primarily due to Swamiji from the VHP. Interestingly, separated by time by an urge for reconciliation, both the conflicting parties now pass the blame to Swamiji for provoking and mesmerizing Odia youths with powerful hate speeches in 2003 and thereafter.

Secularization Halted: Beef-Eating or Cultural Domination Since 2003

Bamunigaon, the conflict between the Pana Sahi and the Odiya Sahi came to the fore due to the pouring of kerosene oil in the beef meet by a few RSS-oriented youths from the Odia Sahi in 2003. In 2007, this conflict snowballed into a major crisis. As stated before, Swamiji is widely held responsible for instigating Odia youths to do so.[28]

The Odia Sahi came under the influence of Swamiji from the 1980s. Whenever he visited the village he used to teach Jangya, Sanskruti, Gita, Bhagavata and Adhyatmikata. He visited this village with a chariot in the year 1988/90. During car festivals in Puri, he used to visit the village on the Jagannath Rath and he did that twice. He allegedly once brought a stone from the Ram Sethu from the Tamil coast. He developed a Sanghathan (organization) here. Whenever he came, he stayed here for one to two hours. His major activities were to preach Brahminical Hinduism and its ritual activities. He was strongly opposed to beef eating and religious conversion. He was also teaching villagers how to stay clean and protect the forest.[29] His major objective was to speak to the people: "Mo dikhya Hindu rakhya" (My duty is to protect Hinduism). He also taught how to improve agriculture, education and health. He set up a Sakha for mobilization of youth and a Bal Bikash Kendra for child education. He used to persuade people how to protect cows and stop conversion to Christianity. He was a social activist and great mobilizer. For his disciples he was like a torch bearer.[30] Swamiji used to admonish Odia youths for not protecting 'cows' from being slaughtered.[31] In 2003, the Sakha members once poured kerosene on the beef meat being cleaned by Panas near the main road. Before doing this, the Sakha membes took photos of people involved in cleaning the meat and filed a police complaint against Pana Christians. Thereafter, police harassment began.[32]

The reaction of Panas was full of surprise. They wondered how the Odia Sahi people could complain against beef eating, when they used to invite them to take away dead animals for food. Panas blamed the Sakha initiated by Swamiji for the spread of hatred against their food habits.

Panas realized that they were dependent on the Odia business families for food materials and groceries. Harassed by the mentalities of the Sakha youth and Odia business families, Panas boycotted their tea stalls, hotels, Kirana (retail) and grocery shops, so on. Because of this confrontation, they initially started with a tea stall in 2003. The tea stall emerged as new Adda (meeting) centre for Panas of this village.[33] Later borrowing money from the local public sector bank, a few unemployed Dalit youth and other Pana elders started different business activities at the Panchayat market complex. In 2005, Panas decided to consolidate their business under the banner of Dr. Ambedkar Banik Sangh. Odia business communities were already having the Vighnaraja Banik Sangh registered since 1994.[34] Now a new contestation began between the two parallel Sanghs from the Odia Sahi and the Pana Sahi. The business of the Odia Sahi communities began experiencing a new low in competition with the Ambedkar Banik Sangh.

Clash of Intolerance

The old business communities did not make huge profits as they did during the past once a new rival emerged on the scene. Though competition became intense between these two communities, their activities continued and provided life and livelihood options for both sections. The Ambedkar Sangh started the celebration of Bada Dina Parva (Christmas Day) in the adjacent to the main road in December 2005 and 2006.[35] During the years of 2005 and 2006, celebrations were organised by the sides of the main road. No conflict took place. Although Panas celebrated the Christmas Day, they did not celebrate social dramas so far. So in the year 2007, it was decided to have a grand festival. Under the banner of Dr. B.R. Ambedkar Banika Sangh, Panas collected some money to celebrate Christmas. Like their neighbouring business rival Vighnaraja Banika Sangh celebrating Dusshera and Ganesh Puja on the grand scale, Panas thought to celebrate their festival by organizing a Nataka (play). The Sangh invested around Rs. 80 thousand in the arrangement of the Medha (podium) alone. They invested much more in arranging music system and arch lights spread across the main road. A Nataka was planned with their own people. The Sangh appealed for the government permission to celebrate Christmas and got the permission from the concerned police officer.[36] Before that happened, objections began to fly, followed by rumours spread by the VHP cadres. During the four days following December 23, 2007, thick objections and rumours flew rapidly that led to the collapse of the social contract in Bamunigaon.

On the 23rd, the Odia Sahi people instigated by the VHP leaders objected to the grand celebration of the Christmas festival.[37] They objected that the main road would be blocked if Panas went ahead with a series of arc lights spread across the main road. Their contention was to celebrate the festival without blocking the main road. Dalit Christians felt that this was how the Odia Sahi people celebrated all festivals like Ganesh Puja and Dussehra and wondered why they should object now. Moreover, they also got police permission for all arrangements. They felt that their objection was more due to caste jealousy and want to humiliate Christian Panas in celebration of their festival. Police tried to mediate between two groups and failed to prevail on Odias. On the same day later, the SP was involved in discussions and saw nothing positive happening. In frustration he retorted that if Odias did not agree with the police for giving permission, then they would die fighting each other. Nothing would happen to him or the local police. When people became very unhappy with his statement, he retraced a bit and said that he would see what could be done by next day.'

On the 24th early in the morning, there were strong rumours claiming that the weekly Hata (market) would not be held due to the tensions in Bamunigaon.[38] Panas suspect that the 'foot soldiers' of Swamiji might be involved in spreading these rumours. The traders came from Ganjam and Gajapati districts to participate in the weekly market in trucks and trollies. Police was asked to negotiate and see that the market would function smoothly. When elders from both communities were trying to reach the police station for a dialogue, police reached the weekly market place to open it and failed to control agitating mobs from either side. Both communities clashed with each other and police got injured too. During the three hours from 8 am to 11 am on the 24th, Christians and Hindus confronted each other and soon clashed in the bazar. A few Odia youth got injured severely. Odia Sahi youth were hospitalised. Panas alleged that their podium, music system and arch lights were all destroyed. Around 6 pm of the same day, a Christian youth burned an Odia shop and this led to a new tense situation once again, alleged by the Odia Sahi people.

Dalit Christians believe that the rumours were spread to prevent the weekly market from opening so that their festival shopping could be spoiled on 24th December. On the 24th evening, a massive rumor was spread through the ETV Odia that Swamiji on his way to visit Bamunigaon was assaulted by the Christian youths in Dasingbadi and admitted in a Daringibadi hospital. This led to a series of retaliatory attacks on Christian communities across the district. On the 25th morning, miscreants phoned local people, informed that Swamiji was injured and hospitalised. Also, Hindus and

Christians clashed in Baliguda and Barakhamba. In retaliation, an Odia mob in collusion with the Hindutva followers from outside burnt down 30 Dalit households and the 43-year-old Church. They also vandalised 25 shops in Bamunigaon. When the Dalits came to know the impending attack, they left for hiding in the Western side hills and a few returned in the evening after the SP and the CRPF company landed in the village.

On the 27th morning, about five thousand Dalit and tribal Christians allegedly in collusion with the Maoists surged ahead to retaliate the destruction of property on the Christmas day. They were armed with axes, spears and fire and burnt down nearly 118 houses of the Odia Sahi and were marching towards the market to burn down shops.[39] When police tried to break their strength by firing rounds in the air and in the legs by 11am, two Panas and one unidentified youth were killed. A young boy was also injured in his leg. When more rounds were fired, the mob once again fled to the forest. Dalit women said that they too fled to the jungle due to the ferocity of violent attack. Even, Odia communities escaped to a separate jungle at the South side of the village. When police arranged relief camps, women first returned followed by Dalit men. They had to hide in the jungles for three to four days without food and water. Three FIRs were filed by each community against a total of 80 people from both groups with regard to the destruction of houses, shops and the Church property. The story of conflict in Bamunigaon began on 24th December and ended on December 27, 2007. Over these four days, already fragile relations between Odias and Panas collapsed. And it could not be revived until the end of 2010, three years later.

III

Adversity as a Teacher, 2007-2010

Over the next three years both the warring communities felt restless owing to a variety of factors. First, the weekly market collapsed depriving business and livelihood options for all. Second, schools stopped from functioning preventing children from further studies nearby. Third, girls were not prepared to marry men from this village as a few of them were involved in litigation. Four, youths started migrating due to the lack of opportunities in this village. Five, politicians were not prepared to settle their conflict through peaceful means. Six, they realized that they would be wasting time and money in court cases while looking for justice. It might take more time than they initially thought. Seven, neither religious peace nor Bhaichara (coordination among brethren) would materialize when justice is delayed through courts. Eight, they felt that social prestige is lost in police cases, arrests, interrogation and public enquiry. Nine, they recalled an Odia saying that 'Golia pani zia ku suhae' (the mud water suits earthworm).[40] The earthworm/crab in this case is the Maoist for Panas and the RSS for Odias. Both participated in perpetuating conflicts (muddy water). However, now they started looking for clean water by removing earthworms. Both groups now wanted to shed their pro-Maoist tags and pro-RSS tags. Ten, both parties observed that due to perpetuation of conflict scenarios, police were more in numbers in the streets of Bamunigaon. Their presence prevented the villagers from visiting the forests for collection of fuel wood and other forest products. This has also prevented relatives and friends from visiting them. In this, they saw a loss of social prestige. Eleven, after 6 pm every evening since 2007, nobody was able to move out of fear and anxieties of life. Cultural anxieties got exacerbated in conflict scenarios. Twelve, government departments like schools, hospitals and banks stopped functioning, forcing communities to think of dialogue for peace and development. Each point is reported to us by respondents from both communities.

These are not our explanations for the need for dialogue and reconciliation. We however think people are reasonable enough to offer rational explanations as they do in Bamunigaon. These are heart-felt feelings of religious communities. Following Gramsci, this could be called 'good sense' which is still part of common sense of the popular.[41] The secular state indirectly contributed to this social imaginary to revive by building up legal pressure on communities but did not politically mediate to address the above issues confronting two warring communities. On the contrary, the secular democratic state is part of the problem being faced by people in Bamunigaon. Secular political parties shied away from solving their problems. But during the 2009 national and state elections, secular parties were there to seek their votes. The BJP won the MLA seat in G. Udayagiri where the village falls and the BJD the MP seat in Phulbani where this village is an integral part. In the aftermath of violence, the secular state provided relief camps and provided relief materials such as cooking items, food and dress materials. It also assisted families with the compensation amount for the construction of houses only. Secular parties controlling state power refused to mediate to resolve Ashanti (unrest or trouble) in the region, despite community leaders approaching them. This is a key feature of crony secularism which does not want communities to settle their own politico-religious disputes and solely relies on the time-consuming legal measure to settle their disputes. The disputes in Kandhamal would have easily travelled the path of major communal riots, if the communities had not taken up 'direct action' to settle their own disputes.

Dialogue in Passive Mode in 2009

Crony secularism enforces the passivity of religious communities and offers them only time-consuming legal remedies. As a tribal leader told us that communities tried to overcome their passivity by directly mediating on their Ashanti and decided for a resolution of Ashanti through dialogue and reconciliation.[42] Communities forced dialogue by dodging the RSS and the Church which were fighting their respective cases in the courts of law. Let us discuss this aspect now. Before the Anchalik Shanti Committee was formed in 2009, 'peace' meetings were conducted by the Revenue Divisional Commissioner (RDC), a senior IAS officer in the first week of January 2008. About five meetings were held under the district administration. The RDC chaired the first meeting and asked the two disputant parties to nominate 5 members in the peace committee. These meetings happened near the porch of the police station. The RDC spoke of how development and peace were affected by riots of 2007. He also spoke of 'Bhaichara' in the village. But his speech did not cut much ice at the meeting where disputant parties aggressively hurled accusations against each other. It led to more acrimony. There could not be any moderation to penetrate a divided social imaginary in the village and its neighbourhood. Communities did not confess mistakes committed by each which led to riots in 2007. It was like a continuation of war in dialogue rather than dialogue in a continued warring condition. As there was no moderation for confession, reconciliation was not even imagined by the communities. Peace meetings were conducted by the district authorities for the next four times without any tangible result. At best, these peace meetings could have prevented communities from indulging in riots in 2008 when Swamiji was killed. But it did not restore peace and development as envisaged by the RDC. These meetings failed as there was a lukewarm response of secular *Netas* (politicians) and Babus (officials) to hold dialogue on a sustained basis. Also, the victims were busy in rebuilding their household life rather than their strained social relations. However, the RDC's speech might have left a mark in social imagination of warring communities as the theme of his speech returned back in dialogue renewed in December 2009.

On December 15, 2009, a meeting was organized by the Inspector in Charge (IIC) of the Bamunigaon police station to form the first Anchalik Shanti Committee (regional peace committee). The committee was formed with ten members under the chair of the Tahsildar on behalf of the state government. A few organic intellectuals of Christian and Hindu communities participated in this meeting which selected the Panchayat Samiti Chairman Luksen Majhi, a tribal leader, as the President of the Committee. The committee hoped that a neutral leader would help the dialogue to take shape and pave the way for reconciliation. But this did not happen. Majhi did not take any initiative for the dialogue. The villagers soon realized that the official committee would not do anything useful for reconciliation. Communities must participate directly in conversation.

Two communities from the Odia Sahi and the Pana Sahi must meet directly and admit the truth and go for reconciliation after discovering each other's sources of Ashanti. The organic intellectuals from two communities activated their respective communities to come forward in the making of the second Anchalik Shanti Committee. Meanwhile, arrest warrants were issued by the Fast Track courts in Phulbani set up in 2008. That put additional pressure and hurried their motivation for dialogue. Then, they started looking for an Abahak (moderator) and 20 members each from Christian and Hindu communities. Invitations were sent to all other villages (nearly 87) under the Bamunigaon police station to attend as observers. The agenda was to 'open up your hearts to each other and discuss': "Hrudaya Kholi Alochana Kariba".[43] Before this new strategy could happen, Maoists killed a local civil contractor, a 'lumpen' and pro-RSS element Manoj Sahu on November 25, 2010 for his alleged role in communal riots in 2007 and 2008. And the dialogue meeting was scheduled four days later. But this killing of an Odia Sahi businessman put a spanner on the inter-community dialogue. However, after the issue of arrest warrant issued by fast track courts looking into communal riots in 2007, police arrested a few youths from either side of the religious divide. This once again triggered the need for dialogue.

Dialogue, Direct Action and Communities During 2009-12

A new strategy was conceived to reconvene the second Regional Peace meeting. On December 29, 2010, each Sahi Sabha was held and chose 10 members each to represent their truth in the regional committee.[44] Both Sahi Sabhas met on the same day. In both the Sabhas, the communities decided to follow decisions taken by their nominees. There was no help from the government and the NGOs for this dialogue to happen. However, villagers themselves arranged funds for the meeting from their own contributions. The 'Solidarity for Developing Communities' (SFDC) with its head office in Brahampur helped in providing transport for participants from neighbouring villages. Local NGOs also claimed to have given small contributions.

On December 30, 2010, the Regional Peace Committee met in the college ground. Men and women of Bamunigaon participated in these deliberations. Villagers from the local police region also gathered. At this meeting, Karmapat Majhi was nominated as the President and Narendra Mohanty as the Secretary. Being neutral to this dispute, Karmapat Majhi, a tribal leader from the Saramuli Gram Panchayat, was chosen as their new moderator. Narendra Mohanty is the state convener of INSAF and the founder of the Vanavasi Suraksha Parishad, Kandhamal.

Members were told to open up their hearts. Majhi asked a few basic questions for members to ponder while narrating their Ashanti: Why did caste discrimination not lead to violent forms before? How did it promote violence now? The Hindus replied that they did not anticipate that this kind of violence would happen. They thought that they should keep Jati and Dharma on top. It led to showing off their superiority complex and domination over Christians. Their ego led them to be losers in life. Panas responded by saying that though they did not believe in discrimination, they resented Odia's domination and became revengeful which is why violence happened. Their mistake lies in taking revenge and retribution. Then Majhi asked them: what do you want now? Both Hindus and Christians stood up and collectively vouched for peace. 'Why peace now?', asked Majhi. Both representatives stood up and stated that due to misunderstanding between groups, they lost property, social prestige, gained more suffering and harassment in court cases. So they wanted peace. Majhi moderated Tarka/Bitarka (arguments and counters) between communities. Both groups decided to drop branding each other as pro-RSS or pro-Maoist.

The peace committee settled for the following resolutions.[45]

1. Both Hindus and Christians formed a local peace committee to resolve disputes by proving the 'innocence' of each other.
2. The committee banned Deshi and Bịdeshi liquor in the village and the liquor trader Satyabadi Sahu accepted the demand at the meeting.
3. It was decided to propagate peace in the region through the use of local media and representatives.
4. Chitra Sen Patra from the Odia Sahi and Kailash C. Nayak from the Pana Sahi were elected as the President and the Secretary to carry out these tasks. They would also lead the Regional Peace Committee which would resolve

Ashanti in the 'region'. The Regional Committee with 32 members from the region and the local committee with 10 members from the village were set up.

At the regional level meeting, it was decided that they would celebrate each festival within the premises of the temple or church or village streets. They would not hold these functions on the main road. The celebration of festivals on the main road was responsible for the riots in 2007. The Dalit Christians also decided that beef cutting and sale should not be displayed in an open space. They would transact cutting animal meat and sale from inside a house in the Pana Sahi only. The Odias recount a local saying, "Nija Ichha Re Khaiba, Para Ichcha Re Pindhiba" (Eat according to one's wish, dress according to other's wish).[46] This local saying was brought into force while reconciling with food habits of each other. They regret that they were provoked by the external elements. Both communities compromised with their exhibitionist stances. It is interesting to note that Dalit Christians also regretted for being revengeful and exhibitionist and gave up 'public' spaces for festival celebration, beef-cutting and sale.

Immediately after the regional meeting, the local peace committee met the lawyers from the RSS and Church to withdraw their respective cases. To their surprise, lawyers told them that cases could not be settled out-of-court but advised them to do the following. During the subsequent witness depositions, they should say that they did not see how violence happened. On January 19, 2011, the local peace committee met in the ground of the cooperative society. They decided that each community would spend money separately while visiting the Daringibadi session court. But they would use a common fund for transportation cost while visiting the Fast Track court in Phulbani.[47] The SFDC also assisted both groups on four occasions. A community was given an amount of Rs. 15,000 for each deposition in the court in Phulbani. It helped them in arranging the transport cost. They said that they visited the court more than ten times for each case. There were about 6 cases filed. Due to this witness deposition process, a new kind of solidarity emerged later. They used to cook and eat food together during their several visits to the court in Phulbani. Such close interaction was unknown in the region before. By March 26, 2012 all cases were dropped.

IV

Anomaly Between Secular State and Secularization

There are certain implications of this dialogue and reconciliation for political secularism. There are anomalies between the secular state and its principles of constitutionalism on the one hand and the principles of secularization process emerging among communities on the other hand. In other words, the legal path followed by the secular state and a dialogue path followed by communities are at variance with each other. It must be admitted that a strict enforcement of law from above and the loss of market and livelihood from below put pressure on the communities and moved them towards dialogue.

Dialogue for Restorative Justice

First, dialogue helps communities to reactivate their social imaginary from which they get alienated by following a legal strategy for justice induced by the secular state. So communities give up the time-consuming process of remedial justice pursued by the state. In the remedial justice usually sought through a court of law, one seeks justice through the punishment of criminals. As communities are involved in committing crimes, the process of delivery of remedial justice is laborious, time-consuming and costly. As a result, both the groups seek restorative justice by using their respective social imaginary. In restorative justice, communities may seek justice through a restoration of pre-existing non-violent life. But when the restoration takes place, life is restored in a higher form. Their 'good sense' in the pre-existing social imaginary gets triggered and helps in the restoration of life in a new form. For example, in this case study, they stopped their opposition to beef-eating by invoking elements in their social imaginary. According to their social imaginary, food must be eaten according to one's own pleasure. Similarly, through dialogue caste Hindus gave up certain superiority and welcomed Dalits to their marriage functions and to sit on the porches of the houses. Though the caste system still exists, the pre-existing social discrimination however changed now. Thus, by connecting with their own social imaginary, they may discover new forms of justice. Through the medium of law, it is likely that they get more and more alienated from their own social imaginary. Law induces passivity. They may manage to overcome the problem of passivity through the medium of dialogue. Just as communities get reconnected with social imaginary, secularism can also connect with social imaginary of communities and try to reshape their imaginary. An immanent engagement with social imaginary is necessary if political secularism must overcome its Lakshman-like isolationism. Just as communities revive a new spirit of friendship, the secular state must become a network of friendship.

Dialogue as Yagna

Second, *politics of self-purification is another feature of dialogue. Dialogue can induce communities to meditate on self-criticism. Without dialogue, they would be only critical of each other. That is how dialogue can contribute to a new friendship.* Any patronizing attitude in friendship is harmful to its growth, whereas a self-critical attitude can take friendship to a newer height. The secularization process may be seen as a self-critical perspective of friendship, not simply as a friendship network. Communities may dialogue by scrutinizing each other closely. They criticize themselves while accusing the other. They subject themselves to what B.R. Ambedkar would call 'Yajna' (not to be confused with Swamiji's Yajna in Kandhamal).[48] What Ambedkar calls self-purification may be called self-criticism, not just satyagraha or war against the enemy. In the present story, the Odia communities criticized themselves for showing caste superiority, religious superiority and cultural superiority in food and other things. What they could not learn from law courts, they learned from their own social imaginary. Their good sense guided them in coming out of their bad sense. They criticized their own exhibitionism. They could recall friendship and fellow-feeling with lower caste Panas from the days of social plays and self-help groups that reduced caste-based untouchability. This helped them ease their Ashanti that inflicted them during 2003-2010. Political secularism must introspect much like our communities here. An introspective politics would do a world of wonders to secular polity. It must begin its journey in Ambedkar's Yajna.

Dialogue and Inter-sectionality of Disputes

Third, the Kandhamal conflicts show that *when dialogue takes place at the intersection of both inter- and intra-religious disputes, it is capable of producing reconciliation. The secular society/state/ political society must adopt a similar strategy.*[49] Two or more paths of criticism of domination must intersect for the progress of secularism. Today, Hindu fundamentalism tries to split political secularism from social imaginary of the popular by simply highlighting inter-religious disputes such as Shuddhi/ conversion. Secular thinking tries reversing this argument by highlighting intra-religious domination within Hindus only. The current debate on 'Ghar Wapsi' in secular thinking seems to have fallen for a trap laid by Hindu fundamentalism. This is a dangerous temptation and a binary thinking. Fundamentalism thrives in binary thinking, whereas secularism can thrive only in dialectical thinking. For these two paths of religious disputes tend to intersect. True, inter-religious disputes may grow by concealing intra-religious reforms as in India today. Conversion-Shuddhi debate may confuse and divert the public from addressing intra-religious disputes. Political secularism, however, must chart its course by addressing both disputes. In Kandhamal, we notice two communities criticized caste domination sanctioned by religion as well as inter-religious domination. While the upper caste Hindus confessed their caste superiority, they also criticized themselves for interfering in beef-eating activities of Dalit Christians. They considerably sacrificed their caste complexes and also their opposition to cultural habits of another religious community. Similarly, Christians gave up beef-cutting and sale in open space and also agreed not to celebrate festivals on the main road. They noticed that by doing so, they tried to show a form of symbolic domination over the Hindu community. The upper caste Hindus carried a dialogue involving a two-line criticism of both intra- and inter-religious domination. Dalit Christians admitted their follies in exhibitionism at the cost of the general public. The story from Kandhamal indicates a double criticism of domination followed by communities and this has ultimately helped in secularization of social imaginary.

The Revival of Good Sense

Four, *dialogue has the ability to offer a synthesizing perspective which the legal route would not. When the agency of communities is directly active in a dialogue, a synthesizing perspective may emerge and help in reconciliation.* But dialogue or no dialogue, agency of the popular cannot be denied. The caste Hindu supporters dodged the RSS, despite the organization helping them in the court cases. Usually, the subaltern followers of the Hindu right are described as 'foot soldiers' by the secular intelligentsia. If followers of the RSS are without their own minds, then it begs a few questions. Does it mean that they lack their own agency/subjectivity especially while supporting the Hindutva's cause? If their minds are poisoned by Hindutva ideology, how could they then develop 'good sense' for dialogue, sacrifice, reconciliation, peace and development? If they act as per dictates of their commanders only, then how could they dodge the Hindu commanders? Similarly, the followers of the Church also dodged the latter, despite the latter helping their legal cases and extending support in their tragedy. In fact, both communities bypassed the legal route shown to them by the RSS and Church. One implication of this case study is that community supporters are not necessarily 'foot soldiers'. They might have been guided by the Right in creating riots. But faced with adversity (bad days), they are capable of recalling positive things from their past social imaginary, develop moral lessons from 'bad times' and forge a 'good sense' for the future. As Gandhi says, adversity is the mother of progress. The secular argument about subaltern followers of the Hindu right as 'foot soldiers' prevents us from seeing that adversity might be an excellent teacher for 'ordinary followers' of fundamentalism. *This good sense emerges from a synthesis of past social imaginary, present adversity and future peace and development initiated by popular elements themselves,* without a direct mediation of the secular state/civil society obsessed with a legalistic solution.

Gramsci advises his comrades not to rush to describe the subaltern supporters of fascism as 'lumpen', without exploring the root causes of their support (Smith 2010: 46). Such a usage would not help comrades from delinking the masses from fascism. In the present case study, we could discern significance of his advice. Needless to argue that the secular state has not played a decisive role in bringing about secularization in Kandhamal after the riots of 2008. The secular state only initiated relief camps, 'fast-track' courts and 'ad hoc' dialogues run by district administration. True, these tactics indirectly put pressure on communities for dialogue. But secular political parties did not play any role in ad hoc or real dialogues in the district. Unfortunately, this story of the secular state is not a stand-alone case in Kandhamal. Faced with adversity, the secular state/parties always resort to relief camps, legal means and ad hoc peace meetings everywhere. In the end, when relief camps and ad hoc peace committees are withdrawn, disputant communities are left at the altar of a time-consuming legal process. In Kandhamal, disputant communities realized follies of a legal path seeking justice, broke with passivity inflicted by crony secularism, reactivated their good sense and asserted their agency to carry out dialogue and reconciliation.

Beyond Constitutional Secularism: From Simple to Complex Differential Sacrifice

Five, *agency-based dialogue must involve a strategy of complex differential sacrifice as it needs to negotiate intersections of inter- and intra-domination in India.* Usually secular political society in India uses a model of simple differential sacrifice.[50] That has been its failing. The Constitution of India follows a 'reform master narrative' based on a strategy of simple differential sacrifice. Following the Indian Constitution, as stated before, most secularists claim that the majority religion must sacrifice conservative practices for the sake of an alliance with religious minorities so that all communities may gain peace and development. This model of sacrifice is extrapolated from intra-religious domination in India (mainly Hindus) as acknowledged in the Indian Constitution. Europeans too followed this strategy as their political secularism needed to negotiate with intra-religious domination only. The Church was asked to sacrifice its domination over the state. This led to the separation of the state from Church and the rise of twin-toleration between Church and the state. As a result, the state emerged as the sovereign power. This strategy seems to have a global reach. For example, in a family the parents are expected to make sacrifices for the sake of securing a better future for children and in turn are expected to ensure their own well-being.

In the Indian Constitution, 'Hindu' elites (vide Articles 15.4, 16.4, 17, 25.2.b, 46, 330 and 332) are expected to sacrifice domination by initiating reforms in access to *all public places,* religious sites and temporal locations.[51] So by safeguarding minority rights in culture, education and propagation, the Indian Constitution asks only Hindus to make a sacrifice for minority religions (vide Article 25 and Article 30).[52] The constitution of India follows what may be called a strategy of simple differential sacrifice and expects Hindus to make sacrifices to build political secularism in 1950. But this constitutional strategy is *not even uniformly applied to all religions.* Even though Sikhism and Buddhism are later added in this reform narrative, Muslims and Christians are still assumed to be egalitarian religions free from caste domination and are kept out of its purview. This assumption is patently incorrect.

As this model is in operation in India since independence, the secular state initially believed in asking Hindus to sacrifice conservative practices with regard to women's issues. The Hindu code bill, for example, asked only majority religious groups to sacrifice certain conservative positions on women, marriage, and property. This bill could not become law due to stiff opposition. It is nevertheless part of modern social imaginary of the intelligentsia being articulated by discourses of various political movements. Thus, the current debates around this bill since its inception reconfirm the constitutional belief that only the majority religion must sacrifice for the sake of political secularism. At least, theoretically, political secularism has not similarly debated women's concerns on marriage and property reforms within Indian Islam, Christianity, Sikhism and others.[53] Thus, a simple differential sacrifice strategy is being followed not merely by the Indian constitution; it has also gained legitimacy in several secular camps ranging from Nehruvian to feminist circles. This model of sacrifice is misleading in a context where conservative practices persist within and outside religious divisions in India. For conservative positions arising from caste and gender domination are found among Hindus, Muslims, Christians, Sikhs and Buddhists and even tribals.

Similarly the tendency to dominate another religion is not merely found among Hindus but also with Muslims and Christians through 'missionary' activities against which the secular state must ensure safeguards too. But the secular state misses altogether a history of inter-religious domination from the pre-colonial and colonial period while giving a false impression that non-Indic religions are egalitarians from within. As Gandhiji forewarns, the secular state should not patronize 'missionary activities' as during the colonial period so that 'other' religious communities would not feel alienated from secularism (Gandhi 1999, Vol. 96: 238–239). Ivan Illich, a Catholic priest, too makes a similar argument against 'corrupted Christianity' that treat neighbouring religions as 'enemies' and hence try to 'civilize' them (Taylor 2007:742). As India is a multi-religious society, reformation of 'corrupted religions' (including corrupted Hinduism) is a very important task.[54] But, this critical reform is absent in India's constitutional law. Thus, in so far as its reform master narrative is concerned, it awaits another round of reforms.

A genuine reconciliation brought about by agency-based dialogue may differ with a politically correct secular thinking such as above. *An agentive dialogue may thus negotiate intersectionality of power relations effectively and offer many varieties of reforms/sacrifices*. We suggest that a story of complex differential sacrifice is emerging in our case study. This new strategy incorporates simple differential sacrifice but assumes that all religious communities must mutually sacrifice for peace and development or for political secularism but Hindus being the majority may have to sacrifice more than Muslims, Christians, Sikhs and other minorities.

The present model of dialogue from Kandhamal rejects that Hindus alone will have to sacrifice for secularization. For political secularism to survive in India, it needs to anchor all religions in non-utilitarian roots. (Patnaik, 2011) If it becomes a maximalist doctrine or a Kamadhenu-like institution for Hindus or Muslims or Christians to squeeze 'milk' for their self-regarding interests only, its project of secularization of conservative social practices within and outside each religion is then doomed. In our story, all religious communities made some sacrifices. Dalit Christians made a few important sacrifices. So also Hindu Savarna castes that probably made more number of sacrifices. Reconciliation develops when all communities mutually sacrifice certain things they usually possess or are engaged with.[55] Only then it does *not* matter if the majority religion makes more sacrifices than minorities.

Conclusion

If political secularism fails to anchor all religious communities in non-utilitarian roots, it would produce 'Hitlers' within each religion as suggested by Ambedkar. *Dialogue must ask communities to offer mutual sacrifice and reform their relations within or outside in order to help secularism grow and agency based dialogue must curb the emergence of Hitlers.* The secularization process in Kandhamal is thus envisaged on a model of sacrifice which goes beyond the underlying principles of constitutional secularism in India. Can political secularism renew a pledge to social imaginary of people? Can it learn lessons from Kandhamal's secularization and Ambedkar's Yagna? Can it learn from the strength of the enemy, while opposing it? Can the secular state pursue a twin strategy of dialogue/law to deliver justice so that what we witness in a locality can be universalized? Without the secular state's proactive role in a sustained dialogue, communities may bring about reconciliation. But with the secular state carrying forward dialogic politics, a nation may usher a new form of reconciliation.

NOTES

1. Lohia describes Ram's 'blemishes' in a very interesting manner. For the killing of the Sudra Sambhuka for reading Vedas, Lohia blames the Guru Vashistha for instigating Ram. This is followed

by his appreciation of Ram as a symbol of limited personality. He examines Gandhi as synthesis of Ram's limited personality (introspective or knowing one's limits), Krishna's exuberant personality (mobilizer) and Siva's non-dimensional mind (universal patience). See, Lohia (2012: 289-90) Also, caste contradictions are presented by him as conflicts between the orthodox Vashistha (s) and the heterodox Valmiki (s). Ambedkar makes a similar statement about Vashistha and Valmiki. See Lohia (2011: 246-270)

2. By reusing Charles Taylor's distinction, this paper argues that secularism may be seen as a norm followed by regime/state/political society for public policies and secularization may be seen as a socio-historical process. We however suggest that both may not correspond to each other in different historical conjectures as in Kandhamal today. For Taylor's distinction, see https://www.youtube.com/watch?v=uaQlWtiZufA (accessed on January 12, 2015)
3. The BJP spokesman Sudhansu Trivedy in an NDTV debate recently cites Ram's advice to Lakshman to learn from the enemy and claims that this can only happen in Hindu civilization. No other civilization makes a similar claim. He forgot to add that Lenin from Russia and Gramsci from Italy advise comrades to do the same thing. This proves that many civilizations make similar claims. Thus, Marxism may also share this moral lesson. Trivedy's claim is culturally sectarian and supremacist. The other TV debaters (Mani Shankar Aiyar, Yogendra Yadav, Irfan Habib and Harsh Mander) did not surprisingly offer any counter-point. Probably, Habib forgot his Lenin. See, http://www.ndtv.com/video/player/the-big-fight/the-big-fight-is-the-idea-of-india-changing/350943, January 3, 2015 (accessed on 08/01/2015).
4. Gowri Viswanathan (2007: 354) argues that the Hindutva tradition is afraid of dialogue for it has implications for conversion. On the contrary, after every war against Christians, the Hindutva leaders ask for dialogue on conversion. Unlike Gandhi, secular forces are wary of any dialogue on conversion for the fear of legitimizing Hindutva's claims. More significantly, she misses out that a two-line struggle (war/dialogue) is being followed by the Hindutva forces.
5. See Shubh Mathur (2008: 124) for making a similar point. Since the 1980s, the Hindutva organizations adopted a mass line approach to mobilize 'Hindu subalterns' in social welfare projects. They thus departed from their Lakshman-like isolationism.

6. Yogendra Sikand's uncritical endorsement (2011) of Ram Punyani's usage of the term 'foot soldiers' for the Dalit supporters of the RSS is deeply problematic. See, http://www.countercurrents.org/sikand290711.htm (accessed on January 8, 2015). Similarly, Ashis Nandy and others (1993: 93) call the followers of the Ramjanambhumi movement 'lumpens', being devoid of elements of faith. There are a series of problems in this position. First, they usually assume that the Hindu right penetrates subalterns from outside. This assumption is also partly flawed. Subalterns may experience partial elevation in its policies offering a connection between the Hindu right and their social imaginary. Second, it denies agency of subalterns, even though there may be a contradiction in their agency. Third, they assume that subaltern followers are fully appropriated by the Hindu right. They ignore that even when subalterns are appropriated by the Hindu right, they retain their 'original thought'. (Patnaik, 1996: 2925-26) An exception to this general thinking is the work by Shubh Mathur (2008:126) who recognizes the agency of subalterns and notes their 'elevation' in the Hindu right projects. But she uses an 'acculturation master narrative' to understand the Hindu right's incorporation of 'subalterns' (ibid: 145) and thereby ignores the 'original and contradictory thought' of subalterns while supporting the Hindu right. (Patnaik, 1988, 1996).
7. B.R. Ambedkar (2014: 268-270), 'Pakistan or The Partition of India', in his *Writings and Speeches*, Vol. 8.
8. Article 25.2(*b*) states that the state shall make laws "providing for social welfare and reform or the throwing open of Hindu religious institutions of a public character to all classes and sections of Hindus". By Hindus, it also means Sikhs, Jains and Buddhists. By implication, a reform imperative in Muslim and Christian institutions is put aside. For, they are assumed to be egalitarian institutions. The Constitutional Order, 1950 reinforces this belief by excluding Dalits among Christians and Muslims from the reservation policy.
9. It is necessary to read together constitutional provisions under Article 25 (1), Article 25 (2B) and the Constitutional Order 1950.
10. See Bosco, Mohammed and others (2010: 18-25 and 113-118) and especially the petition of the Muslim Kathik community (scavenger) published in this book. For the concept of social imaginary, see Charles Taylor (2007: 171-176). For an application of social imaginary via Gramsci's lenses, see Arun K. Patnaik (2011).

11. Interview with S. Baliar Singh, 47 years of age, a member of the Anchalika Shanti Committee (ASC) and NGO worker.
12. Interview with Karmapat Majhi, 56 years of age, ex-Sarapanch of Saramuli Gram Panchayat, Tribal Christian.
13. Interview with K.C. Nayak, Secretary of the ASC, Tailor, Pana Christian, 55 years old.
14. Primary Census Abstract - Odisha, Census of India, 2011.
15. The term 'Odia' commonly used in this village means residents of the Odia Sahi. It does not mean Odia-speaking groups. Interview with Geetanjali Patra, Ex-Samiti member, Odia Sahi, Female, 41 years of age.
16. Interview with Sagar Sahu, founder member of the Vighnaraja Banika Sangha, a liquor vendor, 54 years old.
17. Personal interview with A. Singh, President, a NGO, male and 49 years old.
18. Interview with K.C. Nayak, n. 13.
19. Interview with S.B. Dalei, a member of ASC, Hindu and member of Odia Sahi, and 52 years old.
20. Interview with A. Singh, n.17.
21. Interview with Geetanjali Patra, n. 15.
22. Interview with Rita Nayak, female from Pana Sahi, 37 years old.
23. Interview with A. Singh, n.17.
24. Interview with Rita Nayak, n.20.
25. Interview with K.C. Nayak, n.13.
26. Women from the Paika caste used to work as housewives only. With less public interaction, caste prejudices were very high with them. They were very vocal in humiliating Pana women when they used to meet them at village tanks. The self-help group helped them to come out of the four walls of their homes and induced interaction with Dalit women.
27. Interview with Gitanjali Patra, n.15.
28. P. Kanungo (2008:19) argues that the Orissa Prevention of Cow Slaughter Act, 1960 and the Orissa Freedom of Religion Act, 1967 have helped leaders of the Sangh Parivar to fan out its anti-Christian agenda. We however think that opposition to beef-eating in this case is mixed with religious, caste and cultural dimensions.
29. Interview with S.B. Dalei, a member of ASC, resident of Odia Sahi and 52 years of age.
30. Interview with Ajim Dalei, 30 years of age from Odia Sahi and a highly educated person.
31. Interview with Sagar Sahu, n.16.

32. Interview with Bikash Badaseth, a member of ASC, Christian from the Pana Sahi, a founder member of the Dr. Ambedkar Banika Sangha, and 43 years old.
33. Interview with Bikash Bastiroy and S. Baliar Singh, members of ASC from among the Pana Christians.
34. Interview with S.R. Sahu, Secretary of the Vighnaraja Banika Sangha, businessman and 51 years old.
35. Interview with T. Nayak, President of the Dr. B.R. Ambedkar Banika Sangha, a member of ASC and Christian Pana and 39 years old.
36. Ibid.
37. Kanungo (2008: 19) also states that the VHP's Brahminical Hinduism excludes festivals of Dalits and Christians..
38. Interview with Chitrasen Patra. President of the ASC, contractor from the Odia Sahi and 47 years old.
39. Kanungo (2008: 18) states that Christians retaliated for the first time but the subsequent violence of 2008 sidelined everything.
40. In Odia there is a saying: 'Kankada-ku Golia Pani Suhae' (Kankada=crab; 'To fish in troubled waters' in English)
41. Positive aspects of common sense could be called 'good sense' which has potential to become a new philosophy under certain historical conditions. However, a beginning of new politics may be initiated by the popular through their good sense. (Patnaik, 1988; Coben, n.d.)
42. In the context of inter-religious disputes, a methodology of dialogue must involve multiple strategies of absorption, criticism, self-criticism and mutual sacrifice by contending parties bringing about reconciliation. A model of mutual sacrifice by contending parties is recently announced by the Allahabad High Court (2010) to settle a long-standing inter-religious dispute in Ayodhya. The story from Kandhamal proves right 'the judicial hunches' of the above law court. Dialogue-oriented thinkers like Akeel Bilgrami and Gyan Pandey are conspicuously silent on the need to involve contending parties in a dialogue to promote secularism. The Kandhamal story, as we see below, is a refutation of their self-imposed silence. For a theory of contentious dialogue on inter-religious disputes, see Arun K. Patnaik and Prithvi Ram Mudiam (2014b: 381-88).
43. Interview with Chitra Sen Patra, n.33.
44. There was no woman representative in this peace committee, even though there were a few active women members like Geetanjali Patra (n.13) from the Odia Sahi in the Panchayat

Samiti. This is a notable omission. This indicates the patriarchal nature of the peace committee and dialogue process which incidentally focused on caste and inter-religious disputes only. Despite limitations, the peace committee achieved very interesting results which moulded women's caste imaginary as well.

45. Narendra Mohanty, Secretary of the ASC documented the minutes of the Resolution, *Brahmnigaon Shanti Samadhana Sabha Baithaka Bibarini*, dated December 30, 2010.
46. Personal interview with S.R. Sahu, Secretary of the Vighnaraja Banika Sangh, businessman and 51 years old.
47. The Resolution of Anchalika Shanti Committtee Baithaka, dated January 19, 2011.
48. In the course of his Presidential Address outlining the philosophy of the Mahad Satyagraha at a Conference held in Amravati (November, 1927), Ambedkar makes a distinction between 'Satyagraha' and 'Yajna'. While Satyagraha is like a war/Yuddha for human rights denied to Untouchables, 'Yajna' is meant to purify their 'own vices/complexes' which pin them down as Untouchables. By implication, Satyagraha alone is not enough. (Yadav, 2014: 89)
49. This aspect is adopted from Rajeev Bhargava's theory of Indian secularism which essentially aims to curb inter- and intra-religious domination while respecting multiple faiths in India. The paper too believes in Bhargava's notion of critical respect by the state for all faiths in India. But we would disagree with his belief that such a position is maintained by constitutional secularism in India. We would like to claim that there is an anomaly between moral and political visions of secularism as envisaged by the Indian Constitution. Bhargava discovers moral vision of the constitution but justifies its law by invoking a doctrine of 'differential treatment of religions' (Bhargava, 2010: 89-90 and 2013). We propose a distinction between 'differential treatment *of* religions' which ensures equal respect for religions and 'differential treatment *before* religions' which ensures social equality in religions through reservation. These two are distinct doctrines. The constitutional law does not follow these doctrines *consistently*.
50. In a personal conversation, M.S.S. Pandian alerted us to a notion of differential sacrifice which means groups bear the differential costs of higher law-making so that its pay-offs in lower law-making track offsets the loss suffered under higher law-making

track. See Bruce A. Ackerman (1988:184-185). Pandian claimed that Hindus must sacrifice the idea of the Ram temple in Ayodhya so that their credibility increases immensely among Muslims and other minorities. As a result, *all* would gain peace and development. (Patnaik, 2014a: 22-24) The loss of Hindus will weigh less significantly in comparison with (possible) cumulative gains for Hindus and others. This paper is indebted to his terrific proposal but uses his strategy quite differently.

51. Articles 15.4 and 46 deal with special provision for SC/ST for equal opportunities especially in education; Article 16.4 refers to reservation in services/posts; Article 17 affirms abolition of untouchability; Article 25.2.b initiates reforms for equal access to Hindu religious shrines which is applicable in the case of Indic minorities; Article 330 and 332 provide for reservation in seats in Parliament and State Assemblies.
52. Article 25 underlines "Freedom of conscience and free profession, practice and propagation of religion"; Article 30 provides for educational safeguards for minorities.
53. While commenting on secular sectarianism of feminist politics, G. Ajay and M. Nassim (2014: 16-19) argue that feminist politics could not articulate gendered practices among all religions in India especially after the Shah Bano case in 1985. Feminists could not even initiate dialogue for reforms of personal laws of each religion, due to an acute fear of legitimizing the Hindu right that hijacked the issue of the uniform civil code.
54. The periodic rise of 'confessional religion' in each religious community showing supremacist tendencies has corrupted each religion. It is necessary that the secular state builds safeguards against the rise of 'confessional religion'. Today, the Pentecostal Churches and the VHP represent confessional religion as they, for example, assume that tribal religion is animistic, inferior and is to be 'civilized'. Both must be restrained by political secularism. See Mrinal Miri's reflection (2015) on tribal religion in the conversion debate.
55. Allahabad High Court's judgment on Ayodhya (2010) also articulates this moral vision. See Patnaik and Mudiam (2014).

Bibliography

Ackerman, Bruce A. (1988): 'Neo-federalism?', in John Elster, et al. (eds.), *Constitutionalism and Democracy* (Cambridge: Cambridge University Press).

Ajay, G. and Nassim, M. (2014): "The Politics of Secular Sectarianism", *Economic and Political Weekly*, Vol. XLIX, No. 49, December 6: 16-19.

Ambedkar, B.R. (2014): "Pakistan or the Partition of India" (1946), in *Writings and Speeches*, Vol. 8, Ministry of Social Justice and Empowerment, Government of India (New Delhi: Dr. Ambedkar Foundation).

Bailey, F.G. (1957): *Caste and the Economic Frontier: A Village in Highland Orissa* (Manchester, University of Manchester at University Press).

Bhargava, Rajeev (2013): "Reimagining Secularism: Respect, Domination and Principled Distance", *Economic and Political Weekly*, XLVIII (50): 79-92.

Bhargava, Rajeev (2010): *The Promise of India's Secular Democracy* (New Delhi: Oxford University Press).

Bosco, S.J., Mohammed, A. and others (2010): *Constitutional Rights of Dalit Christians and Muslims* (Chennai: LTD Media).

Chatterji, Angana P. (2009): *Violent God: Hindu Nationalism in India's Present Narratives from Orissa* (New Delhi, Three Essays Collective).

Coben, Diana (n.d.): "Common Sense or Good Sense: Ethnomathematics and the Prospect for Gramscian Politics of Adults' Mathematics Education", http://www.nottingham.ac.uk/csme/meas/papers/coben.html (accessed on January 17, 2015).

Froerer, Peggy (2007): *Religious Division and Social Conflict: the Emergence of Hindu Nationalism in Rural India* (New Delhi, Social Science Press).

Gandhi, M.K. (1999): *The Collected Works of Mahatma Gandhi* (e-book), Vol. 96 (New Delhi: Publications Division, Government of India).

Kanungo, Pralay (2003): "Hindutva's Entry into a 'Hindu Province': Early Years of RSS in Orissa", *Economic and Political Weekly*, Vol. 38, No. 31, August 2-8: 3293-3303.

Kanungo, Pralay (2008): "Hindutva's Fury against Christians in Orissa", *Economic and Political Weekly*, Vol. 43, No. 37, September 13-19: 16-19.

Kanungo, Pralay (2014): "Shift from Syncretism to Communalism", *Economic and Political Weekly*, Vol. XLIX, No. 14, April 05-11: 48-55.

Kapoor, Mastram (ed.) (2011): *Collected Works of Dr. Rammanohar Lohia* (New Delhi, Anamika Publishers).

Lohia, R.M. (2012): *Salient Ideas*, (eds.) B.K. Bhattacharya and Mastram Kapoor (New Delhi, Anamika Publishers).

Mander, Harsh (2009): *Fear and Forgiveness: The Aftermath of Massacre* (New Delhi, Penguin Books).

Mathur, Shubh (2008): *The Everyday Life of Hindu Nationalism: An Ethnographic Account* (New Delhi: Three Essays Collective).

Menon, Meena (2012): *Riots and After in Mumbai Chronicles of Truth and Reconciliation* (New Delhi, Sage Publications).

Miri, Mrinal (2015): "Need to cultivate respect for tribal religions", *The Hindustan Times,* January 19, Viewed on February 5, 2015 (http://www.hindustantimes.com/analysis/need-to-cultivate-respect-for-tribal-religions/article1-1308621.aspx).

Narayan, Badri (2009): *Fascinating Hindutva: Saffron Politics and Dalit Mobilisation* (New Delhi, Sage Publications).

Nandy, A., Trivedy, Mayaram S. and Yagnik, A. (1993): *Creating Nationality: The Ramjanmabhumi Movement and Fear of the Self* (Delhi, Oxford University Press).

Oommen, T.K. (2008): *Reconciliation in Post-Godhra Gujarat the Role of Civil Society* (Delhi, Pearson Longman).

Padel, Felix (2011): *Sacrificing People: Invasion of a Tribal Landscape* (New Delhi, Orient Black Swan).

Patnaik, A.K. (2014a): "Modernity from Below: MSS Pandian's Life and Mission", *Economic and Political Weekly,* Vol. XLIX, No. 48, November 29: 22-24.

Patnaik, A.K. and Mudiam, P.R. (2014b): "Indian secularism, dialogue and the Ayodhya dispute", *Religion, State and Society,* Vol. 42, Issue 4, December: 374-388.

Patnaik, A.K. (2011): "A Critique of India's Political Secularism", *Economic and Political Weekly,* XLVI (43), October 22: 19-22.

Patnaik, A.K. (1996): "Dalit Common Sense Against Hindutva", *Economic and Political Weekly,* Vol. 31, No. 44, November 2: 2925-2926.

Patnaik, A.K. (1988): "Gramsci's Concept of Common Sense: A Theory of Subaltern Consciousness in Hegemony Process", *Economic and Political Weekly,* Vol. 23, No. 5, January 30: PE2-PE10.

"Report of NCM visit to Orissa, January 6-8, 2008", National Commission for Minorities, New Delhi, http://ncm.nic.in/pdf/orissa%20report.pdf

"Report on the Visit of the Vice Chairperson, NCM to Orissa, 21-24. April 2008", National Commission for Minorities, New Delhi, http://ncm.nic.in/pdf/VC%20Tour%20Report%20of%20Orissa.pdf

"Report on the visit of the Vice Chairman, NCM to Orissa, September 11-13, 2008", https://groups.yahoo.com/neo/groups/

MangaloreanCatholics/conversations/messages/28705

Sikand, Y. (2011): "Hindutva and Dalits—Perspectives for understanding communal praxis", http://www.countercurrents.org/sikand290711.htm.

Smith, Keylie (2010): "Gramsci at the margins: subjectivity and subalternity in a theory of hegemony", *International Gramsci Journal,* No. 2, April: 39-50.

Taylor, Charles (2007): *A Secular Age* (Massachusetts: Harvard University Press).

Viswanathan, G. (2007): 'Literacy and Conversion in the Discourse of Hindu Nationalism', in A.D. Needham and R.S. Rajan (eds.), *The Crisis of Secularism in India* (Ranikhet, Permanent Black): 333-355.

Yadav, N. (2014): *Ambedkar: Awakening India's Social Conscience* (New Delhi, Konark Publishers).

10

Impediments in the Way of Secularism

Shuja Shakir

Faith in Western-style secularism is clearly shaking thanks to globalization that is bringing in religion-based politics of intense kind. There is already talk of the "post-secular" era where culture and religion, having been marginalized in world politics thus far, are coming back with a vengeance.[1] The rising tide of religiosity is being attributed to a belief that Western models of governance, be it liberal democracy or communism that proclaimed secularism as their basic tenet, are lacking in the intrinsic cultural and spiritual content, and are thus failing. There is a spurt of unprecedented religio-conservative movements right from Iran, Egypt and Palestine to Indonesia, Pakistan, India and the United States. While these movements do not follow a linear trajectory and there are vast differences in their approaches, they show a surprising similarity in one thing: they are united by a common enemy—secular nationalism—and a common hope for the revival of religion in the public sphere.[2]

Indian secularism, too, feels under the siege as the rise and the success of rightist forces has brought back the debate over relevance of secularism into sharp focus once again. In recent years, Sangh Parivar and its allies have, by and large, succeeded in convincing the majority populace that the so-called Congress-style secularism (dubbed pseudo-secularism) was all about favouring Muslims over Hindus. Therefore, exhortation to ditch this so-called pseudo-secularism, necessary for a Hindu to regain a sense of pride in his culture and a place of respect in the society, has proved to be a successful political plank of rightist Hindutva parties in the country.

This paper is structured around three questions that highlight impediments in the way of secularism:

One, secularism is taking a backseat because secularists the world over have underestimated the importance of religion in the lives of people. Two, in the changed political scenario marked by the rise of extreme religiosity in public life, a revised model of secularism is needed in the country. Three, in the Indian context, the ever-growing hiatus between the preaching and the practice of secularism has been its bane.

Role of Religion

Secularists have tended to react to rise of religious movements in a customary manner: either they have altogether dismissed them as a transient phenomenon or they have chosen to react violently. For instance, the secular elite in Pakistan always treated Taliban as simple tribal who have been brainwashed and would come back on the right path or it has chosen to bomb them. Consequently, a heart-rending attack on school children by the Taliban (Peshawar Killings, 2014) elicited stringent response from the Pakistani army against the Taliban.

In India, too, secularists have been dismissive of the rise of the Hindu right as being transient, a sort of flash in the pan. They feel rightist parties do not have a life beyond five years in the political shelf of the nation. NDA losing in 2004 and Congress regaining its lost citadel for ten years again is cited as an example. Clearly, votaries of secularism have missed out on the need for the deeper evaluation of the role of religion in the society. Marx thought religion was the opium of the masses, a heart of heartless world. That, however, does not seem to be the case at least in the contemporary times. Religion is coming back with a bang and the religious movements, both within and without the country, do not appear anything like transient or on their last legs.

The spurt in the religiosity the world over could be a reaction to the consolidated kind of secularization that was in vogue since the 1950s or so, but is by no means restricted to it. In fact, both secular and religious thinking has existed side by side and we cannot say that secularism has always scored a victory over religiosity in the history. "A proper rethinking of secularization will require a critical examination of the diverse patterns of differentiation and fusion of the religious and the secular and their mutual constitution across all world religions."[3]

Resurgence of religion began in the 1960s. In his inaugural address in 1961, US President John Kennedy not only invoked God three times but also stressed that 'the rights of man come from not the generosity of the state but from the hand of God'. Madan alludes to a number of counter cultural movements in America towards the 60s that were inclined towards the mystical and spiritual like the Hare Krishna Movement, for example. This established one thing that while the people were not moving towards organized religions per se, there was certainly a movement towards some form of 'ultimate values' that were above mundane considerations of secular ideals.

By the 1980s the counter culture movements had gathered enough momentum that could make them go ballistic. A significant assault against secularism came in Iran with Khomeini's Cultural Revolution. Shah had sought to impose the Western values on Iranian society; Khomeini countered it using Islamic ideology that had no place for separation of religion from politics. Khomeini succeeded. Aldous Huxley somewhere says that whenever there is a battle for supremacy between reason and madness, the latter wins. Counter culture, ethnic and religious movements have been attracting huge public support.

Following exit of the erstwhile Soviet Union as a superpower in the late 80s and subsequent collapse of communism as an ideology in East Europe, it was widely thought that liberal democracy had won the day. Fukuyama went gaga over what he termed as 'end of history'. But such hopes stood belied. The vacuum created by the fall of Communism was soon filled in by myriad ethnic and religious movements. "Political boundaries are increasingly redrawn to coincide with cultural ones: ethnic, religious, and civilizational. Cultural communities are replacing Cold War blocs, and the fault lines between civilizations are becoming the central lines of conflict in global politics."[4]

In the post-Communist era, there have been several socio-political revolutions across the globe. Arab Spring, for instance, that swept Tunisia, Egypt, Syria and Libya is one such revolution. While these revolutions significantly differed from each other as all revolutions do, there is some commonality between them. All of them have a distinct religious fervour that is so very evident that experts are highly sceptical about genuine democracy coming to these countries anywhere in the near future. Take Tunisia for instance. It's a country where women are not seen wearing a scarf in public and dress more or less like Europeans. Alcohol is widely consumed, more by locals than tourists and the economy is as advanced as that of southern Europe. Yet in recent elections, people favoured the Islamist party, Ennahada, giving it 43 per cent votes. Likewise in Egypt and Libya, there is resurgence of religiosity and from the kind of public support it is garnering it would not be wrong to conclude that secular democracy remains a far cry there. "Almost all secular Arab governments have failed spectacularly in the modern era. Radical Islam, as a consequence, looks good on paper to millions. It is entirely possible that a large portion of the Middle East will have to suffer under the boot heel of the Islamist regime."[5]

Liberal-secular approach has been focused on marginalizing religion. In fact, secularists were in the fools' paradise when they assumed that modernization and its concomitants—industrialization and urbanization—would soon relegate religion to the background. The underlying notion was that religion along with ethnicity, culture and history and other timeless influences on identity are irrational, private sphere factors that have no place in politics and public life.[6] If liberal secularists have done that, Marxists were not far behind. Marxism has been singularly influential in highlighting the decadent influence of religion on politics and society and has thus been a single most important influence on the modern day secularists. Marx held that religious sentiment is a social product and that humanity makes religion not vice versa.[7] Religion was opium because it blunted man's senses and somewhat diminished the pain of suffering. Religion offers compensation for the hardships of this life in some future life, but it makes such compensation conditional upon acceptance of the injustices of this life.[8]

Weber and Durkheim: A Counterapproach

Emile Durkheim and Max Weber have, however, tended to take a different approach to religion. Durkheim talked about religion as a source of solidarity and identification for the individuals within a society, providing a meaning for life and reinforcing the morals and social norms held collectively by all within a society. It would be wrong to dismiss religion as a fantasy. In fact, it is a critical part of the social system that lends social control, cohesion, and purpose to people. In fact, religion has such an important role in society that that the very idea of "society is the soul of the religion."[9] Insofar as religion is action and insofar as it is a means of making men live, science cannot possibly take its place', just as religion is not 'able to tell science what to do'. But in the face of the advance of science, Durkheim observed, 'religion is itself an object for science!' With its scope delimited but not exhausted, 'religion seems destined to transform itself rather than disappear'.[10]

Weber's important contribution in this context is treatment of religion as an independent variable and source of social change. In treating religion as an independent variable, Weber challenges Marx on the count that religion can have a significant impact on economic institutions. Marx, it may be recalled, had held that religion was a dependent variable that cannot bring about social change. Weber stresses that religious leadership has played a significant role in affecting social change in human history because change requires leaders for motivation as well as direction. He talks of two types of religious leaders or Prophets—exemplary prophets and emissary prophets. Exemplary prophets (Buddha, for example) challenge the status quo by leading an exemplary life, whereas the emissary prophets (prophets of the Book: Moses, Jesus, Muhammad, etc.) call for an active change and thereby usher in modern capitalism and ultimately modernization of the society.[11] Expressing scepticism about science and its techniques being capable of leading modern man to happiness, Weber quoted Leo Tolstoy to the effect that science is 'meaningless' because it does not answer the most important question of 'What shall we do and how shall we live?'[12]

Do We Need Secularism?

That brings us to a question: do we need secularism at all? The question has become important as, in recent times, a number of political activists as well as renowned scholars[13] have been stressing the need to do away with secularism altogether, with some going to the extent of denouncing secularism for having aggravated the very problems it had been created to solve.[14]

Secularism is separation of religion from politics. It means treating citizens as human beings taking their worth independently of religion as any other consideration in treating the worth of the individual other than being human is offensive to democracy.[15]

Secularism in the West meant separation of Church and state as a necessary condition for the modern state. In India it does not mean the same thing because there is nothing akin to the Church in the Hindu religion. Some contend that there is no need for secularism in India because the Hindu religion is already a highly plural religion with no single dogma as such. Its plural character is such that in the past it could accommodate and coexist with various religions like Christianity, Judaism and Islam. So why do we need secularism additionally as a Western import when it was supposed to inhere seamlessly into the practice of Hinduism? Jakob De Roover has raised an important issue in this context, pointing out that while we have been talking about secularism so vociferously but have not been able to clarify what we mean by separation of religion from politics in the Indian context.[16] He argues that semantic confusions about the term secularism have led to its practical problems. Indian secularists need to demonstrate the properties of religion before trying to separate it from politics and this has not happened. When there is no theoretical clarity on what makes some phenomena of Indian culture into religious phenomena or some institutions of Indian society into religious institutions, then there is simply no point in stating that the religious ought to be separated from the political.[17]

Notwithstanding such arguments, India always needed and will continue to need secularism. Indian secularism as Nehru saw it was an instrument to contain the religious strife and establish harmony among the culturally and religiously diverse communities in the country. These culturally and religiously diverse communities could pose danger of overwhelming the state and impose their idea of the "good life" on others.[18] It cannot be denied that beneath the so-called highly diverse and plural society, oppression based on caste and patriarchy lurked in the country. And such evils are by no means gone. The caste oppression is a reality in many parts of the country, Khap Panchayats dispense justice in their own manner as if the constitution does not exist and blood continues to flow as a result of communal violence that keeps taking place here or there. In such a situation, secularism is indispensable. The only issue, however is what form of secularism? Certainly it has to be indigenous as the Western import will not work.

What Form of Secularism is Appropriate?

There is a little doubt that the traditional model of secularism needs to be revised. The critics however remain divided as to the nature of revision. Ashish Nandy who takes an extreme position with regard to the Indian model of secularism says that secularism has exhausted all possibilities and has become positively harmful. Nandy argues that it is the secular state and its elite, with its instrumental rationality and amoral and manipulative technocratic-managerial ethos that has been responsible for the greatest atrocities of this century from the Third Reich to the Gulag to Hiroshima to the anti-Sikh riots in Delhi. What is therefore needed is the alternative to secularism for recovery of India's traditional religious tolerance which must be freed from imperialism of the Western category of secularism.[19]

T.N. Madan, not taking as extreme a position as that of Nandy, talks about the totalizing character of South Asian religions that claim all life of the followers so that religion is constitutive of society and such religions are incompatible with secularism.

However, the critics of secularism do not present any alternative model that would allow smooth negotiation between the worldly and the other-worldly. One simple question: can there be democracy without secularism? If democracy requires a minimum consensus about the basic values and institutions of society and about the rules of the political game, could such a consensus be built on a religious basis in pluralist India, or anywhere else, for that matter?[20] The answer can only be negative. Any alternative to secularism is theocracy and that cannot be compatible with democracy.

Challenges to Secularism in India

Since the 1980s there has been resurgence of what is called Hindu nationalism. It reached its pinnacle in 2014 when the BJP under Narendra Modi captured power at the centre with full majority along with its allies. Although Modi did not explicitly talk of Hindutva or Hindu nationalism in his election campaign, his image as a champion of Hindutva did the trick. Besides, BJP's diatribe against (pseudo) secularism as practised by the Congress convinced a large majority of voters that Muslims under the Congress rule were beneficiaries while Hindus, despite being the majority, suffered.

Congress' secularism consisted in a precarious balancing act meant to keep both majority and minority communities happy. It began with the Shah Bano case, culminated in the Babri Masjid demolition and the rest is history. BJP and its allies succeeded in convincing the Hindu voter that Congress cared more for Muslims, which ultimately drove them to the rightist fold. Muslims were disillusioned with Congress because instead of giving them concrete benefits in the areas of education, health and employment, all it gave them were status-quoist choices. Ultimately neither Hindus nor Muslims were happy with the so-called secular approach of the Congress. Not surprisingly, the 2014 Lok Sabha elections and a few state assembly elections that followed found Congress and its secular stance thoroughly slaughtered.

REFERENCES

1. Scott M. Thomas, *The Global Resurgence of Religion and the Transformation of International Relations: The Struggle for the Soul of the Twenty-First Century*, New York: Palgrave MacMillan, 2005.
2. Mark Juergensmeyer (ed.), *Global Rebellion: Religious Challenges to the Secular State*, London: University of California Press Ltd., 1993, p. 12.

3. Jose Casanova, "Rethinking Secularisation: A Global Comparative Perspective", *Hedgehog Review*, 2006, p. 10.
4. Samuel P. Huntington, *Clash of Civilization and the Remaking of World Order*, New York: Simon & Schuster, 1996, p. 4.
5. Michael J. Totten, "Arab Spring or Islamist Winter", *World Affairs*, January/February 2012.
6. Erin K. Wilson, *After Secularism-Rethinking Religion in Global Politics*, New York: Palgrave MacMillan, 2012, p. 73.
7. Robert C. Tucker (ed.) *The Marx-Engels Reader*, New York: Norton, 1978, p. 54.
8. Malcolm Hamilton, *Sociology of Religion*, New York, Routledge, 1995, p. 84.
9. Emile Durkheim, *Elementary Forms of Religious Life*, Free Press, 1995, p. 421.
10. Cited in T.N. Madan, *Religion in the Modern World*, M.S. Srinivas Memorial Lecture, National Institute of Advanced Studies, Bangalore, 2001, p. 5.
11. Max Weber, *Sociology of Religion*, Boston: Beacon Press, 1963, pp. 54-55.
12. T.N. Madan, op. cit., p. 9.
13. Rajiv Bhargava (ed.) "Secularism and its Critics", Amartya Sen, *Secularism and its Discontents*, New Delhi: Oxford University Press, 1998, p. 455.
14. Ibid., Ashis Nandy, "Politics of Secularism and Recovery of Religious Tolerance", p. 321.
15. Javed Alam, "Ethically Speaking, What Should be the Meaning of Separation for Secularism in India?", *Social Scientist*, Vol. 35, No. 3/4, March-April 2007, p. 13.
16. Jakob De Roover, "Vacuity of Secularism– On the Indian Debate and its Western Origins", *Economic and Political Weekly*, Vol. 37, No. 39, September 28 - October 4, 2002, p. 4047.
17. Ibid., p. 4048.
18. Javed Alam, op. cit., p. 6.
19. Ashish Nandy, op. cit., pp. 321-44.
20. Joseph Tharamangalam, "Indian Social Scientists and Critique of Secularism", *Economic and Political Weekly*, Vol. 30, No. 9, March 4, 1995, p. 461.

11

Secularism and Democracy: Symbiotically Linked Concepts

Asad Bin Saif

Our country has assumed consciously the garb of the Secular Democratic Republic in the post-colonial period. It means secularism is the sine qua non for the health of our democracy which is complementary to each other and inextricably linked. Either of the two if face dilution the other's health is affected. It is the building block where democracy could get sustenance and made meaningful and alive. Secularism is not meant only to maintain peaceful coexistence based on respect and protection of multi-culturalism and multi-linguism but also providing conditions for the progress and development of the people without discrimination. Here one can also see, there should be a proximate relationship between democracy and development. If democracy is defined as a polity where people are considered the ultimate sovereign, then development gives a fillip to the same as development is all-inclusive phenomenon which brings about economic justice. Secularism gives necessary impetus to the rational perspective based on the principle of enlightenment and inculcation of inclusive nation building. So the viability of secularism and imperative of development is sacrosanct which must be insulated from the possible infringement as the very success of democratic polity depends on it.

We have to see how secularism is being reduced and diluted to the worrying level, otherwise so many communal flare-ups and ethnic conflicts, could not have been possible in independent India. It is estimated that since 1960, more than 40, 000 people perished in the communal-related conflicts. The main culprits are police forces as they behave in a partisan manner during the communal riots and caste-based violence as they are well protected by their political and bureaucratic masters, vitiating the atmosphere and aggravating the misery of the people at large particularly of the minority communities. The glaring example of its dilution was the tearing apart of the Babri Mosque in the full glare of law and order machinery and more so in the backdrop of the incumbent Chief Minister, at that time happened to be Kalyan Singh of BJP in UP. Despite submitting an affidavit to the Supreme Court for the protection of the structure, he rather made a worrying somersault, and created conducive conditions for the demolition of the same. The fall out was widespread communal riots that engulfed the country; even our cosmopolitan city Mumbai could not remain unscathed. The unfortunate aspect is that the one who led such an assault on our secular edifice is now at the helm of the affairs of the country. They proclaim the intolerant, exclusive and divisive ideology of *Hindutva* should be the guiding principles of our nation building. The same ideology which has all the ingredients of divisiveness and hegemony of one culture, unfortunately is being touted by them as nationalism. For them nationalism is for the exclusion of others particularly Muslims and Christians. Here an intolerant streak is given vehemence that negates differences in so many ways and aims at achieving homogeneity to finish off alternative narratives and voices.

Now their project is obvious to convert a secular polity based on diversity and plurality into uniformity rooted in the majoritarian and communal concept of Hindutva. For them race and nation are the same and the future of the Hindu race rests on four pillars: Hindu Sanghthan, Hindu Raj, Shuddhi of Muslims and conquests Shuddhi of Afghanistan and the Frontiers. In this way they would accomplish homogeneity based on one race and history of one culture. According to them the religions of Muslims and Christians are alien to the country and Shuddhi (purification) must be applied to these two religions as they could not achieve status of equal citizens. So, it was not surprising to see the conversion of 350 Muslims slum dwellers of Agra by the *Bajrang Dal* and *Dharam Jagran Manch* who were lured with promises of BPL and Aadhar Cards.

(Sandeep Joshi, *The Hindu*, December 10, 2014). The Shuddhi movement began in the 1920s with the declared aim to convert, —'reconvert' according to them the Muslims and thus 'realize the ideal of unifying India nationally, socially and religiously", (R.C. Majumdar, H.C. Raychaudhuri and K. Datta, *An Advanced History of India*, 1950, p. 883). They reacted very sharply when 180 families of Dalits converted to Islam in order to come out from the ignoble treatment meted out to them by caste Hindus at Meenakshipuram, Trinelveli District, Tamil Nadu in 1981. It created considerable furore at national level and the rightist forces blamed the conversion was the sheer case of allurement or inducement made up by the petro dollars. They never accepted it was the direct results of caste oppression which led them to convert.

It must be recalled that the architect of Hindutva ideology V.D. Savarkar, a leader of the Hindu Mahasabha, a fierce nationalist and idealist of rightist mould who wrote a book on Hindutva wherein he exhorted to unite desperate Hindus into a political project which could be in tune with his supremacist designs. His works steeped in a desire for revenge against those who had supposedly humiliated Hindus and tried to erase passive ambience of his co-religionists. 'I want all Hindus to get themselves re-animated and reborn into a marshal race'.[1] Here the proponent of Hindutva, in order to instill supposed virility among his cadres advised them to shun the name of Sita being invoked before the name of Lord Ram as a sign of rationality and gender parity. So the salutation got metamorphosed from *'Jai Sita Ram'* to '*Jai Shri Ram*', the epithet used during the virulent campaign unleashed against the Babri Mosque. He always ridiculed Gandhi's adherence to peaceful coexistence and inclusion for all in the polity of the nation and dovetailed sobriquets on his name like 'crazy lunatic' and 'mealy-mouthed'. He always considered Muslims as savage, immoral, sensual and eager to destroy the Hindu way of life. He even saw two antagonistic nations, an idea which was rooted in religions as the characteristic feature of the nation and declared secular constitution was not in tune with such an exclusive thought. He wrote about himself that when he was 12 years old he instigated an attack against the Masjid in his village during communal riots, 'we vandalized the mosque to our heart's content'. Violence became the creed that he espoused which led to the assassination of the father of the nation by his ideological brothers. His complicity with that crime could not be refuted given the powerful evidence which had accrued against him.

Here another example of vitiated ideology is like: On March 22, 1929 the RSS supremo, M.S. Golwalker declared his exclusive notion of nation in his famous pamphlet 'We Our Nationhood Defined' as all those not belonging to the national, i.e. Hindu race, religion, culture, and language fall out of the pale of real '*national*' life. In his *Bunch of Thoughts* published in 1966, Golwalkar ridiculed those who thought about political and economic unity as for him without cultural and religious unity we could not achieve real vigour to the nation. So, for him cultural hegemony is the paramount panacea for national strength. It was beyond doubt that such perspectives of nation building have been the source of the problem which unfortunately led to the partition of the country. Here idealism of nation building is linked with the ideology and created real impediments in the evolution of secular, democratic and inclusive polity. They played an important role in instilling and disseminating communalism and thus created an obvious dent in the ethos of secularism and consequent waning of our democratic functioning. The game for absorption or flatten diversity under majoritarian communal politics will be utterly destructive and thus possible evolution towards modernism of India will be sent in tailspin. "The communalism of a majority community is apt to be taken for nationalism."[2]

For them such nationalism should be the basis of the dominance of one culture that is cultural nationalism and uniformity could be the panacea for the stability and strengthening of the nation. It is suffice here to say that the monolithic assertion of one culture is not the source of stability but the genesis of restiveness and upheaval the world over including in our country. It is felt the notion of national integration is the manifestation of cultural nationalism a subtle way of creating homogeneity and then hegemonize and for that matter even the genuine grouse of diverse people is flaunted as a challenge to national integration. It would create a great deal of disillusionment which is the prelude to chaos and upheaval. What they want to achieve is not homogeneity but hegemony of the high caste, upper class and status-quoist populace at the cost of the deprivation and marginalization of the large chunk of the population. It is to reminisce here that the theory put forward by Prof. Rashid Ahmed who had the erudite grasp on federal polity suggested about replacing the notion of 'national integration' into 'national cohesion', given the widespread diversity and plurality prevalent in our country.

It is a fallacy to think homogeneity is the solution. Akbar, the Mughal Emperor, had brought '*Din-e-Illahi*' in order to propagate his notion of harmony for all (*Sulh-e-Kul*). We must understand that he was not a religious propagandist but a statesman and empire-builder where his vision was to see homogeneity was the panacea which would provide stability and ultimately peace to the nation. His political instinct was beyond reproach and he was a monarch where his voice used to be the verdict but he failed in his project. Thus, if a monarch failed, how come a project which is perpetuated with the ulterior motive under divisive ideology could succeed, more so under a democratic polity as we have? In fact Akbar had visualized inclusive nation building, whereas these people lacked such a vision. This is the moot point. According to the historian, Stanley Lane Poole, who justly observed 'but the broad-minded sympathy which inspired such a vision of catholicity left creeds and tribes, and for a brief while created a nation where before there have been only factions.'[3]

Thus the Hindu Right's version of nationalism which is, in fact, a discourse of nation building by bringing all the diverse people in its fold through intimidation and propaganda, has been the source of the problem. It has its own insidious dimension as happened in the past elsewhere. It runs counter to the ethos of secular and democratic polity. It is to malign and escalate communal tension, perpetuating polarization, aggression and physical violence and intimidating the religious minorities particularly the Muslims. It led to the social marginalization of the minorities through their propaganda using communal insinuation as conversions in case of

Christians. It is their stand to achieve all-encompassing supremacy over the country's social and political fabric.

It is the preamble to the Constitution which says clearly that secularism is the fundamental value of the Indian State. Though the word secular has been included during the Emergency in 1976 along with socialism, it was made clear by Dr. B.R. Ambedkar during the Constituent Assembly debates that the very ethos of socialism and secularism which were manifested in various provisions must remain inviolable in all circumstances. But unfortunately all these building blocks of our democratic polity have been destroyed to the point of oblivion both by the main political entities Congress and BJP. It was Nehru's idea which laid the foundation of the modern democratic republic which was based on liberalism, socialism and secularism. He was responsible for instilling democratic values and inculcating scientific temper that gives vigour to the rational perspectives which is necessary to come out from the stranglehold of orthodox, obscurantist, feudal and patriarchal systems. It is appropriate to understand that perspective plays a major role in shaping the destiny of society and nation.

Wohi jahaan hai tu kare jise paida
Ye sang-o-khisht nahain jo teri neghain mei hain !

Allama Iqbal

(If you want to build a structure, sands, cements and other ingredients are necessary but they are not enough as your perspective is reflected in that structure. It means perspective plays a major role in shaping the structure. Likewise, nation building needs a perspective of inclusion, otherwise we will not achieve much sought-after enduring peace, stability and all-around prosperity).

In fact, Nehru's prime concern was to carry forward the secular ethos and rejecting an exclusivist approach. It was contrary to what V.D. Savarkar and his ilk under the ideology of Hindutva wanted to force on the nation. According to him, such an exclusivist perspective would create an insidious form of nationality where the majoritarian concept of nationalism would be in full ascendance and inclusive nation building would be given short shrift which would have ominous portents and its own ramifications and repercussions thereon.

As we all know that due to lack of functional autonomy the constitutional institutions are enervated and consequent results are obvious, i.e. so many communal riots and pogroms have happened because the institutions including police failed to live up to the democratic expectations of the people due to the active nexus of political and bureaucratic executives. In fact the onus also lies on the political executives and judiciary as they failed to bring inclusive nation building based on democratic values, rule of law and institutional safeguards. Rather they found it suitable to see the divisive politics through the adoption of communal expediency to be continued to polarize the society and get maximum political dividends. Both the major parties are guilty. One might be overtly propagating communalism and the other covertly doing the same as they always got electoral benefits at the cost of democratic deprivation of the people. What Rajiv Gandhi stated after the assassination of Indira Gandhi at the Boat Club in 1984, that 'when a big tree falls the earth is bound to suffer' was what Narendra Modi invoked as Chief Minister of Gujarat citing Newton's third law that 'every action has its own and equal reaction' during the 2002 pogrom. In both the cases violence had been legitimized and in the ensuing elections they got overwhelming electoral benefits and won the election hands down. In fact the Congress Party got a windfall number, 400 parliamentary seats in the 1984 election. They might have won the election but jeopardized the advancement of our democratic polity.

In both the cases violence was actually the kind of pogrom, genocides, crime against humanity or ethnic cleansing. It means that state complicities were very obvious and people at large suffered immensely both explicitly or implicitly. It can be proved that the exploited and economically deprived youths become the foot soldiers for the execution of the two major parties' nefarious designs. It is an irony that both the executioners of riots and sufferers belonged to the same economic strata. This is a vicious circle.

It is lamentable that the secular polity has been let down by the vicious and communal politics. Even some indictments had been made by the Supreme Court on the deliberate failure of the state government during the communally surcharged situation. For instance, 'the modern day 'Neros' were looking elsewhere when Best Bakery and innocent children and women were burning, and were probably deliberating how the perpetrators of the crime could be saved or protected.'[4]

In fact rule of law is the underpinning of a civilized society and manifestation of the democratic polity. In Gujarat hate-driven polarizations by the communal elements was given unfettered power without any restraint. Police officials, more or less, proved to be on the side of communal elements and whoever among them tried to do their professional and constitutional duties were sidelined. The high echelons among the police officials had been given clear instructions by the political executive in Gujarat to 'let the people vent their spleen'. '*Yeh andar ki baat hai, police hamare saath hai*' (this is the inside story, the police is with us), *was the open boast of one of the Sangh cadres during the communally surcharged situation in Ahmedabad in 2002.* Here the gory story was the huge instillation of hate politics in the minds of senior police officials. The utter failure of large sections of the Gujarat police and for that matter elsewhere was a failure of their constitutional duties according to which they were expected to prevent large-scale massacres, rape and arson—in short to maintain law and order. The administration was influenced, manipulated and bullied to singing a communal tune. So, it is apt to mention here that 'if lawlessness is allowed to override the rule of law, fascism would prevail'. Exact macabre incidents had happened during the 1984 anti-Sikh pogrom.

It is absolutely necessary that secularism as an inevitable attribute of governance must be supported by the institutions of the state. So three pillars of our constitution must function in a forthright manner as a cooperative whole, viz. legislature, executive and judiciary. Unfortunately these institutions have failed to live up to the democratic expectation of just governance of the people. For example, the police institution, the vital component in the governance process, faces at every stage intrusion from the political executives and bureaucrats. It causes undermining of its functional autonomy and efficiency. The politicians and the bureaucrats have used the institutions of the state for their vested interests and in the process have caused the subversion and perversion of these institutions so that they could not work to their optimum potentials without bias and consequently serve the people and protect their rights and dignity. So, the health of our democratic secular polity is dependent on the health and efficiency of the above-mentioned institutions. The principle of accountability should be sacrosanct whereby, anyone, however might be powerful, should feel the heat of the law if there are acts of omission and commission on his part. People need institutional safeguards and the crux of a just system must be based on 'end impunity and hold accountability'. Here one must understand that in a just democratic system 'right is always might' and might must not be treated as right otherwise it would be highly unbecoming of a democratic polity.

There is enough material to prove how the law and order machinery behaved during the communal riots and it was made available by none other than Dr. Vibhuti Narain Rai, a senior most police officer who did extensive work on the communal issue and wrote books (*Shahar Main Curfew*, and *Combating Communal Conflicts: Perception of Police Neutrality during Hindu-Muslim Riots in India*). He stated clearly that no riots could last more than 20 hours if the police did their duties with utmost sincerity. According to him the perception of the police and stereotypes against Muslims causes a biased role of the police during communally surcharged situations. The stereotypical images about Muslims such as being dirty, untrustworthy, violent and pro-Pakistan play a role in the partisan role of the police against Muslims. On the contrary police officials' dominant perception about Hindus is quite the opposite such as they are not aggressive, intolerant and violent. This itself suggests that prejudices about other communities are very deeply rooted in our society including the government and police officials.

The bias against Muslims has been corroborated by the various commissions. For instance, the Srikrishna Commission Report gives the powerful inkling where the malaise is rooted; "the police have an in-built bias against the Muslims particularly among the junior level police officers. The active connivance of the police officials with the rioting mobs and on occasions they behave like passive onlookers and their lack of enthusiasm in registering offences against perpetrators and post haste classifying the case as 'A' (true but not detected) summary".

Justice Madan Commission on the Bhiwandi, Jalgaon and Mahad, Riots, 1970, observed: "The working of the Special Investigating Squad is a case of communal discrimination. The officer of the Squad systematically set about implicating as many Muslims and exculpating as many Hindus as possible irrespective of whether they were innocent or guilty. Deputy Superintendent of Police S.P.Saraf held private conferences and discussions with several leaders of Hindu organizations including many who were implicated in offences like arson and murder against Muslims." Justice Joseph Vithythil Commission on the Tellicherry Riots, 1971, said: "As far as treatment of the minorities is concerned, it is the feeling among them that they are not getting justice, that they are discriminated against, they did not get equal protection of the law. It is their insecurity which veered them towards religious organizations. It is of greater importance that appropriate steps are taken by the government to remove the cause for such feelings in the minorities. There is much truth in the saying that if you want peace you must work for justice."

Justice Ranganath Mishra Commission's observation on the 1984 anti-Sikh riots: "The riots occurred broadly on account of the total passivity, callousness and indifference of the police in the matter of controlling the situation and protecting the people of the Sikh community. Since they did not make any attempt to stop the mob from indulging in criminal acts an inference has been drawn that they were part of the mob and had the common intention and purpose. The commission was shocked to find that there were incidents where the police wanted clear and definite allegations against the anti-social elements in different localities to be dropped while recording FIRs." It is the sheer case of not observing the basic principles of the rule of law consistently flouted by the police officials with the active connivance of their political masters. It tells the sorry tale of a democratic regime that failed abysmally to protect the hearths and lives of the people

Vice-President of India, M. Hamid Ansari, speaking in New Delhi in memory of eminent jurist and human rights activist, V.M. Tarkunde averred: "Even misuse/abuse of draconian law like the Armed Forces (Special Powers) Act has created profound disenchantment with the state. So there is a need for a fuller accountability into the system of governance at all levels so that the culture of impunity ends and the state and its functionaries are held accountable for every act of omission or commission."[7] "The violations of the right to life and liberty by the state were acute in areas of internal conflict such as Jammu and Kashmir, and the North East."[8] It is beyond doubt that despite the constitutional and legal guarantees, religious minorities continue to be the target of violence and discrimination. The pattern of systematic mobilization of hate and divisive politics are discernible in many cases.

It is a lamentable state of affairs that despite a democracy based on modern values with a secular constitution having a prominent bill of rights, our police system functions on feudal and colonial principles that are completely detached from just order. They are part of the patronage system linked to their hierarchies and political executives to serve the regime in power deviating from the just norms of the rule of law. However, there seems to be a significant level of resistance to systematic reforms by the state.

It must be recalled here that when the emergency was declared in 1975 to take away our fundamental rights even Article 21 (*Right to Life with Dignity*) was done away with. Mr. L.K. Advani who was also put behind the bars along with so many leaders had stated at that time that when 'we were said to bend we started crawling'. Such a fear psychosis was created. When the Janata regime came to power after the emergency a National Police Commission was constituted which gave the eight volume report along with the recommendations to do away with the unwanted intrusion in the affairs of the police institution. The most important aspect was that the recommendation that the archaic law of the 1861 Police Act must be reformed so that the police institution should serve the people as it is expected in a just and democratic order. It must be remembered that the 1861 Police Act had been brought into force after the Mutiny of 1857 to repress rebellion. Then the question arises how an Act which has a colonial legacy be compatible in a democratic set up? But the people at the helm of affairs thought it right to continue it as they did not want to see genuine democratic transition to take place and make a law that could be an effective tool of governance based on the principle of service and accommodation. Till now no state has shown real alacrity to go for police reforms in spite of the Supreme Court directives. Unfortunately, nothing substantial has been accomplished so far in order to strengthen the forthright functioning of our democratic polity.

The improved policing is the need of the hour. So, the revamping and restructuring of the police institutions should be done so that their performance meets the expectations of the people. In this way we can preserve and strengthen the rule of law and insulate police from extraneous pressures. Justice Thomas Committee that was formed with the avowed objectives to monitor the implementation of the court's directions also expressed its "dismay over the total indifference to the issue of reforms in the functioning of police being exhibited by the states." The former Chief Minister of Maharashtra expressed the general mindset that the Supreme Court guidelines impinge on their legislative domain.

The seven directives which were laid down by the Supreme Court for Police Reform on September 22, 2006, in response to the PIL filed on July 30, 1996 by the two retired DGPs, Prakash Singh and N.K. Singh, could be the key catalyst for institutional reform of the police in the country. The directives meant to achieve transparency in the system and holding accountability to tackle major ills that plague policing today. The directives are:

1. Constitute a State Security Commission (SSC):
   (a) To ensure that the state government does not exercise unwarranted influence or pressure on the police. (b): lay down broad policy guidelines. (c) evaluate the performance of the state police. The SSC is to have bipartisan representation and members of civil society avoid undue political interference.
2. Fixed Tenure for Director General of Police: Ensure that

the DG is appointed through a merit-based transparent process and enjoys a minimum tenure of two years. This directive aims at combating arbitrariness in the appointment of the highest ranking police officer.

3. Ensure that other police officers on operation duties (including Superintendent of Police in charge of a District and Station House Officers in charge of a police station) also have a minimum tenure of two years.
4. Set up a Police Establishment Board: The Board is intended to bring these crucial service related matters largely under police control like all transfers, postings, promotions and other service related matters of police officers of and below the rank of DSP and make recommendations on postings and transfers of officers above the rank of Deputy Superintendent of Police.
5. Set up a national Security Commission at the union level to prepare a panel for selection and placements of chiefs of the Central Police Organizations (CPO) who should also be given a minimum tenure of two years.
6. Set up Independent Police Complaints Authorities at the state and district levels.
7. Separate the investigation and law and order functions.

Secular polity can only be strengthened when the institutions start working with full vigour and with transparent integrity through the healthy cooperation of each other. But unfortunately the politicians never visualize strengthening our democratic polity through efficacious execution of the institutions with overriding concern to protect people's sovereignty. This should be the crux of the forthright governance. It is the Sachar Committee Report, which made pertinent linkages in this regard vis-à-vis Muslims to link identity with security and ultimately to equity. It means because of their identity, their security is at stake and because of their insecurity their equity is disturbed. Communalism is not merely physical violence inflicted on the members of the Muslim community but economic miseries are also meted out to them.

There is a strong need to bring about police reform so that the institution could function in an effective manner by holding accountable mechanism. The archaic Police Act of 1861 must be amended as according to it the police had been used as force and not as a service with an approach which is in tune with a democratic system. We must also note that execution of community/democratic policing which brought police and people closer to each other in Bhiwandi in 1989, where a proximate relationship between polity and society and the objective of a secular democratic polity were achieved. As a result there was a salubrious development in Bhiwandi. The concept of Mohalla Committee launched under Mr. Suresh Khopade and carried on by Mr. Gulabrao Pol made Bhivandi an oasis of peace and serenity. Consequently, in spite of hypersensitivity of the surrounding areas and the surcharged situation in the post Babri Masjid demolition, when communal spasm was felt even in Mumbai, Bhiwandi remained trouble free. They did it because the the perception about the police is to serve them rather than torment them. The same thing happened in Malegaon because of which this communally sensitive Muslim town in Maharashtra remained peaceful in the aftermath of 2006 bomb blast when 33 people had lost their lives. The reason given by the senior police officer in a more than 65-page document to us when we visited to find out about it, was that they had started community policing and won over the trust of the people so nothing happened. We wonder why such experiments are not replicated elsewhere? This is an important point that deserves to be taken into consideration.

One must keep in mind that community policing is meant to serve the people of the country and not the regime. It implies adherence to the rule of law rather than obedience to the whims and fancies of the public authorities. It protects the democratic and civic rights of the people. It also implies that police should be externally accountable to government bodies and the courts. It also suggests providing a service to uphold the law, rather than using force to impose the law. Thus a democratic policing is characterized by service to society rather than the state.

In a just system power is vested with accountability and nobody, however powerful he is, must not feel immune to accountability. But unfortunately, in India, the laws are taken for a ride by the communal forces and their hangers-on. As the maxim goes, 'where law ends tyranny begins'. Such communal forces could be reined in by providing efficacy to the state institutions. In this way we can checkmate the nefarious designs of the communal people as they are hell-bent on to damage our democratic polity by creating impediments for secularism.

In this way we can achieve much sought-after equity and all around prosperity and consequent stability. In fact secularism and democracy are the notion which could achieve our goal of a strong nation based on inclusion of all and prejudices against none. So, democracy means that governance should be based on law and order, checks and balances, countervailing measures, separation of powers and protection of all including the vulnerable minorities. It also means whoever fails to do his democratic duty he must be held accountable of his deeds of omission and commission. Here is the symbiosis between secularism, democracy and development which could give true meaning to liberty, justice and prosperity.

REFERENCES

1. 'The Man who thought Gandhi as Sissy', *The Economist*, December 20, 2014.
2. Jawaharlal Nehru, on January 5, 1961, *Frontline*, December 13, 2013.
3. Mukherjee L., *History of India, Medieval Period*,
4. Justice Raju Doraiswamy and Arijit Pasayat, April 12, 2004 Judgment on Gujarat Communal Riots.
5. Justice V.N. Khare, on May 1, 2004 on the Gujarat communal situation.
6. Srikrishna Commission Report on Mumbai riots.
7. *The Hindu*, November 23, 2014.
8. Ibid.

12

Muslims and the Indian State

Himanshu Roy

The Muslim question began in the late 19th century specifically after the foundation of the Indian National Congress.[1] The Congress from its foundational years had begun to demand for the Indian representation in the Imperial/Legislative/ Municipal councils of the colonial state premised on the British liberal principle of citizenship. The Congress perceived it as an instrument of political modernity for India based on the British pattern of liberalism, democracy and good governance which essentially meant focus on individualism and application of rule of law transcending the primordial relations of religion, caste and region. The Muslim elite, particularly a segment of it led by Sir Syed Ahmed Khan and The Muhammadan Anglo-Oriental Defence Association (MAO), however, perceived this demand as a medium of Hindu domination and unfit for unhomogenized population and for 'unwilling minority.' In fact, they felt 'that the National Congress is strongly opposed and hostile to the political rights of Muslims'. In a speech delivered at Lucknow in 1887, Sir Syed Ahmed had remarked "they (the National Congress) want to copy the English House of Lords and the House of Commons. The elected members are to be like members of the House of Commons; the appointed members like the House of Lords. Now, let us suppose the Viceroy's Council made in this manner. And let us suppose first of all that we have universal suffrage, as in America, and that everybody, *chamars* and all, have votes. And first suppose that all the Muslim electors vote for a Muslim member and all Hindu electors for a Hindu member, and now count how many votes the Muslim members have and how many the Hindu. It is certain the Hindu members will have four times as many because their population is four times as numerous... And now how can the Muslim guard his interest?" He questioned the audience and then himself answered it. "Let a rule is laid down that half the members are to be Muslim and half Hindu and that the Muslims and Hindus are each to elect their own men."[2] This questioning and proposal was further supplemented by 'A Muslim Manifesto' drafted by the MAO. Defence Association 'dealing with the issue of the representation of Muslims on the Legislative Councils and Municipalities.' The Association had sought 'adequate representation... for minorities' and had argued that 'the Muslim community must be regarded as a political unit with its own interests and sentiments.'[3]

Here it must be noted that Sir Syed was the leading member of this Association. In fact, it was at his residence that the initial meeting was held to form this Association and he was one of the members of its rule-drafting committee. In their defence, he had argued "that as the first essential for inaugurating any system of government, regulated purely and entirely by the majority of votes as such systems must necessarily be, it is indispensable that there should be a tangible homogeneity among the voters in point of race, religion, social manners, customs, economic conditions, and political traditions of history. In other words, the franchise, or the right of voting by the representative system, necessarily presupposes homogeneity, that is similarity among the voters and the population of country in general in regard to the above mentioned points, before the representative system can have any application or be productive of any good."[4] Similarly, their proposal of separate electorate was premised on the logic that Muslims were a separate nation (*Qaum*) who must have equal representatives at par with Hindus. The principle of one man one vote will lead to Hindu domination due to their numerical preponderance and will adversely impact the power relations. It was explicitly posited 'that Muslims can never accept Hindus as their rulers' and that "they are ready to sacrifice themselves for that glory which they still inherit from their forefathers, who were the erstwhile rulers of India." Sir Syed himself had commented that "our nation

(Muslims) is of the blood of those who made not only Arabia, but Asia and Europe, to tremble. It is our nation which conquered with its sword the whole of India, although its people were all of one religion."[5]

Evidently, they treated Muslims as one homogenized community with shared political traditions of history and Hindus as their subjects. Their subjects becoming their rulers under the representative system of one man one vote haunted them. Inevitably, they opposed it with all their might and counterposed it with an alternative proposal of a separate electorate. Unfortunately, the British in later years constitutionalized this alternative proposal through the 1909 Act and institutionalized the minority policy for posterity. More shockingly the Extremists faction of the Congress accepted this policy of the separate electorate in 1916 at the Lucknow Congress which was a volte face of the earlier secular stand of the Moderate faction that had consistently opposed the communal electorate of the MAO Defence Association and of the Muslim League. The Extremists, in fact, in their zeal to counteract the colonial state after the 1909 Act moved a step ahead: (a) they extended the provision of the separate electorate to more number (07) of provinces. Earlier, it was confined to lesser number of provinces and (b) they empowered the representatives of the Muslim community (three-fourth in number) to block any legislation they felt harmful for the community (clause 4 of section one of "The Reform Scheme").[6] In other words they allowed the creation of an Augean stable among them by shutting the doors of reforms on the pretext of safeguarding their cultural-religious identities which objectively benefited their elite and preserved their feudal cultural desideratum including that of their religious personal laws. In the process, the Congress facilitated the existence of and created the conditions for the emergence of two religious social categories—the minority and majority that led to the demand for a consolidated Indian Muslim state in the North West within India[7] (1930), enactment of the *Shariat* Act (1937), and ultimately the partition of the country. It may be recalled here that prior to the enactment of the *Shariat* Act the personal laws of Hindus and Muslims were regional in character and were fused; and it was during the process of their separation (1937) that Iqbal[8] had proposed the formation of 'a free Muslim State' (1937). Derivatively, it was the communal compromise of Lucknow that subsequently catapulted the religious segregation and obstructed the secularization process in the colonial regime and in post-partition India.

Constituent Assembly and Minorities

During the transfer of power, the Constituent Assembly classified the minorities in two categories (a) Anglo-Indians and (b) the rest (Muslims, Christians) and formulated its policy in two different stages. While the policy for the Anglo-Indians remained consistent in both the stages, the policy for the others changed. In the first stage, which was formulated before the partition, the minorities were granted the (a) social and the (b) political safeguards. In the second stage, which was formulated after the partition, while the political and social safeguards for the Anglo-Indians remained in fact as it was envisaged, the political safeguards for the rest (the Muslims, Christians, etc.) were abolished. Only their social safeguards remained intact; and it was enshrined as their fundamental rights. An analysis of them shall elucidate the logic behind their incorporation/retention/deletion from the constitution. A beginning with the special minority right (fundamental rights) may be the appropriate state.

In the fundamental rights category there was one specific minority right which was in the nature of educational right. It was Article 30 that conferred the right to them to 'establish and administer' their educational institutions. It was different from the rest in terms of certain legal privileges and civil immunities. While the rest of the institutions manifested the philosophy of individualism and of modern citizenship of one category, equal before the law and secular in nature, the minority educational institutions were distinct in terms of being representatives of 'religious community.' They were separated from the ambit of legal equality to be conferred special rights known as their social safeguards to preserve their script, culture, language, religion, etc. In other words, it meant that they had the right to be separate as a religious community and administer themselves separately in matters of their educational institutions. The specificity of it was that the educational institutions were (a) free to adopt their own selection procedure for admission of students' (b) were free to choose their teachers and members in the management committee/governing body (c) were free not to subject all the appointments terminations of staff to the prior approval of the Directorate University and (d) were free to formulate their religious curriculum. Subsequently, it was added, by the 25th Amendment Act, 1971, that in case of compulsory acquisition of properties of minority institutions they had to be compensated which (the proviso), was however, not applicable in case of acquisition of property of educational institutions of majority community. Only one limitation was imposed on it (Article 30) that too through the judicial process that evolved after numerous cases came to it for interpretations. It may be stated here that Article 30 itself did not 'lay down any limitations upon the right of a minority to administer its educational institutions.' The judiciary through numerous interpretations in different cases evolved a bunch of regulations on the functioning of this Article. It declared that Article 30 was (a) not absolute, that (b) it must be consistent with the national interest and (c) its right to administer educational institutions must not lead to maladministration. It must follow its laid out procedures and its constitutions which must be 'for the benefit of the institution,' and for the benefit of the minority community. It did not, however, transcend the minority paradigm and in spite of imposing the regulations on the educational institutions it jurisdically recognized them as separate and autonomous bodies and provided them with condition that facilitated their perpetuation.

Now a question arises as to why the Constituent Assembly did not abolish this special minority right even after the partition as it had abolished the other minority rights. A plausible, derivative argument may be that the Constituent Assembly might not have perceived this special minority social safeguard as harmful for the polity in post-1947 period. Instead, it might have perceived it as the safest method to assure the minorities in India even after 1947 without risking the polity. It was more a harmless assurance in the absence of political safeguards which were abolished after the partition. It was also to show that India, despite partition was a secular state and partition did not deter its character. However, in the process, it proceeded against Gandhi's views who had argued that the state should not aid and recognize religious education in educational institutions. It also failed to overcome the fact that the retention of religious personal laws along with the grant of minority right of education occurred because the Indian bourgeoisie was not in a position to risk the possible antagonism of large numbers of the religious population for such 'petty' issues like education and personal laws. More of it, it was also a reflection of the backwardness of a society that treats education and personal laws as low in social ranking compared to the importance of the executive power of the state. Therefore, the Constituent Assembly abolished the political safeguards for the minorities while retaining the minority education. For, the political safeguards were a threat to the executive power of the state. A study of their initial insertion before partition in the constitution and then their subsequent deletion after partition may provide the logic for the changing stance of the members of the Constituent Assembly.

It may be repeated here that the Constituent Assembly had appointed an Advisory Committee on January 24, 1947 to submit its reports on minority rights. In the pre-partition Assembly the Committee formulated its reports as per the then prevailing situation which included (a) the minority right on education and (b) the political rights of minorities. The political rights covered the following points: (a) representation of minorities in legislatures; abolition of separate electorate (b) representation of the minorities as per the Convention based on the 1935 Act in the Cabinets of Centre and Provinces (c) embodiment of an appropriate provision in the constitution for the appointment of minorities in public services (d) appointment of special minority officers (e) and formation of a Statutory Commission for recommending the steps to be taken for their upliftment. It may be noted here that in spite of recommending such rights, "as a matter of general principle (the Committee) opposed the weightage for any minority community."[9] And its recommendations were with utmost restraint. In fact, except for recommending the reservation in legislatures for minorities that, too, after abolishing the separate electorate the Committee did not recommend any kind of reservation for them either in public services or in Cabinets. Instead of reservation it suggested (a) an inclusion of a directive to the Central and Provincial governments, an exhortation to them, "to pay due regard to the claims of minorities" and the (b) the application of the Convention as per the 1935 Act respectively. Both of them were, essentially, to be executive orders in nature rather than mandatory constitutional application (as reservations would have been). In order to make these recommendations applicable, the Committee further recommended the appointment of special Minority officers, both at the Centre and in each province, to enquire into the cases if the rights and safeguards of the minorities were violated/infringed upon and to submit the reports to the appropriate legislatures. The Committee was more concerned with their backwardness; and in order to bring them up to the general community it recommended for the constitution of a statutory commission "to investigate into the conditions of socially and educationally backward classes, to study the difficulties under which they labour and to recommend to the Union or the Unit Government, as the case may be, steps that should be taken to eliminate their difficulties and suggest the financial grants that should be given and the conditions that should be prescribed for such grants."[10] The motive was 'to harmonize the special claims of minorities with the development of a healthy national life.' In fact the approach was "that the state should be so run that they (minorities) should stop feeling oppressed by the mere fact that they are minorities and that on the contrary they should feel that they have an honourable part to play in the national life as any other section of the community."[11]

Keeping in tune with this motive and the general opposition to the principle of weightage to minorities, the committee at the first opportunity after partition debunked their own recommendations and arguments and instead noted that there should be no reservation of seats for religious minorities for their rights and safeguards which the Committee had earlier suggested. For, it led 'to a certain degree of separatism' and was contrary 'to the conception of a secular demoncratic state.'[11] With the abolition of their political safeguards only two aspects remained religious, namely the religious personal laws and a fundamental right for minority education. Since personal laws were religious for all communities so the only religious component that remained special was the minority education. Both the religious rights (personal laws and educational right) remained ingrained in the constitution because, as said earlier, the members of the Assembly were apprehensive in their hearts as to how the people would react once these rights were removed. For, these were the inheritances of the past and were difficult to be removed at once. What followed subsequently after the partition was at least to remove the political reservations and safeguards which were partly an outcome of reluctant measures and partly out of the initiative taken by a section of the minorities themselves.[13] But this was a halfway house. The Assembly could not finish its historical agenda of formulating a Common Civil Code and a common secular educational curriculum. Its unfinished agenda, as a result, continues to haunt contemporary India. It left an indelible imprint to persist and to perpetuate that religious rights are an integral part of a secular state, which these are not, and these rights must increase in number and dimension for greater secularization of the state. But had these religious rights been part of the secular state the Assembly would not have abolished the separate electorate or the reservations for religious minorities in legilsatures. Since the religious rights were not part of the secular state therefore Nehru and Patel called these rights 'poison' and 'evils' and considered these rights as 'one of the main stumbling blocks to the development of a healthy national life.' In fact, they were not in favour of reservation even for the scheduled castes and were relieved when it was conveyed that it was intended, initially, only for ten years.[14]

Contemporary India and Secularism

The development of capitalism since 1950 has created two contradictory trends in contemporary India: one, there is a political perpetuation for the religious rights as the sacred corner stone of the secular state and second, there is a growing secularization of society under the expanding impact of market. While the first is political in nature the second is economic in content. The political perpetuation of the religious rights are more out of electoral politics than for the development of a healthy national life or for allaying the fears of the minorities. No doubt there is one genuine reason for its continuation and that is the minorities, themselves have not come out in the streets against such religious rights. Neither have the other constituents of society come forward. On the contrary, a section of them at least, a section of the elite are demanding for more such rights; and they have picked up all such demands for implementation which the Constituent Assembly had proposed for their implementation in its pre-partition sessions and which it had debunked after the partition. It is unquestionable that the majority of the people among the minorities are backward like the majority of the people among the other constituents and both need upliftment. It becomes, therefore, all the more necessary to formulate holistic policy measures for the benefit of the poor irrespective of their primordial religious affiliation. The benefit of being minorities with special rights along with the addition of reservation in legislatures, public services or allocation of separate grants and aids are untenable.

In fact, minority rights in a secular state are an anachronism. Unfortunately, the possibility of its abolition can only be actuated when the constitutional categorization of majority-minority is abolished. For, the very conceptual paradigm of minority and majority creates divisions among citizens on the basis of religious primordiality which suits political parties. But ironically it is argued that for a thorough secularization of society more special rights be granted to the minorities as they are more backward compared to the majority community. The parameter of the logic is the comparison of economic per capita income between two (minority-majority) religious communities rather than of the secular economic criteria of the class division among the citizens. It is unquestionable that as a religious category average Muslim families are economically backward compared to the average Hindu families in terms of per capita income but then average Hindu families are also backward compared to the average Christian families in similar terms;

and likewise the comparison can be further extended to other religious categories like Parsis, Sikhs, etc. It can be noted here that an average Muslim family is larger in size than an average Hindu family which in turn is larger than an average Christian family. In contrast, the percentage of working women in an average Muslim family is far less than that of an average Hindu family which in turn is slightly less than an average Christian family. As a result, the income per Muslim family is less and expenditure is more. In comparison an average Hindu family has more income and less expenditure on the socially necessary requirements.[15] This leads to the comparative economic backwardness of the religious communities. Analysed in the light of this background the logic of extending more special rights to minorities becomes untenable. Moreover, creation of more such special minority/religious rights, instead of the secularization of right turns the Constituent Assembly on its head which had secularized the rights to a large extent. The existence of two unsecular rights (the religious civil codes and minority education) had pained Nehru, Patel, Ambedkar and other members of the Advisory Committee and its Sub-Committee.

Minority rights were the creation of the colonial state for its divisive politics. The Moderates, akin to the classical liberals of Europe always opposed this act. Like the French and other revolutionary liberals, which never created minority-majority paradigm, the Moderates argued for modern citizenship and put aside any consideration for primordial affiliations. The subsequent praxis in India, however, not only distorted the interpretations of secularism premised on communal compromise (separate electorate, religious personal laws, minority rights) for real politik but also perpetuated it for fruitless argumentative contestation in post-colonial history. Two points are frequently discussed as a result of this perpetuation. It is assumed that (a) minority rights are integral part of secularism and (b) if not secularism then what. The first assumption has been answered in this paper and in the other two articles[16] of mine that minority rights are not integral part of secularism, the second point was answered long ago, in 1948, by M.N. Roy. Roy had argued in his paper *Independent*[17] that modern secularism in India under capitalism is integral part of its existence. It is pointless to argue about it. The important aspect is what kind of secularism India shall have under the Congress rule. That is the real issue.

The fallouts of such developments in the last six decades have been the growth and perpetuation of vested interests among the minorities. A recent case study of growth of minority educational constitutions in Andhra Pradesh conducted by a citizen group aptly reflects this trend. In Andhra, the percentage of Muslim population according to 2001 Census is 9.5 per cent. Their number of engineering colleges are 36 (in 2005), i.e. 15 per cent in proportion to the population with total seat capacity for 11,000 students. About 8,833 Muslim students appeared in the entrance test 2005 (EAMCET, 2005) for admission conducted by the Andhra government. Out of this 4,000 Muslim students qualified for it. The rest of the 7,000 seats were sold out to other non-Muslim students. Similarly, there are 1.44 per cent of Christian population (Census 2001) with 22 Christian engineering colleges and 7,430 seats (2005). 2,831 Christian students appeared in the entrance test, 2005 (EAMCET) out of which 2,176 were selected. The rest of the seats (5,254) were sold out to other non-Christian students.[18] This self-evident interest is the root cause for the protection and perpetuation of minority rights which provide the minorities legal privileges and civil immunities. However, to be different from the rest on the basis of religion is no pretext for being special. The pretext of social safeguards is essentially a chimera that has turned into a pool of vested interests leading to the emergence of a new segment of non-traditional elite among them. The electoral process has fanned the growth of this segmentary interests under the garb of social justice and secularism.

The antidote to this chimera is the expanding and intensifying secular role of the market which through its economic pressure exerted on citizens' every day existence secularizes their religious minds. Like the West, where the mass Christianity has been secularized and only the priestly Christianity in modified form remains as religion, the religious minds in India are too in the process of becoming the citizens. Not only that the market has secularized the content of politics as well as best reflected in the constitution and in its organs. The communal crumbs of the political parties are more a show biz that results out of their competitive electoral politics. But interestingly, under capitalism even their communal policies no longer remain fruitless. It sucks the religious minds from the periphery of politics into the whirlpool of democracy and integrates them with the mainstream politics. Or to put it differently, the alienated/rebels are drawn into the expanding bourgeoisie system from the periphery of politics and get co-opted into it. It is, however, not to belittle the communal role of the political parties in instigating the religious divide for the electoral purposes or for religious bigotry. It may also be simultaneously emphasized that in most cases the communal divide are manifestations of political power struggle, economic impoverishment or for market domination.[19] Religious hatred purely premised on the religious intolerance plays an insignificant role at grassroots level in their routine existence in normal circumstances. For, the market has converted the role of religion from being a serious, sacred affair playing a social role in the public sphere to largely a role of social entertainment. In other words, religion has retracted its earlier stand from public sphere to private domain. Or the serious sacred role of religion has been confined to private sphere. The standardized attributes of the bourgeoisie mode has brought the Western features of mass religion to colonial societies trampling the diversities of feudal mode and of its local production.

Conclusion

The bourgeois mode of production in its history has traversed two different paths in the process of secularizing the religious minds. In Europe, it developed into a revolutionary course and transformed the subjects into the citizens without any divisive paradigm of being religious majority and minority. It uniformly equated every citizen before the law without any discrimination either in civil matters or in criminal acts by radically abolishing the primordial categories from the constitution. It provided legitimacy to the new social relations. In colonial societies, on the other hand, there was differential treatment of the subjects (in certain matters) in the codification of the citizenship statute.

The colonial state, for its divisive politics, had encouraged and created the majority-minority paradigm and deliberately used the varying social categories against each other to perpetuate the social divisions for self-benefit. The post-colonial reformist bourgeoisie subsequently cast away many features of the divisive paradigm but did not abolish it completely. The unfinished agenda, therefore, continues to linger on even in contemporary times. To circumvent it or to uniformalize the citizenship laws, the state has adopted different methods sometimes even apparently discriminatory, to coopt the minorities in universal bourgeois mode of secularism. Some of its recent acts and attempts have been to (a) establish the ministry of minority affairs (b) to establish minority commission and financial corporation (c) to broaden the social base of the minorities by incorporating new constituent groups like Kashmiri pandits, Jains, etc. (e) to modernize *madrasa/* fortification of burial places (f) to register marriages, etc. All these measures under capitalism facilitate the encroachment of the bourgeois laws in the affairs of the religious communities and corrode their traditional foundation or expand the social base of the minorities to such an extent that they no longer remain a ghettoized block. The bourgeois mode, thus, through gradual social engineering, unlike revolutionary Europe, sucks the traditional communities into its vortex.

Ironically, the post-colonial state has picked up all such measures of the Constituent Assembly to secularize the minorities which the Assembly had proposed before partition under the special circumstances but had debunked them after the partition on the ground that these were 'poison', 'evils', etc. The Assembly had to adopt them in pre-partition sessions because these were the least troublesome options available to it in the constrained situation. The post-colonial state has no such constraint. It must, therefore, follow the best course available to it which is unburdened by electoral motives; and the best recourse could be the genuine, need-based economic affirmative action and a non-discriminatory administrative performances of the state.

Unfortunately, the Indian State in its different *avatar*, colonial and post-colonial, has always played the divisive role against the citizens. It used the Indian Muslims against the others during the colonial regime for its own interests, treating the Muslims as one religious homogeneous block transcending the region, caste, class, differences which benefited the feudal-bourgeois segments among them at the cost of obfuscating radical, social, political reforms that would have benefited the ordinary Muslims. The post-colonial Indian state is no different. It continued with the colonial measures of segregation, constitutionally, politically and culturally. Only, the separate electorate was abolished. The abdication of reformative responsibility and poverty alleviation continued to haunt the Muslims. More than that, the use of coercive state apparatus to apprehend the poor Muslims for terror acts abrogating their citizenship rights is a dangerous sign against democracy. Twenty per cent of prisoners in contemporary India are Muslims.[20] Seventy-six per cent of prisoners are under trials who have stayed in jails for years beyond their stipulated time without being convicted and subsequently then released by the courts in absence of evidence. The conviction rate has rarely crossed thirty per cent. Ordinarily, it has been six to seven per cent. This has generated wide degree of alienation and anger in them bringing in more religiosity that abridges the economic divisions in them. The religious divisions among the citizens benefit the ruling class and its state as it obstructs the unity of the poor against the rich. Since, the majority of Muslims are labour and of lower castes, their separation with the other labour on religious premises benefits the upper caste and upper class Muslims and the Indian state.

The Muslim labour need to unite with the other Indian labour for their self-emancipation relegating their other primordialities into the background. For, 13.4 per cent of its population along with 16.6 per cent of dalit and 8.6 per cent of Adivasis who constitute 53 per cent of prison population[21] in contemporary India, there is a world to win.

NOTES AND REFERENCES

1. *The Aligarh Institute Gazette* on 23 November 1886 had aruged that if there is established a parliament for India under the system

of one man one vote which the Congress was demanding 'the Muslims would be in a permanent minority.' See Shan Muhammad (ed.), *The Aligarh Movement*, Vol. 3, Meenakshi Prakashan, Meerut, 1978, p. 970.

2. See his speech delivered at Lucknow on December 28, 1887 in A.M. Zaidi (ed.), *From Syed to the Emergence of Jinnah*, Vol. I, Michiko and Panjathan, New Delhi, 1975, pp. 39-40.
3. See the minutes of the meeting of the MAO Defence Association and the draft of the 'Manifesto' in Shan Muhammad, op.cit., pp. 1059, 1063.
4. See his letter to the editor of the *Pioneer* on September 22, 1893 in Shan Muhammad, Ibid., pp. 1014-15.
5. See his speech in A.M. Zaidi, op. cit., p. 43; See The Aligarh Institute *Gazette* (editorial), September 5, 1893 in Shan Muhammad, Ibid., pp. 1122-23.
6. See "The Reform Scheme" adopted by the Muslim League Reform Committee and The All-India Congress Committee in 1916 in A.M. Zaidi (ed.) op. cit., pp. 575-76.
7. In his Presidential address (1930) Iqbal had only argued for consolidation of numerous Muslim majority provinces of North-West India into one province which was earlier rejected by the Nehru Committee on the grounds of being very unwieldy in size, see C.M. Naim (ed.), *Iqbal, Jinnah and Pakistan: The Vision and the Reality*, Syrocuse University, New York, 1979, pp. 195-96.
8. In a letter to Jinnah, dated May 28, 1937, Iqbal had suggested to him that "the endorsement and development of the *Shariat* of Islam is impossible in this country without a free Muslim state." The 'Muslim State', however, was still within the realm of Indian territorial boundary. Nonetheless, it reflects his growing tendency for religious segregation. See C.M. Naim (ed.), Ibid., p. 65.
9. *Constituent Assembly Debate*, Vol. 5, p. 244.
10. Ibid., p. 247.
11. Ibid.
12. Ibid., Vol. 8, p. 311.
13. See the speech of Nehru in the Constituent Assembly on May 26, 1949, Ibid., p. 329.
14. Ibid., p. 331.
15. See "Role of Religion in Fertility Decline: The Case of Indian Muslims," *Economic and Political Weekly*, January 29, 205; "Hindu-Muslim Fertility Differentials," *Economic and Political Weekly*, January 29, 2005.

16. See Himanshu Roy, "Western Secularism and Colonial Legacy in India," *Economic and Political Weekly*, Vol. XLI, January 2006, Bombay and "The Dharma and Relegere," *Frontier*, Annual Number 2005, Calcutta.
17. M.N. Roy, 'The Secular State', in *Independent India*, August 1, 1948.
18. This was stated by T.H. Choudhury former CMD of VSNL in a Seminar on "Minorities and Minority Rights," held at National Museum Auditorium, New Delhi on March 19, 2006.
19. Asghar Ali Engineer in a series of case studies of communal riots has illustrated these facts. See his *Communal Riots in Post-Independence India* (ed.), 2nd ed., Sangam Books, Hyderabad, 1991.
20. *Prison Statistics of India, 2013*. See *Times of India*, New Delhi November 24, 2014.
21. Ibid.

13

Rise of Majlis-e-Ittehadul Muslimeen (MIM): A Threat to Secularism?

Mohammed Fayyaz

The factors responsible for the establishment of Majlis-e-Ittehadul Muslimeen are rooted in the socio-political history of the erstwhile state of Hyderabad. The aftermath of the police action created a number of problems for the Muslims. The main problems were their political degradation, loss of political power, social demoralization, economic ruin and cultural annihilation.

During the course of accession with India, the Muslims of Hyderabad state felt that they might lose their supremacy particularly their identity as Muslims. Bahadur Yaar Jung started his practical life with proselytizing Islam. Apart from enlightening the Muslims towards their religion, special attention was paid to the construction, improvement and supervision of religious buildings of the Muslims.

Its purpose was to unite the Muslims for the attainment of religious goals. When Bahadur Yaar Jung became the president of Ittehad, the campaign of conversion was precipitated. Earlier there was no mass conversion, there were only a few cases here and there.[1]

In 1926, Mahmud Nawaz Khan, a retired official founded the Majlis Ittehadul Muslimeen.[2] The first name of this organization was Ittehad Bainul-Muslimeen (unity among Muslims) and on November 9, 1928, it was renamed as Majlis Ittehadul Muslemeen. Primarily the limited objectives of this organization were partly religious and partly political.

1. To unite and organize all the Muslim communities for the sake of Islam under the Islamic principles.
2. To protect the economic, social and educational interest of Muslims, and
3. To be loyal to the country and the sovereign and to respect the laws in force.[3]

In December 1933, it reacted to the proceedings of Hindu Mahasabha meeting and defended the Islamic character of Hyderabad. It condemned the charge of indecent Muslim behaviour towards Hindus and explained at length the various facilities given to Hindus. It also complained about the economic plight of Muslims. It asserted the right of Muslims to man the administrative posts on the plea that the ruler in order to perform the state functions, was naturally inclined towards his co-religionists and no claim should be made for a share in the administrative machinery on the basis of population percentage. It asked the Mahasabha to compare the degree of tolerance in Hyderabad with Hindu state like Bikaner in the sphere of public employment.[4]

Thus, the activities of both the Mahasabha and Ittehad geared up and as K.M. Munshi said, were avowedly communal bodies, being left free to carry on their activities unhampered.[5] For about a decade Ittehad continued to believe politics as a command of the ruler and tried to unite Muslims on religious grounds.

The effect of the Government of India Act of 1935, further intensified the local movements in Hyderabad for the establishment of responsible government. The government of India Act of 1935 provided for the establishment of the federal structure for the entire country. The All India State People's Conference under the Congress supervision was active in the princely states for reforms and in February, 1938, Haripura Congress finally decided that it should take part in state movements as well.[6] Thus, the Congress geared up its movement in Hyderabad and established the Hyderabad State Congress. But within three days after its establishment, on September 4, 1938, Congress was declared unlawful on the ground that it was political having loyalties outside the state.[7]

In the absence of Congress, Telangana conference, Kanarese conference, Marathi conference along with the Arya Samaj, defence league and Hindu Civil Liberty Union jointly demanded for:[8]

1. Establishment of responsible government in Hyderabad.
2. Grant of Civil Liberties
3. Accession of Hyderabad to the Indian Union.

The communal riots in 1938 in Hyderabad and communal tension in Nizamabad, Osmanabad and Gulbarga caused the Muslims to think that they must have their own organization. Bahadur Yaar Jung renewed the old organization Majlis Ittehadul- Muslemeen to organize all factions of Muslims to foster a sense of community consciousness. In 1938, he became the president of the Ittehad, and inducted political programme in it. Nationalist Muslims and non-Muslims did not agree with its programme.[9] The Majlis soon became popular largely through public meetings. And Bahadur Yaar Jung used the opportunity of *Majlis Meelad* functions to address the Muslims to popularize it.[10] The demands made by the Ittehad were not acceptable to the Nizam and so he declared, that Jagirdar and Defence Personnel or Government servants could not participate in political affairs. Thus the political activity of Bahadur Yaar Jung was declared illegal.[11] Being a Jagirdaar he had returned his Jagir to Nizam and continued to serve the interest of the Muslims. But later on it was found that Nizam too was inclined towards Ittehad. In 1937, the Nizam's Government prepared a scheme for reforms in administrative set up. According to it 50 per cent of the elected representatives to the assembly were to be Hindus and the remaining 50 per cent Muslims and among the nominated, there were to be two Christians and one Parsi. Bahadur Yaar Jung demanded three things, viz:

1. The state was to be declared as a Muslim state.
2. Separate electorates instead of joint electorates.
3. Three nominees from the *Sarf-i-khas* (Crown Land) were to be Muslims.

He threatened the direct action in case his demands were not met with. Finally, the Nizam had to surrender to the demands of Ittehad and sent a confidential note of assurance to Ittehad on October 4, 1939. This was kept secret till July 13, 1946, which gave unilateral assurance to the Muslims. The council had made two recommendations.

(1) As regards the claim that Muslim representation in the assembly as a whole excluding the council should not be reduced to a minority. Provision may be made in the *Qanuncha* that the three representatives of the *Sarf-i-Khas* to be appointed by H.E.H., will be Muslims.

(2) As regards the necessary percentage which the candidate must secure of the votes cast, of his own community. The *Qanuncha* (by-laws) may also provide that it may be raised from 40 to 51.

Therefore the Muslim community of Hyderabad was assured that when practical measures shall be taken in furtherance of the reforms at its proper time, due effect will be given to this resolution.[12]

Ittehad under Bahadur Yaar Jung became the representative body of Muslims and was successful in getting secret assurances from the government over the constitutional reform scheme.[13] A new constitution was adopted on March 15, 1940 and the following was added to it:

> The ruler and the throne are the symbol of the political and cultural rights of the Muslim community in the State. This status of Muslims must continue forever. It is therefore necessary that the maintenance of the prestige of the ruler must attain first importance whenever a change in the constitutions had to be effected.[14]

Further he suggested Muslim ascendency in Hyderabad State was recognized and the Nizam was recognized as only the symbol of Muslim sovereignty. It was the similar outlook and ideology that was espoused by the Muslim League .It was natural that Bahadur Yaar Jung and M.A. Jinnah came closer to each other. On the question of accession, the Nizam under the pressure of Ittehad decided not to be a part of either India or Pakistan and declared independence on June 11, 1947 by refusing to send a representative to the Indian Constituent Assembly.

After the death of Bahadur Yaar Jung on June 27, 1944, Abul Hasan Ali and later Mazhar Ali Kamil succeeded as presidents of Ittehad but both had to resign due to the clash with its executive wing. Later, in a triangular fight Kasim Rizvi was elected as president of Ittehad by a marginal majority.[15] Rizvi, then 44, a graduate from Aligarh Muslim University, lawyer by profession, a fearless worker and member of the Ittehad executive was firebrand speaker and an emotional leader. After independence, the post-partition riots threatened the very existence of the newly born state. In this situation Rizvi thought of giving prominence to the Razakar wing of Ittehad. Razakar organization was established by Bahadur Yaar Jung in 1938, at a time when the Hyderabad military was over-involved at the Second World War front. Its object was to establish peace and help police in the maintenance of stability and law and order.[16] Rizvi, as the president of Ittehad decided to transform Razakar into a para-military force. Razakars were required to pledge themselves to the supremacy of Muslim power in Deccan. The youths under his influence and charisma started adopting the ranks of Razakars. He had also included the youths of depressed classes in Razakar wing. Venkatrao was the leader of the depressed classes and Shastri was his P.A. It was from them that K.M. Munshi (Agent General of Indian Union) got secrets of Ittehad and Razakars. The Razakars did physical exercise and paraded and saluted the Asafjahi flag. They were conscious of power. It had 52 centres in the state with area commanders. Rizvi acted as a Field Marshall. Every youth was haunted by Rizvi's call and soon the autonomous organization passed into the hands of ordinary leaders and ultimately captured by goondas. This organization was expected to demonstrate and suppress any mutiny, if necessary by violence.

Even after the arrival of India's Agent General, the Nizam, his cabinet and the Ittehad had decided to treat Hyderabad as independent.[17] The relations between Hyderabad and Delhi became worse after the signing of Standstill Agreement.

Rizvi was deadly against the accession of Hyderabad to Indian Union. He became powerful and his party Ittehad had a say in the Nizam's Government. The last Prime Minister Mr. Laiq Ali was his nominee. Ittehad had complete control over the military and the police. Most of the Urdu newspapers toed its line. Even officials were afraid of Ittehad.[18] Many Muslims including Nawab Manzoor Yaar Jung were very perturbed that the destiny of Hyderabad had been placed at the mercy of Ittehad.[19]

Rizvi succeeded in becoming irresistible force in Hyderabad. His strategy was based on miscalculations of the strength of Indian Union and overestimation of that of Razakars. With the militant power and its own press, Ittehad raised the banner of an independent Hyderabad. Rizvi's public pronouncements knew no bounds for instance, "March to Delhi" was his pet phrase.

> "There is a need for the bank of Musi and the bank of Jamuna to combine. We would unfurl the Asafjahi flag on the Delhi Red Fort."
> "The day Hyderabad is attacked I would not be responsible for the safety of the Red Fort. A fire would spread in every direction."
> "If Hyderabad's fate would be that of Junagarh then Red Fort's fate would be worse."

Such type of speeches incited the Muslim youths. Nizam disliked Rizvi. He posed as a prisoner of fear. In fact this posture suited his strategy. Using Ittehad he wanted to present himself as a helpless head of the state before the mounting Muslim opinion. But soon he realized that Ittehad was the real menace for his unfettered survival. Unfortunately Ittehad had to play his game. However in the last phase of the struggle, Ittehad turned against the Nizam as well.[20] Because of the continued refusal of Hyderabad to join India, Jawaharlal Nehru issued ultimatum to stop the terrorist activities of Razakars. It threatened war if Hyderabad refused to join the Dominion. On September 11, 1948, Hyderabad Government appealed to the United Nations. On September 13, 1948, Indian forces converged on Hyderabad on three sides. Rizvi sent unarmed Razakars to the border areas. The majority of them did not know how to operate guns, the area commander had no instructions as what to do in the eventuality of attack. In a few areas the Razakars under enthusiasm resisted and lost their lives. This was styled as Police Action. There was hardly any resistance worth the name. Rizvi had overestimated the Razakar's strength and state forces were ill-equipped.[21]

Nizam surrendered on September 17, 1948 and saved the Hyderabad and his own dignity with a last minute reliance on Agent General of India, K.M. Munshi. The Nizam's forces laid down their arms and surrendered unconditionally and the Police Action ended on September 17, 1948.[22] Over the successful accession of Hyderabad into the Indian Union, K.M. Munshi argued that this was possible due to the vision and strength of Sardar Patel and the tact and executive ability of V.P. Menon.[23]

The Muslim community (particularly of Hyderabad State) was in absolute socio-economic and political chaos when the State was merged with Indian Union. Moreover, the aftermath of the Police Action proved worse for the Muslims. A.M. Khusro writes: "The income of the Jagirdars both in cash and kind declined spectacularly. They were ill educated, untrained and unrealistic in their approach. Hence in other parts of India they failed to obtain their share in employment opportunities. Their expenditure and cost of living forced them to sell out their assets. Their status in society fell and created a deteriorating socio-economic situation not only for them but also a large number of their dependents."[24] All those who were in the Nizam's administration and army in different capacities had to face a similar situation.[25] Muslims of Hyderabad were seen struggling for survival, illiteracy and the feudal past landed them in all sorts of problems. With no jobs and no money left to start their life afresh, they were virtually selling out their properties, both movable and immovable. They were compelled to borrow money on interest by mortgaging their properties and jewellery. The poor and the middle class were naturally the main sufferer but the upper strata which was economically well-off also had to face its consequences.[26] Muslims were economically shattered because their economy was connected with the Jagirdari system. The abolition of landlordism and feudalism also affected the Muslims' economic position. On the other hand, Muslims were retrenched from services on a large scale. The problem of religious education also came up. Urdu was the medium of instruction. After Police Action, English was introduced as a compulsory subject. The Hyderabad Government spent a substantial amount on religious properties and buildings. During the Nizam's regime getting engaged in business was regarded as below their dignity by the Muslims. Thus Police Action signified not only a political change but had shattered the mind of Muslim youths in this area. It brought a "state of frustration" to Muslims in Hyderabad. After partition and Police Action elders migrated to Pakistan and the shattered Muslim youths and students had lost their faith in Islam and were attracted towards the Communist Party.[27]

The Communist influence in Hyderabad started in 1940. The Communist party of Hyderabad was founded by the Comrades Association. Narayan Reddy Alam Khundmeri and Makhdoom Mohiuddin were among the founders of the Party, which had pockets of influence in Nalgonda and Warangal. Andhra Mahasabha and Communist Party of Hyderabad were the wings of the Communist Party. They campaigned against feudal barons in villages and established village *sanghs* and by November, 1946, the communists got control over several villages, rendering them inaccessible to the state officials. When Satyagrah was launched on the issue of the state's accession to India and the introduction of the responsible government, the Communist workers adopted the united front techniques and assumed control over the violent movement of resistance organized by villages against the Nizam's police and the Razakars. The united front paid heavy dividends to the communists at the cost of Congress. By the end of February, 1948, the communists had dropped the make believe of a united front with the State Congress.[28] Communist influence was also extended to the city of Hyderabad. Makhdoom made the Communist Party popular in Hyderabad city and after Police Action it attracted the Muslims and they embraced the Communist ideology.

Under such conditions, the MIM revived itself under the leadership of Salahuddin Owaisi. The All India Majlis Ittehad ul Muslimeen (AIMIM) is a political party to protect and advance the rights of Muslim communities in India. It declared faithful allegiance to Islam. MIM had to change its programme after the Nizam's rule ended and sweeping changes were made in its vision according to the Indian Constitution. It believes in the nation's democracy and strives to protect and enhance its quality by effective representation from local municipal councils to the parliament.

The party has its roots back to the days of the princely State of Hyderabad. It was founded and shaped by Nawab Mahmood Nawaz Khan Qiledar of Hyderabad State on the advice of Nawab Mir Osman Ali Khan, the Nizam of Hyderabad and in the presence of Ulma-e-Mashaeqeen in 1927 as a pro-Nizam party. Then it was styled as Majlis-e-Ittehadul Muslimeen (MIM) and the first meeting was held in the house of Nawab Mahmood Nawaz Khan on November 12, 1927. The MIM advocated the set up of a Muslim dominion rather than integration with India. In 1938 Bahadur Yar Jung was elected president of the MIM which had a cultural and religious manifesto. It soon acquired political complexion and became aligned with the Muslim League in British India.

The Razakars, (volunteers), a Muslim paramilitary organization aimed at resisting merger with India, was linked to the MIM. About 1,50,000 Razakar soldiers were mobilized to fight against the Indian Union and for the independence of the Hyderabad State against Indian integration. After the integration of the Hyderabad State with India, the MIM was banned in1948. The Razakar leader Qasim Rizvi was jailed from 1948 to 1957, and then he was released on the condition to go to Pakistan, where he was granted asylum.

Before leaving, Qasim Rizvi handed over the responsibility of whatever remained of the Ittehadul Muslimeen, to Abdul Wahed Owaisi, a lawyer. Abdul Wahed Owaisi restructured the party and organised it into All India Majlis-e-Ittehadul Muslimeen. After Abdul Wahed Owaisi, his son Sultan Salahuddin Owaisi took control of AIMIM in 1975 and he came to be referred as Salar-e-Millat (commander of the community).

AIMIM demands that 25 per cent reservation of seats and scholarships in public institutions for Muslims. This demand of the party stand since 1962 it raised the demand of. riot investigations followed by payment of compensation through punitive tax on the perpetrators in 1963. The other demands were raised from time to time such as:

Inclusion of Muslims among the backward class quota in 1975.

Proportionate share in the police and army recruitment in 1964.

AIMIM claims that quite a few of its demands have been acceded to such as:

1. The appointment of a national commission to report on the economic decline of Muslims. The Gopal Singh Commission Report, the Sachar Committee Report, the Ranganath Mishra Report, etc.
2. The government to protect fundamental rights of Muslims through the creation of Muslim Affairs Ministry. Union Ministry of Minority Affairs was created in January 2006.
3. The establishment of two Urdu universities. Maulana Azad National Urdu University was established in 1998.
4. Creation of funds for economic rehabilitation of Muslims. In 2008, the central government initiated the "Multi-sectoral Development Programme" under which the government has sanctioned Rs. 3,780 crore for improving socio- economic parameters of the minorities.

Abdul Wahed Owaisi was assisted in his work by his son Sultan Salahuddin Owaisi, who succeeded him as the party president after his death in 1975. He began his political career at the young age of twenty-four. His election to the Andhra Pradesh legislative assembly in 1978 further increased the articulation of Muslim issues and interests. More importantly the youth began to look at him as a role model.

In the legislative assembly, he raised issues which have long been ignored by the mainstream parties including the socio-economic decline of the Muslims, restoration of *awqaf* properties, lack of schools and other infrastructure in Muslim dominated areas, illegal occupation of mosques, ex-servicemen's pension and housing allotments, etc. His electoral success earned him the reputation as a "giant killer" who had defeated tough competitors. Through political maneuvering, he was to force the governments of the day in redressing several legitimate grievances of the community. Sultan Salahuddin Owaisi helped AIMIM get the national prominence by actively advocating the Muslim issues throughout the length and breadth of the country. He participated in a number of national organizations such as::

- The Aligarh Action Committee

- The Babri Masjid Action Committee
- All Indian Muslim Personal Law Board

Through these national platforms, Sultan Salahuddin Owaisi put forward the Muslim demands. His 1984 victory from the Hyderabad parliamentary seat further fortified his stature as a Muslim leader.

He made efforts for the development of the Deccan group of educational institutions, the Dar-us-Salaam Cooperative Bank, and the numerous schools, hospitals, etc. that were established throughout the city of Hyderabad. Thousands of Muslim youths have graduated from these institutions. He was hailed as the "Salar-e-Millat". For quite long the AIMIM was consolidating itself in the municipal councils and the assembly by increasing its tally.

It gradually strengthened its electoral position in Hyderabad. The AIMIM began its electoral debut in1959 when it contested and won two municipal by-elections in the city of Hyderabad. It has retained Hyderabad Lok Sabha seat since 1984. In the 2014 Telangana Legislative Assembly elections, AIMIM won seven seats. Till April 2014, AIMIM was not even a recognized state-level party by the Election Commission of India (because AIMIM did not meet the requirement of securing 6 per cent of the total valid votes polls in the last general election, or winning 9 assembly seats). In June 2014, the Election Commission of India recognized AIMIM as a state party in Telangana. AIMIM was basically a city-based party, with its influence only in Old Hyderabad but later, the party won 2 seats in the Maharashtra Legislative Assembly Election, 2014. The Party president and member of parliament Asaduddin Owaisi won the Sansad Ratna Award for his performance in the Lok Sabha.

In 1960 the AIMIM contested 30 out of 66 seats and 19 seats in the Hyderabad municipal corporation. In 1962, Salahuddin won from Patharghatti assembly seat as an Independent candidate and later from Charminar constituency in 1967. In 1972, he won from Yakutpura and later in 1978, again from Charminar. In 1984 AIMIM emerged victorious in the Hyderabad Lok Sabha Seat and Sultan Salahuddin Owaisi represented Hyderabad till 2004. Since then, Salahuddin's elder son Asaduddin Owaisi represents the seat of Hyderabad. Mohammad Majid Hussain of the AIMIM was unanimously elected as the Mayor of Greater Hyderabad on January 2, 2012. AIMIM was once reduced to a single Assembly seat in Andhra Pradesh in 1994. On November 12, 2012, Asaduddin Owaisi announced the withdrawal of support to the UPA government citing communal policies of the Congress-led government.

In 2009 AIMIM won 43 out of 150 seats in the Municipal Corporation of Hyderabad and appointed the Mayor of Greater Hyderabad Municipal Corporation Mohammad Majid Hussain. Party president Asaduddin Owaisi won Sansad Ratna award for his outstanding performance in Lok Sabha. AIMIM made its entry into Maharashtra state by winning 13 seats in the Nanded-Waghala city municipal council polls held on October 2012. AIMIM made its entry into Karnataka state by winning 6 seats in Karnataka local body elections held in March 2013. In 2014 Elections, AIMIM contested 35 MLA seats (20 in Telangana and 15 in Seemandhra) and 6 MP seats in undivided Andhra Pradesh, but was not able to win any extra seat and won the same 7 Assembly seats and 1 Lok Sabha seat of Old Hyderabad city.

In the 2014 elections, in its efforts to win a majority of divisions in Nizamabad comprising a sizeable Muslim population and also the urban Assembly seat, the MIM this time focused its attention on the constituency giving it the second priority after state capital of Hyderabad. MIM won 16 corporation constituencies, as much as the Congress, of the total 50 in Nizamabad city Municipal Corporation. However, they lost the assembly seat to TRS. Later, MIM made an alliance with TRS for sharing posts in Nizamabad. MIM also bagged the Bhainsa municipality by winning 12 wards after a gap of 10 years.

The party has fielded Hindus in various assembly and local body elections. The AIMIM selected Alampally Pochiah as its First Mayor in the City. MIM had three Hindus as Hyderabad mayors, K. Prakash Rao, A. Satyanarayana and Alampalli Pochaiah. Another Hindu candidate Muralidhar Reddy, was fielded for an assembly seat by MIM from Rajendranagar constituency, though he lost the election.

Interestingly in the 2013 local elections, party fielded a woman candidate from Hindu OBC, V. Bhanumathi and she won the election against Hajira Sultana of the Congress by 1282 votes.

Election History

Lok Sabha

Year	Seats	Contested	Seats Won	Vote Share
1989	1	1	NA	
1991	1	1	0.17%	
1996	4	1	0.10%	
1998	1	1	0.13%	
1999	1	1	0.12%	
2005	2	1	0.11%	
2009	2	1	0.73%	
2014	5	1	1.4%	

Andhra Pradesh Assembly

Year	Seats	Contested	Seats Won	Vote Share
1989	5	4	1.99%	
1994	5	1	0.70%	
1999	5	4	1.08%	
2004	7	4	1.05%	
2009	20	7	0.83%	
2014	15	0	NA	

Telangana Assembly

Year	Seats	Contested	Seats Won	Vote Share
2014	20	7	3.8%	

Maharashtra Assembly

Year	Seats	Contested	Seats Won	Vote Share
2014	24	2	0.9%	

It is appropriate to comment on the recent performance of AIMIM in the Maharashtra Assembly elections. After disappearance of the Muslim League from Mumbai's political scene following the death of Mr. G.M. Banathwala and Mr. Ibrahim Sulaiman Seth, the Samajwadi Party tried to fill the gap by espousing, Muslim causes but failed to make much success. The Muslims, hugely disenchanted with the Congress and Nationalist Congress Party, continued to support them in large numbers primarily because there was no viable alternative. The breaking of the Congress-NCP alliance threw up space that MIM could fill. The MIM allied with the *Dalits.* It brought down the shrill during the campaign and found more on the callousness of the Congress and the NCP in dealing with issues concerning Muslims for example, government had not taken any action following the Sri Krishna Committee Report on 1992-93 communal riots and highlighted how subsequently government, despite contitutiting several commissions to study the socio-economic and political situation of the 14 per cent of the Muslim population in Maharashtra, did nothing to ameliorate their plight. They brought into focus the false cases booked against Muslim youths following the Malegaon bomb blasts and their detention for years. It was a mix of despair and hope that attracted Muslims towards the AIMIM when the results were declared it had won two seats—one from Aurangabad Central and other from Byculla (Mumbai). AIMIM was runner up in three places and secured third place in nine constituencies. It had garnered 5.25 lakh votes giving a huge shock to political parties. The biggest loser in Maharashtra was the Congress.

AIMIM accused Congress and NCP were playing communal politics in the garb of secularism while Congress and NCP accused AIMIM of being an agent of BJP that was out to divide secular votes. AIMIM has no formidable leadership in Maharashtra and has no experienced cadre and lacked money power, yet it won two assembly seats in Maharashtra. Now having assessed its strength, the AIMIM would like to make a go at the municipal elections in Mumbai and Bangalore and also planning to debut in Bihar and UP.

When Asaduddin Owaisi was asked after he took over as the party president following the death of his father in 2008, about future plans, he said, "The time is to consolidate what the party inherited owing to the hard work of the predecessors. There cannot be any unconsidered experiments." Now he plans to broaden the party base by seeking support of the Dalits and the backward classes. But the problem is that the Dalits and BCs have numbers but no strong leadership. So what kind of relationship could there be between the MIM and the SCs and BCs? Could there be a platform where all the Dalits and BCs sit together with the MIM? Or the MIM would try to field more SC and BC candidates? The picture is not clear as yet.

Though AIMIM has improved its position but like many other Muslim organizations, the AIMIM also carried forward the communal legacy of the pre-independence Majlis-e-Ittehadul Muslimeen (MIM) wich was "regarded as remarkably aggressive face of Muslims as it organized the Razakars to defend the independence of Hyderabad State as a Muslim state with the Indian Union". Therefore, the AIMIM is also known as a fundamentalist political party in India that was founded by the radicals among the Muslim population of Andhra Pradesh and the Muslim dominated areas of Hyderabad though it has units in some parts of Karnataka and Maharashtra. To understand the communally provocative character of the AIMIM one has to analyse its role as a pro-Nizam organization which was vehemently opposed to the accession of Hyderabad State to the Union of India. Even their speeches in public places are not in the interest of composite culture of Indian society. Majlis mostly dabbled in passion politics by espousing hate-Hindu sentiments and cashed on the Muslim electorates. (*Party Politics in Andhra Pradesh* by Hanumantha Roy, 1983, p. 164). "In 1957, the MIM was revived in Hyderabad and a decade later was petitioning the Government of India for the foundation of a purely Muslim State on India's eastern coast" (*Encyclopaedia of Islam*—Lieden E.J. Brill, Vol. V, p. 1081).

Even though, the situation in Andhra Pradesh was under control for about a decade following the arrest of Qasim Rizvi, the city of Hyderabad remained under perpetual communal strife and religious tension, particularly after the revival of the MIM with the new name of AIMIM by Abdul Wahid Owaisi.

After the death of Abdul Wahed Owaisi when Salahuddin became the president of the party in 1976, he criticized the

Indian state for allegedly abandoning the Muslims to their fate. Increasingly aligning the party with the fundamentalist ideology of the MIM, he replayed the militant politics of Rizvi and launched an aggressive communal campaign to such an extent that he was popularly known as "Salar-e-Millat" (commander of the community). He reminded his community members of their past glory and "compared the Majlis to the Black Power Movement of America". The mindset of the AIMIM was truly reflected when its legislators opposed the motion which the AP Assembly had placed for condemning the 9/11 attack on America.

Sultan Salahuddin while taking over the presidency of the party from his father in 1976, stepping down from his Lok Sabha seat in 2004 for his eldest son Asaduddin Owaisi and making his second son Akbaruddin Owaisi as leader of the legislative party in the Andhra Pradesh Assembly, the respective three generations of Owaisis have not only converted the AIMIM into a family trust but have also kept the Muslims of Hyderabad under their political control.

Abdul Wahed added All-India, to "MIM" but it has remained the family's fiefdom. There is no denying the fact that the Owaisis feel embarrassed about the party's provenance and have tried to recast its history through selective omissions. Yes, the AIMIM's traces its "roots" to the late 1920s. Yes, it speaks of Bahadur Yar Jung and his role in shaping the party. But it completely glosses over the fact that the MIM spawned Razakars, the dubious role of Qasim Rizvi in the tumultuous 1940s, and that he handed over the MIM to the Owaisis. Leaders of AIMIM are involved in inciting the feeling of hatred among the Muslim youths.

Abdul Wahed Owaisi was arrested under the Preventive Detention Act, 1950 for attempting to rouse communal passions and creating or attempting to create panic, resentment or hatred in the minds of the Muslims against the state and the non-Muslims as disclosed by his speeches at public meetings.

In January 2013, AIMIM Floor leader Akbaruddin Owaisi was arrested for sedition, criminal conspiracy, waging war against India and creating enmity between communities and for his speeches in Nizamabad and Nirmal. Asaduddin Owaisi and Akbaruddin were also booked for charges related to manhandling the Medak district collector in 2005. Some of MIM MLAs have also been booked for hate speeches.

So what does the MIM, as it is being referred to now, stand for? MIM is based in Hyderabad and is led by the Owaisi brothers, who are famous for their vitriolic speeches. It is ironic that one of them, Asaduddin Owaisi even won the Sansad Ratna award for the best parliamentarian.

No doubt, MIM got huge support from the sizeable Muslim population and also benefited from the division of votes in other parties. But the fact is that a voice as vitriolic as Owaisi gets so much support reveals how polarized the Muslim vote has been in Aurangabad. Clips of Owaisi's speeches had been doing the rounds on WhatsApp, and the Muslim youths who feel threatened by the hysteria surrounding Narendra Modi were attracted to them.

As long as their support went to left leaning parties, there was no cause for concern. But if MIM becomes the face of Maharashtra's Muslims, who were so far considered moderate, then we have reason to worry. Like the AIMIM, the RSS has tried to underplay the ideological formulation of its second *Sarsanghchalak*, Guru Golwalkar's views, who had declared that the Muslims either had the option of being assimilated into the Hindu fold or accepting the status of second class citizens. Then again, it disowns the assassin of Mahatma Gandhi, Nathuram Godse. No wonder the rise of the BJP, or the Hindu Right, has also brought into prominence the AIMIM, which represents the Muslim Right. The Hindu Right and the Muslim Right gain from each other, electorally as well as ideologically. Their tactics too are similar. In 2007, the AIMIM cadres sought to assault Bangladeshi writer Taslima Nasrin. In the same vein, the RSS mutants provide a fillip to the politics of identity, from which the Hindu Right and the Muslim orthodoxy will only stand to gain.

How does one deal with the provocative speeches of the types of Akbaruddin Owaisi? What is the remedy? The remedy lies in the political will of the ruling establishment at the Centre as seen on the eve of the accession of Hyderabad to the Indian Union. The second remedy has to be devised by the Muslims themselves. If they want to live a peaceful and dignified life they will have to guard themselves from fundamentalists among them who are still obsessed with the pre-independence mindset of the All India Muslim League, Nizam of Hyderabad and Rizvi, the leader of Razakars, who were opposed to integration of Hyderabad with the Indian Union.

Though the founding fathers of the Indian constitution emphasized on implementation of *secular* principle in political arena, the approach of AIMIM is contrary to the principle of secularism. More than half a century later lip service is paid to secularism without trying to evolve an ethical code that flows from every religious creed. If a religious code, in moral terms, is followed then the realm of religion automatically detaches itself from the political process. It is no accident that a religious America does not have a religious political party. But in a 'secular irreligious' India religion is still a major factor of political mobilization. It is, mainly because of the failure of the formal secular institutions to demarcate the complementary roles of the two realms. There are various reasons for this state of affairs. Prof. T.R. Sharma pointed out that: there had always been a very close link between religion and politics from the earliest time to the present day. The nature and intensity of this interplay has varied from time to time. During the British rule, religion began to be used for political purposes in more subtle ways both by the rulers and the leaders of the freedom movement. Since independence this interplay had acquired a new form and various political parties found it more convenient to mobilize support in their electoral battles with the help of religious factors. The role of AIMIM can be examined in this background.

The post-independence practice of our politics has, in fact, accelerated the process of desecularization. The secular ideas and objectives have been abused by the politicians. The politicians have not only devalued various democratic institutions but also tried to distort the meaning of secularism for their partisan interests. Almost all the political parties in India have the tendency to treat the communities as the vote banks to win elections. During the election period the AIMIM indulges into one of the worst forms of communalism. In order to attract voters, the common and innocent people are subjected to cheap propaganda, based on religion. The AIMIM leaders seize every opportunity to sow the seeds of communal hatred. Mr. Piloo Mody said, "one factor which incites the communal feeling of the people is the way political parties fight the elections. They create their constituencies on communal lines. Political parties use gimmicks to create communal division and these gimmicks become part of mainstream polity."

No doubt the constitution of India is secular and the spirit of secularism permeates all the material provisions of the constitution, however, all these cannot make India a secular state. A secular constitution requires a secular society. It is the habit of the human mind and not the letter of the constitution that matters. Therefore, the main question is how to foster secular politics in a society whose socio-cultural mores and behavioural pattern run on non-secular lines. A conservative, dogmatic and caste and superstition-ridden Indian society has to be transformed into a modern, dynamic and secular society. The struggle in India is not between church and the state but between modernity and traditionalism.

Nomani Rashid says "Indian secularism is a great challenge to all religious communities to cooperate, preserve and promote religious freedom of all the citizens and to create structure for secular society and culture this will make secularism a way of life and strengthen it as the total philosophy of life."[29] Similarly, Sudipta Kaviraj says: "A secular structure was imposed on a society which is extremely religious. A section of Hindus still believe that India is a Hindu state though the government is not admitting it. A secular state cannot become reality until the civil society is secularised. Secularism is not just to become multi religious or tolerant towards other religions. Just as religion, secularism is a way of life, a totality."[30]

It has been suggested by one sociologist "Religion has played a very important role in the life of our country. It is the center round which the whole of Indian social life rotates."[31] The Muslims less exposed to Western education and modernizing forces have tended to be more religious-minded than their Hindu brethren. Consequently, they have all along been more suspicious of the secular state and generally believe it to be a hindrance in the way of a truly religious life. Some Muslim leaders have made matters difficult by distorting and carrying on a false propaganda regarding certain constitutional provisions which permit the state to regulate secular activities of religious organizations and in some cases, even intervene in the interest of public ethics.

Much unwarranted apprehension regarding secularism in the Muslim mind stems from the rather unhappy translation of the term in the Urdu language. The word secularism is translated as *la deeni* or *ghair mazhabi.* As Abid Hussain writing on 'Secularism and the Scientific Attitude of Mind' says: "About the meaning of the secular outlook or secularism, there is a serious misunderstanding among the people of our country and specially among the Muslims. They take it to mean an attitude of mind which completely rejects religion as one of the highest values in life. But as a matter of fact secularism is not necessarily opposed to or indifferent to religion."[32] It would be a good idea if some more appropriate Urdu term, which would convey the positive aspects of secularism, could be found or coined to replace the present negative ones.

In order to make India fully secular, Indian leaders and enlightened men in the country should change their attitude towards the activities of organized religion and start giving every encouragement to scientific-philosophic movements which can shake the foundations of dogmatic religions so that the ideal of secularism may percolate down to the masses.[33] Education obviously can play a vital role in this regard. In short it can help Indians in their social awakening, developing secular attitude by special measures with legal force. Let Muslims sincerely believe that state is seriously concerned to improve their lot and wants them in the mainstream of the Indian nation.

The role of AIMIM in the present political situation, does not contribute much in strengthening secularism in India. On the contrary it creates a situation which could lead to an unhealthy political atmosphere. Professor Zaheer Ali in his paper "Muslims on Suicidal Course" says "Muslims in India seem to be desperate to the extent that a significant section of them is hell-bent on committing political hara-kiri. Those who are familiar with the trajectory of Muslim politics from the point of inception of the Muslim League in 1906 till the partition of India must be awfully astounded to see the Muslims march on the beaten track that has led them, barely 64 years ago, to disaster. In the pre-partition years it was the Muslim League that had spellbound the community with its skewed two-nation theory that viciously communalized the political climate in the undivided India. The catastrophic consequences of Muslim separatism had flung the Muslims, particularly in India, to an abysmal cesspool of poverty and backwardness from where they are still struggling to come out. In the contemporary political scenario we are witnessing the identical drama wherein a sizable segment of the community is repeating the part played by its ancestors, which will, just like the previous one, certainly end in tragedy."

It is necessary for Muslims to act positively, otherwise what Maulana Abul Kalam Azad said after partition will come true. Azad addressing a Friday congregation at the Jama Masjid in Delhi had given expression to his agony: "Do you remember that when I hailed you, you cut off my tongue? I picked up my pen and you severed my hand; I wanted to move forward and you cut off my legs; I tried to turn over and you injured my back". This statement shows the blurry tunnel vision of Indian Muslims and their aversion to prudent advice. Maulana Azad obviously had a sense of foreboding about the community even before partition. Many decades later, Muslim community is still in rudderless boats, sans a proper leadership or awareness, with no real hopes of surmounting their problems.

NOTES

1. Kate, P.V., Impact of the Nizam's Regime on Marathwada (1724-1948), (unpublished Ph.D. Thesis, Marathwada University, Aurangabad, 1978, p. 268).
2. Munshi, K.M., *The End of an Era*, Bharatiya Vidya Bhavan, Bombay, 1957, p. 19.
3. Rehman, Abdul, A Critical Analysis of Nizam Government's Policies regarding Social and Political Problems in the State (1935-1948), (unpublished Ph.D. Thesis), Osmania University, Hyderabad, 1986, p. 235.
4. Ahmed, Munir, *Majlis Ittehad-ul-Muslimeen—A Case Study of*

Muslim Politics, Osmania University, Hyderabad, 1975, p. 46.

5. Munshi, K.M., op. cit., p. 22.
6. Ahmed, Munir, op. cit., p. 11.
7. Munshi, K.M., op. cit., p. 22.
8. Ahmed, Munir, op. cit., p. 11.
9. Ahmed, Nazeeruddin, *Swaneh Bahadur Yaar Jung* (Urdu), Hyderabad 1986, pp. 19-20.
10. Ibid., p. 15.
11. Ibid., p. 24.
12. Ibid., p. 25. see also Kate, P.V., op. cit., pp. 112-13.
13. Ahmed, Munir, op. cit., p. 20. See also Ahmed Nazeeruddin, op. cit., p. 25.
14. Ahmed Munir, op. cit., p. 16. See also Dastoor-al-Amel (Urdu), (Constitution of Majlis Ittehad-ul-Muslimeen), adopted on March 15, 1940, p. 2.
15. Ahmed, Munir, op. cit., p. 21.
16. Ibid., p. 23. See also Rehman, Abdul, op. cit., p. 230.
17. Munshi, K.M., *The End of an Era*, p. 10.
18. Ahmed, Munir, op. cit., p. 27.
19. Munshi, K.M., *The End of an Era*, p. 98.
20. Ahmed, Munir, op. cit., p. 26.
21. Ibid., p. 29.
22. Langer, William, L., (compiled and ed.), *The New Illustrated Encyclopedia of World History*, Vol. II, New York, 1975, p. 1210. see also Choudhari, K.K., op. cit., p. 116.
23. Munshi, K.M., *Pilgrimage to Freedom*, p. 173.
24. Hamid, S.A., op. cit., p. 3. see also Khusro, A.M., *Economic and Social Effects of Jagirdari Abolition and Land Reform in Hyderabad*, Hyderabad, 1958, pp. 173-75.
25. Hamid, S.A., op. cit., p. 4. See Mazharuddin, *Mohammad, Police Action Ke Khaufnak Mahol Mein* (Urdu), Hyderabad, 1981, p. 56.
26. Hamid, S.A., op. cit., p. 4.
27. Interview with Raheem Quraishi.
28. Munshi, K.M., *The End of an Era*, p. 128.
29. Nomani, Rashid, *Text Books for Secular India*, Samradayakta Virodhi Committee, New Delhi. 1970.
30. Kaviraj, Sudipta, The Modern State in India, in Hasan, Zoya (ed.), *Politics and the State in India*, Sage, New Delhi, 2000.
31. Smith, D.E., *India as a Secular State*, Princeton University Press, 1967, pp. 340-41.
32. S. Abid Hussain, *The Destiny of Indian Muslims*, Asia, Bombay, 1965, p. 170.

33. W.C. Smith is of the opinion that secularism will be attained in so far as there is an intellectual understanding of what it is and what it involves; and in so far as there is an effectual supply of men and women whose faith in it, and whose moral commitment to it, are strong. (See, W.C. Smith, *Modernization of Traditional Society*, Asia, Bombay, 1965, p. 57)

14

Secularism in India: Challenges

Asifa Jan

Introduction

Secular tradition is deeply rooted in Indian history. Indian society is a composite whole which is based on the blending of various spiritual traditions, social ethos and different faiths. In ancient times, Bharat has basically allowed the development of a holistic religion by welcoming different spiritual traditions and trying to integrate them into a common mainstream. The development of four *Vedas* and the various interpretations of the *Upanishads* and the *Puranas* clearly highlight the religious plurality of Bharat. From some of the Rock Edicts of the Ashokan era, one can get a clear picture of the spirit of religious toleration in ancient India. Even after the advent of Jainism, Buddhism and later Islam and Christianity into the Indian soil, the quest for religious toleration and coexistence of different faiths continued. It has been seen that there were many temples that existed in the jurisdiction of King Aurangzeb and grants were given to several Hindu temples like the Mahakal temple at Ujjain, the Chitrakoot temple, etc. (Rajendra Prasad: 2010).

The Sufi and Bhakti movements in Medieval India integrated the people of various communities together. The leading lights of the movement were Khwaja Moinuddin Chisti, Baba Farid, Kabir, Guru Nanak, Tukaram and Mira Bai. They contributed to the development of a composite culture which thereof helped in the building of plural culture. It was in this direction when Guru Nanak said that *"There is no Hindu and no Musalman, as there is no distinction between man and man"* (Gurdeep Kaur: 2000).

The Mughal Emperor Akbar also cautiously promoted the policy of toleration of different faiths. His propagation of Din-i-Illahi (Divine faith) and Sulh-i-kul (peace with all) were inspired by the spirit of secularism.

This spirit was strengthened and enriched through the freedom movement in India. In the initial part of the freedom movement, the liberals like Sir Feroz Shah Mehta, G.K. Gokhale, M.G. Ranade, by and large, pursued a secular approach to politics. In fact, Muslim separatism had not taken roots by that time, Mohammad Ali Jinnah was known as an ambassador of Hindu-Muslim unity as said by Gopal Krishna Gokhale and Sarojini Naidu (Singh Jaswant: 2009). The Brahmo Samaj started by Raja Rammohun Roy and the Arya Samaj led by Swami Dayanand Saraswati never treated other faiths with any antipathy. On the other hand, they tried to purify the wrong traditions which had gradually sapped the vitality of Hinduism.

The constitution drafted by Pandit Moti Lal Nehru as the chairman of the historic Nehru Committee in 1928, had the following provision on secularism:

> There shall be no state religion for the commonwealth of India or for any province in the commonwealth, nor shall the state, either directly or indirectly, endow any religion any preference or impose any disability on account of religious beliefs or religious status. (T.S.N. Sastry: 2014)

Secularism is understood in the Indian context as separating religion from state and accommodating religious differences. After independence it was made a fundamental principle of the constitution to help maintain 'unity in diversity', in the Nehruvian sense. In a multi-religious and stubbornly conservative social system the state took up the task of treading on the path of democracy and welfarism with the help of secular values. Besides, it attempted to bridge the differences created by the partition of the Indian subcontinent on communal grounds. Secularism, guided by objectivity and inter-community harmony, bore the fruits of a peacefully democratic system with entrenched belief in 'rule of law'.

Presently, the secular forces are cornered for alleged appeasement of religious minorities and charged with corrupting the so-called ethos of India (clearly depicted in the writings of the Hindu right ideologues like Golwalker, Hedgewar et al). What followed was an environment of mutual suspicion, riots and communal carnages. The alienation of minorities, especially the Muslims, reached alarming levels. This all goes when India is economically growing fast and is poised to become a superpower in the years to come. Secularism acts as a cementing force and tool of social cohesion. Communalism has already done lots of damage to the social fabric of India.

The definition of secularism, accepted worldwide is, (a) complete neutrality by the state in matters of religion, neither supporting nor opposing it; (b) treating all citizens equally, regardless of their religion, without favoring or giving preferential treatment to any particular religion or non-religion; (c) constitutional bar against the state adopting any religion as its state religion; (d) no mixing of religion and politics for vote banks, as religion is a matter of personal faith.

Challenges in India

In a country like India where all major religions of the world flourished for centuries, the ugly head of communalism is all too high. The major challenges to Indian secularism are enumerated below:

Communalization of Education

After independence the right wing Hindu revivalist groups religiously undertook the task of communalizing education in India. The country of multicultural identities and overlapping fragmentations is presented as a Hindu *rashtra* contaminated by the inflow of foreign races. Muslims and other religious minorities are given an ugly representation in historical narratives. The medieval period of Indian history is termed as Muslim period and oppressive to the majority Hindu community. Indian National movement is portrayed as essentially a struggle by Hindus to free their motherland from all impure races. Text books taught in RSS run schools are indoctrinating children to hate people belonging to other communities. It is argued that the early period of Indian history was magnificent in terms of education, art and literature. The decadence was necessarily brought by the presence of other communities. The present government at the union level is asserting to make Sanskrit compulsory at elementary school level and some voices are up for making the recitation of the national song necessary in government aided schools.

Communalization of Society

Communalization of education which in India takes the form of 'Saffronization' is closely related to the creation of a communal society, rather societies. The former is both cause and the effect of the latter. Communal education taught in RSS run schools in particular consistently poison the minds of the learners. They develop an exclusive identity consciousness and fail to appreciate the idea of peaceful coexistence with their heterogeneous neighbours. Today, Indian society is communalized as was never before. The number and intensity of communal riots have increased sharply over the years. The communal political parties are making great strides in politics. Communal politicians are attracting huge crowds, winning elections and awarded ministerial berths in the new dispensation at New Delhi. Be it *love jihad* or *ghai bachav*, consistent efforts are made by the BJP and Sangh Parivar to polarize the communities on religious lines. Thus it is nightmarish for a Muslim person to find accommodation in a Hindu-dominated locality.

Mahatma Gandhi once said that I see a *ray of hope* only in Kashmir while the whole subcontinent was burning in communal flames (Tendulkar: 1958). But now the situation is quite different in Jammu and Kashmir. In the Jammu region, the state created Village Defence Committees (VDCs) on communal lines. In the recent past, these VDCs were found instrumental in infuriating communal riots in the region. Arms are distributed to Village Defence personnel without any training. There is little or no command and control over their activities. Thus the system created a cleavage in the whole region and in the last 15 years we have seen more than 50 communal clashes in Jammu region while no communal violence was reported in the Kashmir division. (Report of J&K Coalition of Civil Society, 2013).

Communalization of Politics

In the political arena when people are mobilized on communal lines it leads to the sense of discrimination and injustice among the minorities. India constitution provides for a secular polity where the state shall not have any official religion, nor shall it discriminate people on the grounds of religious differences. In actual practice, after independence communal groups have only spread like a hundred-headed hydra. The right wing Hindu groups are virtually dictating terms to the present government at the centre. Political benefits are given to people belonging to a certain religious community, nationalism/patriotism is given cultural (religious) colour, right wing communal leaders are venerated and given heroic importance, and secularists are taunted for appeasing minorities. Politics of exclusion breeds only more exclusion and polarization. Political parties religiously sow the seeds of communal disharmony and harvest the seeds of dissension through electoral politics. The Sachar Committee report throws a great deal of light on the appalling socio-economic and political status of the largest minority in the country.

Communal Ballot/Electoral Process

The secular parties, too, cannot exonerate themselves from their share of blame. They cannot ignore the existence of fanaticism in the body politic. It is very often seen that during elections most of the political parties completely forget this noble ideal of secularism and woo the voters even on communal or caste lines. These acts are not done out of ignorance, but are due to compromise of convenience.

The mobilization of voters on the basis of religion or caste is inimical to the health of Indian democracy. These distortions in the body politic of India only serve to weaken and tarnish the image of world's largest secular country in the World

Communalization of Art, Literature and Media

Communalism in India has taken deep roots in the psyche of Indian people. The machinations of the political elite and the divisive education about the embittered history helped inject the venom of communalism in every vein of the social system.

It is therefore quite natural that in the fields of art, culture and literature, the art of the majority Hindu community is venerated and portrayed as 'Indian' art.

Sanskrit, almost the dead language is attempted to be compulsorily revived, study of Vedas is considered to be made part of curriculum. Indenisation of literature is connected with Hindi-isation. Incumbent Prime Minister of a constitutionally secular country with population of more than 160 million Muslims gifts his Japanese counterpart a copy of Bhagwat Gita (religious scripture of Hindus) and calls it a part of 'Indian' culture (*India Today*: August 30,2014). The American historian Wendy Doniger's book, *Hindus: An Alternative History* is banned in the name of preserving Indian culture.

The Bollywood is portraying Muslims as villains, traitors and terrorists. In soap operas the minority religious symbols like a veiled Muslim woman is presented as a victim of male domination and illiteracy. On social networking sites, on blogs and in cartoons, minorities (Muslims, in particular) are treated as the 'Other'.

Recommendations

The Government of India should form an Indian Secular Lobby to promote secular education and secularization of the institutions in India. Educational institutions must be engaged to check the religion going astray and to become a strong cementing force uniting the society in a warm embrace of mutual respect, love and tolerance. The government must invite scholars to produce a standard textbook on Indian secularism and introduce the textbooks in the schools. Let it be set up soon, and be mandated with preparing a basic textbook for all our students, citizens, religious leaders and politicians, for them to inculcate, profess, practise, and propagate India's true secularism.

Inter-Faith Dialogue and Interaction

All communities should firmly pursue the principle that all religions are equal no matter how big or small and powerful or weak they are. Following that, all faiths should develop their relationship on the basis of mutual understanding. All faiths should support and make efforts to safeguard human values and resolve their differences and misunderstanding through dialogue, communication and coordination. Their cooperation will achieve great accomplishments in and outside the nation. Further, there should be an intersectional framework where local and sectoral struggles are connected towards creating mass consciousness about secular and democratic institutions. The programme like the inter-faith dialogue and interaction between the communities will prove a positive step towards a healthy and free society.

Need for Effective Mechanism to Resolve the Internal Issues

The government should establish a secular taskforce in order to identify those issues which lead to the communalization of society. The task force should make an effective mechanism to resolve the long pending internal issues like the Kashmir issue, Naxalism, the discrimination in detentions and delays in trial, etc. These are the main issues wherein the communal actors within and outside the nation exploit the Indian society. Furthermore, they should disband and disarm or should hold answerable and accountable the VDCs. Their recruitment and training must be carried out at a standard that ensures a responsible and accountable force. All arms and ammunition from these groups must be immediately confiscated.

Secular education at School level

Secular education had the potential to produce a vanguard leadership during the freedom struggle which not only secured independence for the millions of people but also laid the foundations of a vibrant political culture and harmony that steered the evolution process of an embryonic nation on a secular, socialist and democratic path. The government should implement and enforce secular education at the school level and should frame and prepare the secular curriculum. Schools have a role in mobilization or building opinion at grass root level so that positive thinking will evolve among the students in all communities. They should increase contacts and familiarity in every walk of life.

Conclusion

This land of Jawaharlal Nehru is now the largest democracy in the world. The father of the nation Mahatma Gandhi was assassinated by the communal forces. The nation woke up and the right wing extremist parties were banned immediately. But unfortunately, the ban on their activities was revoked after few years. Since the 1980's issues like Babri Majid and Article 370 have become the main planks on which the communal ideology is being flaunted all over. Now, India is at a decisive moment where the right wing party BJP holds power at the centre and in most of the states. But all the ministers including the Prime Minister have to abide by the constitution which is a secular and democratic one. If communalism is allowed to flourish with unconstitutional entities like RSS in close conformity with the union government trying to Hinduize the polity and society, then time is ripe for centrifugal forces to tear this county apart.

REFERENCES

1. Mehra, Ajay K., *Emerging Trends in Indian Politics: The Fifteenth General Election*, New Delhi, Routledge, 2013.
2. Shah, Amritlal B., *Challenges to Secularism*, New Delhi, Nachiketa Publications, 1969.
3. Mehra, Chander, *Rashtriya Swayamsevak Sangh, Architect of Hindu Unity: Dr. Keshav Baliram Hedgewar Birth Centenary*, New Delhi, Bharatiya Swayamsevak Sangh, 2012.
4. Sharma, Jyotirmaya, *Terrifying Vision: M.S. Golwalkar, the RSS, and India*, New Delhi, Penguin Books, 2007.
5. Sankhdher, M.M., *Secularism in India, Dilemmas and Challenges*, New Delhi, Deep & Deep Publications, 1992.
6. Narendra Modi gifts book on Vivekananda, copy of Bhagavad Gita to Shinzo Abe, *India Today*, August 30, 2014.
7. Prasad, Rajendra, *India Divided*, New Delhi, Penguin Books, 2010.
8. Kohli, Ritu, *Political Ideas of M.S. Golwalkar: Hindutva, Nationalism, Secularism*, New Delhi, Deep and Deep Publications, 1993.
9. Islam, Shamsul, *Golwalkar's We or Our Nationhood Defined: A Critique*, New Delhi, Pharos Media & Publishers, 2006.
10. Singh, Jaswant, *Jinnah: India-Partition, Independence*, New Delhi, Rupa Publications, 2009.
11. Sastry, T.S.N., *Human Rights and Duties in India: Law, Policy,*

Society and Enforcement Mechanism, University of Pune, Pune, 2014.

12. Tendulkar, D.G., *Mahatma,* Vol. 8, New Delhi, Publications Division, Government of India, 1962.
13. Bhave, Y.G., *Modern Hindu Trinity: Ambedkar-Hedgewar-Gandhi,* New Delhi, Northern Book Centre, 2005.

15

Challenges to Secularism: The Task Ahead

Ramesh Dixit

It is no doubt a very critical phase in our polity and society. The electoral verdict of the 2014 Parliamentary polls has fundamentally altered the course of our political discourse and forced us to rethink certain concepts and concerns in our public life, which were perceived to have been resolved during the last six decades of our secular-democratic constitutional expedition.

Interestingly while communalism has kept changing its strategies and action plans with the passage of time and has to a substantial extent succeeded in mobilizing popular support of a section of Indian masses particularly the urban middle class and also the semi-urban and rural youth, the secular urban elite failed to adapt itself to the changing social political environment and chalk out corresponding new strategies to face the challenge posed by aggressive and violent communalism, strengthened and nurtured by the custodians of global finance capital with the help of modern technology and advance techniques of communication.

The fundamentalist secular urban elite in its self-absorbed arrogance never bothered to evolve a new appropriate language and idiom to communicate with non-anglicized middle and lower middle class semi-urban and rural populace. In fact, the secular discourse during the last two and a half decades has been appropriated by the English-speaking urban elite of metropolitan cities who hardly ever bothered to connect to people outside the boundaries of their "civil society".

This complete lack of dialogue and communication between secular intelligentsia and the ordinary people provided an opportunity to communal elements to capture the vacant space and fill it with rumorous majoritarianism .

During the freedom struggle and thereafter in the Nehru era, secularism remained a predominant ideology not only of the Indian State but also of vast section of Indian masses cutting across provincial boundaries. Nehru's impeccable commitment to the cause of secularism and democracy inspired the masses to meet the challenge of sporadic communal violence with harmony, peace and amity.

This is time to introspect where did we go wrong? Why did we fail to counter the threats of communal forces? Unless we are prepared to answer certain basic questions we shall not be able to meet the challenge of divisive communal elements.

Is secularism only an urban construct or has it got something to do with distant interiors of our multi-ethnic, multi-religious pluralist society? Does being secular necessarily mean being anti-religion/agnostic/atheist or does it allow the people to hold their personal faiths and beliefs and be considerate and respectful to people of different religious and cultural beliefs? Does secularism require the secular Indian state along with a secular and democratic Indian society or do we only need a secular Indian state to preserve and protect the plurality and diversity of our social and religious fabric?

Such queries have to be addressed in the historical context of our independence and democracy. Independent India's first parliamentary general elections were held under the shadow of India's partition on the basis of the two nation theory followed by massive communal violence. According to Prof. Bipan Chandra, Nehru "made communalism the central issue of his campaign. The basic struggle at the time, he said, was between the secular and the communal forces, for the main danger to India's integrity came from the latter. 'If allowed free play', he warned, communalism "would break up India." And he declared: "Let us be clear about it without a shadow of doubt ...... we stand till death for a secular state."[1]

The Indian electorates reposed their complete faith in Nehru's secularism by providing Nehru's Congress Party 364 out of the total 489 Lok Sabha seats. Other secular parties also performed well with CPI getting 23, Socialist Party 12 and Kisan Majdoor Praja Party 9 seats in the First Lok Sabha of independent India. Predominantly religious but secular in their outlook the Indian people outright rejected the communal forces, which despite all their vicious communal propaganda against Nehru and his philosophy of secularism, could bag only 10 seats—Jan Sangh 3, Ramrajya Parishad 3 and Hindu Mahasabha 4.

This indeed was a resounding victory of secularism in a communally surcharged political atmosphere. This was victory of secularism and its substance in the First General Elections. In the 2014 parliamentary election what has suffered an electoral defeat is not the secularism but its hallow rhetoric.

Here it will be pertinent to discuss the factors behind the gradual growth of communalism in the country. What are the factors that are responsible for bringing majoritarian communalism from the peripheries of society into the mainstream of polity and society?

Four Parliamentary by-elections in 1963, immediately after the Third General Election of 1962, witnessed the success of the electoral strategy of anti-Congress opposition parties based on the principle of not fielding candidates against each other. Though all the parties fielded their candidates on their respective Party symbols, they pledged to go for joint campaigning and targeting only Congress Party as their sole adversary. The 1963 Parliamentary by-polls ensured the victory of Dr. Ram Manohar Lohia (Farrukhabad, UP-Samyukta Socialist Party), Acharya J.B. Kripalani (Amroha, UP-Independent), Minoo Masani (Rajkot, Gujarat-Swatantra Party). The only opposition candidate who lost by a narrow margin was Deen Dayal Upadhyay (Jaunpur, UP-Jan Sangh).

The success of this experiment emboldened the major opposition parties to put the first ever no confidence motion against Nehru's government and in the process unite almost the entire opposition against the ruling Congress Party. Although the no confidence motion failed to muster enough support on the floor of the House, it did herald the beginning of a tactical electoral understanding among the anti-Congress political parties.

This electoral understanding among the political parties of divergent ideological orientations was initially conceptualized by veteran socialist thinker and leader Dr. Lohia purely as a strategic alliance which meant proper seat adjustment among non-Congress parties, the sole objective being breaking of the hegemony of the ruling Congress Party and providing the electorate a viable electoral alternative to Congress.

But in course of time, Lohia and his comrades encouraged by the 1963 experiment started theorizing it as a new ideology of non-Congressism, which overshadowed the traditional pattern of right, centre and left politics.[2]

After the Fourth General Election in 1967, when the Congress Party returned to power at the centre with a reduced majority and was ousted from power in more than 8 states, it was hailed as the victory of the ideology of non-Congressism.

The non-Congress governments formed in various states were in fact coalition governments which brought the Jan Sangh and CPI together along with socialists, Swatantra Party, and the breakaway faction of Congress Party in sharing of ministerial berths. In UP the Samyukta Vidhayak Dal government led by Charan Singh as Chief Minister had the presence of Jharkhande Rai of CPI and Ganga Bhakt Singh of the Jan Sangh under the ideological garb of non-Congressism.

The politics of non-Congressism brought the Jan Sangh and its ideological patron RSS, for the first time into the political mainstream of Indian polity and provided them legitimacy which they desperately required at that juncture of their ideological and political journey. Since then they have used all the available multi-party platforms to reach out to wider sections of Indian masses.

The J.P. movement provided them another major opportunity to capture non-Congress political space. According to Bipan Chandra, "During 1974-75, J.P. not only ignored the anti-secular, communal and anti-democratic character of RSS-Jan Sangh and sought their active support in his movement but also gave them good chits and lent them an aura of respectability. On March 5, 1975 he attended the all India session of the Jan Sangh at New Delhi and thanked the party and its members for active support to his movement. In turn, he promised to reciprocate their support. Replying to those who criticized him for relying on RSS-Jan Sangh cadres, he said : "The Jan Sangh and RSS are neither reactionary nor fascist. How can any party which had lent support to total revolution be called reactionary or fascist? And then he went on to the extent of saying: "If the Jan Sangh is fascist, then I too am a fascist."[3]

During the post-emergency Parliamentary Elections under tremendous pressure of anti-emergency political and social forces, the Jan Sangh reluctantly dissolved its identity to become part of Janata Party but RSS tactically retained its separate and independent existence, which ultimately proved to be a major factor in the downfall of Janata government and imminent break up of Janata Party.

When in the 1980 parliamentary mid-term polls, the residual Janata Party comprising the erstwhile Jan Sangh, Swatantra, Congree (O) and other rightist and centrist forces like Babu Jagjivan Ram faced a humiliating electoral defeat, the RSS was prompt enough to leave the sinking ship and float an entirely new political outfit called Bharatiya Janata Party with guidance and blessings of certain prominent, liberal-secular public figures and intellectuals who could successfully persuade the top RSS-BJP leaders to include Gandhian socialism in their policy document. RSS was more than willing to accommodate the suggestions of these renowned personalities as their moral support could provide it sufficient legitimacy and acceptability in non-Congress centrist space. But RSS/BJP did not take much time in going back to its original ideology of majoritarian communalism and giving up its Gandhian socialist pretensions.[4]

Yet, the RSS had to wait till 1989 when after the refusal of Congress, the single largest party, to form the government at the centre, National Front was invited to form the government. V.P. Singh was shrewd enough to garner the support of Leftist parties by addressing them as his natural allies and making a few public statements against communalism. At the same time, he could also solicit the support of the BJP by accepting its pre-conditions, and making certain concessions to its liking. One such overt concession was to allow L.K. Advani to embark on his blatantly communal Rath Yatra from Somnath to Ayodhya which brought the Mandir-Masjid issue into popular discourse.

This was the height of political opportunism of an ambitious political leader who in his sheer lust for power betrayed the cause of secularism and compromised with majoritarian communalism. This was the beginning of an era of unprincipled and unscrupulous power politics where difference between communal and secular became only a matter of convenience.

The following years witnessed the demolition of a 500 years old mosque in full public gaze, when the 'secular' Congress party ruled the country. Though, the apprehensions of connivance or tacit understanding between the then Prime Minister and the perpetrators of this planned act of destruction have been a matter of public debate, the irony is that not a single minister of his council of ministers offered to resign on such an act of betrayal. The self-styled custodians of secularism preferred to observe strategic silence.

Such vacillations on the part of secular Congress leaders not only demoralized the average secular Indian but emboldened the majoritarian communal forces to further polarize our polity and society on communal lines.

In 1996 when BJP after emerging as the single largest party got the opportunity to form the government at the centre, it failed to prove a majority as no other political party even dreamt of supporting it in the Lok Sabha. But within a span of hardly two years, BJP managed to secure the support of not only the secular parties like TMC, TDP and AIADMK but also the fire brand socialists who wasted no time in becoming part of NDA. State-sponsored Gujarat massacre of 2002 was conveniently overlooked by these 'secular' leaders of BJP-led NDA.

In fact, the politics of non-Congressism is responsible for the growth of communal forces in electoral terms. Majoritarian communalism is supported and nurtured by the disciplined and cadre based RSS, which is active at the grass roots level in almost every part of the country.

Now when RSS is openly and blatantly putting forward its divisive communal agenda through central government, secular organizations and individuals should introspect and seriously deliberate the future course of action.

In retrospect it can be said that in the post-Nehru era the secularism in our country has been more a matter of convenience rather than a matter of conviction. The secular parties and organizations have failed to distance themselves from communal outfits which have taken advantage of mass movements and sporadic public uprisings to spread their ideology. They could succeed because of their organizational strength and dedicated cadre, whereas the protagonists of secularism neither have any effective organization to match the RSS nor do they have such dedicated activists who are capable of communicating their ideas to vast sections of society.

Movements like India against corruption led by Anna Hazare and Arvind Kejriwal were also, to a large extent, instrumental in providing a public platform to communal forces. It is suprising that none of us has heard any news about Anna and his revolutionary team since Modi has come to power. Can it be construed that the sole purpose of this movement was to facilitate BJP's entry into the corridors of power?

This is necessary to emphasize that despite minor and periodic vacillations at certain moments, Congress and Leftist parties are only political formations which have demonstrated their will and determination to fight against communalism both ideologically and politically. Therefore any anti-communal front to be effective and purposeful has to have dialogue, if not collaboration, with Congress as well. All talks of non-Congress and non-BJP joint front will ultimately benefit the disruptive and divisive forces only.

The need of the hour is to have the broadest possible joint front of such secular parties and organizations who are prepared to publicly declare their resolve not to have any social or political interaction with communal outfits in future. We know that majoritarian communalism always leads to fascism but proper care has to be taken to distinguish between faith and beliefs of the majority community and the communal propaganda.

It should not be forgotten that communalism is too serious and complex a problem to be handled by NGOs with FCRA or the literary and cultural organizations of Leftist parties. The secular outfits must ensure that there is proper and regular dialogue among different religious, ethnic and linguistic communities at all levels. Most of the problems arise because of the lack of knowledge about each other's customs and behaviour patterns. When there is lack of proper dialogue among various social and religious groups then the false propaganda and the rumours succeed in vitiating the environment.

Extreme care and precaution be taken in the matters of faith and religion to ensure that no religious sensibilities of any community are hurt, though at the same time no concessions be granted to orthodoxy and obscurantism of any variety.

In a democratic polity there are no shortcuts for political or mass mobilisation. Without reaching out to a wider section of masses it is not possible to counter the propaganda of communal forces. Secular activists should stop the habit of working only among likeminded people. This is a futile exercise, which serves no purpose.

Let us start afresh. The minorities understand the worth of secular politics more than anybody else because it affects their basic life and existence. The immediate requirement is to sensitize various sections of the majority community, as a vast section of majority has recently got swayed by false propaganda of majoritarian communal forces. They have to be encouraged and convinced that the plurality and diversity of traditions and beliefs is the strength of our society and any attempt to weaken the bonds of fraternity among the people of this country will only harm our common interests. We have to inculcate a feeling of pride for our composite culture in our neighbourhood.

Indian people by and large do not endure extremism of any sort for long. They adhere to *Majjhim Nikay*, i.e. middle path. Secular activists should also avoid speaking the language of extremes. There is no need for pampering or bashing any community.

A secular state is expected to treat all its citizens as equal. State should neither discriminate nor favour. It has to have no religious preferences. This is the duty of secularist to ensure that Indian state does not vacillate on secularism. This is time for self-introspection and not for empty bravado.

The Indian state just cannot be allowed to shed even an iota of its secular character and credentials but at the same time precautions have to be taken not to hurt the sensibilities of those religious-minded people of all the faiths who do not conform to the views of the urban secular elite but who are equally secular as far as the matter of society and politics are concerned.

NOTES AND REFERENCES

1. Chandra, Bipan, *Indian After Independence*, Penguin Books, 2000, p. 133.
2. Conversations with Mr. Satya Dev Tripathi, a close associate and one of the election managers of Dr. Lohia. He is at present a prominent leader of the UP Congress Party.
3. Chandra, Bipan, *In the Name of Democracy: JP Movement and the Emergency*. Penguin Books, 2003, pp. 145-46.
4. The circumstances following the assassination of Indira Gandhi changed the political environment and BJP could bag only two seats in the 1984 parliamentary elections. But the fact is that the RSS cadre in this election voted for Congress as they perceived Sikh extremism to be a real threat for the Indian nation.

16

Secularism and Annihilation of Caste: Hamid Dalwai and Politics of Muslim Reform

Cybil Vinodan

Introduction

This paper is an attempt to evaluate the contributions of radical Muslim intellectual Hamid Dalwai who was also a founder of the Muslim Satyashodhak movement. He was a vigilant thinker who cautioned the growth of exclusionism in his community fearing it to produce adverse effects on the Hindu fraternity. Though it is over four decades since he passed away, his thoughts continue to gleam with untainted brilliance over the clouds of depression in intellectual life in contemporary India. It is therefore very significant to encounter the thoughts of Dalwai in its sheer originality to overcome many of the fears that produced such depression. This paper will analyse his thoughts after graphically placing them on the table.

The radical thrust Dalwai has given to the understanding of Muslims as a civilization, as a way of life in India is a novel attribute. The constant problem of being a pioneer to recognize the existence of caste amongst Muslims constantly comes through as a criticism of his predecessors, i.e., Muslim intellectuals under colonial rule. It includes the whole array of national-secular leadership as well as the Muslim League. He courted this challenge by leaving behind his profession of a journalist with *Maratha*, a leading daily in Marathi.

Respecting a vernacularized pluralism amongst the Muslims in India with immense attitude, he openly states his longing for Urdu as it is dispersed in all Indian vernaculars spoken by Muslims. He also does not fail to point out the Hindu Kayasth who uses Urrdu as his/her native tongue, rather than any vernacular. His will is a clear statement of his political convictions. As a true adherent of Satyashodak thought he left his remains to be charred to ashes in an electric crematorium. He requested not to set up any memorial after him, but establish research centres for the study of Islam. His atheism could not affect his love for the people who believed in Islam. It could only be strengthened as revealed by his will.

Role of Intellectuals

Dalwai has very clearly analysed the role of Jinnah as a Muslim intellectual, the different phases of the transformation of his approach to the question of India's independence. The first phase of the Lucknow Pact in 1916 and the second phase of demand for Pakistan since the 1930s has been given in a progressive light. His perseverance till the Cabinet Mission to have a united country has been singled out by Dalwai as a complement. The refusal by Congress to abide by the Cabinet Mission of a three-point programme for independence led to a reversal of his position. The possibility of building a Federation, with the provinces of India divided as Hindu and Muslim majority areas with a federal government with limited powers at the centre was refuted by the Congress. They wanted a strong centre and the parity clause of the Muslim League having an equal share in the central government was also unacceptable to the Congress. This inevitably led to Partition.

But the third phase of Jinnah's political transformation happens as the head of the new state of Pakistan. Jinnah's claims to have sought the establishment of a secular state in Pakistan is criticized by Dalwai, who even ridicules how Jinnah feared for his life during the violence of the Partition, especially after Gandhi became a fearless martyr to it. His analysis of Jinnah'a political career has led Dalwai to make some radical conclusions about the fate of Muslim intellectuals in India, as those who fail to connect with their own community and the country as a civilization.

He has particularly focused his criticism on the tradition of intellectual leadership amongst the Muslims since the time of Shah Waliullah in the 18th century who started the Wahabi movement in India that sought after state power for Muslims in the wake of the British conquest and Mughal decline. His inquiries into the reasons for a vacuum of intellectuals amongst Muslims in India takes him to consider even the historic Aligarh movement begun by Sir Syed Ahmed Khan as conservative in its silent acceptance of the Mughal legacy. The failure to adapt to democratic politics, sticking to an old regime and failure to engage with an intellectual class of Hindus emerging under the British rule led to the creation of this vacuum according to Dalwai.

He claims there were three stages in the creation of intellectuals among the Hindus—one which is related to the generation of Raja Rammohun Roy and his reforms to integrate the Hindus, a second stage indicated by the rise of leaders like Savarkar that sought a representation of a Hindu nation from a Rightist perspective and third, the generation of Gandhi that represents the liberal face of Hinduism. He compares the state of Muslims to this and then shows that the first stage though late in arrival for the Muslims in India was represented by Sir Syed Ahmed Khan and the second stage by the likes of Jinnah and the third stage unfortunately failed to materialize because of Partition and the subsequent loss of intellectual heritage that it invoked.

Muslims and Politics of Minorities

In an essay on global Islam and the politics of minorities in India, he has sought attention to the politics of Muslims in India. He has sought to uncover the paradox of a Muslim politics that gets trapped alternatively between states in which Muslims form a minority and those in which they constitute the majority. To begin with he has pointed out the failure of Pakistan to protect the rights of the Ahmadiyas when riots broke out there after Partition. Moreover, Jinnah as well as Maulana Maududi (founder of Jamat-e-Islami) had considered themselves beyond a pale of criticism insofar as the Muslims in India were considered and they held it as the duty of Indian Muslims to be not critical of Pakistan or its treatment of minorities, be they of any religion. Chaudhuri Khaliquzman who headed the Muslim League in India after Partition has been in this way criticized by Jinnah for raising fingers at him for not being able to contain the riots in Pakistan or the killing of civilians.

This leads Dalwai to investigate deeply the propositions for Muslim politics in countries like India. First of all he negates the tendency or attitude of leaders in Muslim majority states to look down upon politics of Muslims in countries where they constitute only a minority. He then proceeds to examine the traces of Wahabism present in all such approaches that ridicule the approach to minorities in Islam. He illustrates the case of the birth of Islam and the creation of its first state in Medina where despite the predominance of Jews and Christians, the prophet established an Islamic state. The Jaziya was duly charged from them, but in later times it came to be interpreted that only the religions of the book shall have the privilege to remain on their own after paying a tax, the rest will be forced to either convert to Islam or be executed. This was the approach to non-believers known as Shafi accepted by Shah Waliullah who sought to experiment it in India. The repercussions or consequences of such experiments showed itself in the decelerated processes of education and adaptation to the democratic processes onset by it under the colonial rule.

Regarding the political history of Islam Dalwai makes certain illuminating comparisons with Christianity. Islam could never establish a united front of religion and politics or church and the state like in Christianity. The Caliph was the most powerful ruler in the Islamic world and this title did not remain stable for long at any one place and shifted from Arab-ruled Spain to Baghdad to Ottoman Turkey. Islam also did not succeed in establishing a clerical order that could align itself globally with the political order. The fall of the Turkish caliphate in the early 20th century also seems to have been repented by none else, but the Muslims of India. The Arabs were by contrast delighted at the defeat of a strong contender to the claim of political supremacy in the Islamic world. The fall of the Caliphate coincided with a time when several Muslim nations were coming into existence. Some of them like Afghanistan were already independent, some like Iran were dependents, and the Arab countries were completely under the rule of the Western countries. There was a strong influence of Western civilization on the Islamic world during this phase. This led to modernization and emergence of an educated middle class in the Arab world. India produced a contrasting effect to this when the Muslims began reacting strongly to the modernized politics of the English-educated Hindu middle class.

He says the failure since the beginning to integrate political and religious authority may be seen in the later history of Islam as well. In countries where Muslims formed a majority they found solace in the fact that they were partners in the government and where they were in a minority, they were hopeful of emerging into partners in government eventually. This was the immediate result of the breakdown of Muslim empires and monarchies, i.e. the Muslim population became divided into two entities-nations where they were in a majority and nations where they were in a minority. Such a decision was guided by the awakening that the days of unlimited authority in government were over with the collapse of the monarchs and emperors, therefore the Muslims now have to ensure a fair share in the respective governments whether they were in majority or minority. Thus one can find a Muslim majority trying to protect the Nizam of Hyderabad who was a recognized Muslim ruler, but a monarch, yet opposing the ruler of Kashmir also a monarch where they were in a majority because there were no prospects for Muslims becoming partners in his rule. This minority-majority politics or a politics of numbers was an invention of the Wahabism begun by Abdul Wahab in Saudi Arabia.

Dalwai also argues that Wahabism analysed Islam as having never accepted a hereditary line of Caliphs since the beginning. Only four of the recognized Caliphs after the death of the prophet could produce a harmonious government for the Muslims. Since the time of the establishment of the first government in Medina by the Prophet, the Muslims have sought political power even when they were in a minority. This is the reason given by both Wahab and Waliullah in organizing Muslims into a political force according to Dalwai. He also cites this as the reason why these two movements turned violently against the Shia Muslims who were not swayed by politics as strongly as the Sunnis. While the Shias accept the Prophet's son-in-law Ali as their leader or Imam, they also consider the line of Imams having ended long ago in Islam. There is no talk about Jihad amongst the Shias because there is no Caliph or Imam to give orders for a Jihad. This is a situation that was found unacceptable by the Sunnis who were adamant like Waliullah or Wahab to organize the Muslims politically. The reason why Islamic society has remained left out in the field of reforms, like those initiated by the Christian church or even Hindu missions like the Ramakrishna Mission (under the influence of Christianity no doubt) is due to this. The absence of social reform in the Islamic context has to be linked with their preoccupation with political authority/power.

Muslim Women and Social Reform

It is with respect to the question of women's rights for Muslims in India that his thoughts take a very serious concern. He was instrumental in convening a Muslim Women's Conference in Pune in 1971, which was probably the first of its kind in the country. It is also famous for its demand for the resolution for a Uniform Civil Code in India for all communities. This is one clause where he has been misinterpreted widely and it is not difficult to see the reasons why. Initially he claims the reasons to it as women becoming a subject for protection as in the case of the abolition of Sati which is owed to the work of Raja Rammohun Roy. He contrasts the case with Europe where a struggle for any class of citizens were fought by none other than the aggrieved or affected and not by a spokesperson or representative. Here in India or most of the non-Western world, representation has been the norm of fight for rights and the strategies have been different. So, the Bengal instance can be also seen as a desperate attempt to bring the Hindu back in fold as one Hindu widow had found refuge in a re-marriage. She had converted to Islam and a court case against her marriage could not be held, because Islam allowed re-marriage of widows. This formed the backdrop of reforms by Rammohun Roy to protect the Hindu community from losing ranks. The

Muslim women's question was there since the time of the Prophet as he had many wives and has been followed since as a tradition. He asks if the Prophet had decreed a man to have more than one wife and asks why then should the Muslims oppose a civil code restricting one spouse per person.

He also points out how Wahabism was focused on destroying the Sufi tradition in Islam. He indicates their call to the destruction of the dargahs and peers that has led to construction of a monolithic Islam. Here he also draws attention to the fact that the Shia women enjoy better education and access to liberal rights than the Sunnis because of a different approach to Islam. He is also trying to address the women's question when he argues that amongst the Adivasis the number of converts to Christianity is higher because women find a better refuge there rather than in Islam or Hinduism.

He compares the case of India with Turkey which had adopted a liberal regime for women as a pioneer in the Islamic world and also seems to advocate in its favour while at another point he is sceptical of the kind of transition to a secular regime in Turkey could be sustainable like a law based more on tradition although he is not here referring to the Sharia. Probably he is indicating a common law based on the collective experience of a people living in a region together as a society despite divisions of faith or religion.

Jati and Dharam are the two words used by him to indicate the orthodoxy. In this context but it has to be understood that he means community by Jati and text by Dharam. Jatiyavad becomes communalism and Dharmnirapekshta becomes secularism. As a founder of the Muslim Satyashodhak Mandal he affirmed his belief in universal principles, but neither community or text. It is difficult to say what exactly he believed in, but from all that he denied it is evident that he chose to align his ideas with the excluded, the victims, the minorities but in such a way that a discourse was generated where a general history could be written of a people. His alienation from Muslims was because of his refusal to admit representation as an idea and the persistent call to create intellectuals as a class bore heavily on his reputation as a Muslim. As he wrote in a note of submission that he always wondered how Muslims in

India could be attracted to only those leaders who never practised any of Islam in their lives while the leaders who practised Islam but spoke for reforms struggled to find any acceptance at all.

Muslims and Secularism in India

Regarding secularism he observes that it has had no connections with nationalism as often believed. The central question he says, whether a country's nationalism is rooted in its religion or the region that it represents. Thus, he refutes claim by Hindu nationalists that after Partition, India has reverted to being the Hindurashtra it had always been, but for the periods of Mughal and British conquest. On the contrary, the Muslim perception argues that this country was never united into a nation till the arrival of the Mughals. It was since the Mughals that it had a history to call its own and also a tradition that gave it its current place in music, arts and performances. He argues that in both these perspectives, religion (dharm) plays the defining role for nationalism. He says that on the contrary, nationalism is always the product of a sense of belonging to a region and a shared sense of history, not a particular phase or period of history.

He further explores the meaning of secularism to the historic context of Europe where it emerged. The crusades which had vitiated the atmosphere of faith and religion in Europe had made it indispensable for the nation states of Europe to create a strict line of separation between religion and politics or church and the state. Protestantism emerged as a winner in this conflict because it was a faith rooted in egalitarianism, individual freedom, human rights and religious freedom. One could see that except for France, all Catholic countries are backward and so also except for Turkey, all Muslim countries have remained backward. France was exceptional because the Catholics sought a way out of this by inventing the notion of secularism for modernizing itself. Turkey also had a similar crisis before accepting secularism as it was left with no other option to modernize. Had it not been accepted, the country's very existence could be threatened.

In India we have accepted a Turkish model of secularism. But the difference is that whereas Turkey was an autocracy when it became secular and therefore could enforce secular laws in the public, India is a democracy and it is not possible in a democracy to enforce secularism in the form of another religion. But if the country is to modernize then secularism and its laws have to be accepted is a foregone conclusion that Dalwai makes.

Anti-Caste Movement and Dalwai

Caste has been always argued to be the one reason in the delay of revolution in India by many scholars. The Muslim Satyashodhak Mandal (an organization based on the teachings of Jotiba Phule) is a testimonial to the claim that the Islamic cause in India has been delayed by lack of understanding of the caste system or else the understanding of the Islamic nation would have been entirely different (Nawalgundkar: 2006: 173). An idea originally mooted by Hamid Dalwai, but has been cited by historians like Ramachandra Guha as a criticism of the present generation of Indian Muslims, who have lacked the strength of a liberal intelligentsia. Ashgar Ali Engineer has responded to this, but not by defending Dalwai. He also blames Dalwai for relying on secondary data on Muslims in India. Yet, in his conclusion, Engineer comes close to Dalwai, that there is a deep stratification in Indian Islam, which led to the collapse of its intellectual class, when they migrated to Pakistan. Dalwai says that amongst his contemporaries, Muslims had no resistance to deter the growth of obscurantism amidst them, while amongst the Hindus a minority class of liberal intellectuals resisted such developments. The reason why he chose the Satyashodhak Mandal as the name for this movement may be due to the fact that he saw in Phule's movement a model of intellectualism for the revival of liberalism amongst the Muslims.

Strangely, the arguments of Dalwai are now being propagated as an excuse for Hindu revivalism. One cannot help not noticing the importance with which his profile is posted on the website of an organization like the Maharashtra Navnirman Sena. His invocation to create a liberal intellectual class of Muslims in India, because as a minority they are better off than the Hindus in Pakistan does not seem to have struck a chord with the secularists in India. The way things are moving, the very early demand for a uniform civil code that was raised by Dalwai (in 1971 at a Muslim Women's Conference in Pune) is also likely to be interpreted heavily in the cause of Hindu revivalism, to the detriment of his own community.

The recurring blame that a Muslim intelligentsia tends to separate itself from orthodox Islam, rather than try and reform it made by Dalwai has been found to be superficial by Ashgar Ali Engineer. His argument that a new middle class—the Ajlaf–that has emerged since the Partition in India is trying to bridge the gap of intellectualism amongst the Muslims. Yet, the early radicalism and individualism demonstrated by Dalwai stands out as singular. I will try and dwell a little more on this problem of the vignettes or isles of singularity of attempts to reform and change amongst 'backward' communities/castes in post-colonial India. How far can such isolation be overcome in order to create a fraternity of castes/communities for the very sake of it, as it also becomes a part of the preamble to the Constitution? Till this far, one can see that such attempts have been few and far between and the word fraternity itself appears to have been kept in a cold storage of identities and at a distance, removed from the context of social movements within which it originally took shape.

One of the serious problems forecast in the ideas of Dalwai is what eventually happens to political orientation of a new middle class that is emerging in an independent country. It is the rootedness of this middle class, which is the larger problem, when addressed at a political level. Hence the problem is not restricted to Muslims and is present in all such communities/castes that have been swept into the nation state at the time of its formation in 1947. This new middle class, which is searching for a political orientation, too fragmented within to have a common face in vying with the politics of identities, has been addressed in a tricky, statist terminology as the SCs, STs, OBCs. It is also true that in its current form, it is a fodder, a brand name for augmenting all forms of statist politics whether it be of the Left or the Right. This is true also in so far as the politics of this middle class is analysed in the context of the centre or the states.

To get to its reasons, we may have to go back to Ambedkar

himself who was the Chairman of the Drafting Committee of the Constitution. The ethos of liberty, equality and fraternity were consistently espoused by Ambedkar in all his mobilizations or struggles of the Dalits for amelioration of their social and economic backwardness. But, fraternity is a hypothetical condition according to the Constitution, because it ensures its citizens, "Justice, social, economic and political; Liberty of thought, expression, belief, faith and worship; Equality of status and of opportunity; and to promote among them all Fraternity assuring the dignity of the individual and the unity and integrity of the Nation". The active participation of the state in promoting fraternity does not indicate any clear origins. I would like to dwell more on this and explore reasons for it.

Fraternity presupposes the existence of both liberty and equality and also foregrounds the idea of endosmosis or the concept by which Ambedkar defined the continuous existence of castes can be, if at all explained in a democratic society. Endosmosis is a concept which comes closest to that of fraternity, which not merely Ambedkar, but also his mentor John Dewey had earlier used after French philosopher Henri Bergson. It is around this concept that one can find the discourse of fraternity unraveling in the Indian context. To quote from Ambedkar, "If you ask me, my ideal would be a society based on Liberty, Equality and Fraternity. And why not? What objection can there be to Fraternity? I cannot imagine any.

"An ideal society should be mobile, should be full of channels for conveying a change taking place in one part to other parts. In an ideal society there should be many interests consciously communicated and shared. There should be varied and free points of contact with other modes of association. In other words there must be social endosmosis. This is fraternity, which is only another name for democracy. Democracy is not merely a form of government. It is primarily a mode of associated living, of conjoint communicated experience."

Conclusion

These words taken from Ambedkar's Annihilation of Caste points in several directions. One is the fact that he was responding strongly to Gandhi's concept of Ramarajya as the future ideal for India. Ambedkar was a pragmatist with respect for the past and hence did not value a past abstracted out of reality of which nothing could be definitely said about in the present. Endosmosis also represented for him an activity by which social movement was ensured. This was not meant to be a vertical mobility of a hierarchical society or a lateral mobility of an egalitarian society. Societies irrespective of the fact whether they were stratified or not, homogenous and egalitarian or not could still have endosmosis. It is a process by which a society communicates with itself, it is an internal mixing of the different groups by the use of porous membranes that separate them but allow communication between them. Ambedkar saw untouchability as a non-porous membrane that held up all the possibility of communication in Indian politics. This was his main reason for arguing strongly for separate electorates for the untouchables.

This is the reason why annihilation of caste has been a key concern of the Dalit movement in foregrounding secularism as a step to contemporary social reform. I will argue that the achievements of the Dalit movement is in shaping new perspectives on community especially those oriented towards fraternity. Secularism, given the neutrality of its proponents in the face of the failure of its projects, never found a resonance in the intellectual life of minority or marginal communities. At least that is what both Dalwai's and Ambedkar's reticence to accept the term to denote the intellectual life of their respective communities indicates.

Dalwai's contention regarding the role of Muslim intellectuals proceeds from the fact that although, they begin with an effort to represent themselves, they end up by becoming anti-Hindu. He says that this has happened with Syed Ahmed Khan as well as with Jinnah and Iqbal. The late processes of modernization amongst the Muslims compared to the Hindus have resulted in this fate. But the twist of this fate is that the stuntedness of the community and the death of its intellectual class can lead to the Hindu community imitating the Muslims. The Hindu liberal who has already paved the way for the creation of an intellectual class, which is exigent for the functioning of a democracy is lauded here by Dalwai who says that neither a Hindu nor a Muslim intellectual can be a secular intellectual like a working class intellectual. Therefore, secularism is only a desirable reality for Indian democracy and not yet a present one.

In pushing the argument further, Dalwai argues for not individual saviors as intellectuals like in the past, but to have an avant garde of intellectuals for Muslims. In overcoming the threats of obscurantism, revivalism plaguing the community only such a class could help. The Hindu liberals have every right to oppose Muslim communalism and can be defaulted in their role as intellectuals if they refuse to do so. But it does not mean that they can show clemency to Muslim communalism, because that way they are also strengthening Hindu fundamentalism.

This interesting inter-connectedness of intellectual life amongst the close-knit community of Hindus and Muslims in India, in their efforts to modernize and democratize in Dalwai indicates a search for new avenues to understand the sociology of India. The same sentiment is expressed in Ambedkar's urge to overcome or shatter the myth that untouchables of India are fully represented in Hinduism. The untouchable or Dalit intellectuals would have to build their own constituencies by fighting the Hindu orthodoxy. In this respect, the anti-caste struggle of Phule and Ambedkar emerges as a beacon light for Muslim liberals in their own fight against orthodoxy and then in the creation of a secular democracy for Hamid Dalwai.

REFERENCES

1. Nawalgundkar, S.N., (2006), Swa.Vinayak Damodar Savarkar, in *Maharashtratil Jatisansthavishayak Vicar* (ed.)Yeswant Sumant and D.D. Punde, Pune, Pratima Prakasan.
2. Guha, Ramachandra (ed.) *Makers of Modern India*, Penguin, , New Delhi, 2010, pp. 490-505.
3. Mukherjee, Arun. P., B.R. Ambedkar, John Dewey and the Meaning of Democracy, *New Literary History*, Vol. 2, Spring 2009, pp. 345-70.
4. Tamboli, Shamsuddin, *Hamid Dalwai: Krantikari Vicharwan* (Marathi), Diamond Publications, Pune, 2009.

17

A Critique of the Critics of Indian Secularism: A Study of Partha Chatterjee's 'Secularism and Toleration'

Noorjahan Momin

Secularism has been a much deliberated concept, both in the realm of philosophy as well as in practice. Its complexities and the diverse ways in which it impacts lives of individuals and groups has led to much deliberation and contemplation, whereby invoking support of its proponents and earning the ire of those who oppose it. Secularism is an integral part of Indian polity, enshrined in the preamble to Indian constitution.

Looking at the mosaic nature of the huge population in India, it would not be an exaggeration to attribute secularism as the cement that has been strongly holding this vast country full of internal diversities together. On the same tone, like many other philosophical ideas when compared with practicality, does not escape the scope of criticism. I would not go in the details about the incorporation of this concept in the Indian Constitution right now. However, its origin and evolution would most certainly be discussed during the course of this paper.

Looking at the complex nature of secularism when implemented in India, it is evident that it has been criticized and explored in great depth. Some of the significant works include those by V.P. Luthra (1964), D.E. Smith (1963), T.N. Madan (1987), Rajeev Bhargava (1994), Akeel Bilgrami (1994), Ashis Nandy (1995), and Javed Alam (1998). In this essay, I would like to limit myself to the work of Prof. Partha Chatterjee

(1994). I would like to do so with the objective of reading and re-reading the 'Secularism and Tolerance' by Chatterjee, so as to explore the different contours of his arguments as well as to see how in some of the instances the thoughts of Chatterjee has benefitted or damaged the cause of secularism in India. Through the paper I would like to situate Chatterjee's arguments in the contemporary scenario where the Right has once again seized the political power and is attempting to establish its supremacy over the secular ethos of the Indian state.

Partha Chatterjee (1994: *EPW* 1768-1777) wrote 'Secularism and Toleration' in times of great turmoil and turbulence. The Babri mosque had been demolished followed by massive bloodshed in communal carnage, and fractured relations between communities. Even though more than 20 years have passed since the publication of this significant academic intervention, the conditions haven't changed much. Muzaffarnagar, Meerut, Mewat and Delhi are some of the recent instances when the communal frenzy and persecution of communities on the basis of their religious affiliations have been raising its poisonous head again. The tilt of democracy in favour of the Hindu Right has once again brought to the fore the need to analyse and evaluate the secular nature of the Indian state. In this paper, Chatterjee questions the adequacy of secularism in standing against this "political challenge [posed by] this Hindu majoritarianism" (1768).

Drawing parallels between fascism in Europe and the Hindu right in India, Chatterjee illuminates his readership about the ways and means through which the proponents of fascism have been using the idea of 'positive secularism'. Chatterjee presents a remarkable insight into the exploration of secularism by the Right and how it has been using or rather misusing the notion of secularism to sideline the other minorities in the country in a hegemonic way. To elucidate it with a relevant example, Chatterjee invokes the historical case of Nazi Germany and Italy where 'the Nazi campaign against Jews as other minority groups did not call for an abandonment of the secular people of the state in Germany'. Chatterjee, in fact, brings to the fore ways in which the fascists have misused the idea to suppress the minorities (Chatterjee 1994: 1768).

In his essay, Chatterjee speaks about the rise and development of the Hindu Right in India as different from the fascist forces of Germany and Italy. For him, the political leadership of the rightist forces have the attribute of camouflaging cotempt towards the minorities and those who exhibit a soft attitude towards the minorities in the recent times is not an inherent feature in the Indian Hindu Right since its inception. According to Prof. Chatterjee, in the inaugural phase, the Hindu Mahasabha had an explicit contemptuous attitude towards the institutions and procedures of the 'Western' or 'modern' state which it has eventually learnt to hide. However, my contention here with Chatterjee's argument is two-fold. While on the one hand, by suggesting differences between the fascists of India and the West in the 1930s-40s, Chatterjee searches for an indigenous fascism that has originated and evolved in India and thus is distinct from that in the West. On the contrary, Marzia Casolari (2000) in *Hindutva's Fascist Heritage* has exposed how the proponents of RSS and Hindu Mahasabha have been drawing inspiration from Mussolini and Hitler. On the other hand, nowhere in the article has Chatterjee, spoken about the inherent similarities between them. It must be kept in mind that, fascism in Europe and in India had originated simultaneously in the backdrop of the Great Economic Depression (during the World Wars) and thus was a universal phenomenon that had economic turmoil as its precursor (Dutt 1934 and Dutt 1949).

Taking the example of the demand for a uniform civil code by the RSS and BJP, Chatterjee elucidates that these are some measures through which the right wing forces try to camouflage their anti-secularism under the garb of a 'principled modernist critic of Islamic or Sikh fundamentalism' and meticulously describe their adversaries as 'pseudo-secularists' (Chatterjee 1994: 1768). A person not familiar with the strategies of the fascist right may assume that due to its allegiance to the notion of a *Hindu Rashtra*, the aspired form of the state in terms of its institutions and procedures must be in conflict with the Western form of the modern state. However, Chatterjee explains how this notion is contrary to the reality and that the 'mature, and most formidable, statement of the new political conception of

'Hindutva' is unlikely to pit itself against the idea of the secular state. In fact, for Chatterjee, "in its most sophisticated forms, the campaign of the Hindu right often seeks to mobilize on its behalf the will of an interventionist modernizing state in order to erase the presence of religious or ethnic particularisms from the domains of law or public life and to supply, in the name of 'national culture', a homogenized content to the notion of citizenship" (Chatterjee 1994: 1768).

Another argument by Chatterjee that appears contentious is where he attempts to contextualize the 'meaning of secularism' in India. For, Chatterjee, secularism is an idea which originated in the West and is best suited for the /or would be applied to the Western state only. This argument is taken further by him by highlighting the specificities of the Indian context and the limitation of the idea of a secular state in India due to this imported nature of its application. For Chatterjee "Indians have their own concept of secularism which is different from the Western concept bearing the same name, that it would be argued, is exactly why the Western concept cannot be applied to the Indian case'' (1769). However, I would like to assert here that even though it is significant to acknowledge the specific reality of the Indian state, it does not alter the concept theoretically. No concept in the world has ever been implemented in its entirely nor has it necessarily obliged to the path of developmental/evolutionary path as envisaged by its proponents. The evolutionary path taken by the Russian state in the first revolution as well as after the disintegration period bears testimony to this fact.

For Chatterjee, secularism is a foreign concept, so alien to the Indian reality that there exists no equivalent to it in any of the Indian languages. Prof. Chatterjee questions the inadequacy of a language specific word to refer to secularism in any of the Indian languages. For him, as a concept has not originated in the Indian soil it lacks proper terminology in Hindi or Urdu, thus leading to a neological deficiency. For him, "there doesn't exist in any Indian language a term for 'secular' or 'secularism' which is generally used in talking about the role of religion in the modern state and society and whose meaning can immediately be explicated without having recourse to the

English terms". According to Chatterjee, this neological deficiency is too 'awkward' (Chatterjee 1994: 1969) to be ignored and works as an impediment in garnering goodwill for a foreign concept in a highly religious country. This point of assertion gains further strength from to the usage of Indian equivalents such as *dharma nirpekshata* and *gair-mazhabi* that in a way represents a disconnection between the state and religion or if said differently, the non-religious nature of the state. For the author, this neological pursuit represents the internal contradiction between the nationalist aspiration and modernist mission of secularization. However refuting this argument by Chatterjee, Prof. Ali (2011: 88-9) asserts that the literal transliteration of the English terminology into Indian languages such as *Dharmnirapekshta* and *Gairmazahabi* in Hindi and Urdu respectively are attempts by those opposing secularism. According to Ali, by doing so anti-secularist in India intends to publicize among the masses a negative connotation of the idea of secularism, an expected hostility towards anything that negates religion. In fact, taking his argument further, Ali suggest that, "an apt Urdu term for the Indian variety of secularism is *mazahabi-rawadari,* i.e. closest to the idea of respect to all religions. Sumit Sarkar regards this attitude of hostility towards anything that is Western and rejecting it as colonial hegemonic project as '... not basically products of lack of authorial competence or quality. They emerge from restrictive analytical frameworks, as *Subalturn Studies* [that] swings from a rather simple emphasis on subaltern autonomy to an even more simplistic thesis of Western colonial domination (Sarkar 1997: 103-4).

Chatterjee's assertion about the implanted nature of secularism in India also lead us to believe that the idea of secularism is completely alien idea and that there was no existence of secular thinking and practice in India, before, it was incorporated by the 'liberal minded leaders of Indian freedom struggle. However, this idea has been contested by Prof. Zaheer Ali (2011) in his monograph *Secularism and its Indian Version* (2011: 35-40) whereby he has in detail explored secularism in its philosophical as well as practical aspects.

Taking a cue from the debate regarding the unwillingness

of the British rulers to interfere with religious matters, thus creating scope of self-management through trusts and other managerial bodies governed by Indians themselves; Chatterjee questions how the willingness of the so-called secular state in India in the post-independence period runs contrary to the notion of separation of the state from all matters of religious nature. Chatterjee here speaks about how on the pretext of maintaining order the state has been meddling with the religious practices and sentiments of the people. Here Chatterjee also justifies the charge of partiality towards the minority community, at the cost of the majority.

The Hindu right has been using the concept of secularism to call for a uniform civil code. According to Chatterjee, this objective is attempted by the proponents of the Hindutva not by demanding legislative enforcement of ritual or scriptural injunctions but by sidelining all the other avenues of thoughts. Hence Chatterjee has very well articulated the subtle mechanisms deployed by the Hindu right in this country, a strategy very different from those in lines when Hindu code bill was drafted. According to Chatterjee 'in its most sophisticated forms, the campaign of the Hindu right often seeks to mobilize on its behalf the will of an interventionist modernizing state in order to erase the presence of religious or ethnic particulars from the domain of law or public life and to apply in the name of 'national culture', a homogenized context to the notion of citizenship (Chatterjee, 1768). However, Chatterjee stops short of responding to such allegations levelled by the opponents of secularism. To any such ludicrous charge a counter-question needs to be asked that why is secularism needed in India? Secularism attempts to challenge primordial practices that breeds inequality amongst different communities.

Placing the modern Indian state in the paradigm of liberal democratic state Chatterjee (1994: 1771) marks out liberty, equality and neutrality as the critical hallmarks of a secular state. For him, when an attempt is made to evaluate the Indian state using these parameters of liberal democracy, there emerges many anomalies. While in theory the Indian state does attempt to fulfil these three preconditions to be categorized as a liberal democracy, it is the application part where it falters leading to great discrepancies. Chatterjee alleges that looking at the evolution of secularism in India "it is clear that whereas all three principles have been invoked to justify the secular state, their applications have been contradictory and has led to major anomalies. He further asserts that these anomalies provide the "Hindu right the most potent ammunition in its campaign against what it describes as the 'appeasement' of minorities" (Chatterjee 1994: 1771-3). An analysis of these points of departure from the Western liberal democratic form of the secular state lead Chatterjee to conclude that like many other aspects of the emerging forms of non-Western modernity, this is one more instance where the supposedly universal forms of the modern state turns out to be inadequate for the post-colonial world. To this it must be added that secularism is not the only idea that has linkages with the Western world. Liberty, equality, fraternity, universal adult franchise, democracy, social justice et cetera are inherent to the socio-political fabric of India and have their genesis outside. However, there has been eagerness on the part of the Indian intelligentsia to single out secularism as a foreign concept and criticize it as being insufficient in catering to Indian realities.

At another instance, Chatterjee suggests that the national freedom struggle itself got entangled into contradictory modernization projects. Maybe Chatterjee gets confused about the nature of the independence movement itself. It should not be forgotten that while the objective of the freedom movement was to acquire political autonomy/independence from the colonial rule, the nationalist project and the usage of modernization in terms of thought and practice were not as such at odds with each other. Here it is also important to note that while the nationalist project was in a way a tool to achieve independence rather than an end in itself.

While giving another reason for non-intervention in the realm of personal law by the colonial rule Chatterjee says that "the reason why personal laws were not brought within the scope of a uniform civil code was precisely the reluctance of the colonial state to intervene in matters close to the very heart of religious endowments, while the British power in its early years took over many of the functions of patronage and administration previously carried out by Indian rulers, by the middle of the 19th century largely renounced those responsibilities and handed them over to local trusts and committees (1769). To this I would like to add that the reason being this reluctance was not a noble one. The events that led to the mutiny of 1857 and the resultant sentiments of hostility among the elites of the Indian populace could be credited for this. Chatterjee here presents a very complicated picture of Indian leaders' hesitation towards letting the colonial state enter into areas that were as crucial to the identity of the nation. According to him, this was not exactly a rejection of any prospect of reform but rather it was a desire for a change in the agency through which such reformist agenda was commissioned; i.e. in Chatterjee's words, 'from the legal authority to the (colonial) state to the moral authority of the (national) community' (1769-70). To this I would like to add that this would be a myopic analysis of the circumstances. The hostility towards reforms was not an attribute not exclusively of the pre-independence era. Even after the colonial rule was overthrown, reforms in socio-cultural practices in India did face stiff competition from the orthodox members of the Indian political elite. By stating this, however, I nowhere intend to discredit the liberal minded leaders of a newly independent India. These contradictions could be validated through an observation of the debates that took place amongst the members of the Constituent Assembly.

Chatterjee has throughout the paper contested the idea of secularism as it exists in the Indian state. However my argument is that, rather than focusing on the inadequacies of the existing form and practice of secularism in India, it would be a more meaningful exercise to acknowledge the fact as Bhargava (1994) has also pointed out that 'it does have a greater scope of improvement' and that is what is desired for an effective functioning of secularism in India.

Another point worth mentioning here is that while there have been innumerable comparisons between secularism in the West and its Indian counterpart, we must acknowledge the evolutionary nature of the concept whereby secularism was incorporated in the private and political lives of the people in the Western world over a prolonged period of time and it has further grown on its own. Whereas in India, it has been reinvented for a modern form of polity only during the independence struggle and consolidated while the constitution was being drafted.

The accession to power by the rightist BJP in May 2014 elections in India, has once again created a deep crisis in front of secularism. The recent developments that stink of sheer disregard for any diversity by the proponents of the creation of a *Hindu Rashtra* as against the democratic, secular, socialist, republic that India has remained so far. In these circumstances, it becomes evident that the attacks on secularism may gain further strength through a systematized patronage provided by the political class. In this regard, it must be asserted that secularism needs to be defended with much rigour. Prof. Partha Chatterjee has very effectively highlighted salient features of the concept. However, his outright rejection of the idea may not serve the cause of secularism in India. While it cannot be negated that secularism as practised in India does have its limitations, however, its being there has itself reassured the existence and sustenance of the diversities of the country.

BIBLIOGRAPHY

1. Alam, Javed (1998), 'Indispensability of Secularism', *Social Scientist*, 26 (7/8), 3-20. [Source: Web] Accessed on 11 December 2014, Link: http://www.jstor.org/stable/3517611.
2. Ali, Zaheer (2011), *Secularism and Its Indian Version*, Occasional Paper Series (3), Mumbai, Dr. Ambedkar Centre for Social Justice.
3. Bhargava, Rajeev (1994), 'Giving Secularism Its Due', *Economic and Political Weekly*, 29 (28), 1784-1791. [Source: Web] Accessed on 25 November 2014, Link: http://www.jstor.org/stable/4401460.
4. Bilgrami, Akeel (1994), 'Two Concepts of Secularism: Reason, Modernity and Archimedean Idea, *Economic and Political Weekly*, 29 (28), 1749-1761. [Source: Web] Accessed on 12 December 2014, Link: http://www.jstor.org/stable/4401458.
5. Casolari, Marzia (2000) 'Hindutva's Fascist Heritage', India, Sabrang Communications and Publishers Ltd. [Source: Web] Accessed on 25 November 2014, Link: http://www.sab rang.com/cc/comold/mar00/document.htm.

6. Chatterjee, Partha (1994), 'Secularism and Toleration', *Economic and Political Weekly*, 29 (28), 1768-1777. [Source: Web] Accessed on 25 November 2014, Link: http://www.jstor.org/stable/4401459.
7. Dutt, R.P. (1934), *Fascism and Social Revolution*, London, Martin Lawrence Ltd.
8. Dutt, R.P. (1949), *India Today*, New Delhi, People's Publishing House. Reprinted in 2008.
9. Luthra, V.P. (1964), *The Concept of the Secular State and India*, London, New York, Oxford University Press.
10. Madan, T.N. (1997), 'Secularism in Its Place', *The Journal of Asian Studies*, 46 (4), 747-759. [Source: Web] Accessed on 25 November 2014, Link: http://www.jstor.org/stable/2057100.
11. Nandy, Ashis (1995), 'An Anti-secularist Manifesto', *India International Centre Quarterly*, Secularism in Crisis 22 (1), 35-64. [Source: Web] Accessed on 26 November 2014, Link: http://www.jstor.org/stable/23003710.
12. Sarkar, Sumit (1997), *Writing Social History*, New Delhi, Oxford University Press.
13. Smith, D.E. (1963), *India as a Secular State*, Princeton, Princeton University Press.

18

Secularism and Livelihood

Neetin K. Sonawane

The rise of Hindutva and the recent electoral success of the BJP can be seen as the culmination of a long-drawn process that began in the 1980s. The rise of right-wing ideologies coincides with the increased socio-economic distress in India. In addition, in 2001, the United States of America's 'War on Terror' and propaganda of 'Islamic Fundamentalism' created ground for the spread of communal ideologies and Islamophobia. In India, that led to increased victimization of Muslims, and such atrocities have intensified due to rise in terror attacks in recent years. This paper argues that one of the central challenges for secularism in the past twenty years has been the neoliberal reforms and the state's inability to treat all citizens as equally entitled to constitutional rights.

The state in its neoliberal form has presented itself as a challenge to the concept of secularism in India. Economic reforms based on neoliberal framework involve restructuring of the state to suit a market-centred global economy. In turn, this essentially involves political and social changes. In a diverse and unequal society like India this has important effects of further marginalization of deprived groups or communities. Thus the idea of secularism has to consider the role of market-centrist ideas in order to deal with the challenge of communalism.

Livelihood and Plight of the Disadvantaged Groups

The issues of livelihood, simply put, involve questions of earning one's bread and butter. These are mainly governed by factors like one's needs, skill level, general conditions of the economy that govern the prospects of getting gainful employment. However, in addition, the above is also governed by social factors of caste and religion that have a serious impact on one's chances of earning livelihood. This is seen mainly affecting Muslims, though other disadvantaged groups like the Dalits and tribals also face similar discrimination. The fact that Muslims in India face such discriminatory treatment has been brought out by the Sachar Committee Report.[1]

Prejudices against makers of Muslim identity can be seen from the fact that often Muslim shopkeepers owning shops in majority areas give non-Muslim names like 'National Bakery' or 'Maharashtra Chicken Shop' or 'Bombay Saloon' or 'Global Computers 'and such others.[2] Further, one also comes across individuals like a barber named 'Manohar' or a plumber named 'Pappu' or an electrician named 'Raju' that are supposedly pseudonyms adopted by Muslims to hide their religious identity, instead of losing out on earnings for belonging to the 'wrong' religion or also 'caste'.

The adoption of neutral names of shops and individuals is a survival strategy in a communal environment. And such individuals do not see this as a compromising or unacceptable situation. It is a simple logic that one's livelihood cannot be compromised for the sake of religious identity.

On the other hand, a fact has been pointed out in no uncertain terms in the Sachar Committee Report; there are those who operate from the safety of ghettoes as compared to living in the fear of a riot or communal violence[3]. The Sachar report and subsequent research clearly point out to severe housing prejudices against disadvantaged groups and mainly against Muslims are found across most cities in India.[4] Further the report notes that Muslims are poorly represented in the employment market across all states. Also, the economic liberalization policies have led to the wiping out of most traditional occupations that were a source of livelihood for Muslims—"such as hand and power looms, silk and sericulture, garment making, leather and automobile repair. Home-based industries like embroidery, zari and chikan work, which provided Muslim women stable but low incomes are also gasping for survival."[5]

In addition, Muslims also face discrimination in government recruitment and private sector jobs.

The neoliberal reforms have definitely gone against the most disadvantaged groups in India. There also exists an unholy alliance between the neoliberal agenda and Hindutva that has come to occupy centre-stage in new politics on the national scene. It is in this arena that secularism is under challenge from communalism and neoliberal agenda. Studies have also shown that neoliberalism and Hindutva have been able to find a common ground.[6]

Neoliberalism and Hindutva: An Unholy Alliance

The rise of Hindutva since the 1980s from a fringe element to the centre of politics has been a long drawn process. It drew partly from the colonial legacy and mainly from the identity based politics that coincides with the introduction of economic reforms in India. Simultaneous deepening of democracy through increased participation of hitherto marginalized groups has been accompanied by majoritarianism and denial of constitutional rights to the vulnerable groups mainly the Muslims and also the Dalits and tribals. This translates into democratic intolerance of other groups by introducing systematic discrimination. Further, the present ascendancy of right-winged group to the centre of democratic process and the compromise of the social transformative agenda has created a legitimation crisis for the Indian state.[7]

It has been often pointed out that India is not a secular state in the Western sense of the term; rather the founding fathers have created a state that is 'religiously impartial' or 'non-communal' in its dealings with the citizens. This can be seen in the fact that it also has been vested with the power to intervene in religious affairs, albeit through the democratic process, in order to protect the rights of citizens or in interest of the general order[8], a fact that has to be understood in light of the role of the modern state mentioned above, i.e. of social transformation. This understanding provides the theoretical framework in which secularism is understood in India. Hence, theoretically India has attempted to build a unique pattern of secularism that is essentially distinct from the West. In other words, the

Western notion of a secular state was neither suitable nor desirable in the Indian context.

The rise of Hindutva as a direct challenge to the Secular State, can be seen, both, as a part of the colonial legacy and partly as a counter to the new social movements in the 1980s. This period coincides with the introduction of economic reforms in India. Such reforms have largely been unopposed due to its piecemeal approach and more importantly through a political process of 'diffusing resistance' without causing major political confrontations.[9] However, in the long run, such reforms may also lead to a credibility crisis for the state.[10] The resultant upheavals caused by the reforms have led to the increased recourse to identity politics and majoritarianism. Hence, the present-day rise of Hindutva-based politics is the result of the culmination of a long-drawn process, that is essentially political in nature but also with socio-economic dimensions, and the same began in the 1980s.

The rise of Hindutva since the 1980s is a culmination of several forces that have played out since Indian independence and before. However it is appropriate to look at only a brief history and then to trace its relevance as far as livelihood issues are concerned.

The RSS ideologues have always had a long term ideological plan to capture power and bring about the formation of a Hindu Rashtra or alternatively a majoritarian democracy where the minorities accept the superior status of the Hindu majority. It is a well known fact that this ambition led to the formation of the 'Jan Sangh', the former's political wing.[11]

Formed in 1925 as a reaction to Khilafat and the majoritarian inferiority complex, the Rashtriya Swayamsevak Sangh was formed by mainly some upper caste Hindus to counter what they saw as an increasing threat to majority interests. It was a long term plan to consolidate and gain control over the political affairs of the country in order to protect the interests of the so-called majority Hindus.

Initially it claimed to be an organization that considered the social sphere as its arena for work and was not much concerned about actual acquisition of power. Subsequently, it launched a political wing with the aim of gaining control over the state affairs in order to assert the interests of the Hindus and to contemplate the realization of the utopian ideal of realizing a Hindu Rashtra. In the post-economic reforms phase, the RSS has been successful in increasing its memberships and *shakhas* in the country.[12] Its political wing, earlier the Jan Sangh, and, later the BJP has been steadily making advances as a significant political force that claims to replace the Congress Party in national politics. The Masjid demolition and the Mandir controversy was an attempt to revive the Hindutva agenda and has since eroded the secular fabric of the country's politics. Here, the Congress also from time to time played its communal cards as a strategy to placate communal interests of the majority and minority communities.[13]

Thus, Mandir issue and the demolition of Babri Masjid, a campaign led by the Bharatiya Janata Party, successfully mobilized and polarized voters along religious lines. The Congress Party also played along the communal card as a strategy for gaining votes and support in the popular imagination. Thus, the secular foundations of the polity were shaken to the core, and, led to further consolidation of the Hindu nationalist network.[14] However, the socio-economic background of the 1980s also contributed to the ascendancy of Hindutva in the said period. It is to this background and the subsequent economic reforms that we now turn to understand the effects of the same on communalization and livelihoods.

Neoliberal Reforms and the State

The present government has set out to do what it had promised to those who invested heavily in it, namely the big business houses. The creation of a conducive atmosphere for business and reform of labour laws followed by increased privatization of services are policies conforming to 'textbook neoliberalism'.[15] Needless to say that, the present government is accelerating these processes that were initiated by the earlier government[16].

It is also essential here to discuss the impact of neoliberal policies and economic reforms on the practice of democracy. The economic reforms initiated since 1991 are radical in the sense that they attempt to incorporate market rationality into structure and practice of state. Principles central to liberal-democracy are being reinterpreted today in terms of political values which are essential to neoliberalism. Increasingly decision-making and implementation is being separated from political and democratic influences. This is justified through the logic of rationality and efficiency of policies and their implementation. In addition, the role of articulation and protection of public interests is being shared with the non-state sector, with greater importance to corporate interests. This results in the marginalization of the voice of the underprivileged groups in society.[17]

The resort to consultation of experts in situations of competing interests has become a new way to subvert the democratic pressures of decision-making. This in turn deprives citizens from right to express themselves and to hold governments accountable. The neoliberal emphasis on citizens as consumers leads to emphasis on individual freedoms and civil rights such as right to property over and above social justice. The redressal of citizens livelihood issues is sought through market-based interventions, e.g. self-help groups promoted to as poverty alleviation measure.[18] In essence, freedom is understood as the choice to participate in market exchanges in neoliberal theories.[19]

Neoliberal Reforms and Democracy in India

The praxis of secularism is said to be based on state autonomy and its authority to intervene in religious affairs to ensure effective implementation of rights in India. Economic reform or neoliberal policies have affected the state autonomy in complex ways. The state plays an important role but has to function as a regulator and not as a provider in a market economy. In this context, the state, expected to play a redistributive role, has shifted to inclusive policies. This has meant that the deepening of democracy has been accompanied by shrinking of the political space in which publicly accountable decisions are made.[20] The issues of livelihood include provision of basic minimum standard of living for citizens. However the hegemony of the corporate capitalist class over the state has meant that the underprivileged sections of society are deprived of an equal voice in the democratic decision-making.

The economic reforms began in India in the 1980s and became full-fledged national policy in 1991-2 under the 'New Economic Policy' announced by the Congress Government in Delhi. The nature of these reforms and their impact has necessary implications on livelihoods of citizens. These reforms that were adopted due to the balance of payments crisis and were able to bring the country's economy out of debt.

However in terms of actual effect on livelihood issues like increase in employment, these reforms have had an adverse effect of declining growth rate of organized employment in the 1990s compared to the earlier decade. It has been also said that these reforms were mainly piecemeal and were brought in a manner as to avoid huge or popular political protests or 'diffusion of resistance'.[21] The point is that the withdrawal of state from key sectors in the economy was considered to be a necessary corrective measure to increase competitiveness, quality of goods and services and overall employment[22]. However, all this was taking place in an atmosphere that was communally charged. It is needless to say, that the socio-political distress of the 1980s and 1990s was also one of the functions of the changing economy and state policy.

The withdrawal of the state from key areas has also serious effects on citizens' daily life. A case in point is the area of policing and law and order. Law and order in India is a state subject, and state government is supposed to ensure law and order as its constitutional responsibility. However reduced financial resources and colonial legacy has meant poor quality of law and order machinery for citizens. Here, one is often reminded of the many police reform suggestions that have repeatedly pointed out the need for maintaining a healthy police personnel ratio as per the population. India is ranked among the lowest in the world as far as population to police personnel ratio is concerned. Needless to say that increased deterioration of law and order, terror-related incidents and the American 'War on Terror' have not helped but further harmed the cause of secularism. In the sense, increased violence instead of being seen as failure of state governments is instead attributed to the presence of certain communities of a certain religion, caste or region. It is easy for communal organizations here to create hatred for Muslims or Dalits or Tribals, by simply blaming the latter for the increased crime!

The practice of free and fair elections is often highlighted as the strengths of Indian democracy. However mere conducting of elections in such manner cannot guarantee of accountability of the elected governments. Moreover, the kind of law and order maintained during election time is absent between elections. The question of law and order and policing machinery has also been affected by neoliberal policies. The understaffing of police in India is something that has been recognized repeatedly in terms of its low world rankings. This is due to a tight control on adequate recruitments in state police. The deteriorating law and order situation is also one of the results of inadequate staffing of the police. This has serious repercussions for secularism. It is important to note here that certain communities; mainly Muslims as well as Dalits and Tribals are perceived as criminals in general and such a perception feeds in to communal ideas. The lack of sufficient machinery to provide basic law and order gets attributed to these communities that are perceived as 'carrying inherent tendency' to indulge in crime or violence. However, during the elections the same machinery gets sufficient powers to deal with any law and order situation and is able to maintain the same for several weeks together. This should be interpreted as an effect of political reforms that have accompanied the neo-liberal agenda.

The hegemony of the corporate or big business class in civil society is self evident in the very fact that there is little disagreement over the adoption of neoliberal policies for development. The 'political society' however comprises those outside the organized sector. The political society organizes itself to negotiate with the state. The state however grants them temporary concessions or benefits as exceptions to the norm. These are nothing but issues of livelihood of most of the members of political society. However the concessions are granted to them as temporary exceptions, and not as citizens' rights. Here the political class is able to fragment the political society into different groups on the basis of their identities like religion, caste, language, etc. This has serious repercussions on the praxis of secularism.[23]

The political class on one hand has attempted to create beneficiaries among different groups of citizens, on the other hand majoritarian perceptions have shaped the ability of the state to intervene and ensure equal entitlement of citizens to constitutional rights. Therefore, secularism has to be seen as a question not separate from, but in fact closely related to, and, an essential part of livelihood issues. In the present-day, neo-liberalism era, the praxis of secularism entails tangible benefits for citizens, especially those who require state intervention for their livelihoods and also for overall improvement in the standard of living. Thus, the discourse on secularism will have to engage with the neoliberal agenda and take into account its economic and political impact.

REFERENCES

1. Mander, Harsh, Barefoot: Promises to Keep, *The Hindu*, February 19, 2015.
2. Ibid.
3. Ibid.
4. Sowmiya, Ashok and Ali Mohammad, Housing Apartheid Flourishes in Delhi, *The Hindu*, July 16, 2012; Vithyathil, Trina and Gayatri Singh, 'Spaces of discrimination, Residential Segregation in Indian Cities', *Economic and Political Weekly*, Vol. XLVII, Issue 37, September 15, 2012.
5. Ibid.
6. Gopalkrishnan, Shankar, 'Defining, Constituting and Policing a New India: Relationship between Neoliberalism and Hindutva', *Economic and Political Weekly*, June 30, 2006.
7. Kaviraj, Sudipta, 'The Modern State in India', in Hasan, Zoya (ed.), *Politics and the State in India*, Sage, New Delhi, 2000.
8. Luthera, Ved Prakash, *The Concept of Secular State and India*, Oxford, New Delhi, 1964.
9. Bardhan, Pranab, 'The Political Economy of Reform in India', in Hasan, Zoya (ed.), *Politics and the State in India*, Sage, New Delhi, 2000.
10. Ibid.
11. Jaffrelot, Christophe, 'The Hindu Nationalists and Power', in *The Oxford Companion to Politics in India*, Oxford University Press, New Delhi, 2011.
12. Ibid., p. 206.

13. Gopalkrishnan, op. cit.
14. Jaffrelot, op. cit., p. 212.
15. Teltumbde, Anand, 'Saffron Neo-Liberalism', *Economic and Political Weekly,* August 2, 2014, Vol. XLIX, Issue No. 31.
16. Ibid.
17. Joseph Sarah, 'Neoliberal Reforms and Democracy in India', *Economic and Political Weekly,* August 4, 2007.
18. Ibid., p. 3216.
19. Harvey, David, *A Brief History of Neoliberalism,* Oxford University Press, England, 2005.
20. Joseph, Sarah, op. cit.
21. Bardhan, Pranab, op. cit., p. 163.
22. Ibid.
23. Chatterjee, Partha, 'The State' in Jayal, Gopal Niraja and Mehta, Bhanu Pratap (eds.), *The Oxford Companion to Politics In India,* Oxford, New Delhi, 2011.

19

Conversion: A Point of Confusion for Secularists and Others

Himanshu Shekhar Mishra

Indian secularism differs from Western secularism in the form of dealing with religions in a neutral way. The Indian secular state is neither anti-religious nor irreligious. In fact, the state function is supposed to be based on, what Rajeev Bhargava says, 'principled distance'. But, instead of maintaining 'principled distance' or 'neutrality' in the context of religious conversion, Indian secular state actually feeds the violence. It ends its fight with the so-called 'Hindu fundamentalism' only. Historically speaking, while the proponents of secularism in India defines secularism as religious neutrality in a liberal state, the anti secularists challenge the notion of 'state neutrality' as a means for the establishment of a plural society. They points that instead of building religious tolerance on good faith and conscience of a small group of de-ethinicized, middle class politicians, bureaucrats and intellectuals... the state system may learn something about religious tolerance from everyday Hinduism, Islam, Buddhism or Sikhism.[2] Thus, the debate between secularists and anti-secularists revolves around one of the basic tenants of contemporary theories of toleration. The clash between them is not the clash between a tolerant, progressive left and an intolerant, conservative right, rather a clash between two frameworks, both claiming to provide a solution to the problem of conflicts between different communities in Indian society. However, in a liberal state like India, while neutrality is a possibility with regard to different issues[1], it is not possible especially with regard to 'religious conversion'. In fact, the liberal secular state has failed to be neutral on an issue like 'religious conversion'.

Conversion is a complex and emotionally charged issue. Fundamentalists exploit it, liberals complicate it, many do not comprehend what the fuss is about, and others shy away from getting involved[3]. In India, it is interpreted mainly in three ways. One way of looking at it is as subversion, as an atrocity, as *adharma* and as a conspiracy to divide India along religious lines. The second way of looking at it is primarily enlightening, saving others by sharing their convictions and beliefs. The third way of looking at it is as a protest against oppression, religious and secular, as an aspiration for betterment, spiritual and otherwise[4] ("Rethinking Religious Conversion", 2008). While the third way of looking at it is related to intra-religious domination, the first and second ways are linked with inter-religious domination. It is non-problematic for secularists and others when conversion is viewed as a consequence of intra-religious domination. Disagreements start when it is viewed from the inter-religious domination perspective. The philosophical basis of first and second views are nothing but the Semitic and pagan positions respectively. Both the positions are mutually exclusive to each other where the state's neutrality becomes untenable especially in the Indian context. While secularists insist that the state should protect the religious liberty of the people (conversion), Hindutva forces want a ban on conversion in India. The reason behind strong aversion towards religious conversion of Hindutva is that many Hindus hold similar views. Mahatma Gandhi, for instance, has said that 'if he had the power to legislate, he would ban all proselytizing...In the Hindu households, the advent of a missionary has meant the disruption of the family coming in the wake of change of dress, manners, language, food and drink...' (*Harijan*, 5 November 1935). This view is still prevalent among contemporary Gandhians. In the words of Manikan Ramaswami:

"In a pluralistic society if people have to live in harmony, one group that believes its assumed form of god is superior and tries to convert the thinking of others will not certainly help. One group trying to impose its views on others based on its unconformable assumption will certainly cause social tension and should not be permitted in a secular society. The pseudo seculars who call it religious freedom to convert, if they apply their mind will understand banning conversion, forced or otherwise, is not a Hindutva agenda; on the other hand not banning conversion is the agenda of aggressive religions" (Ramaswami 2002).

While secularists agree with free proselytization of Muslim and Christian minorities, most of the anti-secularists defend the interest of the Hindus. In such a situation, could the Indian state remain neutral on the issue of religious conversion? By providing the right to propagation in the constitution, the Indian secular state assumes that as if Semitic religions and Hindu traditions are the phenomena of the same kind. However, this assumption has no warrant. Students of religions almost routinely make remarks that Hindu and Buddhist traditions are religions of a different kind (Balagangadhara 2012:203). The secular state cannot assume the opposite of scientific wisdom without compelling arguments. Freedom to convert people into some religions might indicate the presence of a desirable value in society, namely, the value of 'freedom of religious expression'. This value presupposes the truth of the assumption that these religions are rival movements. Indian secularists find no logical difficulty by assuming the existence of multiple religions without postulating that they compete with each other. It is a matter of historical fact that Christianity and Islam have been rivals, wherever and whenever they meet each other. Can the same be said when they meet Hindu traditions and their religion.

The Semitic self-description contains a universal truth claim, which gives rise to a dynamic of proselytization. Proselytizaing is an intrinsic drive of Islam and Christianity. The pagan view, on the contrary, implies that every religion is a tradition. These traditions are upheld not because they contain some exclusive truth binding the believers to god, but because they make some communities. Any attempt at interfering with the tradition of a community from the outside is seen as illlegitimate by pagan. For example, Hindu traditions refuse to accept that their religion is a false one and Christianity and Islam are the true ones. They also do not have the will to say that Christianity and Islam are false religions. They maintain that these traditions can coexist without competing with each other. Given this position between proselytization and non-interference, it is a confusing choice for the secular state to be neutral with respect to these two propositions. In fact, the secular state has to choose between the following premises: (a) no religions could be false; or (b) some religion(s) could be false. There is no neutral ground between these two logically exclusive premises.

These aspects of the Semitic religions and the pagan traditions are bound to collide in a society where Semitic religions encounter pagan traditions as a living force. This is exactly what is happening in India today. The widespread discontent about conversion is not generally caused by the fear that the whole of India will become Christian or Muslim. Many reasonable minds, who do not see an imminent threat of India becoming an Islamic country, still consider religious conversion to be a violation of the social fabric, for it goes straight against the traditional Hindu stance of non-interference. That is why, the Hindutva movement and some Gandhians argue for a ban on conversion. The secularists reply that such a measure would simply make a principle of the Hindus into a 'religious rule', while a truly neutral framework should allow the Muslim and Christian minorities to propagate and spread their religion. The secularists are not as neutral as they think they are. Their plea for conversion indicates that they have made their choice. This choice has been made at the cost of the very principle of state neutrality. It has happened not only in the sphere of conversion, but also in the sphere of reform. The post-independent Indian state has implemented a series of reforms to the 'Hindu religion and its law', while it has not interfered with Islam and Christianity (Chatterjee 1998). This suggests that some interpretations of 'neutrality' and 'liberalism' are at stake here. Andrew Mason formulates an often made distinction between two kinds of state neutrality as follows

"Neutrality of justification requires that the state should not include the idea that one conception of good is superior to another as part of its justification for pursuing a policy. Neutrality of effect, in contrast, requires the state should not do anything which promotes one conception of good more than another, or if it does so, it must seek to cancel or compensate for these differential effects" (Mason 1990:434).

In the context of ethics and normative political theory, one could conceivably endorse Kant's famous dictum 'ought to imply can'. This means 'ought' logically implies 'can'. It generates the following valid theorem: 'Can' logically imply 'ought' and 'cannot' logically implies 'ought not'. If we accept this principle while framing the state neutrality, it would mean that the Indian state ought not to be neutral with respect to religious conversion in India because it cannot be neutral. If the Indian state ought to be liberal and neutral state, then Indian state can be neutral. However, Indian state cannot be neutral on this issue 'conversion'. In other words, with respect to religious conversion, theories of state neutrality oblige the Indian state not to be liberal or neutral.

The Indian state has made a provision in its constitution about the freedom of religion that includes the issue of conversion. Article 25 of the Indian Constitution says that 'all persons are equally entitled to freedom of conscience and the right to freely profess, practise and propagate religion'. It means in the context of secularism and religious pluralism, conversion is legitimate, well within the constitutional provisions, and entirely personal affairs of the citizen' (Radhakrishnan 2002). Not only has this, but also, the Indian secular state put certain legal restrictions on religious conversion. It prohibits all forms of coercion in conversion. It says that religious conversion can take place by means of persuasion only. One can be persuaded to convert only in so far as one accepts the truth of one religion as opposed to the falsity of another. From this the Indian state endorses the belief that religion revolves round doctrinal truth. It may not accept the truth claim of any one particular religion, but it does assume that religion revolves around the truth claim. The failure to be neutral towards the issue of conversion is not specific to Indian secularists. It is a general malfunction of the neutrality of the model of liberal secularism.

All forms of liberalism do agree that a state should not base its policies in any one religion, because it would violate principles such as religious liberty and the equal rights of all citizens. In case of conversion, it appears the liberal state cannot but implement a policy which either presupposes Semitic theology or the pagan stance towards religion and tradition. Hence, it fails to grant equal rights to all citizens, since the notion of religious liberty itself is disputed. However, a liberal state can remain neutral with respect to the competing truth claim of different religions where one does not assume a pro stance with respect to any one of them. This does not preclude the liberal state from accepting that religion is a matter of truth. The western liberal democratic states have accepted this position that means a Semitic theological meta-claim as its factual assumption. It is not able to play the agonistic with respect to the truth value of religious claims because it shares the Semitic beliefs about religions. The reason for not to be agonistic to the issue of truth by the liberal state is because of the fact that the state is unable to say which of the competing religions is true. If the state wants to play the agnostic, the only option is left for the state is to remove the entire issue from the sphere of legislation and let the communities decide about it. But then the state can neither interfere with religious violence nor strive to reduce religious conflict. Western democracy cannot play the agonistic role because it presumes that religious truth is cognitive in nature. The Indian state cannot merely follow Western democracies and hopes to be neutral. It cannot play the agnostic and yet legislate about religious freedom. It confronts choices, which Western democracies never had to face.

The colonial representation of the state, which was fundamentally a protestant description of India, has become the guiding mantra of the 'secular' politicians of India. As Nehru has said himself, he came to India via the West to some extent, therefore he has approached her 'almost as an alien critic, full of dislike for the present as well as for many of the relics of the past that [he] has seen' (Nehru 1988:50). His intention and effects of description can be summarized as the systematic attempts to uphold the claim that the Hindu traditions are degenerate, corrupt and in need of transformation. In other words, he has upheld the Semitic claim about the inferiority of false religions. The secularism of Nehru and his followers is quite simply, a negative attitude towards Hindu traditions. When such understanding of secularism has been pursued under the

Congress government, it has deeply impacted society. Eventually, representatives of Hindu traditions began to articulate a defence of their own tradition with the seduction of this kind of secularism.

From pagan perspective, there is no religious rivalry between the Hindu traditions and the Semitic religions. However, the opposite is the case when viewed from the perspective of the Semitic religions. When the Indian state assumes the truth of a Semitic theological claim and further accepts this claim as its own epistemological position, then it actively creates rivalry between majority (Hindus) and minorities (Muslims, Christians and so on). Strangely, the exacerbation of religious violence does not tell us that secularism has failed in India. The secular state, which secularists continue to wish for, does not prevent religious conflicts: it actively promotes them. By forcing the framework of Semitic religions on Hindu tradition, the liberal state of India is forcing the pagan traditions in India to mould themselves along the line of Semitic religions. The growth of so-called Hindu fundamentalism is the direct result of this coercive straightjacket. Traditions which has never systematically persecuted others on grounds of religious truth, are forced into a systematically persecution of religions precisely on this basis. It is precisely, a liberal and secular conception that generates the phenomenon of Hindu fundamentalism.

The contemporary liberal framework assumes that the Hindu and other Asian traditions are variants of the same phenomenon as Islam and Christianity, namely religion. In the same way, the current analysis presupposes that all cultural movements in the contemporary world can be classified into two basic categories: the liberal tolerant movements and their counterpart of religious fundamentalism. But all religious fundamentalisms are not one and the same phenomena. Hindu tradition cannot be variants of same phenomenon as Islam and Christianity. The seed of religious violence in India is very much rooted within the liberal and secular structures of the state and the rest is carried by the Hindu fundamentalism.

Neutrality of justification is logically impossible for the Indian state. The option is not available because (a) the choices of the state are logically exclusive and (b) the state cannot play the agonistic. The effect of the state policy in a liberal regime may well bring about the decline of some religions and their conception of good. To give up religious freedom and ban religious conversion is both undesirable and retrograde. It would deny freedom to those groups in India who follow the Semitic religions. Instead of doing this, Indian state could look elsewhere to become neutral. It can stimulate explorations into the histories and theories of the Indian cultural traditions and explore the possibility of cultural rejuvenation. It is primarily because of the fact that the traditional pluralism of Indian culture, which is characterized by the coexistence of both pagan and Semitic religions, can be the source of a potential alternative to the liberal model of toleration

In spite of its pretention of neutrality, the liberal model of toleration and state neutrality is itself not a secular, impartial model. In reality, it is a Semitic theological entity which has been dressed up in secular philosophical grab. It is because of the nature of normative theory of the liberal state which tries to provide a universal model to solve the problem of diversity in society; it is bound to fail since it suffers from a profound ignorance of the structure of plural societies other than those of Christian west.

REFERENCES

1. Balagangadhara, S.N., *Reconceptualising India Studies,* New Delhi, Oxford University Press, 2012, p. 225.
2. Chatterjee, P., 'Secularism and Tolerance' in R. Bhargava (ed.), *Secularism and its Critics,* New Delhi, Oxford University Press, 1998, p. 338
3. Heredia. Rudolf C. (2007), *Changing Gods: Rethinking Conversion in India,* New Delhi, Penguin Books.
4. Mason, A.D., 'Autonomy, Liberalism and State Neutrality', *The Philosophical Quarterly,* 40(160), 1990, pp. 433-52.
5. Nandy, A. (1998), 'The Politics of Secularism and the Recovery of Religious Tolerance', in R. Bhargava (ed.), *Secularism and its Critics,* New Delhi, Oxford University Press.
6. Nehru, J. (1988), *The Discovery of India,* New Delhi, Jawaharlal Nehru Memorial Fund and Oxford University Press.

7. Radhakrishnan, P. (2002), 'Conversion Politics I&II', *The Hindu*, November 6-7.
8. Ramaswami, M. (2002), 'Is there God and whose God is he?' *The Hindu*, October 29.
9. "Rethinking Religious Conversion" *Economic and Political Weekly*, Editorial. October 18, 2008, p. 5.

20

Dimensions of Secularism in India

Shamsuddin Tamboli

As we know Secularism is the most discussed but less understood concept, particularly in Indian society. There are not only different opinions and interpretations but a lot of confusion among the people.

The Oxford English Dictionary (*OED*) explains it as: "Secularism is the doctrine that morality should be based solely on regard to the well-being of mankind in the present life to the exclusion of all considerations drawn on belief in God or in a Future State." *OED* also points out that it was George Holyoake (1817-1906) who gave this name to the definitely professed belief. This Central Secular Society states that secularism consists of:

1. Science as the true guide of man
2. Morality as secular, not religious in origin
3. Reason as the only authority
4. Freedom of thought and speech and
5. Owing to the uncertainties of survival, we should direct our efforts to life only.

George Holyoake and Charles Bradlaugh tried to explain the meaning of secularism in detail. Gist of their idea is, according to Holyoake, *ignoring of God was enough*, on the other hand, Bradlaugh insisted that *God should be banished*. This difference of opinion did not affect common conviction that secularism demanded complete separation of the Church from the state and the abolition of all privileges granted to religious organizations and their so called custodians.[1]

When we consider secularism in the Indian context, we

cannot forget the efforts of Prof. K.T. Shah. He was the only member who made efforts to get a provision regarding the secular character of India included in the Constitution. The amendment, moved as Amendment No. 366 was defeated on December 3, 1948. The highlight of the resolution was: "The state in India being secular shall have no concern with any religion, creed, or profession of faith; and shall observe an attitude of absolute neutrality in all matters relating to the religion of any class of its citizens or other persons in the union."

No doubt, it would have put a brake upon the state functionaries freely using the state finance and machinery for pilgrimages and other religious activities. Prof. Shah's amendment would have also prevented the state media, especially radio and television from broadcasting *bhajans*, prayers, religious discourses, etc.

While talking about Indian secularism, social reformer Hamid Dalwai also observed the same thing. According to him the text books used in schools are against the spirit of secularism. In social science books Muslims are mentioned as foreigner. The personalities like Ram and Lord Krishna from our mythology are also projected as gods and it is taught to the students of different faiths. Radio also broadcast the stories, *bhajans, kirtans, sutras,* etc. about Hindu gods. Even down-trodden castes from Hindus are neglected; most of the programmes broadcasted from AIR are of higher castes of Hinduism.[2]

Mahatma Gandhi and Maulana Abul Kalam Azad, were the staunch followers of their respective religions and were propagating that the core of all religions is *humanity* and welfare of all people. They were of the opinion that secular society based on humanity, *mutual tolerance* and respect of different faith is possible. According to Gandhi, Azad's true interpretations of religious books have potentiality for peaceful coexistence, co-operation and understanding of humanitarian principles. The concept of equal regards to all religions was the core of their philosophy. While understanding these personalities we cannot forget that Mahatma Gandhi was assassinated by the follower of the Hindu faith, and Maulana Azad too was targeted by the fundamentalists and the so-called custodians of Islam. This reminds us of the analogy used by Mr. M.R.A. Baig. According to him in the Indian situation "an attempt of secularism is just like making an omelette from a boiled egg."[3]

In our society secularism is coined as *Dharmatitata, Nidharmipana, Dharmavihinata, Dharmatathstata, Dharma-nirpekshta, Sarvadharnasambhav* and *Ihawad*—these words tell us about the society, which is non-religious, beyond religion, without religion, neutrality towards religion, impartiality with religion, equal treatment to all religions, equal regards to all religions and the matter of worldly affairs. The reality of the fact is none of the above words can express the true meaning of secularism. To some extent, *Ishawad* or *Jadwad,* i.e. matters of the wordly affairs come closer to the spirit of secularism. Secularism not only condemns discrimination and exploitation by religion but it is also the concept which tells us about gender equality as well as humanity.

The core of secularism was included in the Indian Constitution through various articles, it is included in the preamble by the 42nd amendment in 1976. Dr. Babasaheb Ambedkar was reluctant to accept the meaning "*non-interference of state* in the matter of religions". According to Dr. Ambedkar, without interference of the state it was highly impossible to bring social justice and the principles of freedom, equality and brotherhood, the spirit of our constitution, as most of the religions are against these principles, major source of discrimination and exploitation are religious beliefs. In this sense Jefferson's "wall of separation between religion and the state" was not accepted by Dr. Ambedkar.

The Constitution of India goes further than Jefferson's definition of secularism. It empowers and directs the state in clear terms to take certain measures which go *counter to the injunctions* of religion in order that values and rights enshrined in the Constitution may for its citizens, be a matter of day-to-day experience instead of remaining mere pledges and oaths to be recited on certain occasions. Secularism is also needed for the process of nation building, national integration, and communal harmony and in the pursuit of the vision of good, well-cultured society as outlined in the Constitution.

While understanding secularism in India we must revisit Donald Eugeme Smith. His book *India as a Secular State* says that "a secular state is a state which guarantees individual and corporate freedom of religion, deals with the individual as a citizen irrespective of his religion, is not constitutionally connected to a particular religion nor does it seek either to promote or interfere with religion." This definition shows the relationship among state, religion and the individual, i.e. relationship between religion and individual, relationship between state and individual, relationship between state and religion.[4]

According to Smith, the basic assumption must be that secular state will have nothing to do with religious affairs, for the purpose of deciding as to whether state is a theocratic or secular state. It is enough if we find out whether the state has anything to do with religion. If it accepts a religion or religions or if it supports a religion or religions or if it incorporates in its constitution religious commands then one can unhesitatingly say that state is a non-secular state. Indian Constitution says that India is a secular state in the sense that–

(i) No particular religion is prescribed as the state religion.
(ii) No preferential treatment is envisaged to any religion or to people professing any particular religion – and
(iii) The right to worship is given to persons professing all religions.

Active or direct promotion or propagation of any religion by the state is not provided for in the Indian Constitution. In this sense it is secular. Articles 14, 15, 16 and 29 also state and establish a secular state.[5]

It is the *constitutional duty* of the political parties and the governments to preserve this secular identity of the state. Unfortunately it is observed that most of the political parties try to use religions or caste as a vote bank during elections—it is also used as a strong instrument to achieve political power as well as to retain power. There are some political leaders who desire to separate the domains of religion and politics, but the state for various reasons involves itself in the regulation—funding as well as the administration of various religious institutions. This is very harmful to maintain the secular identity and policy of the Constitution.

The present BJP led government and its supporters including Sangh Parivar is presenting its true communal nature and hidden agenda. (Actually it is not hidden now, it is open). There are many examples to narrate, describing all Indians as Hindus. The Prime Minister has given the copy of *Bhagavad Gita* to the President of America recently and the foreign minister also given statement that *The Bhagavad Gita* should be declared as the national book. BJP and RSS workers in Ayodhya and Faizabad urged people to fix saffron flags atop temples and houses to mark *bhagava divas* (saffron day) on 6th December, the day of demolition of Babri Musjid in 1992. They have designed a Bhagva Divas logo. According to them Bhagva is a symbol of Hindutva and Nationalism. A Gujarat high court judge also said that if allowed he will introduce Ramayan and Mahabharat in the school curriculum. Efforts of re-conversion in UP by the RSS and Bajarang Dal is the issue of introspection. Silence of the government on these issues also indicates mute-support from its side. This is a big challenge before the secularism.

Even the Congress Party, during its government could not maintain the secular identity of the Constitution. This government also brought *secularism under siege.* We have observed this during the case of Shah Bano, policy of Haj subsidy, and appeasing religious leaders of the community. Now, the emergence of MIM and increasing support of the Muslims to it, is a matter of serious introspection. We know the historical role of MIM. MIM can create a major problem in the attempt of revisiting secularism. Along with political parties, communal organizations, their leaders and activities are not only affecting communal harmony and national integration but also secular development of the society. Azam Khan of the Samajwadi Party in UP has started another debate on Taj Mahal. According to him, this national monument should be handed over to UP Wakf Board. The communalism of the minority is fuelling the communalism of the majority and this is more dangerous for the society.

India is a *multi-religious, multi-cultural* society. Here, secularism has been highly debated, discussed and disturbed by communal organizations and political parties. Here, everyone says he is a secularist. Hindutvadis insist that they are the true secularists and the Congress is pseudo-secularist. Mahatma Gandhi, Vinoba and other liberal leaders propagated secular principles of Hinduism. Nehru has different opinion about secularism. Similarly Maulana Azad (he was agnostic), Dr. Rafiq Zakaria and Dr. Asghar Ali Engineer propound a theory that Islam based upon the holy Quran is secularist.

Hamid Dalwai, the social reformist and the founder of Muslim Satyashodhak Mandal has pointed out the need of Muslim secular and democratic integration in the larger Indian Society. According to him the type of integration that is necessary here cannot be achieved—unless Muslims no less than Hindus—learn to separate religion from the rights and obligations of citizenship of a modern state. And only those can promote such integration who themselves are committed to the values of an open society and to the outlook on man and the universe that is sanctioned by science and scientific method. According to him if secular democratic ideals are to survive, all liberal forces in this country have to really work together on a non-party, non-political basis—one has to go to the root of the problem."[6]

Considering the fact that India is a secular state with multi religious society, we must develop the attitude of our society and people must show *mutual respect* for each other's peaceful coexistence with understanding the fact that:

1. India being a multi-religious and multi-cultural society we must respect the rights of individuals.
2. We cannot enjoy freedom of religion by disturbing peace, order, public health, scientific temperament and constitutional morality.
3. No religion is perfect, permanent and unalterable—if there is need of reform, people should cooperate in the interest of humanity and human rights—Khap Panchayat, Shariat Adalat should have limitations.
4. If there are clashes and quarrels in the society on religious ground we should follow the judiciary system—verdict of the courts must be respected.
5. The citizens must regard and respect the Constitution.

They should accept the supremacy of the Constitution including rights, duties and responsibilities.

Secularism should become a reality instead of a cherished dream.

I wish to make following *recommendations*:

1. As Edmund Burke rightly said "The only thing necessary for the triumph of evil is for good men to do nothing". Hence it is the need of the hour to create secular platform for all like-minded secular organizations.
2. Though it is expected that educational institutes and syllabus should inculcate secular values. It is found that anti-secular elements are in this system. Systematic, alert observations in this regard should be pointed out.
3. Print and electronic media, AIR should promote secular values and discourage anti-secular elements.
4. Personal laws also do injustice to the females of the society—Reform in personal laws, creation of common secular family laws—uniform civil code or registration of marriages under Special Marriage Act, 1954 should be compulsory.
5. Under public interest litigation, petitions regarding communal provocations should be filed.
6. Some measures have to point out to bring transparency and secularization of administrative and police department.
7. There should be prohibition regarding using or displaying religious symbols, photos and statues in public offices.
8. There is a tradition in Maharashtra of performing Mahapuja at Vitthal Mandir of Pandharpur by the government's representative. A serious thought should also be given in this regard.

REFERENCES

1. Ali, Zaheer, *Secularism and its Indian Version,* Mumbai, University of Mumbai, 2011, pp. 27-28.
2. Thatte, Yadunath, (ed.) *Sadhana,* Sadhana Trust, Pune, 1977, 45-46 Issue, p. 12.

3. Baig, M.R.A. (Translated by A. Khondwe) *Bharatatil Musalmananpudhil Pech,* Maharashtra Rajya Sahitya Ani Sanskriti Mandal, Mumbai, 1988, p. 7.
4. Jahagirdar, R.A., *Secularism in India: The Inconclusive Debate,* Paper Submitted at the Seminar of May 11, 2003.
5. Shah, A.B., *The Secularist,* Indian Secular Society, Mumbai, 1988, September-October Issue, pp. 117-18.
6. Dalwai, Hamid, *Muslim Politics in India,* Indian Secular Society, Mumbai, 2002, pp. 76-80.

21

Execution of Secularism Through the State: A Case Study of Pune City

Malika B. Mistry

What is Secularism?

In the West, secularism means separation of the state from religion. In religious and developing societies like India, secularism has to mean that all religions in a nation will enjoy equal status. In India, it is *sarva dharma samabhava.* We are told that originally the secular word was not in the Constitution. This word along with socialism was added during Indira Gandhi's time through an amendment to the Constitution. It is a fact that in spirit, the Indian Constitution has always been secular. So also the Indian society has been.

According to one thinker, Indian secularism is audible secularism. "The religion of those in power at any point of ... time does not matter; for Indian secularism is far more than the law. It is a fundamental social right. India, therefore, is a country with 'audible secularism.' ... In India, dawn is welcomed with the wafting lilt of the azaan, followed by the music of temple bells, the harmony of the Granth Sahib being recited in a gurudwara, and the peal from the church."[1]

Has the Indian State Been Truly Secular?

Though the laws uphold secularism, in reality, in many instances, Indian state has failed to uphold secular values and promote secularism consciously. The politicians who were holding top positions did not really care to promote secularism. Rather they paid lip service to secularism. Innumerable incidences from modern Indian political history support our contention. In order to come to power, the politicians used religion and caste. When they came to power, they used the policy of 'divide and rule' used by the British, the colonial power to perpetuate their power. Installing the idols in the Babri Masjid complex, the Shah Bano case, the demolition of Babri Masjid—all these landmark events in the political history of India, support our contention. From time to time, minorities, specially the Muslim minority, was used—killed, maimed, women raped, properties destroyed—by the political parties and the politicians in high positions to come to power or to stay in power. According to one estimate, communal violence has claimed more than 40,000 lives in India since Independence.[2] If the Indian state was truly secular these precious lives of innocent citizens would not have been lost.

Is Secularism Under Siege?

Yes. The recent events all over India, for example, *Ghar Wapasi* of Christians in Aligarh, banning a priest from entering an area, the fake love-jihad, the outburst by Sadhvi Jyoti and many more incidents, indicate that secularism is under siege. For secularism being under siege, the Indian state is to a large extent responsible. In the true sense, the Indian state has not worked to bring secularism in practice into Indian politics and Indian society. The necessary conditions for entrenching the value of secularism in society are mass education, scientific temper, equal status to all communities and women, not just in law but in practice and economic development ensuring equal opportunities to all citizens in Indian society. Even after six decades of independence, we have not yet achieved universal literacy. Not that India lacks in resources. The political will is lacking. One political scientist rightly observed that if Indian masses were to become literate, they would have questioned the caste-system and would have revolted against the oppression. Also scientific temper has not been promoted. In all developing countries, resources are in short supply. This leads to a number of conflicts. For example, the conflict between Israel and Palestine is more a conflict for resources and less political, though it apparently looks political. It is agonizing to see tribals, Dalits and women at the margins. Poverty is still rampant. According to UN estimates, around 40 per cent of Indian population lives below poverty line. If we take Arjun Kumar Sengupta's criteria, more than 70 per cent of Indian population is poor. Economic development in India has failed to help the masses. The Indian state has failed to provide basic health and education to its masses. In recent decades, economic growth has generated very little employment.

Also increasing fundamentalism in our neighbouring states of Pakistan and Bangladesh is, to some extent, responsible, for secularism not being strong in India. When in our neighbouring states, minorities are persecuted, it will have negative effect on the minorities in India. "One of the fall-outs from poverty-stricken existence with no access to sanitation, education and livelihood of those displaced or stigmatized is the rise of fundamentalism."[3] Welfare of minorities among neighbours (countries) is necessary for the welfare of minorities within India.

If we were to pin-point one major factor for secularism being under siege, it is the RSS ideology and propaganda which has eroded the value of secularism in Indian society. RSS sowed hatred against the minorities to achieve it's goal to bring back the Brahmanical society, by attacking and undermining secularism. In this paper a humble attempt is made to illustrate this argument with the analysis of very recent human rights violation of the minority community in the city of Pune.

The Murder of Mohsin Shaikh in Hadapsar, Pune

Pune has been a peaceful city. It used to be the pensioners' paradise. It has cosmopolitan culture. It is a modern, industrial, thriving city. People here feel safe. So when communal violence flared up, it came as a shock.

On May 30, 2014, on the face-book, some anti-social elements had released some indecent pictures of Shivaji Maharaj and Bal Thackeray. (Till today nobody could prove who were these anti-social elements!) In reaction, a rabid Hindutvadi organization viz. Hindu Rashtra Sena (HRS) made Muslims the target. On May 31, June 1-3, 2014, HRS went on rampage and perpetuated one-sided communal violence. It targeted the

Muslim houses, madarasas and masjids. It destroyed the houses, business tools and burnt vehicles, worth Rs.11,00,000.

On Monday, 2nd June, there was a lot of tension. There was police bandobast in the Sayyad Nagar area of Hadapsar. A Muslim young man, Mohsin Shaikh, (age 28, native place, Solapur) after performing the night prayer in a masjid in the Unnati Nagar was as usual going back to his house. Suddenly 15 to 20 youth miscreants of HRS attacked him. They threw him down. Beat him with sticks and lathis. One of them hit him on his head with a concrete-stone. He started bleeding profusely from his head and died on the spot. An innocent young man, who was the sole bread-earner of his family, was murdered by the lumpen elements of HRS. None of the political parties in Pune condemned this murder or expressed sympathy.

A Fact Finding Committee of the citizens presided by Kumar Saptarshi documented and analysed this one-sided communal violence.[4] Their analysis reveals that if the state wanted it could have prevented this communal violence and the life of Mohsin Shaikh, the innocent young citizen, the sole bread-earner, could have been saved and the properties of the poor and upcoming Muslims would not have been destroyed.

Uncaring Attitude of the State

The Maharashtra Government considered the above communal violence as a law and order issue, whereas the Central Government wanted it to be treated as a communal riot. [5] This shows the callous attitude of the state.

In the Lok Sabha, there was discussion on the communal murder of Mohsin Shaikh. Media condemned the ambiguous stand of the state government on this issue. Sanjay Nirupam, a Congress MP, demanded a ban on HRS. The Home Minister of Maharashtra, R.R. Patil, did not pay heed to this demand.[6]

From the communal violence in Pune, it is clear that the modus operandi of the HRS is to spread hatred against Muslims, instigate communal riots, instill fear and insecurity in the hearts of Muslims, destroy the properties of Muslims and if possible to kill them. Should we not ban such a murderous outfit?

Some social activists have analysed that this violence was inflicted on Muslims to make them scared of a particular political party and motivate them to vote for the party in power. We must remember that the elections were just a few months away. Desai, the Chief of HRS, was paid big money to scare the Muslims and compel them to vote for a particular political party.

The Fact Finding Committee had recorded that the police had an inkling of what was going to happen. But they were not prepared. The State Reserve Force did not arrive on time to save the victims. In the Bhosari area, next to the masjid, there was the fire brigade of the Municipal Corporation. When the HRS miscreants resorted to destruction, the fire-brigade did not come to help them. What does it all show? The deep-rooted hate propaganda against Muslims undertaken by the RSS has destroyed the social fabric and the sympathy and empathy for the Muslim minority.

This pattern is observed all over India. To win the elections, make the Muslims scape-goats. In such negative politics, secularism cannot flourish.

What To Do?

The scenario seems hopeless. Should we lose hope? No. Secularism has to be revived with greater vigour. In course of time, it would.

1. There is a great need to move away from negative/communal politics to positive/development politics. One thinker has observed as follows:

   "A more worrying possibility is that Yogi Giriraj Singh and Sadhvi Jyoti" are acting out the script given to them. There is a strong belief in the BJP that communal polarization helped them win big during the May 2014 Lok Sabha elections and this is a sound tactic. Since the bigger names in the party cannot be seen talking like this it is left to the smaller fry to rouse passions, which in turn bring in the votes. "...A bigger fear is that such a hate speech could end up damaging social harmony and build up an atmosphere of hostility and suspicion among communities. There has been an increase in communal bush fires—any spark could light up a full-fledged conflagration. This is the last thing India wants. It could severely damage Modi's ambitious plans to invite investment—domestic and international—and push the country's growth. Investors look for social harmony as much as friendly economic policies. As PM, Modi has travelled far and wide to assure the world that India has changed, communal tension is the last thing he would want. He needs to act swiftly and keep rogue elements in check. This is a U-turn he and his party must undertake at the earliest."[7]

The example of Singapore will suffice to say that only secularism and communal harmony can bring peace, prosperity, and a good name to the nation. There the state consciously promotes communal harmony and secularism.

2. Another thinker rightly observes that an ideology of partition whether Hindu, Muslim, Christian or Sikh or follower of some other religion, will constantly search for fresh pastures to divide, creating multiple civil wars that break structures at both the macro and micro levels, while the sagacity of shared space will propel the unity that can promise prosperity. When Gandhi made Ram Rajya the symbol of his secularism, he was not suggesting a single faith destiny. Gandhi's vision was inspired by love for all. Gandhi is an icon for all political formations because he fashioned a future from the deep roots of India's civilizational past. His legacy endures.[8]
3. While comparing Erdogan and Modi, the two hard-liners' lives, Amitav Ghosh comments: "When protests break out in India, as they surely will, how will Narendra Modi respond? Will he take a leaf out of Erdogan's book and become more authoritarian and repressive? Will he retreat into Sultanish isolation? Will political pressures ultimately lead to break between him and some of the organizations that helped him bring to power (as has been the case with Erdogan and the Gullenists)? Only time will tell."[9]
4. However, to promote secularism all over South Asia, "a well-thought out strategy to protect the rights of the minorities must be evolved collectively in the face of the

challenge posed by unresponsive state organs, communalization of state and politics and a society which has largely internalized communal attitudes and biases. There should be a sustained campaign on issues related to minorities taken up simultaneously through out the South Asian region.[10]

Conclusion

To conclude, it is only secularism and secular values which can bring peace and prosperity to all Indian citizens and make India a great nation. In this, the Indian state has to play a great role. As Sonia Gandhi in one of her recent speeches spoke, "There could be no Indian-ness, no India, without secularism. Secularism was, and remains, more than an ideal. It is a compelling necessity for a country as diverse as India."[11]

REFERENCES

1. Akbar, M.J. "Hear it? Indian Secularism is both Enduring and Audible" *Sunday Times of India,* Pune Edition, December 7, 2014, p. 18.
2. Dabhade, N., "Report on Session on Rights of Minorities in South Asia: People's SAARC Regional Convergence" *Secular Perspective,* Centre for Study of Society and Secularism, Mumbai, Vol. XVII, No. 23, December 1-15, 2014.
3. Ibid.
4. Action Committee, Pune, *Pune Hadapsar (June 2, 2014) Moshin Shaikh Chi Hatya—Ek Satyasodhan,* Fact Finding Committee, Pune, August 15, 2014.
5. *Times of India,* Pune Edition, June 6, 2014.
6. *Times of India,* Pune Edition, June 8, 2014.
7. Bhatia, Sidharth, "Hate Speak Unbound: Modi's Silence on Communal Speeches Such As Sadhvi Jyoti's is Worrying", *The Times of India,* December 4, 2014.
8. Akbar, M.J., op. cit.
9. Ghosh, Amitav, "Erdogan and Modi : Parallel Journeys?" *Sunday Times of India,* Pune Edition, November 30, 2014, p. 15.
10. Dabhade, N., op. cit.
11. "Secularism is a Necessity for India", *The Times of India,* Pune Edition, November 18, 2014, p. 9.

Contributors

Zaheer Ali, Mumbai-based writer, academician and social activist. President of Centre for Promotion of Democracy and Secularism.

Zeenat Shaukat Ali (Dr.), Director General, World Institute of Islamic Studies and Peace. Author, *Marriage and Divorce in Islam* and *Empowerment of Women in Islam*

Rajesh Bag is a Ph.D. research scholar in the Department of Political Science, University of Hyderabad. His areas of research interest include xenophobia, ethnic nationalism, communal violence and subalterns, secularism and justice.

Rajeev Bhargava (Dr.), Internationally reputed Social Scientist. Professor at the Centre for the Study of Developing Societies, Delhi. Globally recognized authority on secularism.

Ramesh Dixit (Dr.), Former Professor and Head, Department of Political Science, Lucknow University. A well-known activist who has been striving to spread secular ideas for the last forty years in the Hindi heartland.

Subhash Gatade, New Delhi-based social activist and writer having a number of books to his credit.

Murzban Jal (Dr.), Well-known scholar having a number of books to his credit. Currently Director of Centre for Educational Studies, Indian Institute of Education, Pune.

Asifa Jan (Dr.), writer, academician, scholar. Currently Professor, Department of Political Science, University of Kashmir, Srinagar.

Himanshu Shekhar Mishra is pursuing his Ph.D. research at Jawaharlal Nehru University, New Delhi.

Malika Mistry (Dr.), academician, activist and social worker. Currently Associate Professor, Department of Economics, Poona College, Pune.

Mohammad Fayyaz (Dr.), Former Associate Professor and Head, Department of Political Science, Government College of Arts and

Science, Aurangabad. His areas of research interest include Muslim Politics, Political Theory and Indian Political System.

Noorjahan Momin is pursuing her Ph.D. on *The State and the Capitalist Class in Russia, 1991-2012* from School of International Studies, Jawaharlal Nehru University, New Delhi. Her research interests include State and Class, Russian History and Politics, Human Security, International Politics and Comparative Political Studies.

Arun K. Patnaik (Dr.), Professor in Political Science, University of Hyderabad. His research interests include Political Theory, Secularism and Development/Displacement in India.

Ram Puniyani (Dr.), writer activist is Chair of Centre for Study of Society and Secularism, Mumbai.

Himanshu Roy (Dr.), Former Fellow, Nehru Memorial Museum & Library, Teen Murti House, New Delhi. His forthcoming book is *State Politics in India*, Primus, New Delhi.

Asad Bin Saif is involved in social activism, working as Coordinator, Campaign, Communication and Advocacy of Mumbai based NGO, Bombay Urban Industrial League for Development (BUILD).

Shuja Shakir (Dr.), Associate Professor in the Department of Political Science, Dr. Babasaheb Ambedkar Marathwada University, Aurangabad. His areas of research interest include Political Theory and Minority Politics.

Neetin Sonawane is Assistant Professor, Department of Political Science, Abhinav College, Bhayandar (E), Thane. His areas of research interest include International Politics, Political Sociology and Indian Political System.

Karli Srinivasulu is Professor of Political Science and Dean, Faculty of Social Sciences at Osmania University, Hyderabad. His interests include Political Theory, Agrarian and Dalit Movements and Public Policy. His recent work has been on Politics of Special Economic Zones, State Business Relations and Telangana State movement.

Shamsuddin Tamboli is the Executive President of Muslim Satyashodhak Mandal and Executive Editor of *Muslim Satyashodhak Patrika*. Presently lecturer at Marathwada Mitra Mandal's College of Commerce, Pune,

Anand Teltumbde is a writer, political analyst and civil rights activist with the Committee for Protection of Democratic Rights. He currently teaches in a B-school of IIT, Kharagpur.

Cybil Vinodan is Assistant Professor in Political Science, Christ College, Irinjalakuta, Kerala. Presently he is working on Problems in the Study of Left and Dalit Movements in India.